W9-BKY-064

9 1192 01060 6059

920.72 Facts v.5

Facts on File
encyclopedia of Black
c1997.

JAN 0 5 2000

Facts On File Encyclopedia of

Black Women

IN AMERICA

Music

Encyclopedia of
Black Women in America

Facts On File Encyclopedia of

Black Women

IN AMERICA

Music

Darlene Clark Hine, Editor

Kathleen Thompson, Associate Editor

920.72
Facts
v.5

EVANSTON PUBLIC LIBRARY
1703 ORRINGTON AVENUE
EVANSTON, ILLINOIS 60201

☑® Facts On File, Inc.

Facts On File Encyclopedia of Black Women in America: Music

Copyright © 1997 Darlene Clark Hine

All rights reserved. No part of this book may be reproduced or utilized in any form or by any means, electronic or mechanical, including photocopying, recording, or by any information storage or retrieval systems, without permission in writing from the publisher. For information contact:

Facts On File, Inc.
11 Penn Plaza
New York NY 10001

Library of Congress Cataloging-in-Publication Data

Facts on File Encyclopedia of Black Women in America / Darlene Clark
Hine, editor : Kathleen Thompson, associate editor.
p. cm.
Includes bibliographical references and index.
Contents: v. 1. The early years, 1619–1899 — v. 2. Literature —
v. 3. Dance, sports, and visual arts — v. 4. Business and professions —
v. 5. Music — v. 6. Education — v. 7. Religion and community —
v. 8. Law and government — v. 9. Theater arts and entertainment —
v. 10. Social activism — v. 11. Science, health, and medicine.
ISBN 0-8160-3424-9 (set: alk. paper)
ISBN 0-8160-3431-1 (Music)
1. Afro-American women—Biography—Encyclopedias. I. Hine.
Darlene Clark. II Thompson, Kathleen.
E185.96.F2 1997
920.72′08996073—dc20   96-33268

Facts On File books are available at special discounts when purchased in bulk quantities for businesses, associations, institutions or sales promotions. Please call our Special Sales Department in New York at (212) 967-8800 or (800) 322-8755.

Text design by Cathy Rincon
Cover design by Smart Graphics

Printed in the United States of America

RRD FOF 10 9 8 7 6 5 4 3 2 1

This book is printed on acid-free paper.

Contents

How to Use This Volume

SCOPE OF THE VOLUME

The *Music* volume includes entries on individuals and groups in the following subject areas: blues, concert music, gospel, jazz, opera, popular music, rap, rhythm and blues, rock and roll, and soul.

RELATED OCCUPATIONS

Professionals in related occupations covered in other volumes of this encyclopedia include the following: musical theater performers (*Theater Arts and Entertainment*), dancers (*Dance, Sports, and Visual Arts*), music producers (*Business and Professions*), and music educators (*Education*).

HOW TO USE THIS VOLUME

The introduction to these two volumes presents an overview of the history of black women in music. A chronology at the end of the volume lists important events in the history of American music, African-American music, and the participation of black women in music.

Individuals and groups are covered in alphabetically arranged entries. If you are looking for an individual or group that does not have an entry in this volume, please check the alphabetically arranged list of the entries for all eleven volumes of this encyclopedia that appears at the end of this volume, in addition to tables of contents of each of the other volumes.

Names of individuals and organizations for which there are entries in this or other volumes of the encyclopedia are printed in **boldface.** Check the contents list at the end of this title to find the volume where a particular entry can be found.

Introduction

I think, to separate blues from jazz from concert music
from work songs from spirituals—it's like separating
yourself. If someone asked you to come to a meeting to
represent, say, your family, you wouldn't say, "Well,
this meeting is going to be attended by certain people so
maybe I shouldn't bring my left arm," or "This meeting
is going to be attended by certain people, maybe I
shouldn't bring my right foot." You would want to
bring your whole self as a person,
and that's the way I feel about music.

Regina Baiocchi, interview on
Noteworthy Women

She stands in front of an audience in a long dress, her head back and her eyes closed. In the darkness of the theater or the club or the hall, one bright light singles her out. The people wait to hear her sweet, strong, joyous, heartbreaking voice fill the air with music. She is **Bessie Smith, Billie Holiday, Sarah Vaughan, Mahalia Jackson, Aretha Franklin, Diana Ross, Whitney Houston, Mary Blige.**

To most people, this is the black woman musician. The blues queen. The jazz diva. Whether she shouts, moans, scats, belts, croons, or coos, it is her legend that lives in our minds.

And yet, in American music history, one of the first black women known by name was a church organist, and the very first to make a name for herself professionally was a concert singer, a classically trained soprano, who sang operatic arias for Queen Victoria almost fifty years before **Ma Rainey** set foot on a stage.

The music of black women is complex, and its history is no less so. It goes back to the role of African women as storytellers and healers. It goes forward to a leather-clad bass player in a hip hop band.

SINGING A SONG IN A STRANGE LAND

African-American Music in Colonial America

Black American music is a river, huge and wide, like the Mississippi. At its source is a mingling of African and European music in a context of sorrow and slavery. That mingling itself is complex and not always easy to trace, and the river splits into dozens of branches—blues, jazz, bebop, rhythm and blues, soul . . . .

The mistake many people make is to try to find the source of one branch in another. Did jazz come from blues? Did blues come from gospel? The fact is that they all came from that one mighty river, and in the early years of our country, that river was formed. Waters flowed into it from all parts of the black experience and culture, as creeks pour into a river from the melting snow of the mountains.

Colonial America is not usually thought of as a place of joy and music. We imagine the Pilgrims in their stark black-and-white garments walking toward church carrying Bibles and blunderbusses as they pass a wayward neighbor imprisoned in the stocks. There are two things missing in this picture: slaves and songbooks.

The colonists of seventeenth-century America, both black and white, loved to sing. They sang in church, where black slaves sat in pews set aside for them. They also sang outside church. Because theaters were illegal in most places (and television was a couple of centuries in the future), singing and dancing were the main forms of entertainment.

In the Northern colonies, slaves were encouraged and often required to attend church. Because hardly anyone read music, psalms were set to melodies that most people knew; then a member of the congregation tried very hard to keep everybody on tune, usually with unpredictable results. Often, slaves attended classes in religious instruction that included music lessons. Already skilled in African music, black Americans learned, in these classes, how to sing European music as well. (This kind of education did not often occur in the Southern colonies, where slaveowners were fearful of anything that tended to improve the mental capabilities of their slaves.)

Some of these early slaves, in both North and South, learned to play instruments, though not in the church classes; in *The Music of Black Americans*, Eileen Southern speculates that slaves learned to play in a variety of ways. Some men learned to play instruments while serving in white armies—indeed, the usual position of a black man in the colonial militia was drummer, fifer, or trumpeter. The famous painting *The Spirit of '76* would be considerably more accurate if one or all of the musicians were black.

Some house slaves probably learned to play instruments when music masters came to teach the children of the house. Others may have taught themselves; some were probably given lessons by their masters. The fact is that a slave who could make music became a financial asset. The dance-loving colonists made slave musicians sought-after accompanists. The most popular instruments were fiddle, French horn, and flute.

As far as we know, all of these players were men, following in the European tradition that forbade women to be professional musicians. But the situation was very different when black people got together to entertain themselves.

There were slave festivals that were filled with music. "'Lection Day" was a celebration of the election of an honorary ruler of the community. "Pinkster Day" was a celebration that derived from the Christian Pentecost. At these festivals, there were usually instruments such as banjoes, fiddles, and fifes. At other times, dancing was accompanied only by singing, drums, and "patting" —producing music with foot-tapping, hand-clapping, and thigh-slapping. Sometimes the festivals lasted for days, with almost nonstop dancing and singing. From contemporary reports, it seems that the festival music was almost entirely African. The festivals in Albany and Manhattan drew hundreds of black participants and as many white spectators. Men and women joined freely in the dancing, singing, and music making.

A similar kind of celebrating took place in New Orleans' Congo Square every Sunday and on church holy days. Huge crowds of slaves gathered to sing and dance. Thousands of whites gathered to watch them. Historical reports say that the dancing began at three o'clock in the afternoon. Each group, or tribe, took a different part of the square for its own, using its own orchestra of drums, banjoes, and rattles. The dancing would go on until nine o'clock and was so strenuous that dancers frequently had to be replaced as they fainted from exhaustion. The drumming and chanting that accompanied the dancing was performed by both men and women, as was the dancing itself.

Black women in the colonies were also often the singers, or storytellers, in smaller gatherings. Two names have come down to us through the centuries—**Lucy Terry** and Senegambia.

Lucy Terry lived in Deerfield, Massachusetts, from about 1730 to 1821. She married a free black man named Abijah Prince and later gained her own freedom. She called herself Luce Bijah. According to Eileen Southern, she "made her home a gathering place for slaves and freedmen of the community, a place where they could listen to tales and songs of old Africa." Senegambia lived in Narragansett, Rhode Island, also in the 1700s. She, too, was known for entrancing

her listeners with songs and tales of ages past.

These early forms of music making were sources of black American music. Linda Dahl's description of jazz in her book *Stormy Weather* could apply much more broadly: "The root of jazz," she says, "is Africa uprooted; jazz had its beginnings in slavery, when European melodies, harmonies and instruments were combined with, and refashioned for African-born rhythms. And the purpose of the music was African-born, too; perhaps most significant of the elements that made up slave music was the approach to feelings, a codified straining toward personal expression that ignored a preconceived ideal of sound. . . . The music of black slaves married the pain and pleasure of physical life with a permeating spirituality; one of its great, enduring strengths was that it did not sever the life of the body from that of the spirit."

The African songs and dances, with their strong rhythms, their call-and-response patterns, and their repetitions, gradually incorporated the bits and pieces of European tune and harmony that seemed to fit, often from church music.

FROM THE RIVER JORDAN

Religious Sources of African-American Music

Psalms to hymns to spirituals: In the very earliest years of the colonies, the songs sung in churches were Biblical psalms set to music. Then, in the 1730s, the "Great Awakening" happened. Many of the colonists thought religion had become too formal, too much a matter of rules and rituals and too little a matter of feeling and spirituality. Jonathan Edwards started to make the pulpit shake with sermons such as "Sinners in the Hands of an Angry God," and the congregation started to make the rafters ring with lively, "non-psalm" hymns.

The hymns of Dr. Isaac Watts and, later, John and Charles Wesley were very popular among black worshipers. These were the hymns that were widely sung in the Methodist Church, spiritual home of most black Christians in those days.

The first exclusively black churches were in the South and were Baptist. They were founded by slaves in the late eighteenth century and existed for only a few decades before white slaveowners accused them of provoking rebellion. The churches disappeared and did not surface again until the Civil War was over. In the North, black people had been welcome members of the Methodist church since its inception in America. By the turn of the century, however, they had tired of the discrimination they faced in white churches and decided to form their own.

With the formation of the new African Methodist Episcopal Church in 1816 came a new hymnal, called *A Collection of Spiritual Songs and Hymns Selected from Various Authors by Richard Allen*. Richard Allen's hymnal was the first to use what musicologists call the "wandering refrain." He not only added short verses or choruses —refrains—to standard hymns, he added, as Southern puts it, "any refrain to any hymn." It was a reflection of the kind of improvisation that would be a mark of African-American music in the two centuries to come.

As in the white churches of the early colonies, these black congregations would be led in their singing by one of their members, sometimes an older woman. She would sing out two lines, and the others would follow her. The hymns in Allen's collection and the revised editions that followed it were often the basis of the entirely new sort of church music that black Americans would soon create—the camp-meeting hymn, or spiritual.

The way it seems to have worked is that a scrap of lyric from one of the favorite hymns would be sung by the congregation with added choruses, shouts, repeated lines, and exclamations of praise or joy until a new song had been formed. This happened at camp meetings—outdoor revival-type services—that would last for hours. After all the whites went home, the black worshipers would stay and sing for hours more, sometimes all night. While they sang, they clapped their hands, moved their bodies, and even—to the horror of white ministers —*danced*.

Dancing had been a part of the West African religious experience from time immemorial. Asking people from most parts of that region to worship without dancing would be like asking European Christians to worship without praying. But of course, one culture did not understand the other, and the dancing of the black Christians seemed, to the white Christians, to be irreligious. The stillness of white Christians, on the other hand, seemed to black Christians to evidence a lack of feeling.

In the South, however, black Christians often had to be still themselves. As fearful slaveowners banned church meetings, worshipers stole away into the woods to meet in secret. The songs that grew out of the camp meetings and the secret services would take on a new life and a new purpose as the antislavery movement grew.

In the meantime, however, religion was contributing other waters to the river. In many black churches, as opposed to the camp meetings, there was a move toward trained choirs and instruments such as pipe organs. In fact, the St. Thomas Episcopal Church in Philadelphia scandalized the neighborhood by hiring a young woman, Ann Appo, as church organist, a job that thousands of black women have filled with devotion and creativity ever since. These churches contributed to the river of black music through musicians with a thorough grounding in European musical styles. They also provided black women with their most consistent musical outlet. Whatever restrictions were put on them in other places, they could always make music in church.

Outside the established church, black women apparently held considerable power in the community. They were the key figures in the fetish religions, primarily *vodun*, or voodoo, which added another strain to the music of African America. The most famous of the "voodoo queens" was **Marie Laveau,** who lived in the late 1700s and early 1800s. Because of her religious influence, she became exceptionally wealthy and powerful. Other women gained positions of similar power in the subculture. In her book *Stormy Weather*, Linda Dahl draws an interesting parallel: "The defiance, pride, posturing and boastfulness, and the vivid symbolism of these voodoo-queen songs [are] qualities that mark the later compositions of the blueswomen." She then goes on to cite this song, taken originally from a New Orleans newspaper in 1924 and often recorded since.

They think they frighten me
Those people must be crazy

They don't see their misfortune
Or else they must be drunk.
I—the Voodoo Queen
With my lovely handkerchief
Am not afraid of tomcat shrieks
I drink serpent venom!
I walk on pins
I walk on needles
I walk on gilded splinters
I want to see what they can do!
They think they have pride
With their big malice
But when they see a coffin
They're as frightened as prairie birds.
I'm going to put *gris-gris*
All over their front steps
And make them shake
Until they stutter!

Clearly, African rituals, Christian hymns, and underground religions were all sources of the river. In all of these, African-American women were important figures. Other sources were far from sacred, and women were there, too.

MINSTRELS

Music for Dance and Entertainment

The dancing and singing of black street performers in New Orleans inspired the most popular form of American entertainment in the nineteenth century—the minstrel show. It appeared on the scene in the 1830s and remained the biggest thing in show business for decades.

Black women did not have much to do with the minstrel show in these days. But then, neither did black men. What the audience saw onstage was a bunch of white men, wearing burnt cork on their faces to make them look black, performing black dances, singing black songs, and acting out stereotypes of black personalities.

In other words, the music of black people made it onto the stage, and the people didn't.

But what kind of music was it? It was certainly not the spirituals that were evolving in the camp meetings. They would scarcely have been appropriate. What made it to the minstrel stage was a kind of black folk music that seems to have come out of the hours slaves spent together entertaining themselves—and making fun of their white masters. The lyrics were satirical, and the music was strongly influenced by Africa; at the same time, it was usually played on European instruments by people who had been exposed to, and often played professionally, European music.

Much of the music that was later taken by white musicians and adapted for the minstrel show was used by slaves to accompany their dancing. Various men and women would "pat juba (or juber)," making music by tapping their feet to keep the strong rhythm and adding variations by clapping their hands and slapping their thighs. One person, the "juber rhymer," would create verses and recite, not sing, them. The description that has come down to us from historical reports makes the juber rhymer sound much like a rap artist.

On one Maryland plantation, the main juber rhymer was a young woman named Clotilda. From a book by James Hungerford called *The Old Plantation, and What I Gathered There in an Autumn Month*, published in 1859, we have the actual words to some of Clotilda's juba songs. The words tell the dancers what steps to do and make

gentle fun of the people in the community as well. Hungerford's notes indicate the people answering back in short shouts, reproaching Clotilda for her impudence. Most of the juba songs are lost, however.

There was also instrumental music for dancing, called "fiddle-sings," "jig-tunes," and "devil songs." These, too, are mostly lost. They often had nonsense lyrics that must not have seemed worth recording.

Often, the slaves sang songs about animals, especially Br'er Rabbit, in order to express their feelings about their situation. A singer could be satirical about the white masters in these songs, while pretending to talk only about Br'er Fox. Finally, there was the music made up to play for the masters. Again, lyrics were improvised and valued for their humor.

There is much we don't know about the music of slaves, but when it was stolen by white musicians and adapted for the minstrel shows, it took audiences by storm. So we know for certain that it was lively, entertaining, and—judging by its success—a lot more fun than the music most white people were making.

This is one more source of the river. The music that was taken from the plantations and the street singers was often returned. The white musicians would alter the tunes, rhythms, and words of a song. The song would become popular. Then the black musicians would pick it up and play it in its altered form. The waters were mixing.

MAIDENS

Traditional European Music

Well before the end of slavery in the United States, a class of black Americans was forming that had financial security and was interested in pursuing cultural interests, *cultural* usually meaning European. Like their white counterparts, they trained their daughters to paint, embroider, and play music. The daughters did not, of course, play the banjo; they played the pianoforte, the violin—not the fiddle—or the guitar. They also sang.

Unfortunately, these young black women did not play the finest music of the European tradition, any more than young white women did. They played music that was considered appropriate for young women —sentimental, trivial, and pretentious—and like their white counterparts, they were not allowed to perform professionally. Respectable young women did not enter professions. Still, they were often skilled musicians, and they performed for their peers at parties, literary society meetings, and even antislavery lectures.

One black woman did become a professional musician, performing just this sort of concert music. She was able to accomplish this because she was *not* a respectable, upper-class woman. She was born a slave.

Elizabeth Taylor Greenfield, the first African-American musician to achieve a reputation in both America and Britain, was born in about 1819 in Natchez, Mississippi. Her parents were named Taylor and were slaves on the estate of Mrs. Holliday Greenfield, a Quaker. When Greenfield was a year old, her owner released the parents from her ownership and sent them to Liberia, but she kept the child with her.

When the child began to sing, Mrs. Greenfield and her friends encouraged her. After her former owner's death, Greenfield continued to perform professionally at small gatherings. After several years, she was heard by a Mrs. H. B. Potter, who invited her to sing for a number of her friends. A group of them sponsored her in a series of concerts for the Buffalo Music Association.

She was a hit. The press loved her, giving her the nickname "The Black Swan"; soon she was giving concerts all over the United States and Europe. Her career was a frustrating combination of success and humiliation, of support from prominent white Americans, and rejection by much of the white music establishment. While in England, she performed for Queen Victoria at Buckingham Palace on May 10, 1854. She needed the twenty pounds the Queen gave her to help pay her way back home.

Critics universally praised Greenfield's voice for both its range and its power. Her personality won over audiences. There were those who criticized her training, but there is no doubt that she was a remarkable performer. Greenfield formed a black opera troupe that performed in Washington, D.C., in 1862 and in Philadelphia in 1866. Later in her life, she taught music and gave benefit performances for black charities. She died in Philadelphia on March 31, 1876.

One of Greenfield's students, Thomas Bowers, later toured with her. His sister, Sarah Sedgewick Bowers also became a professional singer. In a reference to Jenny Lind, the enormously popular "Swedish Nightingale," Sarah Bowers was known as "The Colored Nightingale."

Other black musicians participating in the classical European tradition performed in sacred music concerts. At the beginning of the nineteen century, many black churches sponsored concerts of arias, anthems, and full oratorios performed by black men and women. One of the foremost concert directors was Susan Paul, daughter of the minister of Boston's Belknap Church.

These sacred-music concerts eventually lost their religious nature and became simply performances of "classical" music. Many troupes of musicians toured the country, performing at these concerts. However, other than Greenfield's company, there were few who made a name for themselves; among those who did was the Luca Family Singers of Connecticut.

The Lucas included father, mother, one daughter, and four sons. The sons all played instruments; the other members of the family sang. They were later joined by another singer, Jennie Allen. The troupe toured widely and, at one point, presented joint concerts with a white group called the Singing Hutchinson Family.

These concert musicians contributed to the formation of black American music in a number of ways. The first—and by no means the least important—was that they gave credibility to black musicians in general: They proved, to the black community as well as the white, that African Americans were singing or playing *any* form of music they chose.

They also contributed as preservationists. Black men and especially black women who received traditional musical training were often responsible for writing down and preserving the music they heard around them. Many of the African-American songs we know about were published in the book *Slave Songs of the United States,* among whose contributors was **Charlotte Forten (Grimké).** She was a young black woman who was born to a prominent free black family in Philadelphia. As a teenager, she committed herself to the antislavery movement and, while attending college, became active in abolitionist activities. Forten became a teacher, but she was also a fine poet and, in 1858, her poem "Red, White, and Blue" was sung by a choir at a ceremony honoring black Revolutionary War hero Crispus Attucks.

Later, black women who played piano for ragtime, blues, and jazz bands would provide the same service, writing down melodies and arrangements that would otherwise probably have been lost. They were often the only trained musicians in the bands.

All of this musical activity faded in significance, though, as the antislavery movement gathered momentum. Now, there were new singers and new songs, and their music carried a profound message.

FOLLOW THE DRINKIN' GOURD

Music Against Slavery

In the South before the Civil War, meetings were not allowed, even in churches. In the fields, the overseer or the driver was always there, alert to any sign of conversation. Written correspondence was impossible: Too few could write; too few could read.

But the slaves could sing. The masters expected it and accepted it. Singing made the work go smoother and faster, and so in the afternoon as the sun shone hot on the cotton, a song would begin—*Follow the drinkin' gourd! Follow the drinkin' gourd. For the old man is awaitin' for to carry you to freedom, if you follow the drinkin' gourd.* The simple message was delivered: The underground railroad was waiting to guide fugitives to freedom if they traveled in the direction of the Big Dipper . . . the drinkin' gourd.

Sometimes the message of the songs was more general, meant to encourage slaves to keep the faith, to believe that they could escape and find their way North to freedom, that help would come soon: *Good news, chariot's acomin'. Good news, chariot's acomin.' Good news, chariot's acomin', and I don't want it to leave me behind.*

Sometimes it was very specific, as when **Harriet Tubman**, the fierce and courageous underground railroad conductor, sang her signature song to alert those still in slavery that she was in the area, ready to take them back with her to the North: *Dark and thorny is the pathway where the pilgrim makes his ways; but beyond this vale of sorrow lie the fields of endless days.*

Sometimes the message was simply one of comfort for those not yet able to go: *Swing low, sweet chariot, coming for to carry me home. Swing low, sweet chariot, coming for to carry me home. If you get there, before I do, coming for to carry me home, tell all my friends I'm coming, too. Coming for to carry me home.*

Hearing these songs now, with all that we know of the underground railroad and the Civil War, of the antislavery movement and the courage of fugitives and their guides, it is difficult to understand why the overseers did not instantly understand the messages of these songs. But the fact is that singing was a constant part of the lives of slaves. There were field hollers—musical cries for help, for food or drink, for consolation. There were work songs to set the tempo for scythes or rowers or threshers. There were songs about children sold down the river and loved ones dead.

Southern quotes an old woman who says of one song, "I like 'Poor Rosy' better than all the songs, but it can't be sung without a *full heart and a troubled spirit.*"

Poor Rosy, poor gal; Poor Rosy, poor gal; Rosy break my poor heart, Heav'n shall-a be my home.

Slaves were also often forced to sing by their masters, before they were put onto the auction block at the slave market, while they were on the forced march back to the plantation, or whenever the masters thought music would "liven them up."

Music was the telegraph of slavery, as well as its inspiration and its balm. Music was also the spur to action for members of the movement, black and white.

Most of us think of **Sojourner Truth** as a powerful speaker for justice and freedom; what is less well known is that she was a singer and songwriter for freedom as well. When she stepped onto stages around the country to rouse audiences to move against the greatest evil this nation has ever known, she used the tremendous power of her speech, but she also sang—and led the audiences in singing—antislavery songs she had written herself. Eugene D. Genovese, in his book *Roll, Jordan, Roll*, quotes abolitionist Harriet Beecher Stowe about hearing Sojourner Truth sing: "She seemed to impersonate the fervor of Ethiopia, wild, savage, hunted of all nations, but burning after God in her tropic heart and stretching her scarred hands towards the glory to be revealed."

All of these songs became a part of the musical river of black America. All of this music entered into the souls of black people and would come out, in many forms, whenever the self demanded expression or the spirit sought release. When the Civil War was over, however, and the century moved toward its end, the river began to branch, to pour forth in all directions.

THE GOSPEL TRUTH

Gospel Music

In 1871, Fisk University had a problem: Since the ending of the Civil War, this fine school had dedicated itself to educating black young people, but money was scarce, and the building fund was always running short. The answer Fisk found to its problem had an impact that no one could have predicted.

Fisk had a young white teacher named George L. White. White had, in his spare time, been providing musical instruction to the Fisk students and had formed a chorus that sang both classical music and spirituals. After a while, he took his chorus to towns in the vicinity to perform. Then in October 1871, he took the small chorus and pianist Ella Shepherd on a tour to raise money for the university. Besides Shepherd, there were four women in the group—Maggie L. Porter, Minnie Tate, Jennie Jackson, and Eliza Walker—and five or six men.

Reaction to the troupe was mixed at first, but they persisted. White named them the **Fisk Jubilee Singers**, after the "year of jubilee" when the slaves had been freed. In 1872, they performed at the World Peace Jubilee in Boston, where an enormous choir of black singers was assembled. When the orchestra started "The Battle Hymn of the Republic" on a pitch that was far too high, the Fisk singers were the only ones of all those gathered with the technical training to handle the song. They saved the day and made their names.

During the next few years, the Fisk Jubilee Singers sang all over the United States and in Europe, introducing the black spiritual to an enthusiastic public. Soon, another black school, Hampton Institute in Virginia, sent out its chorus with a repertoire of spirituals. Hampton's success proved that the world was ready not only for the Fisk choir but for black religious music in general, and other universities followed suit.

Spirituals now, for better or worse, belonged to the world. The branch called gospel music had moved away from the main river. It began with the slave songs, the field hollers, the spirituals made famous by the Fisk Jubilee Singers. But by the time it reached the twentieth century, gospel was its own kind of music. In the second half of the nineteenth century, the revival movement had begun forming a new type of hymn, one more suited to the increasingly urban congregation than the older spirituals. These were the songs that, in the early years of the twentieth century, became the repertoire of the gospel singer.

In *Black Women in America*, Horace Clarence Boyer describes this music as "a more emotional and jubilant black religious music, an urban counterpart of the spiritual and the blues, representing the new freedom of religious, social, and political consciousness of black Americans. Characterized by full-throated tones, blue notes, syncopation, and a performance style of call-and-response, gospel music elicits hand-clapping, foot-patting, and the 'holy' dance, when the spirit is especially fervent."

It was during the twenties that the most important singers and composers began their work, and most, though not all, of them came out of the churches of Chicago or came *to* the recording studios in Chicago.

One of the latter was Arizona Dranes, a blind singer from Texas. She sang and played at the Church of God in Christ prayer meetings as a teenager in Dallas. Then a nearby minister recommended her to Okeh records. She went to Chicago in 1926 for a test recording and was given a contract.

For the next several years, Dranes played in Chicago churches, adding her distinctive singing and her piano playing to the musical style that was forming there. The singing was high pitched and nasal, while the piano playing had a strong flavor of ragtime or boogie.

Dranes recorded for Okeh for several years, receiving $25 for each record side that was issued and $3 a day for living expenses. She was supposed to receive a royalty for every song of hers that was recorded by another artist, but she never did. Health problems and the unscrupulous business practices of the recording company and its employees led Dranes to return to the Southwest and drop out of professional gospel music.

In those few years, however, her style had influenced gospel in a way that would be evident in the music of such stars of gospel as **Clara Ward**, **Rosetta Tharpe**, and Ernestine Washington.

Mollie Mae Gates made her contribution to Chicago gospel in the 1920s and 1930s from her position as director of the Junior Choir at Metropolitan Community Church. She introduced gospel songs to her young choir members, several of whom went on to be leaders of the movement.

About this same time, the "Father of Gospel," Thomas Dorsey, made a break with his blues and jazz past and started to write the gospel songs for which he would become famous. He went around Chicago, from church to church, selling his songs. They were printed on small sheets of paper, called "ballets" by some of his customers, and he sold them for a few cents each. He further stimulated the growth of gospel in Chicago by hiring singers to help him sell his songs. After a time, he organized a group of women who eventually became the first female gospel quartet.

Sallie Martin moved to Chicago from Georgia in 1929 and began singing in church choirs. In 1932, she joined the chorus led by Dorsey at the Pilgrim Baptist Church. A year later, she and Dorsey organized the first National Convention of Gospel Choirs. For years, Martin toured with Dorsey as a song demonstrator, and then she went out on her own. She performed alone or with her own groups, founded a gospel-music publishing company, and formed the first all-woman gospel choir—the Sallie Martin Singers.

Another **Martin, Roberta**, was perhaps the most important woman in Chicago gospel. In the early thirties, she had joined with Sallie Martin to present one of the first gospel concerts for which there was an admission charge. The concert was performed at DuSable High School in Chicago and was part of the movement of gospel out of the church and into the concert hall.

Roberta Martin herself went on to organize the Martin-Frye Singers with Theodore R. Frye, a group which later became the Roberta Martin Singers. Her singing style was smoother and more polished than most of the gospel musicians before her. Her piano style had more refinement and less boogie. Roberta Martin also founded her own publishing company, the Roberta Martin Studio of Music, and composed more than 100 gospel songs. During her recording career, Martin received six gold records and influenced some of the biggest names in gospel music.

But the "Mother of Gospel" was the inimitable Mahalia Jackson. Jackson, who would sing for presidents and monarchs, who sold out every performance at Carnegie Hall for years, who packed Madison Square Garden and stunned the Newport Jazz Festival, started life in 1911 in a shack by the railroad tracks. She grew up listening to the music of the Sanctified Church next door—and to King Oliver. She absorbed the sounds of the Baptist Church her family attended—and the sounds of brass funeral bands. It was as though the whole river of black music flowed down the streets of New Orleans and Mahalia lived on the banks.

Then, in 1927, at the age of sixteen, Jackson moved to Chicago to live with an aunt. She held all sorts of jobs and sang in the choir of the Greater Salem Baptist Church. She was soon first soloist and then a member of a gospel quintet. She toured to storefront churches and demonstrated songs for Thomas Dorsey.

Mahalia Jackson didn't just sing when she sang. She clapped her hands, stomped her feet, and moved her whole body. She was criticized for bringing the feeling of jazz and blues into the church and defended herself with Scripture. But when offers came in for her to sing secular music in nightclubs, she resolutely turned them down. Her first record was issued in 1934, and it was well received.

However, in 1946, Jackson revolutionized gospel music when she recorded the song "Move On Up a Little Higher" for Apollo records and sold more than eight million copies. Her brilliant career was well and truly launched. She had been made a star by the African-American community and would go on to become a world celebrity. Mahalia Jackson recorded thirty albums, received twelve gold records, had her own radio and television programs, and appeared in several films, including *Imitation of Life* and *St. Louis Blues*. When she sang in Paris in the 1950s, she received twenty-one curtain calls.

But perhaps her finest moments came when Dr. Martin Luther King, Jr., called on her to sing for freedom. She toured the nation with him, singing "We Shall Overcome" and stood at his side at the historic 1963 March on Washington.

ONSTAGE

Early Concert Music and Musical Comedy

As we have seen, the route to the stage, for black women, was through concert music. This was as true after the Civil War as before.

When there was no other outlet for black women as professional musicians, those who were able to obtain musical training could tour singing concert songs and opera. There are probably a number of reasons for this: One is the near absolute and apparently unconquerable resistance to the presence of women of any race on the minstrel stages and to black women in burlesque and white saloons; then there was the fact that the black women most likely to have the resources to pay for training and to launch themselves in careers were too "respectable" for most black popular music. At any rate, the concert singers, including the **Hyers Sisters** and **Sissieretta Jones**, were the groundbreakers for all black women musicians.

Anna and Emma Hyers, like Elizabeth Greenfield, were operatic singers, and they began their stage career performing concert music together. They gave their first recital together in 1867 in Sacramento, California. The critics were pleased. Then they went on tour with a baritone, a tenor—their father Sam B. Hyers—and an accompanist. Later, their company included some of the foremost black musicians of the time.

This strictly musical phase lasted for several years and was successful enough that the sisters decided to broaden their scope. In 1875, they formed a troupe called the Coloured Operatic and Dramatic Company and began to produce musical plays depicting the black experience. These were the first plays by African Americans about the African-American experience that were produced in the country. These two black women presented black musical theater at a time where there was no black dramatic theater and no black musical theater other than the black minstrel shows that appeared after the Civil War. Also they did it at a time when there were no black women in any form of theater anywhere in the United States.

Other black women had successful careers as concert musicians in the second half of the nineteenth century. **Nellie Brown Mitchell,** of Dover, New Hampshire, made her debut in New York in 1874 in Steinway Hall and later toured the South. She formed her own company to tour New England in 1886. Marie Selika was born in Mississippi but studied voice in San Francisco, where she made her singing debut in 1876. Her New York debut, also at Steinway Hall, took place five years after Nellie Mitchell's. She then toured Europe with her husband, appearing before Queen Victoria in 1883.

This was just about thirty years after Elizabeth Greenfield's performance for the same monarch.

After touring in the United States and again in Europe, Selika appeared at the Chicago World's Fair of 1893. On October 12, 1896, she appeared at Carnegie Hall with the other two leading black singers of the day—Sissieretta Jones and **Flora Batson.**

Sissieretta Jones was a beautiful woman with a beautiful voice. She was repeatedly compared to Adelina Patti, a magnificent white opera singer of the time. Flora Batson was called "The Double-Voiced Queen of Song" because of her remarkable range from baritone to soprano. In 1885, she became the star of the Bergen Star Company and married its white manager, Colonel John Bergen. Later, she toured with a new manager, the black basso Gerard Millar. Batson, too, sang for Queen Victoria, as well as for Queen Liliuokalani of Hawaii.

There were many more black women among concert artists at this time; indeed, the two decades from the early 1870s to the early 1890s could be called the golden age of the black prima donnas. Even so, their careers were limited to the concert stage, not the great opera companies, and their time would soon be up. By the late 1890s, the public no longer seemed interested, and most of these magnificent singers—with the exception of Sissieretta Jones—retired and became music teachers.

Jones became, instead, a pioneer of the musical stage. Her talent had earned her roles at the Metropolitan Opera in the 1892 season, but, though her contract was signed, the plans fell through. Instead, after spectacularly successful concerts in Madison Square Garden and at a number of European halls, Jones went on the road with a vaudeville company she called the "Black Patti Troubadours." It was billed as a musical comedy, not a minstrel show, and, in the second act, where the minstrel show had a cakewalk, the Black Patti Troubadours show had operatic arias.

The Black Patti Troubadours were a forerunner of a new kind of black theater. As the nineteenth century drew to an end, white audiences were finally getting tired of minstrel shows. All those pre–Civil War plantation characters were getting a little old in the gay nineties. So, at last, minstrel show caricatures changed. They didn't go away, but they changed: The shows were now filled with urban stereotypes, rather than rural, for one thing, and the slow-moving, slow-witted black from the old plantation was gone. In his place was the city dude, the con-artist always trying to make a killing and never quite pulling it off.

In 1890, *The Creole Show* appeared. The basic structure was that of a minstrel show. The star was Sam Lucas, a great star of the black minstrel shows. But now there were black women onstage. They were in the chorus, but still they were there.

The shows were still laden with stereotypes, but now they had performers drawn from what would soon be called vaudeville, and, most important, they had ragtime. The black musical had been born and it would draw huge audiences.

The next big step was taken in 1898 when Bob Cole, having gained his experience with Sissieretta Jones' Black Patti Troubadours, wrote, directed, and produced *A Trip to Coontown*. It was one of the first American musical comedies, black or white. It had a plot and characters, and it was an all-black production from beginning to end.

The new black musicals put black women on stage with black men, not as solo performers but as part of an ensemble, for the first time. Still, men were the stars; only occasionally did a talented black woman move up from the chorus.

One of the first was **Aida Overton Walker**. A talented dancer, she had toured with the Black Patti Troubadours. She married dancer-comedian George Walker when he and his partner Bert Williams were on the verge of Broadway success, and she joined the team. She could sing, dance, and act; she even became their choreographer.

There were many Williams and Walker musicals over the next decade, and Aida Overton Walker appeared in all of them. When Walker became ill and the team broke up, she helped Williams fulfill their bookings by dressing in men's clothes and performing her husband's biggest dance hits in every show. She went on to perform in vaudeville and later became a producer.

In the years to come, many black women would make their names in musical theater as singers and dancers. The most successful black musical of the early part of the century, *Shuffle Along*, produced **Florence Mills**, **Adelaide Hall**, and **Josephine Baker**, all remarkable entertainers. **Ethel Waters**, one of the greatest stars of the American musical theater, black or white, didn't come up from the chorus. She came from another part of the river.

NICE GIRLS DON'T JAZZ

Blues, Jazz, and Popular Music

There were six Goodson girls, and they all played the piano at home in the parlor; then, late at night when their parents were asleep, Billie and Edna, not yet in their teens, would sneak out of the house to go listen to the bands. As often as not, they would find that their sister Sadie had sneaked out first and was playing ragtime with the guys.

"Whenever a show at the Belmont Theater would get in a pinch for a piano player," Billie was quoted in *Stormy Weather*, "the manager would send for a Goodson girl, not caring which one he got." Once, in 1917, when Bessie Smith was singing in Pensacola, she needed someone to fill in for her accompanist for a couple of weeks. Billie got the job. She was ten.

A woman had to love music *that* much in those days to get past all the obstacles. She had to be *that* good to get a chance—and even then, most never made it.

It's difficult to know how to refer to all the black music that is not religious, the music that includes blues, ragtime, jazz, bebop, rhythm and blues, and rock and roll. The term *popular music* is too often used as a contrasting term to refer to music that has no (apparent) ethnicity. However, there are so many black musicians who cannot be placed neatly into one of the subcategories that it seems necessary to find some way to talk about the larger category. This is especially true when looking at the time before the twentieth century.

What kind of music did the black minstrels perform? What do we call the music created by "Mama Lou," the 1880s brothel performer who is credited with the songs "Ta-ra-ra-boom-de-ay," "There'll Be a Hot Time in the Old Town Tonight," and "Frankie and Johnny"? If you were able to go back in time and ask the "Ladies Orchestra" formed in Chelsea, Massachusetts, in 1884 or the "Colored Female Brass Band"

that toured Michigan in the late 1880s just what kind of music they were playing, what would the answer be?

It's important to remember that these black musicians had never heard of jazz or the blues. Those terms didn't exist yet. They played the music that they wanted to play and that their audiences wanted to hear, without regard for what "kind" of music it was. However, for convenience, we can call it dance music.

Although there is no doubt that most African Americans went along with the European-American prejudice against women as instrumentalists, even the earliest reports of black dance music include accounts of women musicians. Linda Dahl, in *Stormy Weather*, refers to jazz historian Curtis D. Jerde's opinion that "black women, especially among the lower classes, participated as instrumentalists in the music that prefigured jazz—particularly in the popular brass and marching bands—much more widely than has been recognized." It is Jerde's belief that women instrumentalists were pushed out of black dance music when it became more a part of the American mainstream.

In other words, when the music was part of the black community entertaining itself, black women could play the saxophone. When it became a matter of entertaining white people, too, black women instrumentalists could go to the back of the bus.

Billie Goodson Pierce was an exception. She left home before she was fifteen, in 1922, and traveled around the South playing blues and jazz. She played in tents and for carnivals and sometimes had to help out with the dancing. She worked in bands called Mack's Merrymakers and the Nighthawks Orchestra and entertained at house parties by herself, playing ragtime and shouting the blues. "I don't know whether it was rough or not," she said. "I was rough right along with it."

There were other women playing black dance music before Pierce, but not many. Some old jazz hands remember a woman named Mamie Desdoumes in Storyville, the red-light district of New Orleans, who had only three fingers on her right hand and played only one tune. In spite of these apparent handicaps, she drew crowds anywhere she played.

And there was Emma Barrett, **"Sweet Emma" Barrett**, "The Bell Gal." Like most of the black women who were pioneers of jazz, Barrett played the piano and played it with power. She was called "The Bell Gal" because she wore knee bells that shook when she played. Her career lasted at least six decades, until 1983.

When the black music scene shifted from New Orleans to Chicago, things tightened up for women. Still, black men accepted women into their musical groups a little more readily than white men—not much, but a little. Women piano players, especially, made their mark.

Lil Hardin Armstrong, for example, studied music at the Fisk Institute, joined the New Orleans Creole Jazz Band as a piano player, was house pianist for a number of nightclubs, and then joined King Oliver's Band. There she met Louis Armstrong and talked him into forming his own band. After they were married, she made a number of recordings with him and often received composer credit. Her strong, four-beat rhythm inspired Armstrong's jazz. As she herself put it in Shapiro and Hentoff's *Hear Me Talkin'*, "I beat out a background rhythm that put the Bechuana tribes of Africa to shame."

Armstrong kept up the beat in one way or another until she died in 1971, onstage, during a television tribute to the late Louis Armstrong. She wrote more than 150 songs.

Lovie Austin was another formally trained pianist who made a career away from the concert hall. She had to take any and every kind of work that came along, but she did it. She was an accompanist on the vaudeville circuit at the beginning of the century. She created an act and toured with it and then moved to Chicago to become house recording pianist for Paramount Records in 1924. Austin composed, arranged, and played for such vocalists as Ma Rainey, **Ida Cox**, and Ethel Waters. She also became a leader of theater bands, composing and arranging music and then playing the piano and conducting the band.

Other Chicago piano players included Irene Armstrong, who was also a composer; Mabel Horsey, who led a group called Mabel Horsey and Her Hot Five; Lil Hardaway Henderson, who played with King Oliver and accompanied Ma Rainey; and Georgia Corham, who was house pianist for Black Swan Records.

Mary Lou Williams got her start far away in Oklahoma City in the twenties, moving later to Kansas City and, finally, to New York. She came as close as any woman ever had to acceptance by the male jazz establishment. Williams was a swing band star in the thirties and one of the greatest boogie-woogie piano players who ever lived. As jazz changed, she changed with it, working with Dizzy Gillespie and composing jazz masses after her conversion to Catholicism. She became one of the most respected figures in modern jazz.

Other women in Kansas City jazz included Julia Lee and Margaret Johnson.

Black women around the country also played in bands, led bands, and composed music. Often, however, they performed in "Ladies' Orchestras" and "All-Girl Bands": In New York, for example, **Marie Lucas** conducted the Lafayette Ladies' Orchestra at the Lafayette Theater after inheriting the baton from her father, Sam Lucas. She also organized and trained bands for other theaters, but most of them were all male.

For many women, black and white, the all-woman bands provided the only opportunity they had to play; they simply couldn't get work in male bands. However, there were dangers in going the "girl band" route, which even further reduced their credibility as musicians. The best-known women often left the women's bands behind and formed their own, with male players: Lil Hardin Armstrong led an all-woman band for a while and then disbanded it to front an otherwise all-male band; clarinetist Ann Dupont led an all-male band for several years, as did **Blanche Calloway**, Cab Calloway's very talented sister.

The most famous of the all-woman bands had its start, like the Fisk Jubilee Singers, in an attempt to raise money for a black school. The principal of Piney Woods School, a boarding school for poor and orphaned children, put together a group of his students to play at local dances and parties. Called the **International Sweethearts of Rhythm**, because the students were from several ethnic backgrounds, the original group included Mexican and Chinese girls, as well as black girls.

The group became extremely good and extremely successful during the thirties and, in 1941, left the sponsorship of the school. Soon, they were joined by white jazzwomen who wanted the chance to work with such

an outstanding band. In the South, these white players often had to try to pass for black. Sometimes it worked and sometimes they spent the night in jail for violating segregation laws and customs.

After about a decade of playing in the most prestigious clubs in the United States and touring the night spots of Europe, the group broke up. But many of the best jazz women of the age were proud to claim a stint with the International Sweethearts of Rhythm.

Still, most women instrumentalists of the time had to do whatever they could, from girls' bands to playing in silent movie theaters to accompanying second-rate singers, just to stay professional.

As the years passed, there was little improvement in the male jazz world's receptiveness to women. However, as the music grew in popularity and commercial appeal, there was room for more musicians, and women often rushed in to fill the vacancies, and the more women there were playing, the more difficult it became for the male jazz establishment to deny their talent.

Una Mae Carlisle became a popular nightclub performer, had her own radio shows in the 1940s and 1950s, and wrote more than 500 songs, including "Glory Day," and "You're on Your Own." **Cleo Patra Brown** helped form the Chicago boogie-woogie sound and had a thriving recording career in the late 1940s. Nellie Lutcher played the nightclubs of Los Angeles for a decade before hitting it big with her first Capital recording, "Hurry on Down" and "The Lady's in Love with You." A prolific songwriter, she also wrote "The Object of My Affections" and "Chi-Chi-Chi-Chicago."

Musician, singer, actress, and activist, the gifted and glamorous Hazel Scott made her musical debut at three and by sixteen was a radio star. Trained at Juilliard, she appeared in Broadway shows and films in the late 1930s and 1940s; in the late 1940s and early 1950s, she became the first black woman to have her own television show. [SCURLOCK STUDIO]

Hazel Scott followed a familiar pattern for black women musicians, but with variations. She was formally trained—at Juilliard. She played with an all-woman band —led by her mother. She had her own radio show by the time she was sixteen and at eighteen, in 1938, was fronting a band, doing blues and boogies as well as classics. Scott's career was based in New York nightclubs, where she was always in demand.

Dorothy Donegan was also formally trained, and her virtuosity became the hallmark of her style. Like Scott, she played the big clubs during the 1940s and later and tailored her music to that milieu. Black women pianists who emerged in the late 1940s and early 1950s included Beryl Booker, Terry Pollard, and Shirley Scott.

For those women who played an instrument other than the piano, life was harder. The big bands such as those of Count Basie or Duke Ellington wouldn't hire them. Period. The smaller dance and club bands wouldn't hire them either, most of the time. They played with all-woman bands and theater bands or formed trios or quartets with other women. Still, they persisted.

Leora Meoux Henderson, a trumpet player, was able to work by creating a band advertised as "The Twelve Vampires—Twelve Girls Who Can Play Real Dance Music." She also played with Lil Hardin Armstrong, with Marie Lucas at the Lafayette, and with the Fletcher Henderson band—but only as a substitute. She was married to Henderson and was his road manager.

Another trumpeter was Dolly Jones. Her mother, Dyer Jones, had been a trumpeter, so Dolly had contacts in the music world. She played with Ma Rainey's band in 1925,

then with Lil Hardin Armstrong, and finally with her own group, the Twelve Spirits of Rhythm. She played in an all-black film, *Swing*, in 1937, and continued in her career until the early seventies.

Better known than either Henderson or Jones was **Valaida Snow;** in part, this was because she drew on other talents to forge her career. She was a singer, dancer, and bandleader as well as a trumpeter. She performed on Broadway in black musicals, made several film shorts, and often headlined at the Apollo. She was known as

Dorothy Donegan, like Hazel Scott, was a formally trained musician, but she had to tailor her style to the big clubs of the 1940s to succeed. She is shown here at the Great Lakes Naval Training Station in 1943. (NATIONAL ARCHIVES)

"Queen of the Trumpet" and "Little Louis." However, while touring Europe, she was interned by the Nazis; although she was released in 1941, her health was seriously affected, and her career, though it continued, was never the same.

Vi Burnside started with the Harlem Playgirls and moved on to the International Sweethearts of Rhythm. A saxophonist, she played in and led small groups after the Sweethearts disbanded. Tiny Davis took the same route, forming an all-woman group called the Hell-Divers after her time with the Sweethearts. The Hell-Divers became Decca Records' first all-woman recording group. One of the Hell-Divers was alto sax player Bert Etta Davis, who became part of **Dinah Washington**'s backup band in the fifties. The Hell-Divers, with various personnel changes, was still performing in Chicago in the seventies.

There were hundreds of other black women instrumentalists from the twenties through the seventies, including sax player Elvira (Vi) Redd, harpist Dorothy Ashby, blues guitarist Memphis Minnie Douglas, a number of drummers, and, of course, **Melba Liston** on the trombone.

Melba Liston was one of the many young black musicians who were encouraged and trained by Alma Hightower. In Los Angeles, Liston joined a youth band sponsored by the parks and recreation department and molded by Hightower. Her first real job, at sixteen, was with a theater pit band, and she went from there to work with the Gerald Wilson band. Liston became a prolific composer, a role she often preferred to performing because of the hostility—and even threats—of male colleagues on the bandstand. But she went on to a remarkable performing career, appearing with Dizzy

Gillespie on two State Department tours. She also arranged much of the music played on the tour.

From there, Liston's reputation grew tremendously, but she survived primarily as an arranger. She arranged music for some of the biggest record companies and biggest performers of our time.

It is certainly true that there were not as many women instrumentalists as there should have been. It is equally true that those who survived often had to use many talents and perform in many venues to make it. But the existence of those who fought to play and the quality of the music they created testify to the capabilities of all women, and to their spirit.

Where black women made their mark in black music in all its forms was in front of the band, singing. At first they were the blues queens, like Bessie Smith and Ma Rainey. Then came Billie Holiday; then **Lena Horne** and **Ella Fitzgerald** came to prominence. Later, there were Sarah Vaughan, **Carmen McRae, Betty Carter, Shirley Horn** and white singers such as Anita O'Day and Peggy Lee. There were also men of both races, such as Billy Eckstine and Mel Tormé. Still, most of the great vocalists in the river of music that includes blues and jazz were—and are—black women.

In 1902, a woman named Gertrude Rainey was touring the South, singing with a troupe called the Rabbit Foot Minstrels. Somewhere in Missouri, she heard a young woman singing a song—a sad one about lost love, about a man who had abandoned her.

Rainey started to sing the song in her act, and the audiences responded as she herself had when she heard that lonely woman singing in Missouri. There was something about the sorrow that reached into their souls, something about the aching loneliness that touched the loneliness in themselves. Rainey, whom everyone called "Ma," started to write and sing other songs with that same feeling.

They were like the songs slaves had sung on the plantations about the pains they suffered, the songs mothers had sung when their children were sold away from them, the songs families had sung when one of their own was taken to the graveyard. Ma Rainey called them the blues. She was the first to call them the blues, she claimed; others said that there was no beginning to the blues, that they had always been there. Both were probably right. Rainey had named the branch, but the others were still looking upstream at the river.

Ma Rainey's blues were down-to-earth, tied to her rural upbringing and those of her listeners. She wrote and sang music about the sorrows of everyday life. Her style of singing was deep, raw, and powerful. Before long, audiences throughout the South were devoted to her. The rest of the country discovered her a couple of decades later, when she recorded "Moonshine Blues" for Paramount Records. After that, she left the tent shows and toured on the TOBA circuit. The Theater Owners' Booking Association (otherwise known as TOBA, or Toby) was black vaudeville, a group of theaters scattered around the South. Most of the early blues queens toured on the Toby circuit.

As her reputation spread, Rainey added the big Northern cities to her tour. In her act, she would make her entrance dripping with glamour and glitter, out of a huge model of a Paramount record player, or "talking machine." Her audiences loved her beautiful dresses and lavish jewelry almost as much as they loved her blues.

In *Black Pearls: Blues Queens of the 1920s*, Daphne Duval Harrison writes, "Her singing retained those characteristics most admired by Africans and Afro-Americans—buzzing sound, huskiness, satirical inflections, ability to translate everyday experiences into living sound." Rainey's longtime accompanist Thomas Dorsey is quoted as saying, "Ma had the real thing she just issued out there. It had everything in it it needed, just like somebody issue out a plate of food say everything's on the plate. And that's the way Ma handed it to 'em—take it or leave it."

Ma Rainey's blues were still very close to the big river and still close to the other streams, such as church music, but Bessie Smith directed the flow a little further away. Born in Tennessee in 1894 to a very poor family, Bessie and her brother performed in childhood on the streets for tips; she sang while he played the guitar. At eighteen, she joined Moses Stokes' traveling minstrel troupe as a dancer and struck up a friendship with Ma Rainey, who was singing with the show. They remained close friends for the rest of their lives.

Four years after she left home, Smith was a headliner, well known throughout the South. In only two more years, she had her own troupe. By 1923, after some resistance because her voice was "too rough," she was signed to record for Columbia Records. Her first album for them sold 780,000 copies in six months. (The first blues recording had been made by **Mamie Smith** in 1920, causing a huge demand for more blues records.)

After Smith started to record, her stage appearances became even more successful. In the big Midwestern cities where there were now large black populations, people would line up all the way around a city block to hear her sing. Actually, according to Langston Hughes, her voice was so powerful and her style so strong that "when she sang in tent shows in the South, nobody needed to pay admission to *hear* her. But, of course, if they wanted to *see* her, they bought tickets."

William Barlow, in *Black Women in America*, explains the appeal of her music. "Taken as a whole," he says, "the blues lyrics immortalized by Bessie Smith had two characteristics of great significance. First, they were drawn from the black oral tradition's repository of rural folk blues; hence, they were very familiar to African Americans. She avoided the more commercialized material from the vaudeville stage or Tin Pan Alley, concentrating instead on verse that evoked deeply felt responses from her audiences. The second characteristic of Smith's blues lyrics was that, although they often addressed far-reaching social issues and concerns, they expressed her own feelings and experiences as a black woman."

When she sang, Smith was sad, angry, and, sometimes, hard as nails. *You can send me up the river or send me to that mean ole jail. You can send me up the river or send me to that mean ole jail. I killed my man and I don't need no bail.*

Singing about poverty, prisons, injustice, urban slums, and gambling, Bessie Smith also touched on sex frankly and forcefully. She became, not just a singer, but an artist who spoke for black women, voicing their concerns and frustrations, declaring their pride and independence.

The blueswomen who followed moved the blues even further from the main stream. Ida Cox and Clara Smith followed Bessie's lead and developed a hard, urban style, "City blues." Mamie Smith and Sara Martin ruled as queens of vaudeville blues. **Alberta Hunter** took the blues into cabarets and nightclubs and even to Europe; Edith Wilson and Ethel Waters took it to Broadway. Each different context added different flavors to the music.

For the decade of the twenties, blueswomen were at the top of the musical heap. Their recordings were hits for the "race records" companies—recording companies that targeted black audiences—and the singers were in great demand as performers. The music they sang came to be known as classic blues, and it was a particularly strong, wide branch of the river of black music, sending out streams all over the landscape.

But when the twenties came to an end, so did the tremendous popularity of the blueswomen. Some fashioned long, creative careers in small clubs or in gospel music; others, like Bessie Smith, were destroyed by despair. But they were followed by a new generation, the band singers.

If the blueswomen were singers with bands standing behind them, the new sound in music was *bands* . . . with singers standing in front of them. The bands belonged to such great musicians as Earl Hines, Count Basie, and Duke Ellington, Tommy and Jimmy Dorsey, Benny Goodman, and Artie Shaw. They all needed girl singers who could carry a tune and look pretty in a fancy gown.

In many cases, they got a whole lot more.

First and foremost, there was Billie Holiday. Holiday started to sing professionally in 1932, when she was seventeen, at a Harlem nightclub called the Log Cabin Club. By 1937, she was singing with Count Basie; after about a year, she left to join bandleader Artie Shaw. In the next few years, Holiday became a star who sang at the New York club Café Society for a couple of years and then toured the country as a solo artist. For awhile, she was the most successful, respected, and envied singer in the business. A major influence on the jazz musicians she worked with, she was said to use her voice like an instrument, like a horn; the musicians who worked with her played off her singing as they would off a sax or a trumpet.

By the early 1940s, however, Holiday was hopelessly addicted to heroin. The next decade was a seesaw of addiction, rehabilitation, more drugs and alcohol, a few more club dates, and, finally, death in an automobile accident in 1959. Still, her influence lived on. Instrumentalists and other singers alike has been touched by her musical sensitivity. Her songs, too, lived on. Holiday wrote such classics as "God Bless the Child," and "Billie's Blues."

In *The Raw Pearl*, **Pearl Bailey** tells this story: In 1934, she was talked into entering the amateur contest at a music hall called the Harlem Opera House, but she got there too late. Down the street, another theater —the legendary Apollo—was also having an amateur night. So she entered that one instead. "I won . . . for 'In My Solitude,' arrangement homemade," she recounts. "Maybe my nice appearance helped, too. I'm grateful I didn't go down the street to the Opera House. I doubt I would have made it there, for that night a young girl walked on stage, opened her mouth, and the audience that had started to snicker ended up cheering. The girl sang 'Judy.' Her name was Ella Fitzgerald. She won, and that voice will go down in history."

Pearl Bailey, of course, did very well herself, with a remarkable career in theater, films, and television, as well as nightclubs. Ella Fitzgerald, on the other hand, simply sang—*like an angel!* She could swing with

Billie Holiday started to sing professionally in 1932, when she was seventeen, at a Harlem nightclub called the Log Cabin Club. By 1937, she was singing with Count Basie. (MOORLAND-SPINGARN)

the best of the big bands and, when bebop developed, she could improvise like no one else; her scatting was legendary.

Lena Horne, Sarah Vaughan, Carmen McRae, Betty Carter, and Dinah Washington were among the other extraordinary vocalists whose careers began in the thirties and forties. Then, for a time, it seemed as though this tradition of great singers was dying out. As rhythm and blues became rock and roll, a musical genre from which women were almost entirely shut out, black women singers became much less visible. Still, the torch was carried by women such as **Dionne Warwick** and **Nancy Wilson**, both of whom were considered uncategorizable during the sixties and seventies.

Warwick was a classically trained musician from a family already prominent in gospel music. She made a career of singing songs by Hal David and Burt Bacharach and appeared regularly at the Apollo Theater in Harlem. In an interview about the Apollo, she said, "I never had any problem relating to the people at the Apollo because that was my heritage. But a lot of people tell me, 'I don't understand how you played the Apollo. They don't understand your music.' What do you mean they don't understand my music? Hal David wrote lyrics that spoke to your heart. Everybody's got one of those regardless of how rich or poor you are, or the color of your skin."

Nancy Wilson also caused problems for people who felt the need to put black performers into neat niches. "Most jazz buffs will say I'm not a jazz singer," she said in *Showtime at the Apollo.* "Most rhythm-and-blues buffs will say I'm not a r-and-b singer, and most pop buffs will say I'm not a pop singer."

The same could be said of **Abbey Lincoln** (Aminata Moseka), **Anita Baker,** and more recently, Whitney Houston and **Toni Braxton.** More and more, there were black women appearing on the scene who chose music that suited them, rather than tailoring their styles to the music.

Pearl Bailey won the amateur contest at the Apollo, which she entered because she was too late to compete in the Harlem Opera House (Ella Fitzgerald won at the Harlem Opera House). It would have been interesting if Bailey hadn't been late. In any case, both have gone on to become musical legends. (SCHOMBURG CENTER)

THE CONCERT TRADITION

Composers and Twentieth-Century Performers in Concert Music

The twenties was a golden era for African-American artists. Paul Lawrence Dunbar and **Zora Neale Hurston, Gwendolyn Bennett** and Langston Hughes were redefining what it meant to be a black writer. The **Lafayette Theater,** under the guidance of founder **Anita Bush,** was planting the seeds of the black theater movement. W. E. B. DuBois was calling for "native art," or art for black people and by black people. This flowering of culture also reached the creators of what we now call concert music, the composers of music to be played by symphony orchestras instead of swing bands, by string quartets instead of jazz trios.

It would be nice to think that, when the first black women put pen to paper—in the last decades of the nineteenth century—to create music out of the rich, painful, fertile experience of black life, they produced pure gold. Unfortunately, they produced the same thing white women of the time did: Respectable music, sentimental music, *nice* music.

"In the music of black women," said Helen Walker Hill in an interview on the nationally syndicated radio program *Noteworthy Women*, "you find the earliest published examples in the field in the area of parlor music, which is true of middle-class white women. . . . The earliest examples of composition by white women in the United States are these sedate little waltzes and sentimental songs and marches and two-steps. And lo and behold, this is the first example of published music that we find by black women."

The issue of respectability, which so limited black women composers and performers in the nineteenth century, had complex origins. Part of it was simply that they were women, and all women were handicapped by the roles and images they were forced into. But for black women, there was more. Respectability was a wall erected against the stereotypes that painted black women as promiscuous and sexually available. These stereotypes had been propounded by white men to excuse their sexual exploitation of black women in slavery and after.

Then, as later, there were many in both communities, black and white, who saw respectability as synonymous with a kind of European-American, middle-class culture

and saw respectable music as European music, untainted by African flavors and rhythms.

Certainly one important factor in shaping this definition was the church. The bishops of the African Methodist Episcopal Church in the early part of the century strongly encouraged the adoption of European music. African music was considered heathenish. In a sense, the church tried to purge the African-American community of its African origins. That included music with African overtones, such as spirituals and blues.

And then there was the problem that black music—ragtime, for example—was so often played in places that no "nice girl" would ever go to. It was, in the minds of many black families and community leaders, "the devil's music."

So the first black women composers erased from their music anything that spoke of their origins, as did the concert singers. An illustration of this comes from a music catalog published by Western University in Quintaro, Kansas, in 1906. In explaining why people should buy their music, students said, "To demonstrate to the world that the Negro is capable of the higher western concepts of music, and not that trashy ragtime music." This was the atmosphere in which the earliest African-American women composers worked.

A few years later, attitudes were beginning to change, but only beginning. **Nora Douglas Holt,** for example, graduated from Western University before going on to Chicago Musical College, where she became the first African American to earn a Masters Degree in musical composition. In 1918, Holt wrote a serious composition with a sound of ragtime, "Negro Dance." Even so, she was careful not to use the word *ragtime* to name or describe her music. She wrote a number of other compositions before turning to music criticism. From 1917 until 1923, she reviewed music for the *Chicago Defender* and, from 1944 to 1952, she wrote for the *New York Amsterdam News*. To the end of her life, she rejected the idea that black popular music forms such as blues and jazz had any place in serious music.

But then, in the twenties, the atmosphere was transformed. Pride in the African heritage was in the air, and it began to reach the music schools. **Florence Price** began to compose not long after Holt, but her music was very different; among her compositions were songs such as "Dances in the Canebrakes," "Arkansas Jitter," and "Bayou Dance."

Price was born and reared in Little Rock, Arkansas, and went on to the New England Conservatory of Music, presenting herself as a Mexican girl from Pueblo, New Mexico, in order to get in. After graduating, she married Thomas J. Price, a successful attorney. The Prices left Little Rock after the Ku Klux Klan lynched a man on the corner of the street where they and other educated African Americans lived. The message had been very clear.

The Prices moved to Chicago, a city that was becoming the center of black music in America. It was an exciting time to be a black artist. Price and other musicians could have told you that the "Harlem Renaissance" was not restricted to New York: There was plenty of art being born in Chicago, too, in part, because the black community was strong and cohesive in Chicago. "It was like a city within a city," says Helen Walker Hill, "run by African Americans themselves—the businesses, the police force, the hospitals. The effort was to create a community that would not be dependent on help from the White population. And while this did have some negative effects, it had the positive effects of creating a great cohesion and great self-help [in the] community. And a very rich artistic environment."

This was especially true for musicians. The first black musicians local of the musicians union was formed in Chicago. The first black-owned theater, the Pekin Theater, opened here. The Prices fit right in.

Inspired by the atmosphere of this strong artistic community, Florence Price composed symphonies, sonatas, and chamber music and wrote pieces for piano, organ, and voice, most of which was strongly influenced by other forms of black music. In 1925 and 1927, Price won Holstein awards and, in 1932, the Rodman Wanamaker Foundation Award for her *Symphony in E Minor*, which was played by the Chicago Symphony Orchestra at the 1939 World's Fair.

Price's eloquent arrangements of black spirituals came to the attention of soprano **Marian Anderson**, who sang them throughout her career. The training and skills of both women in traditional European music were a glorious infusion into black music of yet one more fruitful element.

Another composer who flourished in the rich artistic environment of Chicago was **Margaret Bonds**. She grew up in a home that welcomed and nourished black musicians. Bonds' mother was a church organist and choir director. On Sunday afternoons, the Bonds home was a salon, where musicians from the East, such as **Lillian Evanti** and Roland Hayes, would gather with Chicago musicians and music students. Florence Price's family lived for a time at the Bonds home.

Margaret Bonds began to study with Florence Price during this time. Helen Walker Hill tells how, later in life, Bonds "would tell about many of the people from the black community gathering around the kitchen table to copy out parts for Florence Price so she that she would meet her contest deadline or her performance deadline."

With the encouragement of Price and of her mother, Bonds developed rapidly as a composer. She went to Northwestern University and then approached the world-renowned Nadia Boulanger, asking to be taken on as a student. Boulanger turned her down, not because Bonds lacked talent, but that Boulanger's traditional European approach might spoil something in the younger woman's music.

After Northwestern, Bonds studied at Juilliard and then launched a splendid career, during which she won award after award. As a pianist, she performed with the Chicago Symphony Orchestra, the New York City Symphony, the Scranton Philharmonic, and the Chicago Woman's Symphony. Like Florence Price, Bond had an artistic relationship with one of the century's great concert singers, soprano **Leontyne Price**, who commissioned and recorded a number of Bonds' arrangements of spirituals.

Other black women who were composing concert music around this time include **Undine Smith Moore**, who wrote *Scenes from the Life of a Martyr* and *Afro-American Suite*; **Shirley Graham DuBois**, who wrote the opera *Tom-Toms*; **Betty Jackson King**, who is best known for her choral works; **Philippa Duke Schuyler**, whose *Niles Fantasia* was performed at New York's Town Hall shortly after her death in a helicopter crash in Vietnam; and Evelyn La Rue

Margaret Bonds was a composer who flourished in the rich artistic environment of Chicago. Her mother was a church organist and choir director, and on Sunday afternoons, visiting musicians from New York would gather in her family's home. (LIBRARY OF CONGRESS)

Pittman, who wrote the music dramas *Freedom Child* and *Jim Noble*. Mary Lou Williams, the jazz pianist, also wrote a number of pieces for concert performance, including *Zodiac Suite*, which was performed by the New York Philharmonic in 1946.

Nadia Boulanger, who rejected Margaret Bonds as a pupil, did accept as a pupil another black woman composer, **Julia Perry**. Perry was born in Kentucky in 1924 and studied at Akron University, at the Westminster Choir College, and at Juilliard and Tanglewood. Two Guggenheim awards that she won allowed her to study abroad; besides Boulanger, her teachers in Europe included Luigi Dallapiccola and Emanuel Balaban. She spoke Italian and German well and toured as a lecturer on American music for the United States Information Service.

In the meantime, Perry's reputation grew: As a composer, she was considered one of the most talented women of her generation, particularly for her works *Stabat Mater*, *Pastoral*, and *Homunculus C. F.* Her *Homage a Vivaldi* was enthusiastically received in Italy.

When Perry returned to the United States, however, she was in for a shock: While she was gone, the emphasis on black heritage and black pride had become very strong. Because she had not specifically drawn on black musical forms for her compositions, she found herself rejected by a musical community that wanted its black composers to sound black. She was unable to get performances or commissions, and the few grants and awards she did receive were not what a composer of her stature should have been able to expect. Shortly after her return, she had a nervous breakdown.

But she continued to compose. Moreover, when she had a series of strokes in the early 1970s which left her right side paralyzed, she taught herself to write with her left hand and kept composing. At this time, she wrote her *Soul Symphony*.

Perry's dilemma is a familiar one to black artists in many fields and is particularly acute in music, where, for many people, the lines are so rigidly drawn and have so much symbolic meaning. Ask any random group of people to define *classical* or *concert music* and they will be completely unable to do so; attempts will range from "music that's played in concerts" to "music that is written down" to "music that is in the European tradition." The defining characteristics that

aren't trivial are, usually, culture bound and restrictive.

Contemporary black women composers find themselves in a state of exploration. Their compositions include elements from a variety of sources, including the European tradition and the African-American heritage. They are allowing the river of black music to flow into the concert hall.

Lena Johnson McLin, another Chicago composer, writes cantatas, masses, operas, art songs, and electronic music as well as gospel and soul music. **Dorothy Rudd Moore**, another Boulanger student, has said that the primary influences on her music are Bach and Duke Ellington.

Younger composer **Regina Baiocchi** has written everything from gospel to twelve-tone contemporary music. Music historian Helen Walker Hill compares her to a prism because Baiocchi and her music reflect everything around her. More and more, this seems to be the way black women are making music. However, in the concert music establishment, a question remains: Can a composer who draws on sources of experience and inspiration that are not directly available to white men be accepted fully into the musical establishment?

Historically, even black women performers have had difficulty finding opportunities in that milieu. The earliest concert performers, as we have already seen, were kept out of operas and orchestras. They created careers as solo performers who produced themselves or they joined popular touring groups such as minstrel or vaudeville shows. The only other alternative was to go to Europe.

Pianist **Hazel Harrison**, whose career began at the turn of the century, was first encouraged to pursue her concert career by European musicians, made her debut in Berlin, and often returned to Europe to study and perform. Lillian Evanti made her professional singing debut in Paris. Caterina Jarboro was the first African American to sing with a major opera company—at the Puccini Opera House in Milan.

Not until 1946 did a black woman, Camilla Williams, sign a contract with a major American opera company, but the most prestigious American opera company, the Metropolitan, did not put a black singer on its stage until 1955, when Marian Anderson performed in Verdi's *Un Ballo in Maschera*. Discovering, perhaps, that the presence of a black singer would not send their subscribers running to the exits, the Metropolitan presented **Mattiwilda Dobbs** the next year.

One of the strangest, saddest examples of the plight of the black concert musicians was Philippa Duke Schuyler. Daughter of a prominent black journalist and a wealthy white woman, her genius was proof to the world that interracial marriages can work. As a child, she won awards for her piano performances and compositions and was profiled in the thirties and forties in *Look*, *Time*, and *The New Yorker*.

However, as an adult, Schuyler ran into the same problems faced by other black musicians: She could not get work in the United States. So, she toured Latin America and for over a decade performed in eighty different countries. She played for kings and queens all over the world, but was rejected in the United States. In her letters, she said, "I hate my country and no one wants me in any other. I am emotionally part of nothing. . . . And that will always be my destiny."

In the latter part of her short life, Schuyler created a new persona for herself. She held

Lillian Evanti was one of many accomplished black Americans who had no opportunity to begin their performance career in the United States. She made her professional singing debut in Paris. (SCHOMBURG CENTER)

a passport in the name of Felipa Monterro and tried to establish herself as a new performer on the concert circuit, a *white* performer. She was unsuccessful in this odd and desperate gambit. She died in 1967 in a helicopter crash in Vietnam, where she was working as a journalist.

There has probably never been a clearer example of how terribly strong the need for black pride was in the decades before the civil rights movement and how vulnerable to racist attitudes were those who did not have it. Musicians, among others, are usually dependent for work on the musical judgments of others: When those judgments are slanted by racism, the damage to careers and to personalities is incalculable.

Marian Anderson came to represent the pride of black people. Her early career consisted of a series of concerts that were usually sponsored by black organizations. Then she established her reputation by touring Europe. When she returned to the United States, however, she met with serious resistance from racist policies and groups. The incident that made Anderson a symbol of black pride and heritage took place when, in 1939, the Daughters of the American Revolution (DAR) refused to allow her to

Genius Philippa Duke Schuyler began to compose for the piano at age four. For her thirteenth birthday, she completed her first orchestral work. Scored for 100 instruments, Manhattan Nocturne *was performed by the New York Philharmonic under the direction of Rudolf Ganz.* [SCHOMBURG CENTER]

sing in Constitution Hall in Washington, D.C., a hall that they owned.

The resulting furor made history. Eleanor Roosevelt resigned from the DAR; then she called Secretary of the Interior Harold L. Ickes and asked him to invite Anderson to sing on the steps of the Lincoln Memorial. Anderson was there on Easter Sunday, and so were 75,000 black and white men, women, and children, filling the park and the streets. From that moment, Marian Anderson was a historic figure.

Marian Anderson was the first black singer ever to perform at New York's Metropolitan Opera, when she performed the role of Ulrica in Verdi's Un Ballo in Maschera *in 1955.* [SCHOMBURG CENTER]

In 1939, Marian Anderson performed for an audience of 75,000 in front of the Lincoln Memorial after the Daughters of the American Revolution refused to allow her to sing in Constitution Hall. Secretary of the Interior Harold Ickes, with the help of Eleanor Roosevelt, made this concert possible. Anderson is shown here singing in the same location at the 1952 memorial service for Ickes. [LIBRARY OF CONGRESS]

Barriers did not fall magically after Anderson's magnificent voice rang out that Easter morning. But the talent and determination of black women have made inroads into the musical establishment, more often in concert singing than in most fields. Many black women have built international reputations: Leontyne Price, **Grace Bumbry, Shirley Verrett, Martina Arroyo,** Leona Mitchell, Betty Allen, **Hilda Harris, Kathleen Battle,** and **Jessye Norman.**

In 1989, Jessye Norman sang the French national anthem for the bicentennial of the French Revolution. Given the role Europe has played in encouraging African-American musicians and the struggle for freedom that black women have carried on in concert music, it was an event of great symbolic significance.

WHEN THE WHITE KIDS STARTED TO DANCE TO IT

Rhythm and Blues to Rock and Roll

During World War II, a great many African Americans moved to the big cities, where the radio stations, the record stores, and places to spend their money on music were. So, as in the 1920s, many small black record companies sprang up. They recorded music that this urban black population wanted to hear, the kind that was once called race music. But in a different social climate, that phrase was not acceptable, so they called it rhythm and blues.

Was rhythm and blues a new "kind" of music? Yes and no. A lot of it sounded just like blues; some of it sounded like blues with a little jazz added; some of it sounded like blues with a little country added; some of it sounded like blues with an attitude. If the record companies and the radio stations —and *Billboard* magazine—hadn't needed a way to label it, it would simply have been black music.

In *Black Women in America*, Phyl Garland describes rhythm and blues as "more rhythmically assertive than the popular blues of the 1920s and 1930s." She goes on to say that it "reflected the increasingly confident mood of blacks. Although they had been relegated to segregated units, many black Americans had gotten their first taste of freedom from racism while serving abroad in the military. At home, a huge migration northward by black Americans seeking prosperity in industrial jobs had endowed them with a confident urban edge."

Black women were major figures in this musical movement. In the 1950s, Dinah Washington was known as "Queen of the Blues." She started as a jazz singer with the Lionel Hampton big band, but she had an affinity for blues, and its influence in her music made her an important rhythm-and-blues star. Esther Phillips followed in Washington's footsteps and made her own mark. A favorite of the Beatles, she was nominated for a Grammy as best rhythm-and-blues vocalist in 1973.

Ruth Brown was one of the most successful rhythm-and-blues singers. One of the first singers signed by Atlantic records, she became so popular that she was called "Miss Rhythm," and the record company was called "the House that Ruth built." Other important figures were **LaVern Baker** and **Etta James**.

Later, Aretha Franklin paid homage to many of these earlier women. When she was first called "First Lady of Soul," she protested that "the queen of the blues was and still is Dinah Washington." When she won the 1973 Grammy as best R&B vocalist over Esther Phillips, she gave the statuette to Phillips.

Some of the names of these rhythm-and-blues stars are familiar to anyone who knows the history of rock and roll. This is where talking about "kinds" of music becomes complicated, bringing in issues of racial prejudice, economics, puritanism, and Elvis.

In the early fifties, it became apparent that black people weren't the only ones buying rhythm-and-blues records. Some rhythm-and-blues songs were even making the Top 40 charts. In Cleveland, disc jockey Alan Freed persuaded the management of his station, WJW, to add a rhythm-and-blues program to their schedule; it was so successful that he moved to New York's City's station WINS. He also claimed to have coined the term *rock and roll*.

Ruth Brown, LaVern Baker, and Etta James all became stars in the new climate. LaVern Baker crossed over to the pop charts with "Tweedle Dee" in 1955, followed up by a number of others, such as "I Cried a Tear" and "See See Rider." Ruth Brown was regularly hitting the upper reaches of the rhythm-and-blues charts and, with "Lucky Lips," she made it onto the top forty in 1957. Etta James, a regular on the rhythm-and-blues charts, made it to the top forty in the sixties with "All I Could Do Was Cry," "Pushover," and "Tell Mama."

A *Rolling Stone* interviewer once asked Ruth Brown, "At what point did rhythm and blues start becoming rock and roll?" She answered, "When the white kids started to dance to it." That was also when the problems started to arise. The United States in the 1950s was still a very segregated society, and there were a great many people who wanted to keep it that way. When those people saw white teenagers going to concerts of black music, mixing with black teenagers, they became upset. When they saw white teenagers admiring black musicians, they became upset. When they saw Frankie Lymon, of Frankie and the Teenagers, dancing with a white girl on Alan Freed's TV show, they lost their composure.

Freed's show was cancelled. Rhythm and blues/rock and roll was clearly dangerous, but it was also worth a lot of money. How could the record companies, radio stations, and television stations avoid the danger and make the money? They could do what had been done more than a century before in minstrel shows—put black music onstage without black people.

White performers started to "cover"—record their own versions of—rhythm-and-blues hits. Some did it for love of the music, and others had motivations that weren't so pure. Sometimes the cover artists changed lyrics that were thought to be too sexual for the teenaged audience; sometimes, they made the music smoother and more upbeat. But the major difference between the versions was usually that one musician was black and the other white.

The case of "Hound Dog," first recorded by **Willie Mae "Big Mama" Thornton,** shows several of these forces at work. The song was written for her by white songwriters Jerry Leiber and Mike Stoller. She recorded it using a bluesy, shouting style. The song made the top of the rhythm-and-blues charts in 1953, and Thornton went on tour with a number of other rhythm-and-blues stars.

Three years later, a young white singer named Elvis Presley recorded Big Mama's hit and made music history. Clearly, Presley loved black music: He had grown up with it, been strongly influenced by it, and admired its musicians. But he did clean up the song; the version he sang was faster and more upbeat than Thornton's and was also smoother than his own early recordings.

This advertisement for Willie Mae "Big Mamma" Thornton's single "Hound Dog" is reproduced from Billboard. *It made the top of the rhythm-and-blues charts in 1953. In 1956 a young white singer named Elvis Presley recorded her hit and made music history.* [AMY VAN SINGLE]

Presley's "Hound Dog" was on the top of the charts for eleven weeks.

Still, in spite of white fears and greed, black musicians remained at the heart of rock and roll. The Platters, Sam Cooke, Tommy Edwards, Lloyd Price, Little Richard, Chuck Berry, Fats Domino—the list goes on as long as the beat does. The top of the charts, however, was foreign territory for most black women performers, with the exception of Zola Taylor, a member of the Platters.

Then, in 1961, black women found a way into rock and roll.

You could hear it in the schoolyard, in the apartment building hallway, on the street corner. You could hear it in poor black and Latino neighborhoods, in New York, Chicago, Philadelphia. It didn't take money to do it. You didn't need musical instruments. It was a cappella singing, close harmonies, doo-wop. Many singers who grew up in poor neighborhoods sang doo-wop, but it was especially appealing to women. Boys could start bands, but playing instruments was not considered any more appropriate for girls in the fifties than for girls in the twenties. So the girls sang.

The Bobbettes, the first black girl group to reach the upper reaches of the pop chart, had only one big hit, "Mr. Lee." It was a song they wrote themselves about one of their teachers. They were still very much concerned with teachers at the time: They ranged in age from eleven to fifteen when they signed with Atlantic Records in 1957.

The Chantels had more staying power, but they ran into the kinds of problems that the girl groups were plagued with throughout their tenure on the music scene. They started as schoolgirls, persuading Richard Barrett—manager of a popular men's group

—to give them a chance. He put pressure on a New York record company, and the group began to record in late 1957. Their first record, "He's Gone/The Plea," made it to only number 71 on the pop chart. The second, "Maybe," went up to 15 and got them on *American Bandstand*. In 1958, they had two more hits, "Every Night (I Pray)" and "I Love You So."

But they made no money. They were victims of the systematic exploitation of black recording artists by the record companies, who charged inflated "expenses" against musicians royalties. The very young girl groups were particularly vulnerable to this sort of sharp practice, but they were by no means alone.

In 1959, two of the Chantels left the group in frustration. One of them, Arlene Smith, was the lead singer and had written most of their songs. Barrett replaced them, and the group had two more Top 40 hits. They kept recording through the 1960s, but they never reached higher altitudes on the charts again.

In 1961, a girl group hit the top of the singles charts for the first time. The group was the **Shirelles,** and the song was "Will You Love Me Tomorrow," by Carole King and Gerry Goffin. The Shirelles had ten more hits in the Top 40 during the next two years, including five in the Top 10; they were also very influential in forming what Gillian G. Garr in *She's A Rebel* called "the first major rock style associated explicitly with women."

What probably made the girl groups so popular is that they sang, with innocence and sincerity, about the things adolescents cared about—love, dating, boyfriends, girlfriends, breaking up, making up. Charlotte Greig put it this way in her book on the girl groups, *Will You Still Love Me Tomorrow?*: "The Shirelles were go-betweens, emissaries between the sexes, summoning up their emotional courage on behalf of teenage boys and girls too shy and inarticulate to speak directly to each other. They were the first group to clearly fulfill this role, and they were dearly loved for doing so." They wrote many of their own songs, brought a kind of sweet intensity to the songs written for them by others, and could sing like the very dickens. They were good musicians.

The Shirelles were hugely successful in a music field that was not congenial to either women or African-Americans. From July 9, 1955, when the first rock-and-roll record hit the top of the charts, until January 30, 1961, when "Will You Still Love Me Tomorrow" did the same, there were fifty-nine number-one hits by white men, nine by black men, seven by white women, four by groups of white men and women, and three by a group with black men and a black woman. In other words, in the first five-and-a-half years of rock and roll, the only black woman to participate in a number one record was Zola Taylor of the Platters. Then the Shirelles came along.

What the Shirelles accomplished was remarkable any way you look at it, but they have seldom been counted among rock-and-roll pioneers. Male rock and rollers, as well as historians of the rock-and-roll era, tend to speak as though any four pretty girls with a minimum of musical talent could have pulled off the same thing. The implication is that the songwriters, arrangers, producers, and record companies were really responsible for their success; this charge is seldom or never made about male musicians, whatever their race.

The Shirelles confronted the same practical problems the Chantels had: Though they followed up "Tomorrow" with another number one hit, "Soldier Boy," and remained in the Top 10 with "Baby It's You," "Mama Said," and "Dedicated to the One I Love," the Shirelles stayed broke. When the first group members turned twenty-one, they found that the money they thought had been held in trust for them was not there. It had been used for "expenses."

About a year later, another black girl group, the **Marvelettes**, had a number one single with "Please Mr. Postman." It was the first Motown record to make the top of the charts. Another particularly fine group, **Martha Reeves** and the Vandellas, came out of Motown. Their string of hits included "Dancing in the Streets" and "Nowhere to Run." There would also be hit records for the Crystals, the Chiffons, and the Dixie Cups before the biggest girl group of all time came out of the motor city.

The Supremes were a cultural phenomenon. From August 22, 1964, when "Where Did Our Love Go?" hit number one, until December 27, 1969, when "Someday We'll Be Together" heralded the end of Diana Ross' stay with the group, The Supremes had twelve number-one singles. They were the most successful American rock-and-roll group of the sixties and one of the most successful of all time.

However, as solo performers in rock and roll, black women were still nowhere to be seen.

It's true that Ruth Brown had a number of crossovers onto the pop charts in the late fifties. In 1962, a young black woman singing under the name Little Eva hit number one with "The Loco-Motion," and followed that up with several more top-forty singles.

Between August 22, 1964, when "Where Did Our Love Go?" hit number one, until December 27, 1969, when "Someday We'll Be Together" heralded the end of Diana Ross' stay with the group, the Supremes had twelve number-one singles. They were one of the most successful musical groups of all time. (PRIVATE COLLECTION)

In 1964, Mary Wells had a number one single with "My Guy," but she never made it into the top thirty again.

That, during the rock-and-roll era, was the history of black women solo performers on the pop charts, and yet they were pretty much holding their own with black men and white women. Looking at pictures of rock-and-roll stars of the sixties is like flipping through a fraternity photo album: You've never seen so many young white guys.

In the late sixties and early seventies, things began to change: There were more

black faces, and there were more women's faces. Diana Ross' solo career took off. But far more important, Aretha Franklin moved from Columbia records, where she was recording "Over the Rainbow" and "Try a Little Tenderness" to Atlantic, where she recorded "I Never Loved a Man (The Way I Love You)" and "Respect." She started to sing soul.

THE (MANY) SOUNDS OF SOUL

Soul Music

Nobody has ever really been able to define *soul*. It's what Ray Charles and James Brown and Aretha Franklin sing—that much is easy. But what *is* it? In *Showtime at the Apollo*, Little Anthony tells a revealing story:

> The Imperials needed something to make that audience come out of their seats. The thing you do in church is reach their sensitivity mark, the emotional thing they can relate to. I remembered a gospel thing we used to do in church, and I said, "Wait a minute." I told my guitar player, "Give me that thing that we do in church, you know, that run that everybody gets up on." We worked on it in the Apollo. I called it, from an emotional standpoint, "I'm Alright." It became a legend with the Imperials. I just did a gospel thing, and fell to my knees and started reaching.

At that point, the song had few words besides the tag, "I'm Alright." But then, Little Anthony goes on to say, the owner of the Apollo, Frank Schiffman, sent Sam Cooke to work with the Imperials on some lyrics.

So Sam took a little paper and started writing: "When my baby holds me in her arms—I'm alright, I'm alright. When I taste her many charms—I'm alright, I'm alright." So it went from a religious gospel thing to what you see today—realizing that you can take an emotional thing and turn it into a spiritual thing to a sensual thing. We opened up a can of worms that I regret to this day.

Revealing as this story is, Little Anthony takes too much guilt—and credit—onto his shoulders. That element of expressing, and even of churning up, emotions has been part of African-American music from the beginning. As we quoted Linda Dahl earlier, " . . . perhaps most significant of the elements that made up slave music was the approach to feelings, a codified straining toward personal expression that ignored a preconceived ideal of sound. . . . The music of black slaves married the pain and pleasure of physical life with a permeating spirituality; one of its great, enduring strengths was that it did not sever the life of the body from that of the spirit."

Gospel had perhaps developed that aspect of the music more than some of the secular genres, but it neither invented nor had sole claim to what could be called the "soul" of black music.

Soul in that sense is what Aretha Franklin offered the rock-and-roll world. She was not the first and would not be the last, but she was the Queen. "Respect" became an anthem, a rallying cry, a theme for the time. Franklin followed it with "Baby, I Love You," which also broke into the pop charts' top ten and "(You Make Me Feel Like) A Natural Woman." "Chain of Fools" was another major hit. During the next couple

of years, she would have eleven more top forty songs and four more top twenty albums. By 1970, she was one of the most important recording artists in the country. She was the "Queen of Soul."

A broader definition of *soul* developed as the movement toward black freedom and identity grew. It was possible for a white artist to have soul in the sense just discussed. However, in a different sense, *soul* was defined as what black people bring to music from their experience and their heritage. It is at once a broader and a narrower definition. It takes in fewer people, but it allows black musicians a greater freedom of style and expression. In that second sense, the seventies were the beginning of a time for black women to explore the different sounds of soul.

Tina Turner was still with the Ike and Tina Turner Revue, enjoying more success in Britain than in the United States and more success onstage than on records. Still, she did have three top-forty hits in the early seventies—"I Want to Take You Higher," "Proud Mary," and "Nutbush City Limits." In 1976, she left her abusive husband Ike and set out on her own. Her massive comeback in 1984 with the album *Private Dancer* won her three Grammy awards. Turner's style is hugely energetic and sexy in an almost athletic way, owing more to James Brown than to Bessie Smith.

The same could probably be said of **Patti LaBelle**. With the Bluebells—Cindy Birdsong, Nona Hendryx, and Sarah Dash—LaBelle developed a "girl group" image in the 1960s. In the seventies, they changed their name to Labelle, lost Cindy Birdsong to the Supremes, and broke the mold as far as image was concerned. With the help of a creative fan, they became glitteringly futuristic, rivaling the most glamorous of the "glam rock" superstars; their live shows became spectaculars. *Rolling Stone* said, in 1974, "Labelle owns New York. The city which is supposed to be the performer's ultimate conquest bows in unashamed surrender any time the group takes the stage."

That same year, "Lady Marmalade," a single from their album *Nightbirds*, hit number one. Three years later, the group disbanded so that each member could pursue a solo career. Labelle herself went on to become a multifaceted entertainer, starring in *Your Arms Too Short to Box with God* on Broadway, and releasing a number of chart-topping albums and singles.

Another group that played with images was the **Pointer Sisters**. They came on the scene with a 1940s look and a jazzy singing style. But they ranged widely in their performances, breaking out of the nostalgia pigeonhole to develop a powerful performance style on such songs as "Fire" and "Slow Hand." Their 1983 album won two Grammy awards and launched a string of four hit singles.

Gladys Knight and the Pips were a highly successful rhythm-and-blues group as early as the late fifties, with a number of Top 40 singles in the early sixties. Originally from Georgia, they won an amateur night contest at the Apollo and became regular Apollo headliners. They've had a number of hits over the years, including "I Heard It Through the Grapevine," "Neither One of Us (Wants to Be the First to Say Good-bye)," "Midnight Train to Georgia," and "Love Overboard" and have won a number of Grammy awards in both pop and rhythm-and-blues categories. Knight has always felt that the group was unfairly pigeonholed as rhythm-and-blues performers.

Other black women who had an impact on the seventies and eighties include the disco artists Sister Sledge and **Donna Summer**. Summer later transcended her disco roots and became a popular singer of ballads.

In 1985, the most successful woman in popular music made her debut. The album *Whitney Houston* included "You Give Good Love," which went to number three on the pop charts; "Saving All My Love for You," which went to number one and won a Grammy; "How Will I Know," which went to number one; and "Greatest Love of All," which went to number one. Obviously, the album also hit the top of the charts. It was the first time in history that a solo female artist ever had three number-one songs from one album. Houston has never looked back.

The music industry has stopped counting the records Houston has broken. She seems to be the magic combination: The daughter of gospel singer Cissy Houston and cousin of Dionne Warwick, she has a strong grounding in black music, is lovely and wholesome, and has a remarkable voice. She is, simply, one of the most popular singers in history.

All of these women have developed their own voices and styles that go beyond labels. What became clear in the fifties and sixties is that mainstream rock and roll was not a hospitable place for women. What became clear from the seventies on is that black women were making too many different kinds of music to be pigeonholed anywhere.

ROXANNE RAPS BACK

Rap Music

At first, it seemed that rap music was going to be an even more exclusively male club than rock and roll: There was political rap,

African nationalist rap, message rap, crossover rap, but all of it was guy rap—or so it appeared.

Actually, the roots of female rap go back to a woman named Sylvia Vanderpool, who was part of a duo called Mickey and Sylvia in the 1950s, cowrote "Love Is Strange" with Bo Diddley and played guitar on Tina Turner's "It's Gonna Work Out Fine." With her husband, Joe Robinson, she formed the Sugar Hill recording company in 1975. After producing several other rap groups, she released "Funk You Up," by The Sequence in the early eighties. Lisa Lee followed, in a collaboration with Afrika Bambataa. In 1984, she formed Us Girls with Sha Rock from the Funky Four Plus One More.

Female rappers loudly announced their presence in 1985, when fourteen-year-old Lolita Shante Gooden released "Roxanne's Revenge" under the name Roxanne Shante. It was an answer to the UTFO's "Roxanne, Roxanne," which put down a young neighborhood woman named Roxanne for being stuck up. The answer song triggered a whole series of Roxanne songs and, in the end, gave success to another female rapper, Joanne Martinez, who called herself the Real Roxanne.

A rivalry grew up between the two women. Martinez was sponsored by UTFO, who wrote and produced most of her material. Shante wrote much of her own material; understandably, therefore, Shante's records were harder on men, striking out against sexual harassment and other sexual exploitation. However, by 1988, Martinez, too, was writing some of her own material. Her "Respect" was inspired by both the Aretha Franklin anthem and Helen Reddy's "I Am Woman."

The first female rappers to hit the Top 40 charts came on the scene in 1985: Cheryl James and Sandy Denton's first record released under the name **Salt-N-Pepa** was "I'll Take Your Man," a reworking of the Pointer Sisters' "How Long (Betcha Got a Chick on the Side)." With that record, they had a DJ, Latoyah, who was called "Spinderella." She was soon replaced by Dee Dee Roper. Salt-N-Pepa's debut album, *Hot, Cool, & Vicious*, was released in 1986 and became the first female rap album to reach the Top 40 and to go platinum.

As Salt-N-Pepa's career took off, **Queen Latifah** (Dana Owens) crossed over; her first album, *All Hail the Queen*, released in 1989, sold more than a million copies, but Latifah really hit the pop mainstream when she rapped on the David Bowie record "Fame '90." Her "Ladies First" was a strong statement of pride in womanhood, and in a remarkably short time, she was a major figure in black entertainment, with her own production company, roles in a number of films, and a part in the hit television series *Livin' Single*.

Women rappers address a multitude of social issues in their music, from poverty to urban decay to sexual abuse. Controversy about the antifemale lyrics of male rappers also puts the spotlight on black women who choose to participate in the hip-hop culture. They have been expected to respond to the sexual attitudes expressed in male rap, and the majority do, with strong statements of female pride. Queen Latifah exemplifies this in her name, in her rhetoric, and in her life; at the same time, her approach to male rappers is more often educative and consciousness raising than confrontational.

The range of identification with feminism is wide. Queen Latifah rejects the title, one that the women of Salt-N-Pepa wear proudly, while Yo-Yo (Yolanda Whitaker) even formed the Intelligent Black Women's Coalition, which is, in their own words, "devoted to increasing the self-esteem of *all* women."

There are also women of rap who compete with male rappers on their own terms, with explicitly sexual boasting. These groups call themselves by the disrespectful terms male rappers apply to women, declaring that they are trying to take back some of the power those words have when used negatively.

When these groups began releasing records, they were met with hostility from other women in the hip-hop culture, who believed they were "disrespecting" themselves and other women. However, a strong argument could be made that they were attacking the double standard of the music world, and that their records certainly addressed serious social issues that face women.

A maverick on the female rap scene was **Sister Souljah**. She is perhaps more a social activist than a musician. Her speeches assailing drug abuse, U.S. politicians, male rappers, and black-on-black crime are at least as famous as her records. She gained further notoriety in 1992 when President Clinton made an ill-judged attack on her first rap album, *360 Degrees of Power*, claiming that it contributed to the violent climate that resulted in the Los Angeles riots of that year.

Whatever else can be said about rap, it is clear that black women musicians have come a long way from "Please Mr. Postman."

AND THE RIVER FLOWS

Tina Turner had the energy of a rock-and-roll star, but she was consistently labeled rhythm and blues. Aretha Franklin had the soulful delivery of a classic blues singer, but she was the first woman inducted into the Rock and Roll Hall of Fame. Nobody knows *what* category Nancy Wilson or Dionne Warwick fits in. And what about Abbey Lincoln (Aminata Moseka)?

Today, apart from saying that Queen Latifah is a rap artist, it is almost impossible to label *any* black woman musician, and it seems very likely that Latifah won't stay labeled long. When you listen to the music of Whitney Houston, Mary Blige, Toni Braxton, and Vanessa Rubin, you hear so many sounds, so many echoes of voices past. The same is true when you listen to new composers of jazz and concert music.

Maybe the branches of the river have reached the sea. It is certain that the waters are mixing; it is equally certain that the time has come to recognize that music is not composed or performed by races or ethnic groups, but by individual artists. While it is easy to generalize about "women's music" or "a black sound," about concert musicians or female rappers, there is only one generalization that can be truthfully made about black women's music: It always has been and always will be whatever music is made by the magnificent artists who are black women.

[This introduction incorporates material from the following articles in *Black Women in America: An Historical Encyclopedia*: "Blues and Jazz," by Daphne Duval Harrison; "Composers" and "Concert Music," by Mildred Denby Green; "Gospel Music," by Horace Clarence Boyer; "Rap Musicians," by William Eric Perkins and "Rhythm and Blues," by Phyl Garland.]

A

Addison, Adele (1925–)

Adele Addison, soprano, is best known as a recitalist but has made distinguished appearances and recordings in oratorio and opera; she is also recognized as a teacher and scholar with special interests in German lieder. Born July 24, 1925, in New York City, her early education took place in Springfield, Massachusetts, where her family moved during her childhood. She received the B.Mus. from Westminster Choir College in 1946 and then studied with Boris Goldovsky at the Berkshire Music Center and Povla Frijsh in New York City.

Addison made her recital debut in Jordan Hall, Boston, Massachusetts, in April 1948 and four years later gave a recital in Town Hall, New York City. Tours of the United States and Canada were interspersed with teaching. In 1962, she was soloist in the opening concert at Philharmonic Hall at Lincoln Center, and in 1963 made an acclaimed tour of the Soviet Union under a cultural exchange program. She has taught at the Eastman School, Philadelphia College of the Performing Arts, Aspen Music School, and the State University of New York, Stony Brook.

Indicative of Adele Addison's standing among American singers and her intelligent musicianship is the fact that she has participated in several significant world premieres of contemporary music, such as John La Montaigne's *Fragments from Song of Songs* with the New Haven Symphony (1950); Poulenc's *Gloria* with the Boston Symphony Orchestra (1961); and Lukas Foss' *Time Cycle* with the New York Philharmonic Orchestra. In addition, she has appeared with most of the other major American symphony orchestras. She was awarded an honorary doctorate by the University of Massachusetts in 1963.

DORIS EVANS McGINTY

Acclaimed soprano Adele Addison was soloist at the opening concert of Philharmonic Hall at Lincoln Center in 1962. (LIBRARY OF CONGRESS)

One of the most prolific and influential composers in the history of gospel music, Doris Akers was one of the first musicians to bridge the gap between the black and white gospel traditions. (J. C. DJEDJE)

Akers, Doris (1923–)

At a very young age, Doris Akers (gospel composer, choir director, singer, and publisher) listened to sermons to get ideas for songs. She became one of the most prolific, influential composers in the history of gospel music. Born May 21, 1923, in Brookfield, Missouri, Akers moved with her family to Kirksville, Missouri, when she was five. By the time she was six years old, she was playing the piano "by ear"; her first song, "Keep the Fire Burning in Me," was written when she was ten. As a young person, not only did she play at church and school activities, but she also organized a five-piece band called "Dot Akers and Her Swingsters," a band that featured swing jazz

and other styles of popular music in vogue during the 1930s and 1940s.

After her arrival in Los Angeles in 1945, Akers performed with the **Sallie Martin** Singers for a year and later organized her own gospel group, the Doris Akers Singers. In 1948, she joined **Dorothy Simmons** to form the Simmons-Akers Singers. During the ten years that the group was together, the Simmons-Akers Singers became nationally known through concert tours, recordings, and the establishment of a publishing company, the Simmons and Akers Music House. The company published and distributed songs written by Akers. Akers came into greater prominence in the late 1950s and the 1960s when she became a solo artist and director of the Sky Pilot Choir, one of the first racially mixed choirs in Los Angeles that featured the singing of black gospel music. In the late 1950s she also became affiliated with the white-owned publishing company Manna Music, giving her music even wider distribution. Thus, she is noted as one of the first musicians to bridge the gap between black and white gospel music.

In 1970, Akers moved to Ohio. Before leaving, she made several recordings with RCA, Capitol, and Christian Faith; appeared on nationwide television on many occasions; and received numerous awards for her contributions to gospel music. For example, in 1961 Akers was acknowledged as "Gospel Composer of the Year." During the 1970s and 1980s she continued to be active in the field of gospel music, particularly within the white Christian community.

She became known as an established gospel composer in 1947 with the publication of "A Double Portion of God's Love" by Martin and Morris Music; such standards as "Grow Closer" (1952), "Lead Me, Guide

Me" (1953), "God Is So Good" (1957), "You Can't Beat God Giving" (1957), and "Sweet, Sweet Spirit" (1962) are just a few of the hundreds of songs that she has composed. Not only are her songs found in various hymn and religious song books of all denominations, but some have been used as themes for musicals (e.g., *Praise House* and *Me and Bessie*) as well as the titles of hymn books (*Lead Me, Guide Me*).

JACQUELINE COGDELL DJEDJE

Allen, Geri (1959–)

Detroit-born pianist-composer Geri Allen sets modern standards that stem from patterns laid out by jazz greats, from various continental styles, and from a personal sensibility that honors and preserves past traditions. Allen is respected as an intelligent and gifted musician, with connections to the pulse of modern music, and is a creative mediator of fused sounds.

Geri Allen's encyclopedic use of sounds grows out of the vocabulary built by the grammarians of keyboard jazz composition —**Mary Lou Williams**, Thelonious Monk, and Duke Ellington—but her expansions fuse the funk, hip-hop, and soul styles that are closer to the taste of her generation with the ancestral musical sounds of Africa, the Caribbean, and South America. Her concept of musical inclusiveness may be called postmodernism in music.

Allen was graduated with a Bachelor's degree in jazz studies from **Howard University** in Washington, D.C., and, after several years as a touring performer, earned a master's degree in ethnomusicology at the University of Pittsburgh. Her musical colleagues include avant-garde saxophonist Oliver Lake, flutist James Newton, and Motown's Mary Wilson. She also has been active with the radical groups M-Base and Black Rock Coalition.

Her 1991 recording, *The Nurturer*, features and honors her mentor, trumpeter Marcus Belgrave. Three of the nine tunes on the album were composed by Allen, and the others (except one by Lawrence Williams) were composed by members of the sextet. This democratic assignment of talent, as well as the musical qualities of the album, suggest a dedication to experimentation and newness. The album's title piece, Allen's "Silence and Song/The Nurturer," comprises piano statements that range from clean lyricism to mystical harmonic coloring to aggressive and complex rhythmic statements that delicately balance the horn and percussion lines.

Other projects include the recording of Jimi Hendrix's compositions (scored for three pianos) and the composition of a large experimental work commissioned by the avant-garde American Music Theater Festival in Philadelphia. Her album *Maroons* (1992) is an "improvisation-happening" that recognizes ex-slaves as warriors who freed themselves and who created their own cultures in the Americas. Allen leads her own trio, the Geri Allen Trio, that tours Europe, Japan, and the United States.

LORNA McDANIEL

Anderson, Ernestine (1928–)

Ernestine Anderson was described by *Time* magazine in 1958 as "the best new voice in the business." That voice has gotten even better over the years, and Anderson should easily make anyone's list of the top ten jazz vocalists active in the 1990s.

Born in Houston, Texas, on November 11, 1928, Anderson was exposed very early to the blues. Her parents played blues records constantly, giving their daughter an early taste of bluesmen such as John Lee Hooker and Muddy Waters. This may account for Anderson's strong blues-based style. The church also was a big influence; young Ernestine sang hymns in her neighborhood Baptist church. She also heard jazz whenever the bands of Jimmie Lunceford, Billy Eckstine, Erskine Hawkins, and Count Basie came through Houston.

As a teenager, Anderson began to sing at Houston's El Dorado Ballroom and at other venues outside the church. When the family moved to Seattle, Washington, she continued to sing with local bands, touring with several groups led by Russell Jacquet, Johnny Otis, Eddie Heywood, and, finally in 1952 and 1953, Lionel Hampton.

In 1956, Anderson found herself in Sweden with an all-star jazz group led by trumpeter Rolf Ericson. Although she had made her first recording the previous year with Gigi Gryce, it was the album *Hot Cargo*, recorded in Sweden, that made U.S. critics and audiences take note of her.

Critical acclaim notwithstanding, Anderson's popularity waned in the early 1960s, and in 1965 she moved to England. When she returned to Los Angeles a few years later, she decided to retire from singing and took a succession of nonmusical day jobs. She also took up Nichiren Shosha Buddhism.

In the 1970s, several musicians, including Ray Brown and Benny Carter, urged Anderson to resume her professional career. She signed a recording contract with Concord Jazz and has made a number of excellent albums for the label and garnered several Grammy nominations. Her concert and club appearances have further enhanced her reputation as one of the best song stylists on the scene today.

VINCENT PELOTE

Anderson, Marian (1897–1993)

When she was just eight years old, Marian Anderson sang on a church program in which she was presented as the "Baby Contralto"; her aunt, who had arranged the program to help raise funds for the church, asked her to sing. Two years earlier, Anderson had joined the junior choir at her church, Union Baptist Church in Philadelphia. She loved to sing more than anything, and music and musical instruments always caught her attention at home and in school.

Anderson was born on February 27, 1897. Her parents, John and Annie, were hardworking but not well off financially. In her autobiography, *My Lord, What a Morning*, Anderson recalled her father's devotion to his family and the warmth and joy they all felt when they were together. For a time before she was two years old, the Andersons lived with John's parents. After her sister Alyce was born, the family rented a small house near the grandparents. Another sister, Ethel, was born while they lived there.

Anderson recalled playing "music" on a table while her mother worked. She pretended that the table was a piano and kept rhythm with her feet and hands as she sang a melody with nonsense syllables. She always enjoyed singing with her family at home. Neither of her parents had been particularly talented singers, but Annie Anderson had sung in church choirs.

John Anderson was very active in his church, serving as an usher, and took his daughter with him every Sunday to attend Sunday school and morning worship services. She loved to hear the choirs and sing in the congregation. When she was six, she joined the church's children's choir, which responded well to volunteer director Alexander Robinson, singing with great spirit and enthusiasm. In a short time, Robinson noticed Anderson's beautiful voice and vitality and selected her to sing a duet with her friend, a soprano, in both Sunday school and the worship service, her first public appearance.

Anderson was about eight years old when her father bought a piano from his brother. She tried to play immediately, even attempting a major scale by placing her thumb under her fingers as she had seen others play. With no money for music lessons, she taught herself by means of a card with the names of the keys and notes that could be slipped directly behind the keys; later, she saw a black woman playing the piano and decided that she too could develop her skill.

She also made an attempt at being a violinist; seeing a violin in a pawn shop, she scrubbed her neighbors' steps to earn money to buy it. Having saved $4 and buying the violin for $3.98, she again tried to teach herself, but it was not long before she decided that the violin was not her instrument.

When she was ten, her father received an accidental blow to his head at work and never recovered. Following his death, the family returned to his parents' home.

Anderson went to William Penn High School with the idea of following a commercial education course to prepare her for a job so that she could earn money to help care for her mother and sisters. These studies did not interest her, but she did enjoy her once-a-week music class. Noticing her talent, her

Racism was a constant in Marian Anderson's life. The photo above from the National Archives shows her "performing at the Great Lakes Naval Training Station, for the officers and men of Negro regiments." (NATIONAL ARCHIVES)

music teacher invited her to sing with the school chorus, and she was occasionally given solos. After singing solo in a school assembly, she was called to the principal's office and encouraged to change to a college preparatory course, which would permit her to pursue more music studies. Anderson transferred to South Philadelphia High School and continued to perform in assemblies with the support of her new principal, Dr. Lucy Wilson.

In the meantime, her singing began to attract attention at church, where she had joined the senior choir and visited other churches with the choir. As she became increasingly well known, Anderson learned to play the piano well enough to accompany herself, and accepted invitations to sing at other churches and at larger church-related events. In 1919, she sang at the national meeting of the National Baptist Convention, U.S.A., Inc., in Atlantic City. Gospel composer Lucie Campbell, the convention's music director, introduced Anderson to the thousands attending the meeting and accompanied her.

Along with the many opportunities to perform and her growing success, Anderson felt the need for formal training. While still in high school, she began vocal studies with black music teacher Mary Saunders Patterson. Teaching without charge, although a family friend agreed to pay for the lessons, Patterson made Anderson aware of vocal technique and inspired her to find an accompanist to work with her on a permanent basis. She also studied with Agnes Reifsnyder for a short time.

At this point, she was encouraged by her mother and others to consider attending a music school and decided to get information about enrolling in a school in downtown Philadelphia. She was abruptly turned down because of her race; when she described the humiliating rebuff, her mother encouraged her to keep her faith and never give up the pursuit of her dreams.

During her senior year in high school, her principal introduced Anderson to Giuseppe Boghetti, a teacher of great reputation, but she could not afford his expensive fees. When it appeared that she would have to wait until she could save enough for lessons, church members and friends came to her rescue. A special concert at the church was arranged, with Roland Hayes, whom she

admired and respected, as one of the soloists. She was greatly moved by this gesture and considered singing on the same program with Hayes to be one of the highlights of her life. The concert raised $600 for her singing lessons.

Boghetti further developed her technique —especially her breathing—and taught her songs in German, Italian, and French, written by Schubert, Brahms, and other classical composers.

Her accompanist, Billy King, was a talented musician who served as organist at an Episcopal church and had accompanied artists such as Roland Hayes; eventually King took over the duties of managing her concerts and publicity. Sponsored by a variety of black organizations, Anderson toured and gave concerts at colleges and churches and other venues with black audiences. As her earnings increased, she was able to help her mother purchase a home, in which she set up a studio for her music practice.

Her growing audiences and larger fees also gave her assurance that she was ready to advance in her career. She felt she could gain national recognition by performing at Town Hall in New York City. On the night of the concert (in 1922), she was shattered by the poor attendance, and her confidence was shaken by a performance she felt was not especially good. The few reviews verified that her New York debut was premature. The incident threatened to end her career, and she retreated for some time. However, with the comfort and encouragement of her mother, she recovered and continued singing.

Entering a contest sponsored by Philadelphia's Philharmonic Society, Anderson won, marking the first time a black American had won first prize. In 1925, her victory in a competition held in New York City under the sponsorship of Lewisohn Stadium Concerts won her an appearance with the New York Philharmonic at Lewisohn Stadium, and many of her friends and family members were able to hear her perform. This tremendous career boost enabled her to acquire the top professional concert management of Arthur Judson. Her career advanced for a while, but eventually she felt the need for further study and considered going abroad to try to gain a reputation in Europe, as Roland Hayes and others had done. In New York, she studied briefly on a scholarship with Frank La Forge, vocal teacher to several famous singers. La Forge

Marian Anderson traveled throughout the world to perform. She is shown here in 1943 receiving the Liberian Redemption Award from Walter Walker, Liberian Consul General. Eleanor Roosevelt looks on. (NATIONAL ARCHIVES)

felt she did not need to go abroad and was not particularly encouraging when she decided to do so.

In the summer of 1929, armed with names of people she could contact for assistance, Anderson sailed to England on a second-class ticket. Billy King had given her a letter of introduction to Roger Quilter, who had assisted and encouraged Roland Hayes. Lawrence Brown, Hayes' accompanist, had written to Raimund von zur Muhlen, a famous teacher of German lieder.

Upon arrival in England, she called Quilter, only to discover that he was in a nursing home. Remembering black actor John Payne, who had visited her home in Philadelphia, she reached him and was invited to stay in his home. Later, she telephoned Muhlen and made an appointment to sing for him at his house. When he accepted her as a student, she moved closer to his home, but unfortunately, after only two lessons, he became ill and discontinued all teaching. Quilter, somewhat recovered, recommended Mark Raphael, a student of Muhlen and a specialist in lieder; although Raphael was a good teacher, Anderson was quite disappointed about not being able to continue with Muhlen.

After a concert in 1931 for the **Alpha Kappa Alpha Sorority** (she was an honorary member), Anderson was greeted backstage by a representative of the Rosenwald Fund. Upon learning of her desire to study in Germany, he encouraged her to apply for a fellowship, which she received. During her studies in Berlin, she gave concerts throughout Europe for the next several years. When she sang in Finland at the home of composer Jean Sibelius, he remarked, "My roof is too low for you." Her popularity, after two successful Scandinavian tours, was noted in Nazi Germany, and she was invited to sing there until it was discovered she was not 100 percent Aryan.

In June 1934, at her third Paris recital, she met and signed with the internationally known American concert manager Sol Hurok, beginning a long professional relationship. In spring 1935, she sang two concerts at Vienna's Wiener Konzerthaus and one at Salzburg's Mozarteum; a second Salzburg recital, held in a hotel ballroom, was arranged by American Gertrude Moulton. Following this concert the great conductor Arturo Toscanini uttered his famous statement, "Yours is a voice such as one hears once in a hundred years." Her first trip to the Soviet Union came in 1935. Returning briefly to the United States, she performed at Town Hall again on December 30, 1935; this time the outcome was much more successful. In 1936 she made a second, more extensive trip to the Soviet Union.

Although her fame throughout the world had helped break some racial barriers, Anderson was still denied many opportunities. Hurok's organization attempted to protect her from the prejudice they met when they tried to book her in certain areas. However, the most infamous incident associated with her career was the refusal in 1939 of the Daughters of the American Revolution (DAR) to allow her to perform in Constitution Hall in Washington, D.C. During a great surge of public protest, Eleanor Roosevelt resigned from the DAR and was instrumental in getting Secretary of the Interior Harold L. Ickes to issue Anderson an invitation to sing at the Lincoln Memorial. On Easter Sunday, April 9, 1939, she sang before a crowd of 75,000 in one of the most significant concerts in American music history. Eventually the policy of prohibiting black performers in Constitution Hall was changed.

In 1943, Anderson married architect Orpheus H. Fisher. They had met years before, become friends, and remained in touch through the years. They made their home on a farm in Connecticut.

After World War II, Anderson resumed her travels abroad. She made her television debut on *The Ed Sullivan Show* in 1952, and toured South America, Korea, and Japan in 1953. Her historic debut with the Metropolitan Opera Company in January 1955 marked the first time a black singer had ever sung at the Met. She sang the role of Ulrica in Verdi's *Un Ballo in Maschera*. In 1957, she traveled 40,000 miles throughout Asia as a goodwill ambassador sponsored by the U.S. State Department. The tour, recorded by CBS television, included Thailand, Korea, Vietnam, Singapore, Taiwan, Burma, Malaysia, and India. Both Anderson and her program, *The Lady from Philadelphia*, won praise.

During her career Anderson received numerous awards and honors, including the Spingarn Medal, Bok Award, and Page One Award. She sang at President Eisenhower's inauguration in 1957 and at President John F. Kennedy's in 1961. In 1958, Eisenhower appointed her an alternative representative in the United States delegation to the Human Rights Committee of the United Nations. In 1964 and 1965, she gave more than fifty farewell concerts before retiring from a rich career that lasted more than thirty years.

Anderson suffered a stroke in March of 1993 and died on April 8 of congestive heart failure in Portland, Oregon, at the home of her nephew, the celebrated conductor James

The Ed Sullivan Show *(1952) served as Marian Anderson's television debut. She is shown here starring in an NBC Christmas special in 1959.* (SCHOMBURG CENTER)

DePriest, music director of the Oregon Symphony.

The noted soprano **Jessye Norman** once said: "At age 10 I heard, for the first time, the singing of Marian Anderson on a recording. I listened, thinking, 'This can't be just a voice, so rich and beautiful.' It was a revelation. And I wept."

MILDRED DENBY GREEN

Armstrong, Lillian ("Lil")   (1898–1971)

Singer, pianist, and composer Lillian Hardin Armstrong was an internationally celebrated musician and one of the first women to become a giant in the jazz world and then successfully maintain an elevated position for the duration of her long—and "hot"—career.

Lillian Hardin was born on February 3, 1898, in Memphis, Tennessee. Classically trained in a childhood environment where popular music was considered vulgar, Armstrong received piano and organ lessons as a child and went on to play for both her church and school. Her family moved to Chicago in 1914 or 1915, whereupon Armstrong's formal music education moved from Fisk University to the Chicago College of Music, where she earned her teacher's certificate in 1924. In 1929, she graduated from the New York College of Music.

One of her first jobs was selling sheet music as a song-plugger at Jones's Music Store in Chicago, where she learned and demonstrated the store's music. Billed as "the jazz wonder child," Hardin developed her abilities as a player of popular music and made many contacts with musicians who later would become useful to her in her career as a jazz pianist. Among these is said to have been Jelly Roll Morton, one of the greatest jazz pianists of the era, who swayed her toward the musical style for which she became famous, a hard-note hitting, powerful rhythmic style.

Hardin's early jobs involved accompanying singers, among them **Alberta Hunter,** but her first major break came with the Original New Orleans Creole Jazz Band, playing the swinging New Orleans style to audiences full of such prominent artists as Bill ("Bojangles") Robinson and Sophie Tucker. One night, Hardin was heard by King Oliver and Johnny Dodds, who were so impressed with what they heard that they invited her to join their band, King Oliver's Creole Jazz Band, one of the great jazz bands

of the era, bringing the New Orleans style north to Chicago's Lincoln Gardens. A short time later, Louis Armstrong joined the band. The two musicians hit it off from the start, and Hardin and Armstrong were married in 1924. She is credited with aiding and encouraging Louis Armstrong in his career during this period, teaching him how to read music more proficiently and urging him to form his own band. Thus, between 1925 and 1928, the Hot Five and the Hot Seven were formed, bands that Lillian Armstrong played with during many of their concerts and recordings and for whom she composed such hits as "Lonesome Blues" and "Jazz Lips." During these busy years, she also appeared in the Broadway shows *Hot Chocolates* (1929) and *Shuffle Along* (1933).

Armstrong's talent and determination enabled her to ride out the difficult years of the Great Depression as a musician, playing in several bands, such as those of King Oliver, Freddie Keppard, and Elliot Washington. A combo of her own making was the all-women swing band the Harlem Harlicans, which played between 1932 and 1936, as well as another group out of Buffalo that comprised former members of Stuff Smith's band.

Although the couple were divorced in 1938, Lillian Armstrong's career suffered no setback. During the late 1930s, she recorded under the name Lil Hardin and worked as a session pianist for Decca Records. Armstrong returned to Chicago in the 1940s, playing local venues such as the Three Deuces. She toured several times, including one tour of Europe in 1952. Two of her songs, "Bad Boy" and "Just for a Thrill," became huge hits in the 1960s. In 1971, Armstrong collapsed and died of a heart attack on stage at Chicago's Civic Center Plaza during a memorial concert in honor of her former husband.

Composing and playing some of the greatest music in jazz history, Lillian Hardin Armstrong was a key player in an era that set the tone in the development of jazz. Her style of "hot" jazz succeeded in setting new standards within the industry. Many of Armstrong's superb compositions remain popular today, with fans both old and young.

FENELLA MACFARLANE

Arroyo, Martina (1937–)

"'The keeper of the seal of Italian melody' was the title Verdi is said to have conferred on Puccini, as his successor; but singers as well as composers are needful guardians of that historic possession. In the nineteen-twenties it left its native land for a time, won by the more fluent and lyrical Germans and Austrians. In the sixties, like a good many European treasures, it appears to have crossed the Atlantic. . . . It is hardly Anglo-Saxon, however, when one reflects that a very considerable part of the American achievement has been played by . . . Price, Arroyo, Bumbry, and Verrett."

J. B. Steane, *The Grand Tradition* (1974).

Born in February 1937 of African-American, Native American, and Spanish descent, Martina Arroyo was encouraged by her parents to follow her dreams but always to have something to fall back on. Thus, her work as a schoolteacher and as a case worker for the New York Welfare Department might appear simply to have been vocational insurance. However, although singing lessons, opera workshops, and the selected movies her parents took the family to all stimulated her interest in opera, Arroyo thought of teaching as equally glamorous, and her career offers ample evidence that she sees service to humanity as much more important than mere personal glory or attainment.

Arroyo studied music and ballet as a child and in high school began voice lessons with Marinka Gurewich, who remained her principal teacher and mentor until Gurewich's death in December 1990. Even as a teenager Arroyo was described as self-directed, able to stand up to bullies, and not put off by the jealousy of peers who could not understand why she aspired to more than the usual. As her teacher later recounted, "How far a voice will go you can only guess. To be a great singer means more. . . . What struck me was this personality of straightforward determination without any of the unkindness that is so often included." Arroyo took the initiative in figuring out what she needed to study. "[She] had her own program for herself, which is rare in a teenager. . . . [She had] intelligence and talent centered in just the right way, plus the awareness that being a human being is still the main thing in life."

Arroyo raced through Hunter College in only three years, graduating in 1956, all the while keeping up with her academic studies and her deep involvement in music and taking part in all the usual college activities. Within two years of graduation she had made her New York debut in the American premiere of Pizzetti's *L'Assassinio nella Cattedrale* at Carnegie Hall on September 17, 1958. Her debut at the Metropolitan Opera on March 14, 1959, was as the offstage celestial voice in *Don Carlos*. Onstage stardom at the Met came as the result of her last-minute substitution for Birgit Nilsson as Aida on February 6, 1965. As the performance progressed, the originally disappointed audience was transformed into a wildly enthusiastic fan club. For more than a decade after that, Arroyo was a mainstay of Met casting, known particularly as a superb interpreter of Verdi. She starred in numerous major roles, especially in *Ernani, Macbeth, Il Trovatore, Lohengrin, Don Giovanni, Aida, Un Ballo in Maschera, La Forza del Destino, Andrea Chenier, Madama Butterfly,* and, more recently, *The Flying Dutchman* and *Turandot.* She was the first soprano in twenty years to sing two consecutive opening nights at the Met—as Elvira in *Ernani* in 1970–71 and as Elizabeth in *Don Carlos* in 1971–72—followed by a third opening night as Leonora in *Il Trovatore* in 1973–74.

Beginning in 1958, Arroyo began to expand her activity beyond the Met, touring in Europe, South America, and South Africa, as well as middle America. During this time she built an impressive international reputation for her singing, not only of opera but also of oratorio and other large works for voice and orchestra. Unlike most dramatic opera singers, she also is known for her technical mastery of works by contemporary composers such as Varèse, Dallapiccola, and Stockhausen. "It is not every dramatic soprano who knows how to hum one note while whistling another one a third higher."

In 1959, Arroyo embarked on her first of many major tours of Europe, appearing at the Vienna and Berlin state operas and in the opera houses of Frankfurt, Dusseldorf, and Zurich. Her initial engagements in Britain in 1968 were a London concert performance of Meyerbeer's *Les Huguenots* and a Covent Garden appearance as Aida; in 1973, she made her Paris Opera debut. At home, in addition to her performances at the Met, she was a frequent soloist with the New York Philharmonic and other top orchestras and a favorite soloist of conductors such as Bernstein, Giulini, Böhm, Schippers, Hindemith, and Mehta.

Throughout her career, Arroyo has garnered consistent praise for her vocal opulence and technical control in the classics as well as in the contemporary repertoire. Her vocal presentation has been described as "rich, powerfully projected, staggering in size and beauty . . . heard to greatest advantage in the Verdi spinto roles . . . yet flexible enough for Mozart;" as "flooding the vast auditorium with wave after wave of golden sound;" and as "tenderly sung, excels in the clarity of its triplets and the florid whorl of the second part."

Of a 1965 performance with the Cleveland Orchestra, R. Widder wrote that Arroyo "contributed her formidable vocal talents to two widely diversified numbers and . . . scaled the heights of expressive vocalism in both. Her classic style (in Scarlatti) left nothing to be desired, but in [Barber's concert scene, 'Andromache's Farewell'] Arroyo realized a stunning performance of a magnificent composition. Her success and the acclaim of this tremendous work by an enthusiastic audience was overwhelming."

Referring to 1968 as "the winter of her content," J. Frymire wrote of Arroyo's January 29, 1968, debut as Elsa in *Lohengrin* as "a performance which should establish her in the front rank of contemporary sopranos . . . a diversified exhibition of the lyric art . . . not seen since Rethberg was in her prime. A full-throated voice of great beauty is given free rein but never pushed; and it is backed by first-rate musical taste, vocal technique, and dramatic credibility."

Of her performance of Leonora's aria "Pace, pace, mio dio" from Act IV of *La Forza del Destino*, J. B. Steane wrote that probably no performance stays more "in the memory . . . than Arroyo's saddened tone at 'profondo il mio sospir' and her vividly acted change of mood at the start of the final section. In all respects—beauty of voice, technical control, musical and dramatic feeling—she belong[s] to the tradition."

In his review of the recording "There's a Meeting Here Tonight," Irving Kolodin described the fully versatile Arroyo performing with **Dorothy Maynor** as "a meeting in time of two particular people whose voices together symbolize what has happened in civil rights to correct uncivil wrongs over the last few decades." Referring to the emotional force of Arroyo, who by that time was an established personality on television as well as in concert halls, he added that "success has not deflected her from fidelity to the objectives to which she originally addressed herself nor . . . has it imparted the least bit of pretension to her as a performer."

The list of her recordings is astonishing. In 1974, Steane observed, "If she were to record nothing more than she has done up to the present, she would still have earned an honourable place among her contemporaries . . . or indeed, among the century's singers."

Aspiring young artists can benefit from Arroyo's clear-eyed perspective expressed in her comments: "While it's great to be Black and beautiful . . . it's even better to be Black and beautiful and prepared" and "work is the key . . . to me, charisma is just a fancy word for rehearsals."

Martina Arroyo continues to embrace the multiple loves of her life as they appeared to her when she was a teenager. In addition to performing all over the world, she followed up her first master's class at the Mozarteum in Salzburg (1983) with classes at other locales around the globe. She has also taught voice at Louisiana State University and Bowling Green University in Ohio.

EILEEN T. CLINE

Ashby, Dorothy Jeanne (1932–1986)

Jazz harpist and bandleader Dorothy Jeanne Ashby was born August 6, 1932, in Detroit, Michigan, and died April 13, 1986, in Santa Monica, California. Ashby began as a pianist and switched to harp in 1952. Her father, Wiley Thompson, a jazz guitarist, taught her harmony; she continued her musical education at Bass Technical High School and Wayne State University, where she pursued advanced studies in harp, piano, and vocal technique, also playing harp in the university orchestra.

In 1953, she began her professional career as a harpist, performing in Detroit and throughout the Midwest and Northeast. From 1960 to 1966, she was both a staff harpist and show hostess for radio music programs and a harpist in pit orchestras for musicals produced by her husband, John Ashby, and her father. During her career, Dorothy Ashby performed or recorded with a diverse group of jazz musicians, including Louis Armstrong, Duke Ellington, and Woody Herman, and she recorded with Jimmy Cobb, Miles Davis, Richard Davis, Roy Haynes, Terry Pollard, Art Taylor, Gene Wright, and Frank Wess. Ashby also toured regularly with her own trio, appearing in concert halls, nightclubs, and on television shows. In addition to her performance credits, Ashby also was active in other areas; she participated in the Detroit public schools harp programs, hosted a Detroit jazz radio show, composed several jazz tunes, and wrote a book about modern harmony for harp and piano.

After moving to California in the early 1970s, Ashby became a much-sought-after studio musician. Her harp style combined traditional harp and jazz performing techniques. Known for her unique choral voicings and impeccable technique, which led scholars such as Linda Dahl to compare her with Wes Montgomery, Dorothy Jeanne Ashby was one of the best jazz harpists of her time.

EDDIE S. MEADOWS

Austin, Lovie (1887–1972)

One of the outstanding blues pianists on the Chicago jazz scene from the 1920s through the 1940s was Lovie Austin. Born Cora Calhoun in Chattanooga, Tennessee, in 1887, Austin was formally trained in music theory and piano at Roger Williams University in Nashville, Tennessee, and later at Knoxville College. Her musical talents and training enabled her to play, record, and arrange for some of the great early blues singers.

In the early 1900s, after a brief first marriage to a movie house operator in Detroit, Michigan, Austin worked the vaudeville circuit as piano accompanist to her second husband, Tommy Ladnier. However, she continued to use her first husband's last name, Austin. She had a great predilection for musicals and revues and formed her own band, the Blues Serenaders, a trio that featured Tommy Ladnier on trumpet and Jimmy O'Bryant on clarinet, and with whom she toured the Midwest and the South. Austin also managed, composed, arranged, and directed her own musical shows, including *Sunflower Girls* and *Lovie Austin's Revue*, which played Club Alabam, a black nightspot in New York.

Austin was one of the first female pianists to accompany early blues singers such as **Ida Cox, Ma Rainey,** Chippie Hill, Edmonia Henderson, and **Ethel Waters.** After recording companies started to use black artists, Austin made her first recording for Paramount Records in 1923 with **Ida Cox,** with whom she worked for many years. She played with jazz musicians Buster Bailey, Louis Armstrong, Kid Ory, Johnny Dodds, and **Alberta Hunter;** in fact, Austin and Hunter shared composer credits on two hit records, "Nobody Knows You When You're Down and Out" and "Down Hearted Blues." The latter became a huge success when **Bessie Smith** sang it in 1923, and Austin later wrote "Graveyard Blues" for Smith. Among her hundreds of early records, Austin's other hits included "Steppin on the Blues" and "Travelin Blues" in 1924 and "Heebie Jeebie" and "Peepin Blues" in 1925.

In the mid- and late 1920s, Austin composed and arranged music for many so-called race records and arranged vaudeville-improvised tunes for the orchestra at Chicago's Old Monogram Theater, where she remained as musical director for twenty years. During the Great Depression, which put most black women artists out of work, Austin became well known as director of theater pit bands at the Monogram, and she played with many of the great performers of the period. After leaving the Monogram, she worked for nine years at Joyland Theater.

During World War II and in the late 1940s, Austin toured her own shows for a time and then became pianist at Jimmy Payne's Dancing School in Chicago. In 1946, when Chippie Hill recorded on the Circle label, she was backed by Austin on piano, Lee Collins on trumpet, John Lindsay on bass, and Baby Dodds on drums.

Austin was a well-respected musician with a powerful, rhythmic style of piano playing. In 1926, a writer for the *Chicago Defender* newspaper described her approach as "percussive, pushing the beat along, filling in the bass parts with her right hand maintaining a steady flow of countermelody." She was a pioneer at the piano and had a consistent and dependable musicianship that supported the performances of other singers and performers. She kept a balance and completeness of sound while making use of stop-time, arranging the chords and harmonies in such a way as to occasionally require the musicians to play in double-time.

Austin's well-rounded musicianship and musicality made her a role model for women pursuing a career in music. Famous jazz pianist, composer, and arranger **Mary Lou Williams** described how she, as a young performer, felt after seeing Austin perform at a Pittsburgh theater:

> On seeing this great woman sitting in the pit and conducting a group of five or six men, her legs crossed, a cigarette in her mouth, playing the show with her left hand and writing music for the next act with her right. WOW! . . . My entire concept was based on the few times I was around Lovie Austin. She was a fabulous woman and a fabulous musician, too. I don't believe there's any woman around now who could compete with her.

Williams was so fascinated by Austin, finding her superior to many men of the period, that she later incorporated some of Austin's playing style into her own.

With new jazz styles coming onto the national scene and the number of positions for black women artists waning, Austin's career took a drop in the 1950s. Complicated legal problems kept her from enjoying any financial benefit from most of her reissued recordings and compositions. She made her last recording with Alberta Hunter in Chicago in 1961 and died in Chicago in 1972.

DELORES WHITE

B

Bailey, Pearl (1918–1990)

Born Pearlie Mae Bailey on March 29, 1918, to Joseph James Bailey and Pearl Bailey, this versatile entertainer spent her earliest years in Newport News, Virginia. When she was four, her family moved to Washington, D.C., but her mother and father, who was a preacher, soon separated. Although Bailey initially remained with her father, she eventually joined her three older siblings—Virgie, Willie, and Eura—in Philadelphia, where their mother had remarried.

By the time Bailey reached her early teens, her brother Willie (now calling himself "Bill") had established himself as a successful tap dancer. With his encouragement, she entered an amateur contest at the Pearl Theater in Philadelphia as a singer and won first prize. She was fifteen. Although she originally wanted to become a teacher, her attendance at William Penn High School became sporadic after the Pearl Theater performance. When she won another amateur night a few months later at the prestigious Apollo Theatre in New York City, any residual teacherly ambitions vanished. From then on, she devoted herself to show business full-time.

Throughout the rest of the 1930s, Bailey performed extensively as a singer and dancer on the Philadelphia-area entertainment circuit: One summer she toured with singer Noble Sissle's band as a specialty dancer; another summer during her late teens, she performed in the red-light districts of tough Pennsylvania mining towns like Pottsville, Wilkes-Barre, and Scranton. It was during this wild time that she married for the first time; the marriage—to a drummer—lasted only eighteen months.

In 1940, after her mining-town stint, Bailey moved to Washington, D.C.; soon after her arrival she landed a job as a vocalist with pianist-composer Edgar Hayes' band. For the next few years, she found herself on the move: With the Hayes band and later with the Sunset Royal Band, she performed in high-caliber New York City nightspots such as the Savoy Ballroom and Apollo Theatre, as well as in Washington, D.C., and Baltimore clubs. When the United States went to war in December 1941, Bailey did her part by singing for the troops in a cross-country tour with the USO—the first of many USO tours she made during her long career. The tour ended in Los Angeles, where Bailey lingered long enough to perform at the Flamingo Club.

When Bailey headed back to New York to sing in jazz trumpeter Cootie Williams' band, she stayed put. In 1944, she performed solo at the Village Vanguard, a popular nightspot; then her manager, Chauncey Oldman, lined up an eight-month stint at the Blue Angel, another famous New York club. Her successes at these two clubs led to a run at the Strand Theater with Cab Calloway in 1945. Although she was to have been only a temporary fill-in for ailing diva Sister **Rosetta Tharpe**, Bailey found herself

In reviewing the 1960 film All the Fine Young Cannibals, *the critic for* Variety *noted that Pearl Bailey gave the best performance, but that "even she can barely cope with a preposterous role of a celebrated blues singer who dies of a broken heart when jilted by 'that man who played blues for her'(Robert Wagner). Fortunately, the plot takes a brief break to enable Miss Bailey to render one or two numbers in her inimitably casual, well-timed and phrased style."* (DONALD BOGLE)

booked permanently; she was soon performing regularly with Calloway at the Zanzibar nightclub on Broadway.

In 1946, Bailey made her Broadway theater debut as Butterfly in *St. Louis Woman*, a musical extravaganza. Even though she appeared in only two numbers ("Legalize My Name" and "A Woman's Prerogative"), Bailey upstaged the rest of the cast, including the celebrated tap-dancing Nicholas Brothers. With her appealing mix of comedy and sensuality, she won the 1946 Donaldson Award for most promising newcomer of the year.

Following the success of *St. Louis Woman*, Bailey kept busy both on Broadway and in Hollywood. She appeared onstage as Connecticut in *Arms and the Girl* (1950) and as Madame Fleur in *House of Flowers* (1954) and performed in the revue *Bless You All* (1954). After her film debut in *Variety Girl* (1947), she acted in numerous other films, including *Isn't It Romantic?* (1948), *Carmen Jones* (1955), *That Certain Feeling* (1956), *St. Louis Blues* (1958), *Porgy and Bess* (1959), and *All the Fine Young Cannibals* (1960).

Between movie and stage jobs, Bailey was constantly in motion, performing in nightclubs across America and sometimes appearing with Count Basie's band throughout the 1950s and 1960s. She was often booked in glitter meccas such as Las Vegas and Atlantic City. Her albums did brisk business: *The Bad Old Days, The Cole Porter Song Book, For Adult Listening, Tired, It Takes Two to Tango, Legalize My Name*, and *Echoes of an Era*. Some of Bailey's own compositions were included on these albums: "A Five Pound Bag of Money," "I'm Gonna Keep on Doin'," "Don't Be Afraid to Love," and "Jingle Bells Cha Cha Cha." During this period she also became a television variety-show fixture, appearing primarily on the Ed Sullivan and Perry Como shows.

In 1952, Bailey married Louis Bellson, another drummer. Although controversial because Bellson was white, their union was by far Bailey's happiest. In addition to her brief early marriage, she endured a turbulent 1948–52 marriage to John Randolph Pinkett, Jr., with whom she had a son, Tony, and daughter, DeeDee.

The late 1960s to mid-1970s saw a continued flowering and diversification of Bailey's career. In 1967, she was named entertainer of the year by *Cue Magazine*. In 1968, she won a special Tony Award for her performance as the title character in an all-black production of *Hello, Dolly!* on Broadway (1967–69); in the same year she won the March of Dimes Award. In 1969, she was named the United Service Organization Woman of the Year. Bailey penned several

books, ranging from her 1968 autobiography, *The Raw Pearl*, to a 1976 collection of poetry and personal observations, *Hurry Up America and Spit*. Her other books were *Talking to Myself* (1971), *Pearl's Kitchen* (1973), and *Duey's Tale* (1975). She appeared in a film drama, *The Landlord* (1970), and starred in her own ABC-TV series, *The Pearl Bailey Show* (1971).

Even after announcing in 1975, at the age of fifty-seven, that she was retiring from show business, Bailey remained in the public eye by numerous TV appearances on commercials, game shows, sitcoms, dramas, and specials. In 1975, she was named a special advisor to the U.S. Mission of the United Nations General Assembly; costarred with comedian Redd Foxx in the 1976 film comedy *Norman . . . Is That You?*; received a Britannica Life Achievement Award in 1978; and was feted with an "all-star" TV tribute in 1979. In 1981, Bailey provided the voice for Big Mama, the owl, in *The Fox and the Hound*, an animated film.

In the early 1980s, Bailey went back to school to complete the education she had abandoned in the 1930s, and in 1985 she received a B.A. in theology from Georgetown University in Washington, D.C. Her last book, *Between You and Me* (1989), detailed Bailey's experiences with higher education. She was awarded the Presidential Medal of Freedom by Ronald Reagan in October 1988.

She died on August 17, 1990, in Philadelphia.

SARAH P. MORRIS

Baiocchi, Regina Harris (1956–)

"It is important," writes composer Regina Harris Baiocchi, "for the reader to be reminded of the fact that what they read about me is merely a snapshot of who I am at the time of the writing. And, before the ink is dry on the page, I am already a different person."

Regina Harris Baiocchi was born on July 16, 1956, to Elgie Harris, Sr., a Roman Catholic deacon, visual artist, and truck driver, and Lanzie Mozelle Belmont Harris, a teacher. She was the fourth of nine children. Her paternal grandmother was an organist at Notre Dame Chapel in South Bend, Indiana, and at Roberts Temple Church of God in Christ (COGIC) in Chicago.

As a child, Baiocchi attended first public and then parochial schools. She credits the nuns as well as all four of her grandparents with giving her a profound awareness of black history. "The nuns in my grammar school," she says, "were members of the Sisters of the Blessed Sacrament whose mission was to educate African Americans and

Composer Regina Baiocchi has written everything from gospel to twelve-tone contemporary music. Her work has been performed by the Chicago Symphony Orchestra, among others. (PRIVATE COLLECTION)

Native Americans. Our curriculum was steeped in black history."

Music of every kind was also a part of Baiocchi's childhood. "As a child I attended African Methodist Episcopal churches before my family converted to Catholicism. I was exposed to the tail end of Latin masses, African-infused AME hymns, and foot-stomping, sweat-back-your-hair COGIC gospel music." But music was not limited to church: Her mother listened to a jazz station with female disc jockeys or to gospel and soul, and her father played bluegrass fiddle and harmonica.

Baiocchi was an honors graduate in instrumental music from Paul Laurence Dunbar Vocational High School, married Gregory D. Baiocchi, a systems design engineer, in 1975, and then went on to receive a bachelor's degree in music composition and theory from Roosevelt University in 1979. After graduation, she taught science and mathematics while she discovered her voice as a composer. Most of the pieces she wrote at this time were for the churches where she worked as choir director.

By 1989, however, Baiocchi's work was well enough known to be performed by the Chicago Symphony Orchestra at Orchestra Hall, and later by the Detroit Symphony Orchestra and the Chicago Brass Quintet, among others. She has been commissioned to create pieces by AT&T, the city of Chicago, Arts Midwest, Mostly Music, Inc., and the American Society of Composers and Performers (ASCAP).

Baiocchi has written everything from gospel to twelve-tone contemporary music. Music historian Helen Walker Hill compares her to a prism: she and her music reflect everything around her. Baiocchi also writes and speaks with great eloquence about her experience as a black woman and as a composer. She shows great generosity of spirit as she writes of other musicians and a profound unwillingness to be pigeon-holed when she speaks of herself and her own work.

In addition to her composing, Baiocchi writes lyrically straightforward poetry. Her poetry about her family reflects the openness, confidence, and affection that characterize all of her work. In recent years, Baiocchi has begun gathering and preserving the stories of musicians whose words and works are about to be lost to the history of black women in music. She identifies herself strongly with such pioneer composers as **Florence Price**, **Margaret Bonds**, and **Betty Jackson King**. "They got a lot of rejections from the white males—their music was often barred by the establishment. Things haven't changed that much. People can still lock you out," she says. Locking Baiocchi out, however, may be more than the music establishment can manage.

KATHLEEN THOMPSON

Baker, Anita (1958–)

Sultry, romantic, and tough as nails—these have been used to describe Anita Baker. A balladeer and diva devoted to a pure and technically clean sound, Anita Baker has been talented enough to become a star and strong enough to challenge the powers that be in the entertainment industry.

Born in Toledo, Ohio in 1958, Baker was raised in Detroit by her maternal grandmother, Mary Lewis Baker; because she knew that she might not live to see her granddaughter grow up, she did her best to instill in her self-reliance and a sense of responsibility. Baker split her time between school and church and worked part-time jobs in between. It was in church that she first began to learn how to sing.

Baker was thirteen when her grandmother died. Only then was she told that Mary Lewis was not her real mother: The woman who gave birth to her actually lived down the street but never showed any interest in her daughter. This shock reverberated through Baker's life and career.

Taken in by other members of her church, Baker began to sing in clubs by the age of sixteen; at eighteen, she graduated from Central High School in Detroit and became the lead singer for a local soul/funk group called Chapter 8. When its record label folded, so did the band. Baker spent the next two years singing in the evenings and making ends meet with jobs as waitress, cook, and receptionist.

In 1982, at the age of 24, Baker got the chance to go to Los Angeles and record her first album, *Songstress*. The album received critical acclaim, and she toured the country opening for another musician. Continually hearing requests for her album, she thought it must be selling; however, the recording company kept insisting that she owed *them* money. Finally, she sued the label for a proper accounting and won a release from her contract.

In 1986, Baker signed with Elektra and recorded her first hit album, *Rapture*. This time acting as executive producer, Baker sought a simple, pure recording that would let the quality of her voice shine through. This album included the hit single, "Sweet Love," which ensured her success. Her next album, *Giving You the Best that I Got* was a multiplatinum hit and was considered one of the best pop albums of the 1990s. Next

came *Compositions* in 1990, featuring a number of well-known backup musicians.

By this time Baker was exhausted from nonstop touring and recording. One day in 1991, she walked into a hotel on her concert tour and decided she simply couldn't stand it any more; she canceled the tour and went home.

For the next three years, Baker reevaluated the priorities in her life, began to come to terms with her mother, and started a family with her husband, Walter Bridgforth. Thinking of how she had been taken advantage of in the early days of her career, she and Bridgforth began to hold workshops around the country, teaching young musicians how to stand up for their rights.

Finally, in 1994, she was ready to perform again: Returning to the stage with the Boston Pops, singing a jazz arrangement of the classic "Summertime," Baker was given a spontaneous standing ovation from the orchestra. Later that same year, she brought out her new recording, *Rhythm of Love*, another hit.

After fifteen million albums and seven Grammy awards, Anita Baker knows who she is: She's a strong, gifted woman, who has learned to make a life on her own terms.

ANDRA MEDEA

Baker, LaVern (1929–)

Influenced by her aunt, blues great Memphis Minnie, LaVern Baker began her illustrious singing career in 1947. Credited with many popular rhythm-and-blues anthems, including "Tweedle Dee," "Jim Dandy," "Tra La La," and "I Cried a Tear," Baker is known as a pioneer rhythm-and-blues artist with a style that *Billboard* magazine once described as "full-throated, vibrant belting with a sexy tease."

Born Delores Williams in Chicago, Illinois, on November 11, 1929, Baker made her singing debut in a Baptist church at the age of twelve. She was dubbed "little Miss Sharecropper," perhaps to compete with the popularity of a singer known as "little Miss Cornshucks." Her astounding vocal abilities led her to make her professional debut while still a teenager. With a powerful, commanding vibrato and a mastery of melodic explorations, she began to perform at Chicago's famed Club DeLisa in 1946, receiving an almost unprecedented six-month booking. She moved on to appear at the Flame, a show bar in Detroit, Michigan, where she cut a test record for Columbia Records under the direction of legendary manager Al Green. In 1949, she made her recording debut on RCA-Victor with the Eddie Penigar band. In 1952, she joined the Todd Rhodes Orchestra and toured internationally, both with the orchestra and as a solo artist.

Baker's repertoire, aptly described as raucous, consisted of jazz and urban blues. Her short-lived contracts with Columbia and, later, King Records generally were unrewarding, and in 1953 she signed with Atlantic Records, which was then developing a historic roster of rhythm-and-blues artists. From 1955 to 1960, Baker topped the pop and rhythm-and-blues charts with a stream of hits for Atlantic Records, becoming one of the first rhythm-and-blues artists to cross over to white audiences. In 1958, she recorded a compilation of songs made famous by the great **Bessie Smith**, with a command of both the blues and the lyrical content that landed her rave reviews.

Although Baker had hits with white audiences, racism kept her from being successful on the pop chart. An unabashedly imitative cover, or remake, of "Tweedle Dee" by white artist Georgia Gibbs went gold, effectively derailing Baker's chances of a pop hit. Not one to sit idly by, she lobbied her congressional representative to introduce a bill that would make it illegal to copy an arrangement, but to no avail. Several years and thirty-three singles later, Baker left Atlantic in 1965 for Brunswick Records. The following year, "Think Twice," a duet with Jackie Wilson, rose only to number thirty-seven after three weeks on the charts.

In 1965, Baker began working with the United Service Organizations (USO), entertaining American troops with her rich, soulful stylings. Her USO tours crossed Europe and the Far East, including Japan, Taiwan, Vietnam, Guam, and the Philippines. In the Philippines, Baker served as show director, mistress of ceremonies, and vocalist for the U.S. Marine Corps at Subic Bay.

In 1988, Baker made a triumphant return to the States for Atlantic Records' Fortieth Anniversary Celebration at Madison Square Garden. It was an honor to be included as part of the pioneer artists for Atlantic Records. In November 1989, she was honored by the Rhythm and Blues Foundation during its first annual Career Achievement Awards Celebration, receiving an award of $15,000 in recognition of her contributions to rhythm-and-blues music. Later that year, two of her songs were featured on the soundtrack of the movie *Shag*, and Baker was signed to perform a new song written by songwriter Doc Pomus for the 1990 film *Dick Tracy*. In February 1990, performing on the U.S. mainland for the first time since 1969, Baker appeared at the John F. Kennedy Center for the Performing Arts in Washington, D.C.

LaVern Baker lives in New York City, where she continues to perform with gusto. In 1991 she was inducted into the Rock and Roll Hall of Fame.

SUZAN E. JENKINS

Barnett, Etta Moten (1902–)

From Broadway to Hollywood to Africa, Etta Moten Barnett lived a life of remarkable achievements and experience. Then, in her late sixties, she became a strong advocate of women's rights and made her mark in an entirely new field.

Etta Moten Barnett was born in Weimar, Texas, in 1902, the daughter of Freeman Moten and Ida Norman Moten. Her mother came from a ranching family, and her father's family owned a large farm. Freeman Moten was a minister in the African Methodist Episcopal (AME) Church, and Ida Norman Moten was a schoolteacher he met at his first church.

An only child, Barnett early began to sing with her mother in the church choir. When she was ten years old, in the fourth grade, she went to an AME secondary school and junior college called Paul Quinn College in Waco, Texas. She was given a scholarship to the school so that she could sing with the Paul Quinn choral group. Boarding at the school and singing with the group, which raised funds for the school, were experiences Barnett remembered fondly in an interview with Ann Feldman, producer of the radio program *Noteworthy Women*. As one of five "little girls" who were under sixteen and therefore not allowed to have boyfriends, she remembered that "up until that time, we carried notes from the boys to the girls and the girls to the boys. And we had play mothers and a regular family thing. . . . I loved it."

After Paul Quinn, Barnett went with her family to California, where she attended public schools for two years. When her family moved to Kansas, Barnett went to Western University in Quindaro, Kansas, for her high school years. At the age of seventeen, she married Curtis Brooks, the head of the business department at Western, and moved to Okmulgee, Oklahoma; she and Brooks were married for six years and had three daughters before they were divorced.

Returning to Kansas to live with her parents, Barnett enrolled at Western University and later at the University of Kansas. Her daughters lived with her parents while she was at school; she saw them on weekends and conducted a local church choir to earn money. However, her major source of income during these years was the Jackson Jubilee Singers, a well-known choral group based at Western University.

The Jackson Jubilee Singers toured on the Chautauqua circuit in the summer. The Chautauqua Company sent performers to small towns where, in each town, a tent was raised for one week. In the evenings, there were performances by singers, actors, and reciters, as well as lectures. During the day, there were classes for children and more lectures. The Jackson Jubilee Singers performed in the afternoons and starred in the evening performance. "We did classics and spirituals. They hadn't discovered gospel yet, at that time. . . . We were the only blacks on that twelve-week circuit."

The group also accepted some engagements during the school year. When they performed in Kansas City, where Barnett's children were living with her parents, they had told her, "'Well, mother, you gonna flunk all the way down that hill'—because we called the campus at KU 'up on the hill'—'you gonna flunk all the way down that hill if you keep coming away from school like this.'"

Barnett didn't flunk, even though she also had her own radio program on a local station, and when she graduated from the University of Kansas in 1931, the renowned singer and choral conductor **Eva Jessye** read about her senior recital in the newspaper. Jessye invited Barnett to come to New York to join her choir. Barnett accepted.

As part of the Eva Jessye Choir, Barnett was at the center of musical and theatrical activity for black performers in New York. Two weeks after she arrived, Jessye recommended Barnett for a role in the Broadway show *Fast and Furious*. **Zora Neale Hurston** and **Jackie "Moms" Mabley** were both writers on the show, which closed after two nights but led to another role for Barnett.

The musical *Zombie* played for two months on Broadway then toured to Chicago and California. In Chicago, she became reacquainted with a man she had met only briefly but heard a great deal about. Claude Barnett was head of the Associated Negro Press, and she had been corresponding with him since meeting him on a visit to Chicago the year before. He even published some parts of her letters on his wire service.

When *Zombie* closed, Barnett went on to *Sugar Hill* and *Lysistrata*. She sang for a number of films but did not appear onscreen until *The Gold Diggers of 1933*. She sang the song "Remember My Forgotten Man." As a white woman mourned the death of her husband in the war, Barnett sang of the death of her own husband, whose sacrifice had been forgotten. Because she performed

a song of such power and relevance to their lives—and because she did not appear as a maid—black audiences flocked to see the movie. "When you stop to look for me," she told a *Chicago Tribune* interviewer, "you have to look real fast, but it meant so much to the Negro people to break the stereotype of blacks playing menial roles."

Because of her appearance in the film, Barnett was cast in *Flying Down to Rio* with Ginger Rogers and Fred Astaire. Again, she sang one song—"Carioca"—but this time she got screen credit. In black neighborhoods, she sometimes got top billing.

Etta Moten and Claude Barnett were married in 1934. Her children moved in with them and were adopted by their mother's new husband.

The tremendous response to Barnett's two brief film appearances should have led to a film career; however, her color stood in her way. Instead, she went into radio. She had her own show in San Francisco and was a soloist for the program "Carefree Karnival" on NBC radio. She was also mistress of ceremonies for the West Coast salute to Radio City Music Hall when it reopened in 1932. Barnett also appeared on the vaudeville circuit and toured to theaters and women's clubs. Her accompanist at this time was **Margaret Bonds,** the notable black woman composer, and her program was primarily classical music. When composer **Florence Price** recorded her classic "The Negro Speaks of Rivers," Barnett's picture adorned the cover of the album.

While she was rehearsing for a concert debut at Town Hall, Barnett was heard by a staff member of the about-to-be-produced *Carmen Jones* and she was asked to audition. At her audition, the conductor, Alexander Smallens, insisted that she was needed, instead, to replace **Anne Wiggins Brown** in the 1942 revival of *Porgy and Bess*. Barnett had turned down the role in the original production because she felt her voice was not yet right for it. This time she accepted.

For three years, Barnett sang the role of Bess almost every day. It was a soprano role, though, and she was a mezzo-soprano. Although some of the songs had been lowered for her voice, the strain was too great. She was forced to stop singing for a time, to rest her voice. "I never sang *well* after Bess," she says. She and her husband took advantage of this time off to tour Africa for the Phelps Stokes Fund, of which he was a trustee. For African Americans at that time, she says, "it was just part of living to know about Africa."

For some years, the Barnetts became official representatives of the United States government to African nations. Most of her singing appearances were in Chicago so that she could remain close to home. In 1970, she became head of the international program of the **Links** and involved the group in the International Woman's Year activities. She then headed the U.S. nongovernmental delegation to the conference in Mexico City.

Since that time, Barnett has attended each of the international conferences on women and speaks movingly of her experiences at these gatherings. She tells of the women from countries with little sexual equality— "those who dared"—speaking out about their lives.

In the 1995 interview with Feldman, she spoke with acuteness and sophistication about people such as the Gorbachevs, whom she knew and to whom she gives much credit for increased freedom in the world today, and Newt Gingrich, who she believes is giving the American people the illusion of freedom and change without the substance. She believes that integration has had many advantages, but she is firm in her conviction that the black community has lost some of its precious self-reliance.

At the age of ninety-three, she declares that the world was so interesting that she was "very eager to see what happens at the end of the century." When asked what advice she would give young people, she said, "Read, learn, keep your mind open."

KATHLEEN THOMPSON

Barrett, "Sweet Emma" (1898–1983)

Emma Barrett, also known as "Sweet Emma the Bell Gal," was born March 25, 1898, in New Orleans, Louisiana. Her father, William B. Barrett, was a captain in the Union army during the Civil War. She had one son, Richard Alexis. Barrett's entire career as a pianist and singer was associated with the New Orleans jazz style. Because she disdained giving interviews, many details of her life are unconfirmed. Although the origin of the name "Sweet Emma" is in dispute, she reportedly created it herself, believing that it described her personality. In the 1950s, a Bourbon Street tavern owner gave her a pair of garters with bells; these bells, along with a red beanie inscribed with "The Bell Gal," became a trademark. She was very discreet in discussing her personal affairs and reacted strongly to intrusive individuals. Her distrust in banks was partially the reason she lost her life savings when her house was robbed in 1961. When friends staged a benefit concert and presented her with $1,000, she was robbed again.

In the early 1900s, Barrett played with George McCullum, Sr.'s dance bands and the Original Tuxedo Orchestra and then joined Oscar "Papa" Celestin's band in 1923. Though Barrett was among the many New Orleans musicians who did not read music, she worked with the city's top reading bands, including Bebe Ridgeley's Original Tuxedo Orchestra, Sidney Desvigne's Orchestra, and the Piron-Gaspard Orchestra.

In the following decades, she toured with trumpeter and bandleader Percy Humphrey. Though she refused to travel by airplane, she played distant venues, including Disneyland, the Stork Club in New York, and the Guthrie Theatre in Minneapolis. By 1960, her popularity enabled her to start her own group—one that included some of the musicians whom she had worked with for decades.

In 1961, Barrett substituted for Lester Santiago, in Louis Cottrell's band at the famed Preservation Hall in New Orleans. This concert began an association with Preservation Hall that continued for the remainder of her life: At Preservation Hall, she sang songs such as "Just a Closer Walk with Thee," "Won't You Come Home Bill Bailey," and "I Ain't Gonna Give Nobody None of This Jelly Roll." Her energetic approach to playing the piano occasionally damaged the sounding board of the instrument.

During the 1960s, Barrett formed an all-star band that included Percy Humphrey, Willie Humphrey, Jim Robinson, Narvin Kimball, and Josiah "Cie" Frazier. This band recorded two albums, *New Orleans' Sweet Emma and Her Preservation Hall Jazz Band* and *Sweet Emma the Bell Gal and Her New Orleans Jazz Band at Heritage Hall*. She recorded several albums with the Preservation Hall Jazz Band that featured her singing and playing the piano. In the

1960s, Barrett appeared on *The Ed Sullivan Show* and in the motion picture *The Cincinnati Kid*.

A stroke in 1967 paralyzed Barrett's left side, but she continued to perform, beating time with her left hand while providing full right-hand parts. She made frequent television appearances and played at many elite Mardi Gras functions, arriving at performances in her wheelchair. Her last Preservation Hall performance was January 18, 1983, ten days before her death. She died in New Orleans on January 28, 1983.

ARTHUR C. DAWKINS

Barton, Willene (1930?–)

Willene Barton was born in Georgia, where she lived until she was ten years old. She taught herself to play the saxophone because, as she explained in an interview for *Stormy Weather*, "At that time, remember, all the bands were either made or broken by the tenor player. It was all saxophone players."

After her family moved to New York, Barton finished school, graduating from Manhattan High School. While still in school, she saw the Sweethearts of Rhythm at the Apollo Theatre several times and was enthralled. She identified especially with saxophone player Vi Burnside. After graduation, she studied music with private teachers, receiving particular help and encouragement from Eddie Durham, who managed an all-women's band called the Darlings of Rhythm.

By 1952, Barton was playing with another all-women's band that was led by Anna Mae Winburn, a former Sweetheart of Rhythm. While on the road, she ran into her idol, Vi Burnside, who had formed a group of her own after the Sweethearts disbanded.

Burnside was extremely popular and far more established than Barton, who describes an encounter in the *Stormy Weather* interview:

> I think it was the first weekend we were there that she came down to our club, the Ebony Lounge. And the place was packed. Now, I had a brand-new instrument, all pretty and shiny. So Vi asked if she could borrow my horn. I said sure. And she got up there and turned the place *out*. She played every note that was supposed to be in everything! So I knew that was it. The next week I went over to see her at *her* club, a place called Gleason's. When the people saw me, they demanded that *I* play, so she gave me *her* horn. And when I left there they put so much money in the bell of that saxophone! I'll never forget it. I had a bell full of money and a chicken dinner!

Barton was too young and raw to have actually defeated Vi Burnside, but she was always popular with the audience, and Burnside, like the other established women in jazz, was always encouraging to Barton.

Barton left Winburn in 1953 to form a group with Myrtle Young, another ex-Sweetheart. In 1955, she broke away from Young to form her own group, the Four Jewels. She then led an all-men's group, which included George Tucker on bass and Gildo Mahones on piano. She was with organist Dayton Selby for about six years and then joined the great **Melba Liston**.

During this time, she often sat in with male bands, playing with Ben Webster, Illinois Jacquet, Sonny Stitt, and Gene Ammons, among others.

Then, when the sixties came along, Barton found that her kind of music just wasn't selling. "It got so bad in the sixties," she said, "some kids didn't even know what a tenor saxophone was. They would ask me, 'Lady, what's that?' All they knew was the guitar." Barton found that she couldn't bring in enough money to hire the musicians she wanted to work with. She got a regular job and played music only occasionally.

Then, in the 1970s, sparked by the feminist movement's increasing interest in music by women, a group called The Jazz Sisters of New York City got together; white piano player Jill McManus led the group, and Barton played tenor sax. The group played around the New York area, at the New York Jazz Museum, the Village Gate, Storyville, the Five Spot Cafe, and other clubs and at colleges and universities.

In 1979, Barton performed with the "Big Apple" Jazz Women Ensemble at the Kansas City Women's Jazz Festival. The response was wildly enthusiastic. On July 4, 1981, Willene Barton and a pick-up band she put together for the event became the first women's jazz group to be a part of the Newport Jazz Festival, playing at Carnegie Hall. She considered it the highlight of her career to date.

Also in the early eighties, Barton had her first chance to play in Europe, going to Switzerland and France with Sandra Reeves Phillip's show "Great Ladies of Jazz." The following year, she went back with the same show, with Tunisia and the North Sea Jazz Festival added to the itinerary.

For the past few years, Barton has been playing in street festivals and clubs around New York. When asked about her career, she said, "Very often life doesn't come out as you planned. Things come out of the blue. I'm not in the ground yet; who knows what might happen?"

KATHLEEN THOMPSON

Battle, Kathleen (1948–)

A soprano with a distinctly sweet and expressive voice, Kathleen Battle was born in Portsmouth, Ohio, and received her B.M. and M.M. degrees at the Cincinnati College-Conservatory. Thomas Schippers was responsible for her debut as the soprano soloist in the German requiem of Brahms, at Spoleto in 1972. She made her first appearance at the Metropolitan Opera as the Shepherd in Wagner's *Tannhäuser* in 1977, following this as Blonde (*Die Entführung aus dem Serail*), Despina (*Così fan Tutte*), Elvira (*L'Italiana in Algeri*), Pamina (*Die Zauberflöte*), Rosina (*Il Barbiere di Siviglia*), Sophie (in both *Der Rosenkavalier* and *Werther*), Zdenka (*Arabella*), and Zerlina (*Don Giovanni*). In such soubrette roles, she appeared often with the major opera houses of Europe and was a frequent soloist and recitalist internationally, moving toward midcareer with an enviable reputation. As a recording artist, her repertoire also includes spirituals, wherein gospel ornamentations enhance the intensity of her interpretations.

In 1991, Battle and **Jessye Norman** performed together at Carnegie Hall, and in 1993 Battle premiered a song cycle she had commissioned with lyrics by **Toni Morrison** and music by André Previn.

A five-time Grammy Award winner, Battle recorded and co-produced in 1995 an album entitled *So Many Stars*, a collection of love songs, lullabies and spirituals, with music performed by black jazz and Brazilian music artists. It reached the top of Billboard's Classical Crossover chart. She has also recorded with jazz trumpeter Wynton Marsalis and pop superstar **Janet Jackson**. Battle says, "I am a classical trained singer who loves folk music, who loves jazz, and who loves classical music . . . why can't I embrace all music?"

DOMINIQUE-RENÉ de LERMA

Blige, Mary J. (1972–)

"If it can be said that **Whitney Houston** represents the 'good' middle-class black girl, then Mary J. Blige is the rags-to-riches role model for the hip-hop generation," said Deborah Gregory in *Essence Magazine* in March 1995.

Born in the Bronx, New York, Mary J. Blige is the second child of four born to Cora Blige, a nurse who reared her first two children by herself. Blige's father played the bass guitar in a band; "He was never really around" Mary is quoted as saying. Her family lived in Savannah, Georgia, until she was nine; they then moved back to New York, this time to the Schroeder Street Projects in South Yonkers, called 'Slow Bomb' by its residents. Of her childhood, Mary told *Essence*, "Growing up in the projects is like living in a barrel of crabs. If you try to get out, one of the other crabs will try to pull you down."

Her climb out of the barrel began when Mary made a cover of **Anita Baker**'s "Caught up in the Rapture" at a karaoke joint. Her mother's boyfriend gave the tape to a friend of R&B singer Jeff Redd. Redd played the tape for the CEO of Uptown records who signed Mary J. Blige to his label.

In 1992, her first album *What's the 411?* was released and reached double-platinum status. The album blended the hard-edged sound of neofunk with the softer soul of R&B and earned her the title "Queen of Hip-Hop Soul." She toured the nation with hip-hop headliners such as Bobby Brown, Boyz II Men, Jodeci, and TLC. *Rolling Stone* magazine gave her a rave review when she toured with Bobby Brown saying, "Mary J. Blige was the most impressive of the opening acts, gliding with a jazzy sophistication over an edgy street beat."

Her second album *My Life* was released in December 1994 and debuted at number one on the R&B charts. This second album marked a change for Blige: She has a songwriting credit on every song on *My Life* except a remake of "I'm Going Down." The album is usually described as being more mature and textured than her first, with shades of classic **Aretha Franklin** and **Billie Holliday**.

"All I want to do is sing. So I'll sing as long as my voice lasts," she told *Essence*. "I'm very hungry for success right now. Nobody ever looked up to me before for anything. Now kids and even grown-ups look up to me because of my music. It really makes me *feel* like somebody."

HILARY MAC AUSTIN

Bonds, Margaret (1913–1972)

Margaret Bonds was born on March 3, 1913, in Chicago, Illinois. Her mother, Estella C. Bonds, was a church organist as well as her first teacher. Their home was frequented by young pianists, singers, violinists, and composers such as Will Marion Cook and Florence B. Price. It was a natural environment to nurture her own talents as both singer and composer.

As a high school student, Bonds studied with William L. Dawson and **Florence Price**. She received bachelor's and master's degrees in music from Northwestern University in Evanston, Illinois, and continued graduate studies at the Juilliard School of Music in New York City.

The recipient of a Rosenwald Fellowship, a Roy Harris Scholarship, a National Association of Negro Musicians Award, and a Rodman Wanamaker Award during her career, Bonds taught at the American Theatre Wing and performed with several orchestras, including the Woman's Symphony, the New York City Symphony, and the Scranton (Pennsylvania) Philharmonic, and she was the first black guest soloist with the Chicago Symphony at the Chicago World's Fair in 1933. From 1968 to 1972 she

The first black guest soloist with the Chicago Symphony Orchestra, Margaret Bonds was also a noted composer, many of whose arrangements of spirituals were commissioned and recorded by Leontyne Price. (SCHOMBURG CENTER)

worked with the inner-city Cultural Center in Los Angeles and she also served as music director for several musical theater institutions in New York.

Bonds composed music for the theater as well as ballets, orchestral works, art songs, popular songs, spirituals, and piano pieces. Her works for piano and orchestra are programmatic, and each depicts her sense of ethnic identity through the use of jazz harmonies, spiritual materials, and social themes. **Leontyne Price** commissioned and recorded many of her arrangements of spirituals.

Margaret Bonds died in Los Angeles, California, on April 26, 1972.

SANDRA CANNON SCOTT

Braxton, Toni (1967–)

"She sounds like a man." Toni Braxton remembers hearing this as a teenager; yet, Toni Braxton's distinctive alto voice has made her famous enough to vie for **Whitney Houston**'s crown as the pop voice of the nineties.

Born in 1967 in Severn, Maryland, Toni Braxton is the eldest child of six born to Michael and Evelyn Braxton. Michael Braxton was an electric company employee and a part-time preacher in the Apostolic Church; her mother had sung in the Baltimore doo-wop group the Vue-ettes and was an amateur opera singer when Toni was young.

The Apostolic Church of her childhood demanded that Braxton and her family shun popular culture of all kinds; as a result, Toni wasn't allowed to listen to popular music on the radio or to watch television. Toni would listen to the radio when her parents went shopping and would sneak out to watch *Soul Train* on the sly. After her parents converted to the less-conservative United Methodist Church, Toni was allowed to sing at talent shows.

While studying to be a teacher at Maryland's Bowie State College, she and her sisters formed The Braxtons. They released their first (and to date, only) album in 1990. "It went zinc and copper," Toni told the *New York Times*. "In other words it didn't do well."

It did, however, get the attention of the Atlanta-based production team of Kenny "Babyface" Edmond and Antonio "L.A." Reid. Just starting their own label, LaFace, they offered Toni a solo deal. "I hesitated at first but I talked to [my family] and they said, 'Go do your thing, make a name for yourself and then you can bring us up,'" Toni told the *Washington Post*.

She sang two songs for the Eddie Murphy film *Boomerang*, both of which became number one hits. In August 1993, her solo debut entitled *Toni Braxton* was released and stayed on the charts through much of 1993 and early 1994, topping 3 million in sales. She received two American Music Awards for favorite new artist in both the soul-R&B and adult contemporary categories, a Grammy for best new artist, and another Grammy for best female R&B vocal performance for "Another Sad Love Song." Two Soul Train Music Awards, best female R&B album for *Toni Braxton* and Best Female R&B for the song "Breathe Again" followed.

Toni Braxton has had a spectacular entrance onto the music scene; it will be interesting to see where her unique voice takes her in the future.

HILARY MAC AUSTIN

In addition to a long career in musical theater, Carol Brice (on right) also distinguished herself as a classical singer and was one of the earliest black classical singers to record extensively. (MOORLAND-SPINGARN)

Brice, Carol (1918–1985)

Carol Brice was born on April 16, 1918, in Sedalia, North Carolina, to a highly musical family. The Brice Trio, with which she was active from 1932, included her brothers Eugene and Jonathan, each of whom had his own individual career. She studied at the Palmer Memorial Institute in her hometown and Talladega College in Alabama before enrolling at New York's Juilliard School of Music, during which period she began a long career on the musical stage with *The Hot Mikado* (alongside Bill "Bojangles" Robinson).

Prior to becoming the first black musician to win the Walter Naumburg Award (1943), she was soloist at St. George's Episcopal Church in New York, where Harry Burleigh had enjoyed a prodigiously long tenure as baritone soloist. In 1944, she presented her debut recital as contralto at Town Hall and the next year appeared on network television. Few black singers of her generation had access to the American opera stage; her career was initially confined to musical theater, in works by Harold Arlen, Jerome Kern, and George Gershwin, although she was cast as the Voodoo Princess in Clarence

Cameron White's *Ouanga* in 1956. In the 1970s, she was active with the Volksoper in Vienna, returning to the United States in 1974 with her husband, expatriate baritone Thomas Carey, to serve on the faculty of the University of Oklahoma where together they established a regional opera company. She died on February 15, 1985, in Norman, Oklahoma.

With **Marian Anderson**, she was one of the earliest black classical singers to record extensively. In addition to those works she performed on stage, her recorded repertoire included arias and lieder by Bach, Beethoven, Carpenter, Dett, Falla, Franz, and Mahler.

DOMINIQUE-RENÉ de LERMA

Brown, Anne Wiggins (1915–)

Had it not been for Anne Wiggins Brown, George Gershwin's folk opera of the African-American experience might have come to be known by its original title, *Porgy*. To make it into a star vehicle for Brown, Gershwin revised the work and retitled it *Porgy and Bess*.

Currently a citizen of Norway, Anne Wiggins Brown was born to Dr. Harry F. Brown and Mary Wiggins Brown in Baltimore, Maryland, in 1915. At an early age, she was obsessed with being a stage star, although she realized that blacks were cast only as servants or in degrading comic roles. Her mother, recognizing this extraordinary talent who was now all of seven years old, attempted to enroll Anne in a local private Catholic school, where the prodigious child caused great excitement among the nuns. When school officials discovered that the family was not Spanish but black, however, Anne was denied admission, even though

her father was a prominent Baltimore physician. She was to encounter the same discrimination a few years later at the now famous Peabody School of Music, currently located in Baltimore, Maryland.

Not to be discouraged, Brown always kept her dream of becoming a star in the forefront of her numerous activities, which included plays and musicals in which she sang everything from Bach to blues.

Her talent captured the attention of Constance Black, wife of the owner of the *Baltimore Sun*. After having presented Anne in numerous private performances, Black encouraged the young woman to enter the Juilliard School of Music.

Brown's vocal teacher at Juilliard was Lucia Dunham. Following participation in many competitions, Brown won the prestigious Margaret McGill Scholarship. She then attracted the attention of George Gershwin and auditioned for him; still wanting to become a "serious" singer, she auditioned with the typical Western European repertoire, but Gershwin requested of her an unaccompanied rendition of the spiritual "City Called Heaven" because the spiritual was more akin to the idioms of his forthcoming opera, *Porgy*. This spiritual was soon to become internationally known as one of her signature selections.

Having found his "perfect" Bess, Gershwin worked closely with Brown. He not only rewrote act three of the opera in order to have Bess sing the lullaby "Summertime," but he also changed the title of the opera to *Porgy and Bess* so that Brown would share equal billing with the promising young black baritone Todd Duncan.

The much anticipated premiere of the opera took place at New York's Alvin Theatre on October 10, 1935. The event was met with mixed critical reviews; however, critic Olin Downs had much respect and praise for the two lead voices, Brown and Duncan. Anne Brown, now twenty, had achieved her dream.

The opera, which had a run of 123 performances, was not a financial success but did embark upon a national tour. Brown married, for the second time, to Jacob Petit. Her first marriage, to Floard Howard, which ended in divorce, occurred while she was a student at Juilliard. To Dr. and Mrs. Petit was born her first child, Paula.

In 1942, she returned to Broadway in a more upbeat version of *Porgy and Bess*. This version proved to be more successful financially.

Feeling her career a bit stagnant, Brown embarked upon a concert career. Upon the expiration of her contract with *Porgy and Bess* and declining the lead in Oscar Hammerstein's new musical, *Carmen Jones*,

Creator of the role of Bess in George Gershwin's Porgy and Bess, *Anne Wiggins Brown led cast protests to desegregate audiences for the opera at the National Theatre in Washington, D.C. Here she is seen christening the S.S.* Frederick Douglass. (SCHOMBURG CENTER)

Brown was to be managed by Albert Morini. She successfully toured the United States, Canada, and Europe. Her performance with the Robin Hood Dell Orchestra in Philadelphia broke, at that time, all attendance records; however, her most celebrated performances between 1942 and 1948 were the appearances at Carnegie Hall and with the Los Angeles Philharmonic.

Brown's 1948 European tour, especially the performance in Norway, was extremely well received. Divorced from her second husband, she was married to Norwegian ski jumper Thorleif Schkelderup. While raising her family, she continued to perform in Europe, South America, and Asia; she was not to return to America for twenty years.

Although now an adopted Norwegian, she had never forgotten her racial struggles during her formative years in America. Always a civil-rights advocate, Anne Brown in 1935 led the *Porgy and Bess* cast in protest when they learned that the performances at the National Theatre in Washington, D.C., were to be before segregated audiences. The theater relented in its segregation policies for these performances; however, the general policy of segregation was not to change for another twenty years.

During a 1953 tour in Europe, Anne Brown developed respiratory problems. Consequently, she did not quite achieve her new goal as an Italian opera diva, but she did continue to study and sing. Upon her return to Norway, she was diagnosed as asthmatic, a condition that ended her singing career. One of the most sought-after teachers in Norway, Brown's celebrated students include actress Liv Ullmann and jazz singer Karen Krog. Her time is spent with her family of two daughters and four grandchildren.

Anne Brown has been the subject of a Norwegian television documentary and authored a best-selling autobiography, *Sang Fra Frossen Gren*.

J. WELDON NORRIS

Brown, Cleo Patra (1909–)

Cleo Patra Brown has had two careers in music, one from the 1920s through the 1940s as a jazz pianist and the other, beginning in the 1970s, in religious music. She was born on December 8, 1909, in Meridian, Mississippi, and began to study piano at four. As a youngster, this daughter of a Baptist minister, played in her father's church and continued her music studies when her family moved to Chicago in 1919.

Cleo's older brother, Everett, was also a pianist—but of a different breed. He played ragtime and boogie woogie in Chicago nightclubs. Although her parents were strict about her style of playing, she managed to learn the style from her brother. Envious of her brother's artistic freedom and better pay, she ran away from home and got married.

She toured briefly with a traveling orchestra at fourteen, before returning to Chicago to perform in Chicago's clubs and on select radio stations during the 1920s. In 1935, she replaced Fats Waller on his New York radio series and began to record shortly thereafter.

With the exception of a brief illness in the 1940s, Cleo Brown played regularly until 1953. She is credited with popularizing the "eight-beat-to-the-bar" style of playing when she remade Pine Top Smith's "Boogie Woogie" classic. Despite her popularity, she recorded only twenty-four tracks during her career, eighteen of those during the year 1935–36.

Cleo Brown retired from music in 1953 and took up nursing. In 1973, she switched careers again to return to music—but this time she played religious and inspirational tunes under the name C. Patra Brown.

In 1979, C. Patra Brown had a weekly feature on a radio station in Denver, Colorado, playing religious melodies. She still resides in Denver and plays the piano for a Seventh-Day Adventist Church.

PAULETTE WALKER

Brown, Ruth (1928–)

Ruth Brown has presence. She has it when she performs at Rainbow and Stars, wearing a gown that glitters so much it rivals the view of the city skyline. She fixes the audience with a gaze of regal imperiousness, then dismisses any airs with a slyly lifted eyebrow and sings, "If I Can't Sell It, I'm Gonna Keep Sittin' on It," which is not necessarily about secondhand furniture.

The New York Times, December 7, 1995

Crowned "the fabulous Miss Rhythm" by legendary vocalist Frankie Laine, Ruth Brown recorded such hits as "Teardrops from My Eyes," the million-seller "5-10-15 Hours," "Mambo Baby," and "Mama He Treats Your Daughter Mean," all for Atlantic Records. Born in January 1928 in Portsmouth, Virginia, the oldest of eight children, Ruth Brown has seen it all: With five number-one and two dozen top-ten hits on the rhythm and blues charts during the 1950s, Miss Rhythm sold so many records for Atlantic that the fledgling company was dubbed "the house that Ruth built."

Born on January 30, 1928 in Portsmouth, Virginia, Brown first performed profession-

During the 1950s, singer Ruth Brown sold so many records for Atlantic Records that the fledgling company was dubbed "the house that Ruth built." (SCHOMBURG CENTER)

ally in 1947, but she made her debut singing spirituals as a teenager in her mother's Baptist church choir and her father's Methodist church choir, eschewing the blues because her father thought of it as "the devil's music." As a girl, Brown's primary exposure was to white, popular music and country and western; after she was exposed to so-called race records in late 1940, however, she won amateur night at the famed Apollo Theater in New York by singing the ballad "It Could Happen to You." She began to sing with Lucky Millinder's renowned band in 1948, but her first real professional experience came from touring with big bands in the South during World War II and as a pop singer for United Service Organizations (USO) shows in 1950. The circumstances under which the performers of that day had to perform in the South were less than optimum; yet sharecroppers and farmers alike shared in the rhythmic and lyrical expressions of her music. Brown has noted that "the music came out of a very trying period; a period where people were fighting for self-esteem, for dignity and equal rights . . . that was the struggle." While touring in the South she went to jail more than once in protest of Jim Crow laws but continued to sing fervently in the musical tradition borne out of true living experience.

After listening to recordings of **Billie Holiday** that her uncle had brought from New York, Brown began to shape her vocal style to encompass the blues-tinged sounds she grew to love. When she was finally convinced to switch to rhythm-and-blues in the late 1940s, her career skyrocketed. She recorded more than eighty songs for Atlantic Records, consistently topping the rhythm-and-blues charts with hits like "So Long," "Oh What a Dream," and many others. In the late 1950s, she shared star billing at the Apollo Theater with many greats, including Miles Davis and Thelonious Monk.

Attracting white audiences through her performances in promoter Alan Freed's rock 'n' roll shows in 1956, Brown hit the pop charts the following year with her first crossover hit "Lucky Lips" and continued that success in 1958 with "This Little Girl's Gone Rockin'," "Jack o' Diamonds," "I Don't Know," "Don't Deceive Me," and "Shake a Hand." Brown left Atlantic Records in 1962 and moved to Philips Records. Two years later, after a few minor hits, she went into semiretirement in order to raise her family, often working under a pseudonym as a domestic worker and bus driver to make ends meet.

Following a ten-year hiatus, Brown reemerged on the music scene with stints at Hollywood's Cinegrill and Michael's Pub in New York. In 1988, she appeared in Atlantic Records's Fortieth Anniversary Celebration at Madison Square Garden. Her work as Motor Mouth Mabel in John Waters's feature film *Hairspray* (1987) introduced her to yet another new audience. She received both a Tony Award and a Keeping the Blues Alive Award in 1989 for the best performance by a leading actress in a musical for her role in the critically acclaimed Broadway show *Black and Blue*, a Grammy Award (1989) for her album *Blues on Broadway*, and the Rhythm and Blues Foundation Career Achievement Award in November 1989 for her contributions as a trailblazer in the development of rhythm and blues. In 1990, Brown became host of National Public Radio's weekly syndicated program, *Blues Stage*. She also hosted NPR's *Harlem Hit Parade*; was included in a documentary entitled *That Rhythm, Those Blues* (1988), funded, in part, by the National Endowment for the Arts; and has performed to standing-room-only audiences internationally.

Brown was inducted into the Rock and Roll Hall of Fame in 1993. Her autobiography *Miss Rhythm* (written with Andrew Yule) was published in 1996.

SUZAN E. JENKINS

Bryant, Clora (1925?–)

It isn't easy to play the trumpet. It certainly wasn't easy in the 1940s to play a trumpet in a jazz band, not if you were a woman, but Clora Bryant could, and she still can.

Clora Bryant was born in Denison, Texas. Her mother died when she was two, and her father, a single parent, brought her up. In public schools, she learned to play the trumpet. She didn't exactly choose the instrument she was going to play; her brother did. He played the trumpet, and the family couldn't afford two instruments, so Clora ended up a horn player by default.

In high school, Bryant's teacher encouraged her talent. By her senior year, she was playing in a jazz band that performed at proms and other social events. "In high school," she said in an interview for Linda Dahl's book *Stormy Weather*, "you find girls playing instruments all the time. It's *after* you get out of high school, when you get that union card and you start competing one to one with guys, that it's hard. They don't like competing with each other, let alone a female!"

Bryant attended Prairie View College in Texas, a school she chose because they had an all-women's orchestra. The orchestra made an East Coast tour while Bryant was playing with it, appearing in 1943 at the Apollo Theater in Harlem.

In 1945, Bryant left Prairie View and went to California to study at the University of California at Los Angeles (UCLA). At the same time, she became active in the Los Angeles music scene. When she had to leave college for lack of money, she worked with the internationally acclaimed Sweethearts of Rhythm, before going on to smaller women's bands.

In 1951, she appeared in a band led by Benny Carter on a local television show that featured black talent. Again on local television, she played in all-woman jazz combo that featured Jackie Glenn on piano, Anne Glasco on bass, Ginger Smock on violin, Matty Watson on drums, Willie Lee Terrell on guitar, and Vivian Dandridge—sister of actor **Dorothy Dandridge**—doing vocals. However, when she played with an otherwise white band at about the same time, the station received so many negative phone calls that she was removed from the band.

In the meantime, Bryant was playing with all the important male bands she could, even if it was just in jam sessions. Then, later in the fifties, she went to Las Vegas in the backup band for singer Damita Jo. While there, she made friends with Harry James and Sammy Davis, Jr., those friendships led to an appearance in the film *Pepe*, playing with an otherwise all-male orchestra.

Bryant left Damita Jo to play with Billy Williams. The band did six months a year in Las Vegas and then played in New York City, the Catskills, and New Orleans. From there, Bryant went on to dozens of other groups, large and small. She played at small clubs where she got in trouble for refusing to sit and drink with the male customers, and in large show bands—in the trumpet sections of bands led by Duke Ellington, Lionel Hampton, Count Basie, and Stan Kenton.

In 1981, when she was interviewed by Linda Dahl, Bryant was leading and playing with a number of groups in Los Angeles. She was in the trumpet section of Bill Berry's L.A. Big Band. "I took trumpeter Blue Mitchell's place in fourth chair in that band, and I don't know how Bill Berry swung it, but I've been accepted. . . . And I'm the only woman in the band. You do see *one* woman in a band, never two or three."

Still, she points out that she has received a great deal of support from some male musicians, especially Dizzy Gillespie. When asked to name women trumpeters worthy of mention as jazz players, Gillespie immediately said, "Clora Bryant." Bryant says, "The *real* musicians, they are *proud* of what you can do."

In the 1980s, Bryant started studying composition at her old school, UCLA. She also received a grant from the National Endowment for the Arts for a five-part piece she calls "Suite for Dizzy."

KATHLEEN THOMPSON

Bryant, Hazel Joan   (1939–1983)

Hazel Joan Bryant, actress, opera singer, director, and playwright, became one of the most prominent visionaries and producers off Broadway as executive director of the Richard Allen Center for Culture and Art (RACCA) from 1969 to 1983. Born September 8, 1939, to African Methodist Episcopal Bishop Harrison James Bryant and Edith Holland Bryant, the third of six children in their Zanesville, Ohio, home, her childhood was dominated by the excitement of religious rituals and church functions. Her musical talents, nurtured in the church, were refined at the Peabody Preparatory School of Music, **Oberlin College** and Conservatory of Music, and the Mozarteum School of Music. She studied acting with Stella Adler and Harold Clurman and did graduate study in theater administration at Columbia University.

Prior to her years as a director/playwright/producer, she was a working performer. In 1962, she toured Europe with Robert Shaw; on Broadway, she appeared in *Funny Girl* as Emma with Barbra Streisand, *A Taste of Honey* as Helen, *Hair* as Sheila, and *Lost in the Stars* as Irina; and

on tour in Europe performing such operatic roles as Mimi in *La Bohème*, Bess in *Porgy and Bess*, Fiordiligi in *Così fan Tutte*, Tosca in *Tosca*, and Butterfly in *Madama Butterfly*.

She established the Afro-American Total Theater in 1968, initially to produce musicals and operas, but later to stage one-act plays and eventually full-length plays. In 1974–75 the name was changed to the Richard Allen Center for Culture and Art, commemorating the founder of the Methodist tradition of her childhood. RACCA produced more than 200 performances, highlighting numerous special events and spearheaded by Bryant. In 1971, she developed a special youth project in South America; as a result, RACCA was endorsed by the Bishop's Council as the cultural arm of the AME Church. She was the cofounder of the Lincoln Center Street Theater Festival (1971–81) with Mical Whitaker and Geraldine Fitzgerald; produced the first Black Theatre Festival USA in the summer of 1979, featuring ten black theater companies from around the country to celebrate RACCA's tenth anniversary; and produced the first International Black Theatre Festival in the summer of 1980, featuring companies from Africa, London, the Caribbean, and the United States. In 1982, Bryant launched the Holland Limited Touring Company (named after her mother) and took Langston Hughes' *Black Nativity* to the Vatican in Rome for Pope John Paul II. She wrote several plays that were produced by RACCA: *Circles*, *Star*, and *Making It*. In 1978, the RACCA production of *Long Day's Journey into Night* was presented at the Public Theatre, and in 1982, it appeared on television starring Ruby Dee and Earle

Hyman, winning ACE awards for best production and best actress (Ruby Dee).

RACCA received numerous AUDELCO (Audience Development Committee) Award nominations for its productions. Hazel Bryant received the Mayor's Award of Honor for outstanding contributions to the arts in 1978 and a special citation from the governor of New York for the Black Theatre Festival in 1979. Her spirit was summarized in the words of Mical Whitaker, former artistic director of RACCA, who said, "She was a visionary who was always thinking of new things to do and getting new things done."

LINDA NORFLETT

Bumbry, Grace (1937–)

Grace Bumbry, the self-described "shy, very shy girl" from St. Louis, Missouri, achieved international acclaim in roles that established her as one of the outstanding operatic divas and concert artists of the twentieth century. She was born on January 4, 1937, to Benjamin and Melzia Bumbry, who recognized early her unique musical talents. She studied piano with her mother from the age of seven and joined her musical family in choirs at the Union Memorial United Methodist Church, where she was a soloist by age eleven. She sang in vocal ensembles at Sumner High School, directed by Kenneth Billups, who tutored her in voice and influenced her early career development. She received scholarships from the National Association of Negro Musicians and was inspired by **Marian Anderson,** for whom she sang at the age of seventeen; impressed by her "magnificent voice of great beauty,"

Anderson called her to the attention of Sol Hurok, whose roster of artists she later joined. Bumbry studied at Boston University; at Northwestern University, where she became the student and protégé of Lotte Lehmann, the German-born operatic legend, who encouraged her to pursue a career in opera; at the Music Academy of the West; and with Pierre Bernac and with Armand Tokatyan. Lehmann presented her in a solo recital in 1958 in a performance that received critical acclaim.

Bumbry made her opera debut with the Paris Opera Company as Amneris in Verdi's *Aida* in 1960 and made operatic history in 1961 as the first black performer at the Bayreuth Festival when she sang the role of Venus in Wagner's *Tannhäuser*; she made her American debut in 1963 at the Chicago Lyric Opera in the same role and her Metropolitan Opera debut in 1965 in Verdi's *Don Carlo.* Her leading roles include those in Verdi's *Macbeth, Nabucco,* and *Ernani;* Strauss's *Salome;* Janacek's *Jenufa;* Ponchielli's *La Gioconda;* Donizetti's *Roberto Devereux;* Mascagni's *Cavalleria Rusticana;* Meyerbeer's *L'Africaine;* and Gershwin's *Porgy and Bess.* She sang in the world's leading opera houses and concert halls and in a 1962 command performance at the White House. Recordings of opera, lieder, and oratorio document the extent to which she succeeded in performing repertoires that covered the range of her rich and powerful voice.

She lives in Basel, Switzerland, with her husband, Polish-German tenor Erwin Jaekel.

REBECCA T. CUREAU

C

Caesar, Shirley (1938–)

"Baby Shirley, the gospel singer," as she was called by the age of ten, has had three incarnations in gospel music: At age twelve, she was traveling throughout the Carolinas and Virginia as soloist for the one-legged preacher Leroy Johnson; by age twenty, she was one of the leaders of the Chicago-based gospel group, the Caravans; and by age thirty-two, two years before the death of **Mahalia Jackson**, she was dubbed "Queen of Gospel."

Caesar was born on October 13, 1938, in Durham, North Carolina, to James and Hannah Caesar. Her father, known as "Big Jim," was legendary throughout the Carolinas as the powerful lead singer of the gospel quartet, the Just Come Four; Caesar observed the quartet in rehearsals and by age ten was singing solos in their concerts. Her life was changed in 1950, however, when her father died in his sleep and she was left to care for her invalid mother. She began to appear in solo concerts and, at twelve years old, joined the troupe of the evangelist Reverend Leroy Johnson. She appeared regularly on his television show out of Portsmouth, Virginia, in 1950 and in November 1951 made her first recording for the Federal label, "I'd Rather Have Jesus." From age fourteen to eighteen, she traveled alone throughout the South on bus and train, appearing in solo concerts and often arriving home with only a few minutes before she was to attend classes. After graduation from high school, she enrolled at North Carolina College in Durham (now North Carolina Central University), pursuing a major in business education.

In 1958, while a student at North Carolina State, she attended a concert by the Caravans, a female gospel group, and was so impressed that she wanted to become a member. With the help of gospel singer Dorothy Love Coates, leader of the Original Gospel Harmonettes of Birmingham, Alabama, Caesar was granted an audition. The audition was successful, and after she withdrew from college, she was immediately taken into the group. The three members of the Caravans each had distinctive singing styles: the leader, Albertina Walker, was known for her ability to stand "flat-footed" and sing the old hymns with wrenching sincerity and coloraturalike embellishments; Inez Andrews, known as the "High Priestess of Gospel," was a contralto with a three-octave range who could shatter glass with her powerful, high-pitched screams; and Sarah McKissick was a soft-voiced gospel ballad singer. Caesar brought a unique quality to the Caravans, for her style was one of energy, percussive attacks, explosive releases, and a florid treatment of melodic lines. Though Caesar was a Baptist, she had adopted the practice of Sanctified singers of dramatizing songs; she would act out each of her solos, often moving into the auditorium to shake hands with members of the congregation.

She made her first recording with the Caravans in 1958 and, from the first session, scored success with "I've Been Running for Jesus a Long Time, and I'm Not Tired Yet." The song was set to a lively tempo, and in performances, Caesar would run down the aisles each time the word *running* appeared in the chorus. She found her true style, however, with the 1961 recording of "Hallelujah, It's Done." During the choruses of the song, Caesar ad-libbed in the style of the African-American folk preacher and found that she possessed a special gift for adding text to the song to illustrate important points. She cultivated this technique, called song-and-sermonette, a device created by Mother **Willie Mae Ford Smith** and developed by Edna Gallmon Cooke. This device was to become her trademark in later years, both in her singing and as an evangelist, which she became in 1961.

She scored tremendous success with her 1962 recording of "I Won't Be Back," dramatizing the song by walking through the auditorium, looking for a door by which to leave, and at the end leaving the auditorium and remaining outside for a short period of time. "Sweeping through the City" was the next big hit for Caesar; during the performance she would mimic sweeping the floor.

Caesar left the Caravans in 1966 and organized her own group, the Caesar Singers; with this group, she discovered her ability to generate excitement through her "mother" songs. Her first big hit with these songs was a 1969 ten-minute song-and-sermonette entitled, "Don't Drive Your Mama Away." The song recounts the story of a mother with two sons, one of whom leaves home while the other remains, completes college, and marries. Tired of her mother-in-law's old-fashioned ways, the successful son's socialite wife commits her to a senior citizens' home, but the wayward brother returns home to tell his brother that if he drives his mother away, he will surely need her someday. The African-American sense of family was touched by this rescue of the mother, and the song became a huge success. It was followed by "No Charge" in 1978, the story of a small child who, when asked by his mother to do chores after school, submits a list of his charges for such work. The mother responds by stating that for carrying the child for nine months, for breast feeding him when he was a baby, for washing and ironing his clothes, for cleaning his room, and for praying for him each night, there would be no charge.

In 1980, Caesar garnered a crossover audience with her recording of "Faded Roses," set to country-and-western accompaniment, which again tells the story of a wayward child. On this occasion, though, a mother dies without the opportunity to say goodbye to a son who has not contacted her since he moved to Germany. His sisters notify him of her death, but by the time of his arrival at the cemetery, the roses on her grave have faded. Besides her poignant "mother" songs, Caesar is lauded for her standard "house-rocking" songs, such as "This Joy I Have, the World Didn't Give to Me." In such songs she elects a fast or medium tempo, sings at the very top of her range, uses abundant embellishments, adds extra notes, scoops, and growls to the melody, and executes her runs and shouts for Jesus.

Caesar currently makes her home in Durham, performing around 150 concerts each year in addition to a few reunion concerts with the Caravans. In 1984, she returned to college at Shaw University in Raleigh and earned a bachelor's degree in business education. She served on the Durham City Council from 1987 until 1991; is the pastor of the Mount Calvary Word of Faith Church in Raleigh, one of the sixty churches of the Mount Calvary Holy Churches of America, of which her husband, Harold I. Williams, is the presiding bishop; and is the founder and president of Shirley Caesar Outreach Ministries, an organization providing emergency funds, food, clothing, and shelter for the needy. She is the recipient of an honorary doctor of humane letters degree from Shaw University.

Caesar won a Grammy Award for her 1971 recording of "Put Your Hand in the Hand of the Man." In addition to winning the Grammy for gospel in 1971, she has been nominated eleven times, winning five more Grammys. Out of ten nominations for the Dove Award for Gospel, she has won six, as well as five Stellar Gospel awards and two NAACP Image awards and has been inducted into the Gospel Music Hall of Fame.

HORACE CLARENCE BOYER

Calloway, Blanche (1902–1978)

Blanche Calloway was a consummate entertainer who carved out a remarkable career despite race and gender discrimination.

Born on February 9, 1902, to Eulalia and Cabell Calloway, Jr., in Baltimore, Maryland, Blanche was the oldest of six children. Her father was a lawyer, and her mother was a teacher and organist at the Presbyterian church, where young Blanche sang in the church choir.

In 1921, Oma Crosby and her five Cubanolas, a song-and-dance show, passed through Baltimore. A young married woman at the time, Calloway auditioned, won a part in the show, and left town as a Cubanola. Her husband followed but, not being in the business, did not stay long. The act went to New York, and Calloway landed a job singing in the wings in *Shuffle Along*, a Broadway revue. Before the show closed, she sang in front of the chorus line as a soubrette.

Later, Calloway appeared in *Plantation Days* in Chicago. Traveling with the show to Baltimore, she came home to find her brother Cab playing drums with a local band; she took him back to Chicago with her and enrolled him in school with the aim of helping him follow their father's footsteps into law. Cab dropped out of school, however, and became an entertainer himself, famous for the "hi-de-ho."

Blanche Calloway performed as a regular at the Sunset Cafe, a haven for jazz musicians such as Louis Armstrong and Earl Hines. While doing vocals with her brother's band, she was noticed by the manager of the Pearl Theater in Philadelphia, who suggested that she front her own band. Calloway became the first woman in the country to lead an all-male band. Beginning in 1931, for thirteen years she toured with "The 12 Clouds of Joy," singing, conducting, and dancing in a particularly energetic acrobatic style.

Eventually the difficulties of life on the road and the unrelenting pressures of racism made Calloway decide to leave the band. That same year, 1944, she remarried and settled in Washington, D.C., where she managed the Crystal Caverns. Here, such groups as the "Orioles," who hold a place in the Rock and Roll Hall of Fame, got their start. Later she moved to Philadelphia and managed the Jim Jam nightclub; became deeply involved in civil rights and other political activities, and took the significant financial risk of managing **Ruth Brown**, a brown-skinned singer, at a time when even light-skinned women such as Calloway herself sometimes dusted white flour on their faces to get jobs.

After moving once more, to Miami, Florida, Calloway became the first woman disc jockey on American radio; later, as hostess of her own daily show, *News, Views, and Interviews*, she interviewed many of her former show-business colleagues. Her career in radio lasted twenty years. Calloway was also founder and president of Afram House, Inc., a mail-order cosmetics firm that reportedly was the first of its kind in the nation to be both black owned and black operated.

In about 1972, Calloway's health began to fail, and after the death of her fourth husband, she returned to Baltimore. She died on December 16, 1978, at the age of seventy-six.

MARGARET D. PAGAN

Campbell, Lucie E. (1885–1963)

Lucie E. Campbell once said, "Teaching is my vocation, music is my avocation." She taught American history and English in the public schools of Memphis for fifty-five years, retiring in 1954; concurrently, she was music director of the Sunday School and Baptist Young People's Union Congress of the National Baptist Convention for forty-seven years, from 1916 until her death. As music director, she exerted great influence over the dissemination, growth, and development of African-American religious music in black Baptist churches nationwide.

She has been called "the great song composer of the National Baptist Convention."

Campbell was born on April 30, 1885, in Duck Hill, Mississippi, the youngest of eleven children of Burrell and Isabella Wilkerson Campbell, both of whom were former slaves. Burrell Campbell died before his daughter was two years old, and Isabella moved the family to Memphis, where Lucie was educated. After graduating from Kortrecht High School in 1899 as class valedictorian, she was assigned to teach at her alma mater (later named Booker T. Washington High School), where she remained until her retirement. She received a bachelor of arts degree from Rust College, in Holly Springs, Mississippi, in 1927, and a master of science degree from Tennessee State University in 1951.

Essentially a self-taught musician, Campbell possessed an outstanding contralto voice and played piano and organ at the Metropolitan Baptist Church in Memphis, where in 1909 she began to teach the young people's choirs. By 1904, she had organized and was made president of the Music Club, a local affiliate of the National Federation of Colored Musicians.

In 1916, she was made music director of the Sunday School and Baptist Young People's Union Congress; in this position, she was responsible for helping to create and maintain an atmosphere of optimism and religious fervor at the annual sessions to keep the organization intact and to discourage churches from defecting to the convention that had split from the parent body in 1915. For these meetings, she organized and directed 1,000-voice choirs; composed songs; wrote and staged original musicales and pageants, such as *Ethiopia at the Bar of Justice;* and selected soloists and organized ensembles to provide music. She was a member of the Music Committee that compiled hymn books for the denomination, such as *Golden Gems*, *Inspirational Melodies*, *Spirituals Triumphant*, and *Gospel Pearls*. Compiled in the 1920s, these books contain such Campbell songs as "Something Within" (1919), "He Understands, He'll Say 'Well Done'" (1950), "Heavenly Sunshine" (1923), and "The King's Highway" (1923).

The songs she wrote in the 1920s, 1930s, and early 1940s are considered outstanding examples of gospel hymn writing; the texts are full of imagery and the melodies are memorable. By the mid-1940s she began to compose in the new gospel music style of the Chicago School of **Mahalia Jackson**, **Roberta Martin**, and Thomas A. Dorsey. Her compositions in the new genre included "Jesus Gave Me Water" (1946), "There Is a Fountain" (1948), "When I Get Home" (1948), and "Footprints of Jesus" (1949). She wrote anthems, such as "Praise the Lord" (1946), which sold a record 30,000 copies, and songs for liturgical use for Christmas and Easter, such as "This Is the Day the Lord Has Made" (1947).

She was a dynamic orator and rivaled the famous Nannie Helen Burroughs in popularity as a sought-after Woman's Day speaker; also like Burroughs, she was frequently at odds with ministers who resented her forceful manner. Her positions of leadership included president of the Tennessee Education Congress (1941), the first woman to hold the office; vice president of the American Teachers Association (1944); member of the National Education Association's National Policy Planning Commission (1946); and president of the Women's Convention, Auxiliary of the Tennessee State Regular Baptist Missionary and Education Convention (1948).

Campbell composed approximately eighty songs, some of which have been lost. She did not copyright her music until 1950, having given much of it to the Baptist denomination. Today her songs are heard more frequently at the Grand Ole Opry in Nashville than at Baptist conventions and congresses, but contemporary singers such as Take Six are taking an interest in her output.

On January 14, 1960, she married the Reverend C. R. Williams in Memphis after a forty-year courtship and moved to Nashville. Following a testimonial in her honor given at the Sunday School and Baptist Training Union Congress in Denver in June 1962, she became ill. She died at Riverside Hospital in Nashville on January 3, 1963.

LUVENIA A. GEORGE

Capers, Valerie (1935–)

Valerie Capers is a concert musician who has made a music video with Dizzy Gillespie, or she is a jazz musician who has performed Mozart—regardless of labels, she is a remarkable woman.

Capers was born May 23, 1935, in the Bronx, New York, to Alvin and Julia Capers. Although her father was a professional jazz pianist and a close friend of Fats Waller's, he supported his family with a job at the post office. Her mother was a civil-service worker in New York hospitals. Before he died, her older brother, Bobby, played tenor saxophone and jazz flute with Mongo Santamaria.

When Capers was six years old, she contracted a misdiagnosed viral infection that damaged her optic nerve and left her totally blind. Undaunted by this challenge, Capers learned to play piano by ear. In 1953 Capers graduated valedictorian from the New York Institute for the Education of the Blind, where she studied piano formally. After high school, Capers was advised to spend a year preparing for college. Capers practiced eight to ten hours daily and, in 1954, was offered full scholarships to Barnard College and Juilliard School of Music. Capers still regards Thode as her "guiding inspiration."

Capers was the first blind student to receive a bachelor of music (1959) and master of music (1960) from Juilliard. After college, Capers' brother convinced her to learn jazz so that she would be as proficient in the American traditional music as she was in the European. Since then, Capers has remained active as a composer, arranger, and educator.

Still, it was difficult for Capers to find a full-time teaching job because of her blindness. The Bronx Neighborhood School of Music was the first to give Capers a chance to teach full time. Capers describes her time there as the happiest five years of her life. Since then, Capers has taught at several New York area colleges, including Bronx Community College of the City University of New York (CUNY), where she chairs two departments.

Once she gained confidence as a jazz pianist, Capers formed her own trio and soon recorded three albums. Her debut album *Portrait in Soul* (1967, Atlantic Records) was followed by *Affirmation* (1982, KMA Arts). On *Come On Home* (1995, Columbia/Sony) Capers sang and played piano music she wrote; the album also features Wynton Marsalis, Paquito D'Rivera, Mongo Santamaria, Bob Cranshaw, John Robinson, and Terry Clarke.

In 1976, Capers received support from the National Endowment for the Arts (NEA) for her jazz opera, *Sojourner,* which in February 1981, premiered at St. Peter Lutheran Church on Lexington Avenue (known for its ministry to jazz musicians through its jazz vespers). Opera Ebony mounted a production of *Sojourner* in 1985.

Capers' *Portraits in Jazz* (1974–75) are twelve student piano pieces inspired by great jazz artists, with interpretative notes. **Billie Holiday**, Ron Carter, and Duke Ellington are among those Capers portrays. *In Praise of Freedom* (1976) is a chamber work for chorus and jazz ensemble, based on Martin Luther King's March-on-Washington speech.

In 1978, Capers made her conducting debut at Carnegie Hall when she directed her gospel-inspired jazz Christmas cantata *Sing About Love.* which featured Slide Hampton, Donald Byrd, Nat Adderly, a chamber orchestra, and a 20-voice choir. Her song cycle, *Song of the Seasons* (1987) for soprano, cello, and piano, was commissioned by and premiered at the Smithsonian Institution in D.C. *Celebration*, a work-in-progress for jazz orchestra, is Capers' tribute to John Coltrane.

Capers performed Mozart's *Piano Concerto in A* with the New York Bronx Arts Ensemble Orchestra (1992) and at the Strawberry Music Festival in Malibu (1992) and appeared with **Kathleen Battle** at New York's Riverside Church (1993). Her trio has appeared on commercial recordings and in festivals and clubs, including North Sea Jazz Festival in Holland, Grand Parade de Jazz in France, Kool Jazz Festivals, the Piano Jazz series with Marian McPartland, Cafe Lido and Fat Tuesdays, and *Jazz in America* (1985), a video with Dizzy Gillespie and Ray Brown.

Pianist and composer Valerie Capers is a musician who is equally at home with Mozart and Dizzy Gillespie. The first blind student to receive a B.A. and master of music from Juilliard, Capers and her jazz trio have made numerous recordings and have appeared in concerts and music festivals throughout the world. (PHOTO:VALERIE CAPERS)

In 1987, Capers was the first musician to receive *Essence* Magazine's Woman of Essence Award. In 1988 and 1989, Capers served as an NEA jazz fellowship panelist. The jazz curriculum developed by Capers serves as a model for schools nationwide.

Capers writes and reads braille fluently. Her compositions, prose, lyrics, and poetry are written in braille and translated for those who are braille illiterate. Capers said, "The last thing I remember seeing was snowflakes as my father carried me up the stairs of our brownstone on East 168th Street." Today Capers is left with light perception, sensory memory of blue, red, yellow, green, and a lot of soul in her music.

REGINA HARRIS BAIOCCHI

Cara, Irene (1959–)

Irene Cara was catapulted to stardom by two major hits. The first was the hard-driving "Fame," and the second was "Flashdance . . . What a Feeling." Also an actor, dancer, and keyboard musician, the multi-talented Cara embodied the ambition and intensity of the 1980s.

Born in the Bronx on March 18, 1959, to Spanish-speaking parents, Cara first performed when she was seven. Her entire family was musically talented: Her father and brother were musicians, and her great-aunt played five instruments.

As a girl, Cara's mother had not been not allowed to pursue a career in show business, so when the young Irene showed talent, her mother would not hold her back. Cara was enrolled in singing, dancing, and piano lessons and made her first appearances on Spanish-language broadcasts in New York City at the age of seven; a year later, at eight, she made her Broadway debut; by the time she was ten, she won an invitation to sing at a tribute to Duke Ellington in Madison Square Garden; before she entered her teens, she won another Broadway role, in the Obie award-winning musical *The Me Nobody Knows*. Not satisfied with performing alone, she also began to write song lyrics at the age of twelve.

Cara was still in her teens when she made her film debut. She was sixteen when she won a supporting part in *Aaron Loves Angela* and then was offered the lead in *Sparkle*. Soon after, she won parts in two television productions, the famous miniseries *Roots* and *The Guyana Tragedy: The Story of Jim Jones.*

She had barely hit twenty when she got her real break, a part in the motion picture

Fame, about New York teen-agers at a school for the performing arts. Cara sang the title song. Her passionate, soaring rendition made her an international star. The song won an Oscar for best original song in 1980, and the sound track album earned a platinum record. She also was nominated for two Grammy awards for the same work, and received a nomination for a Golden Globe award.

In 1983, Cara did it again with the title track from the picture, *Flashdance.* The song hit number one and brought her two Grammy awards. The first was for best pop vocal performance, and the other was for best album of an original score.

This second song, produced by **Donna Summer**'s producer, carries a strong disco style; at times, Cara was criticized for sounding too much like Donna Summer, which simply annoyed Cara: "There are so many records made by male artists today that sound alike. But nobody makes an issue of that. That's why I'm very supportive of other female artists, especially those trying to make their own statement and not be controlled. Trying to do what they want instead of being somebody else's Barbie doll. There are too many people in this business who just want you to look pretty and sing. That's the last thing I consider I do."

Carlisle, Una Mae (1915–1956)

Una Mae Carlisle was born on December 26, 1915, in Xenia, Ohio, of American-Indian and black parentage. She sang at three and studied piano shortly after.

In 1932, at the age of seventeen, Carlisle worked at a Cincinnati radio station. Fats Waller heard her play and asked her to join his band; she had intended to make a career of singing, but the opportunity to play piano with Fats Waller was too compelling to decline. She left Fats Waller's band in 1934 to audition for the Cotton Club in New York and then rejoined him four years later to sing on his album *I Can't Give You Anything but Love* (1939).

In the late 1930s, Carlisle performed solo and recorded in Europe. She worked with the *Blackbirds* stage show during their European tour in 1938, worked in clubs and in the film industry in France, and operated her own club in Montmartre while studying music at the Sorbonne.

In the late 1940s and early 1950s, singer/pianist Una Mae Carlisle had a popular radio show. A protégée of Fats Waller, Carlisle at one time operated her own nightclub in Montmartre in Paris. (SCHOMBURG CENTER)

When World War II began, Carlisle returned to the United States and recorded *Walkin' by the River* (1940) and *I See a Million People* (1941) for Blue Bird Records. She became a popular nightclub performer and had her own radio show in the late 1940s and early 1950s.

In 1940, Carlisle performed with Her Jam Band, with Slam Stewart (bass), Benny Carter (trumpet), and Zutty Singleton (drums). She recorded with tenor saxophonist Bob Chester and with Don Redman.

Becoming ill in 1954, Carlisle retired. She died two years later, on November 7, 1956, in New York City.

PAULETTE WALKER

Carter, Betty (1930–)

Born Lillie Mae Jones on May 16, 1930, in Flint, Michigan, Betty Carter has used several other stage names, including Lorraine Carter and Betty Bebop (coined by Lionel Hampton). Carter studied piano and, as a teenager, worked as a singer in clubs in Detroit, where she grew up; she also sat in with visiting artists such as Dizzy Gillespie and Charlie Parker. From 1948 to 1951, she toured with and wrote several arrangements for Hampton and made her recording debut. She accompanied Hampton to New York in 1951, thereafter worked in various nightclubs and theaters including the Apollo, toured with Ray Charles (1960–63), and visited Japan (1963), London (1964), and France (1968).

After she married in the mid-1960s, Carter went into a brief retirement in order to raise her children. She returned to the stage with her own trio in 1969 and her own recording company, Bet-Car Productions in 1971. Since 1969, Carter has worked with several young, virtually unknown, but talented pianists such as John Hicks, Danny Mixon, Mulgrew Miller, and Benny Green; simultaneously, she expanded her musical palette to include a part in Howard Moore's musical *Don't Call Me Man* (1975) and to sing with string orchestras conducted by David Amram in New York (1982) and Boston (1983).

Betty Carter's style was initially inspired by **Billie Holiday** and **Sarah Vaughan** but is now more instrumentally than vocally focused. It is common to hear melodic fragmentation of text and melodies as well as reharmonization of harmonies: Carter appears to feel that the audience knows a given tune and that it would therefore be redundant for her to restate the specific musical elements of that tune throughout each performance. Her approach to singing also includes a myriad of horn sounds, vocal effects, an excellent ear, and a strong sense of harmony and rhythm. Betty Carter is a jazz singer's singer.

EDDIE S. MEADOWS

Chapman, Tracy (1964–)

In a world that becomes more high-tech every day, singer/songwriter Tracy Chapman relies primarily on her voice and her acoustic guitar, but she owes the biggest break in her career to a computer.

Chapman was born in Cleveland, Ohio, on March 30, 1964. Her parents, George and Hazel Chapman, divorced when she was four, and she and her older sister lived with their mother. As a child, Chapman loved books and music. She listened to folksingers Bob Dylan and Joni Mitchell, gospel stars **Mahalia Jackson** and Al Green, and pop singers as diverse as Barbra

Streisand, **Gladys Knight**, and Cher. Chapman also began to make music herself, first with the ukelele and later with the clarinet, the organ, and the guitar.

Chapman won a scholarship to the Wooster School in Danbury, Connecticut, a private high school. Her fellow students and the faculty were so impressed by her performances at school functions that they took up a collection to buy her a new guitar in her sophomore year, and the yearbook predicted that she would "marry her guitar and live happily ever after." She went on to Tufts University in Boston and graduated cum laude with a degree in anthropology in 1986; while at college, she continued to write and perform her songs.

Chapman's style found an appreciative audience in the coffeehouses of politically liberal, arts-friendly Boston, but she had doubts about pursuing a career in music. She was no Gloria Gaynor, no Gladys Knight, no **Tina Turner**. She was a folk singer, a woman who stood alone onstage with her guitar and sang dark, simple, intense songs in a deep, almost shy voice. Some of the songs were about love, but more of them were about racism, poverty, and domestic violence, and these were the 1980s, not the 1960s. Record buyers were yuppies now, not hippies. Out in the real world, would anybody want to listen?

Fortunately, Charles Koppelman, whose son was a classmate of Chapman's at Tufts, thought they would. He signed her with his music publishing company, SBK, and helped her get a record deal with Elektra. Her first album, *Tracy Chapman*, was released in 1988. While she was in London on the promotional tour for it, the organizers of the Nelson Mandela seventieth birthday tribute concert hired her to do a short set on a small

side stage, filling time between headliners. It started out as just another gig, but at the last minute Stevie Wonder withdrew from his scheduled appearance because a computer disc needed for his equipment couldn't be found. A worldwide TV audience and 75,000 people in Wembley Stadium were waiting, and the producers chose Chapman to fill in.

Suddenly, she was a star. Her album went to number one in both the States and the UK,

Singer/songwriter Tracy Chapman was a complete unknown until she filled in for Stevie Wonder at a London concert in honor of Nelson Mandela's seventieth birthday. Suddenly, this intense performer, who prefers to accompany herself on an acoustic guitar, was a star. (PRIVATE COLLECTION)

and "Fast Car," which told the story of a couple trying to escape a life of poverty and disappointment, was a Top Ten single in both countries. She won three Grammys, including Best New Artist. Her next two albums, *Crossroads* (1989) and *Matters of the Heart* (1992), disappointed some reviewers, who felt that she was becoming too introspective or falling back on "the vocabulary of generic 1960s folk anthems," and delighted others, who said that she "sustained the brilliance that she displayed on her debut." Her album, *New Beginning* was released to critical acclaim in December 1995.

For Chapman herself, being number one is less important than making music that will "challenge people and give them contexts for issues." One of her songs begins:

She's got her ticket/ I think she gonna use it/ I think she going to fly away/ No one should try and stop her/ Persuade her with their power/ She says that her mind is made up.

Chapman may not always get to first place on the charts, but she travels on her own ticket.

INDIA COOPER

Chiffons, The

It was the early 1960s, and the performers making the top of the charts were Steve Lawrence crooning "Go Away Little Girl," the Rooftop Singers folk-rocking their way through "Walk Right In," and Paul and Paula making everyone's teeth hurt with the saccharine sweetness of "Hey Paula." The world of popular music welcomed a group of New York teenagers who called themselves The Chiffons, chanting "doo-lang, doo-lang, doo-lang."

Judy Craig, Barbara Lee, Patricia Bennett, and Sylvia Peterson had gone to high school together, had spent their lunch hours singing together and had recorded a number of singles for tiny record labels such as Big Deal.

Then, in 1961, a songwriter friend of theirs named Ronnie Mack asked them to cut a demo of some of his songs; while they finished school and went out to look for jobs, Mack took the demo around New York.

After a great many refusals, Mack finally interested a group of four men who sang as The Tokens and who had just signed a production contract with Capitol Records. The Tokens in turn signed Mack and scheduled a recording session with the four young women. When the Chiffons—a name they chose for themselves—walked into the studio, they found their new bosses waiting to be their backup band. The Tokens, it turned out, didn't have enough money to hire musicians, and it was the recording engineer who suggested that the "doo-langs" in the background of "He's So Fine" were kind of cute and should begin the song.

Then Capitol didn't want the song, so the Tokens shopped it around to thirteen other companies. It was only after turndowns from Columbia, MGM, and ABC-Paramount that they turned to the smaller Laurie Records. Released at last, "He's So Fine" went quickly to the top of the charts, where it spent five weeks at number one.

Shortly thereafter, Ronnie Mack died of Hodgkins' Disease. The Chiffons had lost a friend and a talented songwriter who believed in them. However, their success attracted the team of Carole King and Gerry Goffin, who had written a song called "One Fine Day," which they thought could tie into the "fine" theme established by the Chiffons' first hit. It had already been recorded, with Little Eva singing and King on the piano, but the recording had not been released. So, the Tokens erased Little Eva and recorded the Chiffons over the demo. The Chiffons had another hit: "One Fine Day" went to number five.

Their third "fine" song was "A Love So Fine," which made the Top 40, but not the top ten. Their last Top 40 hit was "Sweet Talkin' Guy," in 1966.

Ten years later, the estate of Ronnie Mack sued former Beatle George Harrison, claiming that his song "My Sweet Lord" was too similar to "He's So Fine" for coincidence; a judge agreed. The Chiffons then had a little fun by recording the Harrison song, but it wasn't a serious contender for airplay.

KATHLEEN THOMPSON

Coates, Dorothy (1928–)

Dorothy Love Coates is one of the protean gospel talents, celebrated as a singer, group leader, composer, and arranger. She was born Dorothy McGriff on January 30, 1928, in Birmingham, Alabama; after her father, a minister, abandoned his wife and six children, McGriff quit school to support her mother. Her verbal fluency and political acumen were such that she could have become a social force, another Rosa Parks; instead, she applied her talents to gospel music. She became the piano accompanist for several local choirs and in the mid-1940s formed the Royal Gospel Singers. Composed of McGriff; her sisters, Ruth and Jessie McGriff; her brother, Fred McGriff; and three friends, the Royals were the first gospel group to have their own radio program in Birmingham. During the week, McGriff worked standard menial jobs, but on weekends she performed as a soloist, inspired by Queen C. Anderson and **Mahalia Jackson**.

In 1946, Coates married Willie Love, a quartet luminary who sang for years with the Fairfield Four; her second husband, Carl Coates, was another quartet veteran who sang bass for the Sensational Nightingales. In 1947, she brought a quartet drive to the Original Gospel Harmonettes, Birmingham's top gospel group, with whom she toured for more than twenty years, becoming a gospel legend.

Coates never had a majestic voice, but her irresistible rhythms and singularly impassioned delivery more than compensated. She seemed to be made up of raw energy, but her intelligence was never in doubt. She was not only an animated performer, but also an astonishing lyricist. She began by interpolating original verses into other composers' songs, but the response convinced her to start writing full time. She has composed a dozen standards, including "That's Enough," "He's Right on Time," "You Must Be Born Again," "Come on in the House," "I Won't Let Go," and "You've Been Good to Me."

Deeply committed to the civil rights movement, Coates spoke about the problems of segregation, a particularly insidious condition for an itinerant performer in the 1950s. Like her idol, composer W. Herbert Brewster, she intends her songs to work doubly as encouragement to worldly political advancement and as meditative or testifying "rave-ups."

Coates now travels with an ensemble that includes her sister, Lillian McGriff Caffey, and her daughter, Carletta Coates. In recent years, she has appeared at the New York and New Orleans jazz festivals, at New York's Central Park Summer Stage, and in Germany and Switzerland. In 1990, she appeared in *The Long Walk Home*, a film about civil rights starring **Whoopi Goldberg** and Sissy Spacek.

ANTHONY HEILBUT

Cole, Natalie (1950–)

Can you follow in your father's footsteps and still be yourself? For Natalie Cole, the

When Natalie Cole was signed by Capitol, her father Nat King Cole's record label, she was afraid it was only because of nepotism. But she soon proved herself as a musician and a star in her own right. After a long struggle with drug and alcohol addiction, Cole made a courageous comeback in 1987. Her 1991 album Unforgettable *was both a tribute to and a collaboration with her father.* (PRIVATE COLLECTION)

answer turned out to be yes, but it wasn't easy.

Cole was born on February 6, 1950. In the upper-class Hancock Park section of Los Angeles where she grew up, hers was the only black family. Her mother, Maria Hawkins Cole, had been a singer with the Duke Ellington Orchestra; her father, Nat King Cole, was an enormously successful pop singer and one of the few black performers ever to have his own TV variety show. When Natalie was fifteen and attending prep school in Massachusetts, he died. The pain of that loss would stay with her for years.

Cole was surrounded by music in her childhood, both the rock she favored and the jazz her father preferred to listen to. When she was eleven, she sang an **Ella Fitzgerald** song for him. "She's got the voice," he boasted to his friends. However, her parents discouraged her from going into show business, and she graduated from the University of Massachusetts in 1972 with a major in child psychology. But what she really wanted to do was to sing professionally; she had already begun to build this career for herself and concentrated on it after graduation.

In 1974 she began to work with the songwriter/producer team of Chuck Jackson and Marvin Yancy. They got nowhere in their search for a record contract until they went to Capitol, her father's label. Cole signed reluctantly, fearing that she would never be anything but Nat King Cole's daughter to them, but it turned out to be the right move: Her first album, *Inseparable* (1975), went gold and brought her Grammys for Best New Artist and Best Rhythm and Blues Female Vocalist. Her next two were equally successful, and audiences loved her live onstage. In 1976 and 1977, she received NAACP Image Awards.

Then Cole's life took a bad turn: She had become involved with drugs and alcohol in college and now became seriously addicted. Driving under the influence, she had several accidents. Her three-year-old marriage to Yancy collapsed; her mother had to take control of her finances, and her efforts to stay sober failed. "I did it for everybody but me," she said, "and as soon as I got out, I went right back to doing what I was doing before I went in." Finally, a six-month stay at a clinic in 1983 brought her back to herself, and she was ready to start again.

Several years, several albums, and several thousand hours of hard work in the studio and on tour later, she had her next major success with *Everlasting* (1987). Then she focused on a risky project that had been lurking in the back of her mind: making her late father's music her own. *Unforgettable* (1991) contained twenty-two of his hits; on the title song, thanks to state-of-the-art technology, she and her father "sang" together. Professionally, the album was her greatest triumph: It soared to number one and won seven Grammys and other awards. Its personal impact may have been even more important—"All the things that a young girl might never have had a chance to say to her dad, and all the things she *wished* he could have said to her are on this album," she said.

Cole explored more music from her father's era on *Take a Look* (1993), and in 1994 she interpreted traditional Christmas songs on *Holly and Ivy* and made her acting debut in the cable-TV movie *Lily in Winter*. Being "just" Nat King Cole's daughter is one thing she won't worry about again.

INDIA COOPER

Coltrane, Alice (1937–)

Alice Coltrane describes her music as an endeavor to create a feeling of spiritual perfection. As a pianist, organist, harpist, vibraphonist, and composer, she epitomizes a tradition of great black musicians who have elected to pursue their art outside the confines of the commercial industry. Coltrane is perhaps best known as a member of the John Coltrane ensemble, arguably the premier avant-garde jazz group of the 1960s. Since the early 1970s, her performances of secular music have been limited to infrequent benefit concerts in Japan, Holland, Poland, London, and New York, although she occasionally has recorded religious music with other jazz musicians.

Born Alice McLeod on August 27, 1937, in Detroit, Michigan, she is the mother of four children: one daughter, Michelle, and three sons, Ravi, Oranyan, and John, Jr. (who died in an automobile accident in 1982). Coltrane descends from a family of musicians: Her mother, Anna, played piano and sang in the church choir, and her mother's brother, Ernie Farrow, was a professional jazz bassist. Alice McLeod began piano study when she was seven and later studied organ and music theory privately. Her development into an accomplished pianist and organist was influenced early on by Earl "Bud" Powell and Thelonious Monk.

Coltrane launched her professional career when she joined the Terry Gibbs Quartet in 1960; prior to that she gained experience with other groups led by Kenny Burrell, Johnny Griffin, Lucky Thompson, and Yusef Lateef. In 1963, she married John Coltrane; she joined his group in 1965. After her husband's death in 1967, she continued

Through her music, Alice Coltrane endeavors to achieve a feeling of spiritual perfection: "To me, to bring music to an exalted transcendental level was the reason for the engagement with music in the first place." (SCHOMBURG CENTER)

to record and tour with her own groups until she settled in Woodland Hills, California, in the early 1970s. Among those touring with her as members of her groups were, at various times, saxophonists Pharoah Sanders, Archie Shepp, Joe Henderson, Frank Lowe, and Carlos Ward; bassists Cecil McBee and Jimmy Garrison; and drummers Rashied Ali, Ben Riley, and Roy Haynes. In 1975, following a journey to India to pursue spiritual studies, Alice Coltrane received a Sanskrit name, Turiyasangitananda, and founded the Vedantic Center.

Displaying a wide range of musical interests throughout her career, Coltrane has recorded with Laura Nyro, the Rascals, and other pop groups and has also performed excerpts from Stravinsky's *Firebird Suite*. In 1987, she led a quartet, which included her sons, in a tribute to John Coltrane at New York's Cathedral of Saint John the Divine. She continues to play devotional music on her organ at home and occasionally practices classical music on her Steinway concert-grand piano.

Alice Coltrane's current musical orientation may be best captured by her own words: "Avant-garde music is very highly technical music, but I saw instrumental music elevated to a higher plateau, where it was no longer avant-garde, but was spiritual, or devotional, music. To me, to bring music to an exalted transcendental level was the reason for the engagement with music in the first place."

TOMMY LOTT

Cotten, Elizabeth   (c. 1896–1987)

Born around January 1895 in Chapel Hill, North Carolina, "Libba" Cotten became interested in music as a child. She began to play her brother's banjo and guitar shortly after the turn of the century and taught herself to tune and play them left-handed (upside-down). Cotten came of age at a particularly rich time in the history of Southern rural music: The just emerging blues along with the large body of fiddle/banjo dance tunes, minstrel show songs, ballads, and religious songs formed her repertoire.

Chapel Hill was her home until the early 1940s, when she joined the great migration northward, settling in Washington, D.C. Cotten eventually became the housekeeper for the famed ethnomusicologist Charles Seeger, whose family discovered her talents and diverse storehouse of songs.

In the late 1950s, during the beginning of the "folk revival," Cotten slowly began a professional music career. She eventually became a regular performer at folk festivals throughout the United States and Canada and was identified with the country dance tune, "Freight Train." During this period, Cotten recorded three albums for Folkways Records and one for Arhoolie Records that featured her broad repertoire.

Cotten continued performing into the early 1980s as one of the few black women on the folk-music circuit. She eventually received awards from the National Endow-ment for the Arts as well as a 1984 Grammy Award for *Elizabeth Cotten Live!* Washington, D.C., remained her home until she moved to Syracuse, New York, to be closer to relatives. She died there on June 29, 1987.

KIP LORNELL

Cox, Ida (1896–1967)

Ida Cox sang the blues in minstrel shows, vaudeville, nightclubs, and on records during the heyday of blues recording in the 1920s. She was born Ida Prather on February 25, 1896, in Toccoa, Georgia, and received her early musical training in the church. Her theatrical career began in her teens when she ran away to join White & Clark's Black & Tan Minstrels, at first performing "Topsy" roles in blackface. For the next decade, she traveled as a singer with some of the best minstrel troupes of the day, including the Rabbit Foot Minstrels, Silas Green from New Orleans, and the Florida Cotton Blossom Minstrels. During this period, she married Adler Cox, whose name she kept throughout her career, although she remarried twice.

She began to record for Paramount Records in 1923, and by 1929 she had made more than forty records in classic blues style, often accompanied by a pianist or by a small jazz combo. Cox's most frequent accompanists were **Lovie Austin**, a pianist and arranger for Paramount, and Jesse Crump, who became her third husband.

During the height of her popularity in the 1920s she toured extensively, playing theaters and clubs in major cities with major jazz figures, among them Ferdinand "Jelly Roll" Morton and "King" Joe Oliver. When the Great Depression hit, Cox produced her own shows, *Raisin Cain* and *Darktown Scandals*,

The strains of "Freight Train" performed left-handed on Elizabeth Cotten's (upside-down) guitar were a familiar sound at folk festivals around the country from the late 1950s through the early 1980s. (SCHOMBURG CENTER)

and took them on the road. In 1934, billed as "The Sepia Mae West," she appeared with **Bessie Smith** at the Apollo Theater in New York in the *Fan Waves Revue*. When impresario John Hammond put together his second "From Spirituals to Swing" concert at Carnegie Hall in 1939 with the intention of introducing black music to a white highbrow audience, Ida Cox was on the program.

After 1929, Cox did not record again until 1939 when she made recordings for John Hammond with a group of jazz greats who were billed as her "All-Star Orchestra." These were issued on the Vocalion and Okeh labels. Cox continued to tour until she suffered a stroke in 1945, but she came out of retirement in 1961 to record an album, *Blues for Rampart Street*, on the Riverside label. She spent her final years living with her daughter in Knoxville, Tennessee, where she died of cancer on November 10, 1967.

Ida Cox was a blues queen in every way. Her shows were always high class, and though she is remembered as imperious and demanding, she was a good manager and a fair employer. She combined glamour and sophistication with a singing style that was both sultry and emotionally appealing. She performed and recorded many of her own songs, and though she was, in the words of Lovie Austin, "always a lady," her lyrics are often salty, laced with sexual allusions and sly humor directed at men. Her song "Wild Women Don't Have the Blues" has become a feminist anthem among modern blues lovers, a situation "Miss Ida" would probably have appreciated.

SUZANNE FLANDREAU

D

Davis-Barnes, Gail (1950–)

Pianist Gail Davis-Barnes is a champion of the cause of African-American composers. She has toured both the United States and the Middle East telling the story of black music.

Barnes was born May 22, 1950, in Dayton, Ohio, the second of three daughters, to Rev. James Thomas and Elease M. Davis. Her father was a minister in the United Methodist church; her mother, a nurse and social worker.

Barnes, who sang in the choir and served as piano and organ accompanist for various church functions, graduated from Paul Laurence Dunbar High School in Dayton, where she played xylophone in the marching band, and viola in the orchestra and concert band and also sang in Dunbar's choir.

Her early piano teachers included the husband-wife team of Audley and Barbara Wasson. The Wasson technique impressed her so much that she is using it today with her students. Barnes knew her life would never be the same after she heard a recording of Susan Star playing Mendelssohn's *Concerto in G-minor* with the Philadelphia Symphony Orchestra. Barnes knew then she wanted to be a pianist.

Barnes continued her piano studies with Marilyn Neely, George Hadad, and Rosemary Platt while pursuing an undergraduate degree. In 1971, she was awarded a bachelor of music in piano performance, with a double minor in music history and organ from Ohio State University. She moved to Ann Arbor, Michigan, to study with Marian Owen Hunt and Charles Fisher while pursuing a master of music degree (1972) in piano performance, again minoring in music history.

In 1972, she married Ray Barnes and continued postgraduate studies by attending master classes and working with her present coach, Joseph Hurt. Her love for history and for the oral tradition grew from her ethnomusicology classes. Through these classes and recordings by Natalie Hinderas, Barnes came to know such composers as George Walker, William Grant Still, and Hale Smith.

While the music of these black composers inspired Barnes to develop her concert-lecture series, she soon found that the music was not easily accessible; music by black women composers was even more difficult to find. By 1977, Barnes had completed her first concert-lecture recital on keyboard music by African-American composers. What began as Barnes' passion became a pilot program for the concert-lectures she conducted worldwide. A typical recital-lecture consists of a brief composer biography, a discussion of the music, the actual performance, and a question-and-answer session. Barnes' roster includes **Florence Price**, R. Nathaniel Dett, **Margaret Bonds**, John Work, and others.

From 1980 to 1983, Barnes' family lived in Dhahran, Saudi Arabia, where Barnes taught general music and music appreciation to an international group of children from ages seven to twelve. Her concert-lectures were so well received in Saudi Arabia that she could not honor all the requests for appearances. Despite her success in Dhahran, Barnes was happy to return to the States, where she enjoyed more freedom. Saudi laws dictated that she had to have her husband's written permission prior to each performance; additionally, she and her daughters could not leave their compound without Ray Barnes' written permission.

Barnes is the author of a series of workbooks of music theory for pianists entitled *Theory for Two*—the title refers to the parent-student relationship suggested by the Suzuki method, upon which the series is built. Books I through III were published by GDB Music Service in Ann Arbor. Books IV and V are scheduled for publication in 1996.

Barnes is the minister of music at Glacier Way United Methodist Church and Church of the Good Shepherd in Ann Arbor. For twenty-three years, Barnes has maintained a private studio in Ann Arbor where she teaches piano and organ, using conventional and Suzuki methods, and lives with her daughters Regina and Regan. She plans to produce a commercial recording of music by African-American composers. Another goal is to fill a void by publishing music by African-American women composers.

REGINA HARRIS BAIOCCHI

Dawson, Mary (1894–1962)

Mary Lucinda Cardwell Dawson, opera director, emerged during the 1950s as a noted leader in the field of music in the United States. She opened the Cardwell Dawson School of Music in Pittsburgh, Pennsylvania, around 1926 and was a well-known choral director in Pennsylvania for more than twenty years. She served as the tenth president of the National Association of Negro Musicians (NANM) from 1939 to 1941 and founded the National Negro Opera Company (NNOC) in 1941–42.

Mary Lucinda Cardwell was born February 14, 1894, in Madison, North Carolina, to James A. and Elizabeth Cardwell. She was the oldest of six children—two brothers and three sisters—several of whom were active in music. The family moved to Homestead, Pennsylvania, where Dawson attended local schools and began her early training in piano. In 1925, Dawson graduated from the New England Conservatory of Music and then continued her studies at Chicago Musical College and the Metropolitan Opera Studio, training in organ, voice, staging, and opera technique; in choral music under Arthur Hubbard, Clara Huhn, and Harvey Gaul; and in opera technique under Vincent Sorey and Clayton Gilbert.

She married Walter Dawson around 1926, and they moved to Pittsburgh. There she started the Mary Cardwell Dawson School of Music, which became a highly regarded Eastern private school. The Cardwell Dawson Choir won the Pittsburgh *Sun-Telegraph*'s Harvey Gaul Award for musical excellence in 1937 and 1938 and performed at the New York World's Fair in 1939. Meanwhile, Dawson performed recitals as a pianist and singer throughout Pennsylvania and in Washington, D.C., and Chicago. In 1941, the Dawsons moved to Washington.

As a direct outgrowth of her work as president of NANM, Dawson founded NNOC to provide opportunities for trained black singers to perform. The company's first production, Verdi's *Aida*, was staged in Pittsburgh during the twenty-first annual

NANM convention in 1941. The leading roles were sung by LaJulia Rhea, Napoleon Reed, Nellie Dobson Plante, William Franklin, Shelby Nichols, Reginald Burrus, and Thelma Wade Brown; Frederick Vajda staged the opera and conducted the orchestra. The NNOC received its first charter from the State of Illinois, where *Aida* was restaged on October 10–11, 1942.

Dawson started opera guilds in Chicago, Pittsburgh, Washington, D.C., and New York to assist in subsequent productions of *La Traviata*, *Faust*, *Aida*, and *Ouanga*. The last, written by black composer Clarence Cameron White, had its premiere at the Metropolitan Opera House on May 27, 1956, conducted by Henri Elkan, and several more performances were sung the following September at Carnegie Hall.

The NNOC presented staged operas with orchestra from 1941 to 1956; between 1946 and 1961 the company performed an operatic version of *The Ordering of Moses* by Nathaniel Dett. The National Negro Opera Foundation was formed by Dawson in 1950–51 to provide a broader cultural and national base for the company's activity. However, from its inception NNOC was constantly in debt, and Dawson and her husband often used personal funds to underwrite the financial costs of productions.

Although NNOC used both black and white musicians and technical staff in its productions, Dawson accomplished her goal of giving talented black singers opportunities that were denied them by white companies. Singers such as Camilla Williams, **Muriel Rahn**, Robert McFerrin, LaJulia Rhea, **Lillian Evanti**, and **Carol Brice** gained valuable experience as leading NNOC soloists. The company had the support of many national figures, including Eleanor Roosevelt, **Mary McLeod Bethune, Marian Anderson**, and W. C. Handy. NNOC became a member of both the national council of the Metropolitan Opera Association and the Central Opera Services.

In 1961, Dawson was appointed to President John F. Kennedy's National Committee on Music. She also held memberships in **Delta Sigma Theta Sorority**, the **National Council of Negro Women**, the **National Association of Colored Women**, and the National Association of Negro Business and Professional Women's Clubs.

Following a visit to Chicago in July 1961, Dawson became ill and on March 19, 1962, she died of a heart attack in Washington, D.C. She was one of a cadre of black women who assumed positions of national importance at mid-century and was praised for her determination to provide artistic and cultural opportunities for musically talented black Americans.

ELLISTINE P. LEWIS

de Haas, Geraldine (1935–)

Some voices soar in the concert halls and the clubs. Others ring out in the service of humanity. The voice of jazz singer Geraldine de Haas, in her lifetime, has done both: She frequently put her musical career on hold to promote unity through the medium of jazz.

Geraldine de Haas was born the seventh of nine children on January 16, 1935, in Newark, New Jersey. Her role models include her father, who was a window washer and advocate for African-American health and culture, and her mother, who was a homemaker.

As a child, de Haas used to sit in movie theaters day after day, learning musicals verbatim. When they were in their teens, de

Jazz singer Geraldine de Haas has performed throughout Europe and North America. She is the moving force behind the soon-to-be-built Jazz Museum of Chicago. (PRIVATE COLLECTION)

Haas, her sister Salome, and her brother Andy formed a trio called Andy and the Bey Sisters. Their break came after Andy appeared on New York television in the locally produced variety show, *Star Time.*

In the 1950s, the Beys performed in England, Spain, France, Belgium, Germany, Holland, Yugoslavia, Canada, and the United States. They recorded *Andy and the Bey Sisters* (1961, RCA), *Round Midnight* (1963, Prestige), and *Now Hear Andy and the Bey Sisters* (1963, Prestige).

Andy played piano and wrote; the sisters harmonized. The Beys opened for Bud Powell, Horace Silver, Dizzy Gillespie, Redd Foxx, Flip Wilson, **Carmen McRae**, and Cab Calloway; Their act was also sought by **Sarah Vaughan**, Count Basie, Miles Davis, and **Lena Horne**.

When Geraldine married guitarist/bassist Eddie de Haas, Andy and the Bey Sisters disbanded. Shortly afterwards, Salome married and moved to Toronto where she still thrives as a playwright, as well as a composer and singer. Andy travels between New York and Austria and enjoys an international career as a composer/pianist and an educator.

When de Haas moved to Chicago in 1968, she was pregnant with her second child. It was the "city of neighborhoods," where African Americans were warned, "Stay out of my neighborhood!" In 1968, Chicago was the site of civil-rights marches, the Democratic national convention, and a bloody riot following a rock concert in Grant Park. This was the de Haas family's welcoming committee.

Geraldine herself devoted her time to raising her family, earning a B.A. from Chicago State University, and singing. Then, in the 1970s, she became involved in the beginnings of the organization Jazz Unites, Inc.

It all started in 1974 with Duke Ellington's death. A group of musicians in Chicago wanted to salute Ellington. De Haas wanted the concert in Grant Park for all of the city, not just in the "'hood." Thanks to a little media pressure and a lot of perseverance, she united the Chicago Park District, the musician's union, and people from all neighborhoods. The tribute was a great success and became a pilot for an annual event. In 1981 Jazz Unites, Inc., was born to facilitate it.

In 1995 Jazz Unites' eighteenth annual Ellington tribute featured Ellis Marsalis.

Jazz Unites also presents annual tributes to **Marian Anderson,** Paul Robeson, and a festival of jazz stars. The festival roster has included **Betty Carter,** Jimmy Smith, Willie Pickens, and Von Freeman, with sponsorship from the MacArthur Foundation, Budweiser, Absolut Vodka, and Coca-Cola.

The Jazz Unites Festival started a trend in Chicago. Summer in the city now resounds to the music of the Chicago Jazzfest, Bluesfest, Gospelfest, and Countryfest. All of these musical events, which have contributed enormously to the quality of life as well as the finances of Chicago, are modeled on de Haas' original. Only musical insiders, however, are knowledgeable enough to give her credit. She has not yet been given formal recognition by the city.

She has, however, become a valued member of the musical community in Chicago and the country. She has served on the boards of the National Endowment for the Arts, the Illinois Arts Council, Arts Midwest, the Center for Black Music Research, and the City of Chicago Department of Cultural Affairs. She has received honors from Mayor Harold Washington, *Chicago Tribune* magazine, and *Chicago Jazz* magazine. Other accolades include the Paul Robeson Award and Sculptor Chicago.

De Haas' radio and television appearances include *Newport Jazz Festival* and *An Evening with Ella Fitzgerald* on the Public Broadcasting System (PBS) and *Classical Black* with William Warfield on WUIC in Chicago. Her Chicago live performances include the *Commemorative Ellington Sacred Concert, Jazz Matazz,* and *Women in Jazz.* Theatrical credits include roles in *To Be Young, Gifted and Black, Don't Bother Me, I Can't Cope, Hair,* and the films *Let's Get Lost* and *The Paris Jam Session.*

De Haas is now in the process of building the Jazz Museum of Chicago on East 75th Street. She has secured a building, $400,000 from the state of Illinois, and the services of architects from Skidmore, Owenings, and Merrill. De Haas' vision of the Jazz Museum of Chicago includes a 1000-seat theater, practice rooms, radio station, A/V facilities, convention space, classrooms, and archival and office space for Jazz Unites, Inc.

Photographer John Tweedle once captured the spirit and regality of Queen Geraldine at a tribute to Ellington. His photograph shows de Haas with a perfectly shaped *Free Angela Davis* afro, her dashiki hem brushing her sandaled feet, and her slender hand holding a microphone; the audience is figuratively in the palm of her outstretched hand. This is the performer whom de Haas the organizer eclipsed to make jazz a force to unite people of all neighborhoods.

REGINA HARRIS BAIOCCHI

Dixon, Lucille (1923–)

Classical and jazz bassist, orchestra manager, and artistic activist, Lucille Dixon has devoted much of her life to providing opportunities for young black musicians to achieve orchestral playing experience.

Dixon was born in Harlem on February 27, 1923, the daughter of a Baptist minister. In her early years, she studied piano first with her mother and then with Carmen Shepperd, a popular black piano teacher in Harlem. During this time, she played for her father's church services, earning fifty cents each Sunday. At Wadleigh High School, she began to study the bass viol and was encouraged to audition for the All-City High School Orchestra, which performed at various sites around New York City. After she passed the audition and was accepted into the orchestra, arrangements were made for scholarship study with New York Philharmonic bassist Fred Zimmerman.

Dixon's participation in various other symphonic groups began in 1941 with the National Youth Administration Orchestra, an organization that served as the country's clearinghouse for symphony orchestras. During her association with the NYA, she was also enrolled at Brooklyn College (1941–43) and played bass with the Juilliard Orchestra. It was during this time that all-girl orchestras were becoming quite the rage in the United States, but because of her race, Dixon's requests for auditions were denied, even for radio broadcasts.

Because of the racial discrimination experienced by black classical musicians, Dixon became active as a jazz bassist, beginning with a two-year tenure with Earl Hines from 1943 to 1945. However, needing more flexibility than Hines' rigorous touring schedule allowed, she formed her own band, the Lucille Dixon Orchestra. This group remained together from 1946 to 1960 and included at various times such luminaries as Tyree Glenn, James Taft Jordan, Buddy Tate, Sonny Payne, Bill Smith, and George Matthews.

Lucille Dixon has performed and recorded with some of the great names in the music industry, including **Ella Fitzgerald,** Johnny Hartman, **Sarah Vaughan**, Billy Daniels, Earl Coleman, Tony Bennett, **Dinah Washington**, Vincentico Valdez, Machito, Joe Franklin, Georgia Gibbs, Frank Sinatra, Jan Peerce, **Billie Holiday**, and Eubie Blake.

Although Dixon had a prominent career as a jazz musician, she did not give up on the idea of playing in a symphony orchestra.

From 1960 to 1964, she played with the National Orchestral Association and in 1964–65, with the Boston Women's Symphony, where she was principal bassist. Her other orchestral affiliations include the National Symphony of Panama (1954–56), Radio City Music Hall (1960), Dimitri Mitropoulos Competitions (1965–67), the Westchester Philharmonic (1962–72), the Ridgefield Symphony (1973), and the Scranton Symphony (1970–72).

In 1965, she was a founding member of the Symphony of the New World and became its manager in April 1972, a position she held until 1976. This organization provided valuable performing experience for young black musicians whose opportunities were few.

She is married and the mother of three children.

CAROL YAMPOLSKY

Dobbs, Mattiwilda (1925–)

Mattiwilda Dobbs is an internationally renowned coloratura soprano who has the distinction of being the second black woman to sing with the Metropolitan Opera Company. Born in Atlanta, Georgia, on July 11, 1925, one of six daughters of Irene Thompson and John Wesley Dobbs, she grew up in Atlanta, starting piano study at age seven and singing in the First Congregational Church choir. She earned a B.A. from **Spelman College** in 1946, where she studied voice with Naomi Maise and Willis James. Continuing her education in New York, she attended Columbia University Teachers College (M.A., 1948, in Spanish language and literature) and studied voice privately with Lotte Leonard (1946–50). She also studied at the Mannes Music School

(1948–49), at the Berkshire Music Festival at Tanglewood (1950), and with Pierre Bernac in Paris (1950–52). During this period she won the **Marian Anderson** Award (1947) and the John Hay Whitney Fellowship (1950–52).

Mattiwilda Dobbs' career opportunities surged when she won first prize in the International Music Competition held in Geneva, Switzerland, in 1950. She studied with Lola Rodríguez de Aragón in Madrid in the next year and began to concertize under the management of Sol Hurok, giving a highly successful series of recitals and appearances with orchestras in European capitals. Her first operatic success occurred during the Holland Festival of 1952 in Stravinsky's *Le Rossignol* and was followed by appearances in other celebrated opera houses such as La Scala in Milan (1953) and the Royal Opera House at Covent Garden (1954) where she sang a command performance for the British royal family and the king and queen of Sweden (1954). She was decorated with the Order of the North Star by King Gustaf VI of Sweden. In one way, 1954 was a tragic year for the singer, for her husband of one year, Louis Rodriguez, died four days before the Covent Garden command performance.

However, in 1954, American audiences gave Dobbs full recognition in the wake of the critical acclaim accorded her Town Hall appearance as Zerbinetta in the Little Orchestra Society performance of the Strauss opera *Ariadne auf Naxos* (Hermann Scherchen, director). Her American operatic debut as the Queen of Shemakha in Rimsky-Korsakov's *Le Coq d'Or* took place in the San Francisco Opera House (1955), and in the next year she appeared at New York's Metropolitan Opera as Gilda in Verdi's *Rigoletto* (November 9, 1956), following

The American operatic career of Mattiwilda Dobbs was given great impetus by her highly successful tour of European capitals in the 1950s. (SCHOMBURG CENTER)

Marian Anderson and Robert McFerrin as pioneer black singers with that group.

Dobbs married journalist Bengt Janzen of Sweden in 1957 and, in 1959, settled in Stockholm, continuing to perform in Europe, America, Australia, and Israel as recitalist and opera singer. She returned to the United States and taught on the faculty of several American institutions including Spelman College, the University of Texas at Austin, and the University of Illinois. She retired as Professor of Voice at **Howard University** in 1991 after a tenure of fifteen years. In 1989, she was elected a member of the Metropolitan Opera Association National Board. She made several recordings of operas and art songs.

DORIS EVANS McGINTY

Donegan, Dorothy (1922–)

Educated hands moving across the keys as if controlled by some manic force, legs kicking out gleefully at the pedals, eyes shut tight, coif glistening with perspiration: this is a portrait of Dorothy Donegan when she is thoroughly caught up in the muse. Records do not do her justice. Her spirit is not easily captured in a recording studio, and she must be seen in order to be properly appreciated and believed. Although steeped in the classics, Donegan inevitably chose jazz, the art of improvisers, because no page of notated music could possibly harness her talents and interests. Honored as a Jazz Master by the National Endowment for the Arts, she has been caught up in the muse since the tender age of six.

A native of the south side of Chicago, one of the crucibles of African-American cul-

Hands moving across the keys as if controlled by some manic force, legs kicking out gleefully at the pedals, coif glistening with perspiration, Dorothy Donegan becomes thoroughly caught up in the music when she performs. Here, she entertains black troops during World War II. (MOOR-LAND-SPINGARN)

ture, Donegan began her musical odyssey almost from the moment she entered Willard Elementary School and her parents enrolled her in piano lessons at the studio of Alfred Simms. Her interest in music accelerated greatly when she entered the famous DuSable High School, coming under the tough and learned tutelage of Captain Walter Dyett. Known for encouraging a raft of celebrated jazz musicians, Dyett practiced a kind of tough musical love that gave Donegan the boost she needed.

Donegan's first professional job was playing with the Bob Tinsley Band at the age of seventeen. From there, she played solo at a downtown grill; in 1942 the owner of one of the grills where she worked presented the twenty-year-old Donegan at Orchestra Hall in a concert featuring a winning mix of jazz, boogie-woogie, and European classical music. Donegan was the first jazz pianist to take the stage at Orchestra Hall, a venue previously graced only by classical talents such as Vladimir Horowitz.

That 1942 concert proved to be a portent of the future, as Donegan has gone on to a rich, globe-trotting career that often finds her straddling disparate musical spheres. Fluent in the classics as well as jazz, she truly belongs to that special class of orchestral jazz piano playing occupied by such masters as Art Tatum, Erroll Garner, and Oscar Peterson.

WILLARD JENKINS

Douroux, Margaret (1941–)

"Gospel music is energy. Whereas you can sing a hymn academically, gospel music demands a soul kind of deliverance. The energy is what gives gospel its character." Because of her sensitivity to and under-standing of both the technical and spiritual characteristics of different religious music genres, Margaret Jean Pleasant Douroux (composer, arranger, and publisher of gospel music, hymns, anthems, and spirituals) has been able to write more than 115 sacred songs.

Born March 21, 1941, in Los Angeles, Douroux is the daughter of Los Angeles gospel pioneer Earl Amos Pleasant (1918–1974) and music teacher Olga Williams Pleasant (b. 1920). Douroux and her husband Donald are the parents of one daughter, Mardoné Patrice Douroux.

During the three years that Douroux attended Southern University (Baton Rouge, Louisiana) in the 1960s, she was actively involved in civil rights movement sit-ins and later became the West Coast music director for Operation PUSH (People United to Save Humanity). Douroux received her B.A. degree in music from California State University, Los Angeles. Her master's degrees in education and educational psychology were earned at the University of Southern California. She received a doctorate in educational psychology from the University of Beverly Hills. During her thirteen-year career in the Los Angeles school system, she served as elementary teacher, guidance counselor, and psychologist.

Douroux acquired much of her religious music training from working in her father's church (Mount Moriah Baptist Church) where she was greatly influenced by contacts with Los Angeles gospel musicians Thurston Gilbert Frazier and **Gwendolyn Lightner**. In recent years, she has served as choir director for various television shows —including 227 starring Marla Gibbs, and Billy Graham's twenty-fifth anniversary special. Since the late 1970s, she has served

"Gospel music is energy." The energetic Margaret Douroux has composed more than 115 sacred songs. In 1981, she founded the Heritage Music Foundation, whose mission is to establish a gospel music hall of fame and museum complex. (J. C. DJEDJE)

as minister of music at Greater New Bethel Baptist Church. Douroux also regularly conducts gospel-music workshops around the United States.

Several of her compositions have become standards in various hymn books and religious communities: "Give Me a Clean Heart" (1968), "I'm Glad" (1970), "What Shall I Render" (1975), "The Lord Is Speaking" (1976), "He Decided to Die" (1976), "Trees" (1979), and "Follow Jesus" (1981). Songs that have won awards or been recorded and featured in special projects include "God Is Not Dead" (The Mighty Clouds of Joy won a Grammy Award for Best Gospel Performance with this song) and "I'm Glad" (**Nikki Giovanni** used this song as background music for a recording of poetry). In addition, several songs have been featured on recordings by James Cleveland and his Gospel Music Workshop of America, as well as by other established gospel musicians (e.g., **Shirley Ceasar**, Clay Evans).

Not only have a number of music awards been presented to Douroux—the Best Song Award (James Cleveland and the Gospel Music Workshop of America), the Music Accomplishment Award (A Corporation for Christ Church News), and the Gospel Academy Award (Daviticus)—but she has also received a host of proclamations and official tributes from cities around the country. She is the founder and president of her own publishing company (Rev. Earl A. Pleasant Publishing Company); has made three recordings—*Revival from the Mount* (1970), *The Way of the Word* (1982), and *Signs of the Advent* (1987); and is the author of several publications: *About My Father's Business* (1977), *Christian Principles That Motivate and Enhance Education among Black Children* (1979), *Why I Sing* (1983), and *Find the Kingdom* (1985).

In 1981, Douroux established the Heritage Music Foundation, an organization whose mission is to build Gospel House in Los Angeles (a monument, hall of fame, and museum complex that would be devoted to the nurturing and preservation of gospel music). Country music has the Grand Ole Opry, and Western classical music has Carnegie Hall: Douroux believes that gospel music should be recognized and supported in a comparable manner.

JACQUELINE COGDELL DJEDJE

E

En Vogue

"En Vogue updates the Motown dream-girl act for a brave new world," announced *Vogue* magazine in September 1992. But when it comes to comparisons, the group itself prefers Sister Sledge and Emotions to the Supremes.

Created by producer-songwriters Thomas McElroy and Denzel Foster, En Vogue is made up of vocalists Terry Ellis, Cindy Herron, Maxine Jones, and Dawn Robinson, all of whom were born between 1967 and 1969. Beginning as a high concept group put together from auditions, the four chosen women have melded to form an integrated musical whole.

The group debuted with the platinum-selling *Born to Sing* in 1990. The first single from the album, "Hold On," reached the top of the charts, and two others—"Lies" and "You Don't Have to Worry"—both became hits; the albums went platinum and won five nominations at the Soul Train Music Awards; and "Hold On" won as the best single by a band or group. The song also earned En Vogue a Grammy Award nomination.

Their follow-up album, released in 1993 and entitled *Funky Divas*, went platinum-plus. While *Born to Sing* established En Vogue as a group to watch, *Funky Divas* broadened En Vogue's audience and their repertoire. The mix of rap, funk, hip-hop, hard rock, and reggae on the *Funky Divas* album seems to have given them the cross-over audience many groups find elusive. As *Spin* magazine noted, "En Vogue didn't just try on a few different hats; it set up a chapeau shop."

The first single, "My Lovin' (You're Never Gonna Get It)" immediately climbed the charts and was followed by "Giving Him Something He Can Feel," "Free Your Mind," and "Give it Up, Turn it Loose." The video of "Free Your Mind" won four awards at the Music Video Producers Association Awards, and the album won the American Music Award for soul/R&B album of the year.

The members' backgrounds reflect the variety of their sound. Terry Ellis explained to Seventeen magazine, "We all sing lead. Dawn's sound is funky, Maxine's sort of sultry/gospel and Cindy's more jazz-oriented."

Ellis traces much of her own sound to her sister, who was a nightclub singer and who encouraged her to sing from a very early age. Always interested in a musical career, Ellis nonetheless finished college before pursuing it.

Cindy Herron studied classical voice, opera, and jazz. Living with her mother in a predominantly white neighborhood gave her a strong pop-music influence at a young age; when she and her sister moved in with her African-American father, new musical influences were added.

Dreaming of stardom since childhood, Dawn Robinson grew up and developed her

En Vogue consists of singers Terry Ellis, Cindy Herron, Maxine Jones, and Dawn Robinson. Their 1990 debut record, Born to Sing, *went platinum, won five nominations at the Soul Train Music Awards, and earned En Vogue a Grammy Award nomination. Their platinum-plus record,* Funky Divas, *reached a broad crossover audience with its mixture of rap, funk, hip-hop, hard rock, and reggae.* (PRIVATE COLLECTION)

voice and style at A.M.E. Zion Church where she was a member of the Youth Voices of Zion Choir. She began to sing in clubs at age 16.

Raised by her father, Maxine Jones graduated from East Side High School in Paterson, New Jersey, and then attended junior college in Oakland, California. She grew up singing in church and loving gospel music but she later turned to jazz.

In addition to its awards, the group has many other badges of success, including guest appearances on *In Living Color* and *Saturday Night Live,* singing the theme song for "Hangin' With Mr. Cooper," a performance at the 1993 presidential inauguration celebration in Washington, D.C., and a film role for Herron. Musically, they have clearly transcended their packaging.

HILARY MAC AUSTIN

Ennis, Ethel (1932–)

Pianist, jazz vocalist, and bandleader Ethel Llewellyn Ennis was born November 28, 1932, in Baltimore, Maryland. Her mother, Bell, was a housewife, and her father, Andrew, was a barber. Before she expressed an interest in music, Ethel was shaped and nurtured by the strong moral and religious values of her family, especially by her mother and her grandmother, "Honey" Elizabeth Small.

Ennis' musical interest surfaced in the second grade when at age seven she started to play piano; her first job as a pianist was playing for her church Sunday school at fifty cents a week. By the age of fifteen, Ennis was surrounded and influenced by rhythm and blues, absorbing the work of R&B artists

Versatile song stylist Ethel Ennis, whose first job was playing the piano at her church's Sunday school, sang at President Richard Nixon's second inauguration. (SCHOMBURG CENTER)

LaVern Baker, Hadda Brooks, Savannah Churchill, Camille Howard, and Rose Murphy among others. Additionally, Ennis was influenced by tunes like "I'm Tired Crying over You" by Ella Johnson, "Fine Brown Frame" by Nellie Lutcher, and "Please Don't Freeze on Me" by Ruth Brown.

In the late 1940s, Ennis joined a jazz octet led by Abraham Riley, where she honed both her piano and vocal skills. It was during this period that Ennis met and collaborated with William Everhart to write a rock 'n' roll composition entitled "Little Boy" (published and produced by Savoy in 1950). The song was recorded by several artists, including Little Richard. Also in 1950 she entered and won the *It's High Time* talent show, her first exposure on local television (WAAM). The prize for winning was an all-expense-paid trip to Philadelphia to appear on the *Paul Whiteman Teen-Age TV Show*.

After high school graduation (1950), Ennis' musical career began to blossom. By day, she studied shorthand and typing; at night, she performed with an R&B group called the Tilters, the JoJo Jones Ensemble, and in such clubs as the Red Fox (Baltimore), the Village Vanguard (New York), the Red Onion (Aspen, Colorado), and the Astor Club (London), to name a few. In addition, she performed at the Apollo Theater (Harlem) and with Benny Goodman, sang for eight years on *The Arthur Godfrey Show,* and made numerous additional TV and nightclub appearances and recordings.

Despite a bad first marriage (to Jacques Leeds), Ennis married again; her second husband was Earl Arnett. Ennis' strong moral and religious values catapulted her to significant musical heights. Her style is imbued with influences from Billie Holiday, Sarah

Vaughan, and **Dinah Washington**. In her vocal stylings, one can hear a flair for humor, impersonations of Holiday, Vaughan, and Washington; equal competence whether singing a ballad or up-tempo composition; and the ability to personalize her lyrics. Ennis can also fit diverse musical situations, whether singing at Richard Nixon's second inauguration or on *The Arthur Godfrey Show* or performing with her trio. Ethel Ennis is a national treasure of African-American music.

EDDIE S. MEADOWS

Evanti, Lillian Evans (1890–1967)

Lillian Evans was born in Washington, D.C., on August 12, 1890. The daughter of Anne Brooks and Bruce Evans, M.D, the lyric soprano was the first black American to sing opera with an organized company in Europe. As a protégée of Lulu Vere Childers, she studied at the **Howard University** School of Music, graduating in 1917. The name Evanti was a combination of her maiden name and the last name of Roy Tibbs, a Howard University professor of music

Lyric soprano Lillian Evans Evanti scored successes in Europe, the United States, and the Caribbean. She is seen here with her son. (SCURLOCK STUDIO)

In 1925, lyric soprano Lillian Evans Evanti (shown here costumed for the role of Lakmé, circa 1924) was forced to go to France for her operatic debut, but in 1943, she sang Violetta in La Traviata *with the National Negro Opera Company in Washington, D.C.* (SCURLOCK STUDIO)

whom she married. Five years of study and performance beginning in 1925 included voice lessons with Mme. Ritter-Ciampi in Paris and Rosa Storchio in Italy and acting lessons with M. Gaston Dupins. Her most notable performances in Italy and France were at the Casino Theater in Nice, France (1925), and at the Trianon Lyrique in Paris (1927) in the title role in *Lakmé* by Delibes. After her return to Washington, D.C., Evanti made her Town Hall debut in 1932 and gave recitals throughout the United States, Europe, and the Caribbean.

Lillian Evanti was honored by an invitation to sing at the White House for President and Mrs. Roosevelt in 1934, and she won critical acclaim for her performance as Violetta in the National Negro Opera Company production of Verdi's *La Traviata* in Washington, D.C. (1943). She was sent by the State Department to Argentina and Brazil with Arturo Toscanini and the NBC Orchestra as a goodwill ambassador in 1940. One of her compositions, *Himno Panamericano* (1941), was well received in Latin American countries. Lillian Evanti died in Washington, D.C., on December 6, 1967.

DORIS EVANS McGINTY

F

Fisk Jubilee Singers

> Wherever they have gone, they have proclaimed to the hearts of men in a most effective way, and with unmeasurable logic, the brotherhood of the race.
>
> *The Jubilee Singers: With Their Songs,*
> by J. B. T. Marsh

This great tribute introduces us to the original Fisk Jubilee Singers. These singers were a band of emancipated slaves who toured to raise money for Fisk University and to introduce the world to the beauty of the songs of a people. These songs told of an unvoiced longing for a truer world, where people were free from rejection, disappointment, and sorrow.

The Fisk Jubilee Singers were led by George L. White, a man of vision and purpose, who began training a group of young people in 1866. From this band of singers,

This photograph of the renowned Fisk Jubilee Singers was taken in 1882, when three of the five original women members were still performing. They are, seated at left and center, Ella Sheppard and Maggie L. Porter, and, standing at far right, Jennie Jackson. (MOORLAND-SPINGARN)

112

he organized the original Jubilee Singers composed of four black men and five black women, so that they could sing for the world as they had sung for him. The five women in the original group were Ella Sheppard, Maggie L. Porter, Minnie Tate, Jennie Jackson, and Eliza Walker.

Ella Sheppard was born into slavery in February 1851. Rescued from slavery by her father at an early age, she found her way to Fisk School in Nashville, Tennessee, when she was thirteen. Her musical ability greatly developed both as a singer and a pianist, and she eventually served as pianist for the Jubilee Singers.

Maggie Porter lived in slavery for twelve years. She was born on February 24, 1853, in Lebanon, Tennessee, and later moved to a plantation in Nashville. At thirteen, having attained freedom, she entered Fisk School. Her vocal ability soon won her the role of Queen Esther in the cantata *Esther*. She continued vocal instruction there and joined the Jubilee Singers.

Minnie Tate was the youngest of the Jubilee Singers. Born in Nashville in 1857 to free parents, she entered Fisk School to pursue musical training. Minnie Tate had been taught from infancy by her mother, who, having received educational training, opened her home to teach other black children.

Jennie Jackson was born free. Her grandfather was a slave and the body servant of General Andrew Jackson. After several years of work, she began to sing at Fisk School and became a member of the Jubilee Singers. She enrolled in Fisk School in 1866.

Eliza Walker was born into slavery near Nashville in 1857. Her freedom came with the release of her mother from slavery. In 1866, at the age of nine, she entered Fisk School and sang with the group until 1870.

In 1871, the Jubilee Singers began a successful singing tour to save Fisk School from imminent closing due to financial difficulties. They toured the United States and England, Scotland, Ireland, Holland, and Switzerland, bringing back $50,000 to save Fisk School and found Fisk University.

CATHERINE KING CLARK

Fitzgerald, Ella (1918–1996)

After being orphaned at an early age, Ella Fitzgerald, the "First Lady of Jazz," spent most of her formative years in Yonkers, New York, where she began to nurture her musical interest while attending that city's public schools.

In 1934, she won the legendary Apollo Theater's amateur contest; the prize was a week's work with the theater's band, whose director was seminal big-band drummer William "Chick" Webb. The Baltimore-born Webb was so impressed with the aspiring vocalist that he immediately asked her to join his group. Her association with Webb led to two of Fitzgerald's most memorable recordings: "A-tisket, A-tasket" (1938) and "Undecided" (1939). After Webb's death in 1939, Fitzgerald assumed directorship of the band, which she continued for three years.

Following her stint with Webb and his band, Fitzgerald embarked upon a solo career, most notably with the sponsorship of renowned jazz impresario Norman Granz, whose Jazz at the Philharmonic tours introduced the singer to immensely appreciative audiences in the United States, South America, the Orient, and Europe. She also dabbled in motion pictures, with notable cameo

The first lady of jazz, Ella Fitzgerald turned scat singing into a fine art. (SCHOMBURG CENTER)

appearances in *Pete Kelly's Blues* (1955), *St. Louis Blues* (1958) and *Let No Man Write My Epitaph* (1960).

In 1956, Fitzgerald signed with Granz's Verve record label and, with the aid of late arranger Nelson Riddle, produced a string of what many critics and fans have deemed definitive readings of songs by George and Ira Gershwin, Johnny Mercer, and Richard Rodgers and Lorenz Hart, among others. Her association with Granz continued into the 1960s, as did her notable recordings with jazz greats such as Duke Ellington, Louis Armstrong, Oscar Peterson, and Count Basie. Subsequently, she collaborated with guitarist Joe Pass on a series of classic duet sessions for Granz's Pablo label.

Fitzgerald received the first two of her fourteen Grammy Awards in 1958; she received more Grammy Awards than any other female jazz singer. She was also honored by countless organizations for her contributions to the American art form of jazz

and was considered by many to be the ultimate jazz vocalist. Her artistry incorporated a stunning technical range, including a dazzling command—reputedly the most dazzling of any artist to date—of what has come to be known as scat singing. The most recent of several biographies is Stuart Nicholson's 1994 book *Ella Fitzgerald: A Biography of the First Lady of Jazz.*

Although age and bouts of illness had diminished her once-astounding technical faculties, Fitzgerald, like other legendary jazz artists, had learned the deceptive art of distilling a composition's melodic and emotional essence into a comparatively minimalistic series of musical gestures. She was capable of great jazz singing even while simply meandering her way through a composition's theme. More than a year after amputation of both legs because of diabetes, Fitzgerald died in the summer of 1996.

REUBEN JACKSON

Flack, Roberta (1940–)

Would she have been missed had it not been for the 1971 movie *Play Misty for Me?* Maybe not, but the inclusion of her 1969 love song "The First Time Ever I Saw Your Face" in that film made Roberta Flack a household name and a gold-record winner in 1972. The success of her single "Killing Me Softly" quickly followed in 1973, and she has been dazzling our ears ever since.

Born in 1940 in Black Mountain, North Carolina, Flack grew up in Arlington, Virginia. She played the piano by ear at age four and began lessons at age nine. Later, while teaching music in Washington, D.C., she moonlighted by accompanying opera singers on the piano. When her own singing began to attract crowds at a local Washington eatery, the owner built a showcase room for her called Roberta's. Jazz pianist Les McCann heard her there and brought her to the attention of Atlantic Records.

Known for her intense, yet soft, singing style, Flack presents a sharp contrast to the gospel-inflected style epitomized by **Aretha Franklin** in the late 1960s and early 1970s. Her ability to cover, or restyle, songs by other artists so that they take on new meaning and new life makes Flack more of an artist than a mere pop singer. For example, her versions of "To Love Somebody," originally released by the Bee Gees, and "Bridge Over Troubled Water," a Simon and Garfunkel hit, are vastly different from the originals.

After her recording of "The First Time Ever I Saw Your Face" was featured in the film Play Misty for Me, *Roberta Flack became a gold-record winner and a household name.* (SCHOMBURG CENTER)

Roberta Flack's album *Set the Night to Music* was released in 1991. The title song was a top-ten hit.

ARTHUR J. JOHNSON

Franklin, Aretha (1942–)

In her 1967 recording of "Respect," Aretha Franklin transformed Otis Redding's mixed appeal for civil and sexual rights into a compelling demand for the equality of black women. Cast in a crucible of vernacular musical styles that evoked images of the black experience, "Respect" resonated with a moral certitude embodying contemporary notions of soul. That the song's feminist message would exceed the confines of race and gender owed to the profundity of Franklin's singing and to the enabling power of African-American performance; that her soulful declaration would at times take a secondary position to trivializations about her personal life, dress, and business dealings underscored the disrespect that she and other black musical figures consistently have endured.

As was true with so many performers in the soul and rhythm-and-blues genres, Franklin's formative musical education took place in the black church. Born on March 25, 1942, in Memphis, Tennessee, she moved with her parents and siblings first to Buffalo and then to Detroit, where her father, the Reverend C. L. Franklin, would become famous as an evangelist and pastor of the New Bethel Baptist Church. Performing and recording locally in New Bethel's gospel choir (Chess Records 1956) and appearing on the gospel circuit as the featured soloist with her father's evangelical troupe, Franklin literally grew up in the music profession at a time when gospel had begun to reach beyond the boundaries of the church and into the popular realm. Models who inspired her to pursue her teenage avocation as a career included her mother, Barbara Siggers Franklin (a gospel singer who had left the family in 1948), and three women who were national successes and her closest mentors, **Clara Ward**, **Mahalia Jackson**, and **Dinah Washington**, all family friends. With encouragement from pop-gospel star Sam Cooke and guidance from another family friend, jazz bass player Major Holley, Franklin directed her ambition toward the contexts of mainstream popular music and jazz.

In 1960 she moved to New York, where with Holley's help she auditioned with John Hammond, the Columbia Records executive who had overseen the recording careers of Count Basie, **Billie Holiday**, and other major jazz artists. Under contract with Columbia from 1960 to 1966, Franklin recorded ten albums, beginning with a jazz-oriented mixture (accompanied by a group led by Ray Bryant) seemingly crafted in the image of Holiday's style and presence. When Franklin failed to secure a major following, Columbia assigned her to other producers, who introduced lush accompaniments and a repertory of standards and novelties that led her even further from the stylistic drama of the black church. Although she earned a respectable following among nightclub audiences–notably for *Unforgettable* (1964), a recorded tribute to Dinah Washington following Washington's death–Franklin gained only marginal national success; she was limited by the conventions of a style that had foundered in the wake of an emerging rock-pop style.

The turning point in her career came in 1966 when Franklin signed with Atlantic

The immortal Aretha Franklin demanded R-E-S-P-E-C-T in 1967. (SCHOMBURG CENTER)

Records, one of the premier labels specializing in black rhythm and blues. Collaborating with producer Jerry Wexler, she recrafted her popular style against the background of gospel and blues, replacing Columbia's studio orchestrations with the rough-and-ready accompaniment of a white soul band from Muscle Shoals, Alabama. Her initial Atlantic LP, *I Never Loved a Man (the Way I Loved You)* (1967) was an immediate popular success, generating two number-one hit singles, "I Never" and "Respect." Remarkably, the latter not only capped *Billboard* magazine's rhythm-and-blues chart but also crossed over to earn the top position in the white-oriented pop category.

Franklin's next albums–especially *Lady Soul* (1968) and its singles, "Chain of Fools" and "(Sweet Sweet Baby) Since You've Been Gone"–established her as the dominant presence in black popular music; she was the new "Queen of Soul."

Record releases from the early 1970s, moreover, reflected efforts to widen her stylistic scope and audience by attenuating the soul sound without lessening personal artistry. *Live at the Fillmore West* (1971), crafted for a white rock audience, highlighted previous hits and popular songs accompanied by a soul band led by King Curtis. *Young, Gifted, and Black* (1971), a deeply introspective, autobiographical portrait, also sought a broadly popular audience. Here, Franklin provided a series of deeply moving performances despite lackluster accompaniment and frequently insipid arrangements. The capstone of the early Atlantic period was *Amazing Grace* (1972), a live performance that marked her return to the traditional gospel setting. Featuring accompaniment by the Rev. Mr. James Cleveland and the Southern California Community Choir, the album represented a watershed moment in musical intersections of sacred and secular, arcane and popular, black and white.

What made all of these recordings so compelling, so profoundly moving, was Franklin's ability to materialize a character, a way of being, summed up in the purposely vague term *soul*. Mixing themes of love, sex, struggle, joy, pain, and affirmation, Franklin succeeded by crafting profound images out of the seemingly mundane, everyday experiences of ordinary life. Her recorded performances of "Respect," "A Natural Woman," and "Do Right Woman" acknowledged inadequacy as they celebrated perseverance, granted fallibility as they voiced optimism and hope. These messages were powerful because they were sung with such conviction by a singer whose voice evoked human qualities of rightness and integrity at a time of dynamic struggle. They were her vocalized symbols of the African-American experience, of resistance, of affirmation, of celebration–symbols enhanced by the down-home, down-to-earth certainty of her blues and gospel accompaniments. For white audiences, moreover, Franklin's message carried similar depth of meaning, and her crossover appeal spoke positively about the successes of a musical-based racial dialogue during a period of extreme contentiousness and misunderstanding.

However, the condescending portraits to which Franklin was subjected during moments of personal difficulty showed how her successes could easily be undermined. Notable among these negative representations were commentaries on her love life, judgments about her embrace of African style and dress, and a 1968 *Time* feature that deteriorated into a silly comparison of soulful and not-so-soulful historical figures.

After the extraordinary creative and popular successes of the late 1960s and early 1970s, Franklin seemed unable to sustain the energy and vibrancy that so enlivened her initial Atlantic recordings. As civil-rights activities declined, soul music correspondingly lost much of its captivating power, and Franklin herself began to move whimsically from style to style. From 1974 to 1979, she recorded a series of albums with various producers, and despite some success from her collaborations with Curtis Mayfield—*Sparkle* (1976) and *Almighty Fire* (1978)—none seemed to measure up to her earlier dramatic achievements. Significantly, while the limited appeal of these records may have said more about the evanescence of popularity than about the limits of her creative talents, commentators rarely sought to contextualize or explain. Even her biographer worked from the assumption that popularity defined value, as he cast her so-called decline as a reflection of poor judgment in the studio and on stage as well as of unfortunate choices in style and dress.

The reality of declining economic success did, however, have tangible effects, leading to a break with Atlantic Records in 1980. From Atlantic she switched to Clive Davis' Arista label; that move, staged publicly as the comeback of the soul diva, helped to revive her distinctive sound within the disco inflections of the era. Despite an extended legal dispute with Arista, Franklin gained considerably from the label's marketing powers, which capitalized on her stature as the grand figure of black pop.

An appearance in the film *The Blues Brothers* (1980) and collaborations with major rock artists—George Michael and Annie Lennox on the album *Who's Zoomin'*

Who? (1985) and Keith Richards as coproducer of *Aretha* (1986)—renewed her appeal among interracial youth audiences. The collaboration with Lennox, "Sisters Are Doin' It for Themselves" (*Who's Zoomin' Who?*), became something of an interracial feminist anthem in rock and rhythm-and-blues circles.

By the late 1980s, Franklin had reemerged in mainstream markets, this time symbolically as the voice of liberation when "Respect" was heard on the soundtrack of CBS's prime-time television show *Murphy Brown*.

Her honors and achievements simply confirm her position as the "Queen of Soul": the vocalist chosen to sing at the funerals of Martin Luther King, Jr., and Mahalia Jackson; the youngest individual ever to receive Kennedy Center Honors; recipient of fifteen Grammys, more than any other female performer; and the first female inductee into the Rock and Roll Hall of Fame (1987).

RONALD M. RADANO

G

Griffin, Bessie (1922–1989)

"I'm a gospel singer in the old mold . . . traditional. I sing gospel songs that are taken from the hymnal, from the old *Gospel Pearl* book, gospel music that was started in the thirties." Regardless of where and for whom she sang, Bessie Griffin never strayed from her belief that "gospel was the good news that you did through your feelings."

Born Arlette B. Broil on July 6, 1922, to Enoch Broil and Victoria Walker Broil in New Orleans, Louisiana, Bessie Griffin died April 10, 1989, in Los Angeles. She was educated in the Arlean Parish schools of Louisiana and was a graduate of McDonough Number 35 Senior High School. After her first marriage, to Willie Griffin, which ended after two years, she married Spencer James Jackson, Sr. They had one son, Spencer James Jackson, Jr., a railroad detective who died in New Orleans in 1981.

Because her mother died when she was five years old, Griffin was raised by her "grandmother" (actually her mother's cousin), Lucy Narcisse, from whom she learned to sing. Growing up in New Orleans, she sang in church choirs and various gospel singing groups (e.g., the Brent Quillon Four Gospel Singers and the Southern Harps). In 1951, **Mahalia Jackson** invited Griffin to Chicago to sing at Jackson's anniversary celebration, and in 1953, Griffin joined the Caravans, a female gospel group founded by Albertina Walker, and traveled with them for a year before settling in Chicago. Leaving Chicago in 1955, she toured with W. Herbert Brewster, Jr., the son of gospel songwriter W. Herbert Brewster, Sr. Later, she returned to New Orleans where she became the host of her own radio program and was crowned "Queen of the South."

Griffin first visited Los Angeles in June 1956 when she was invited to be one of the featured artists in a gospel festival ("Cavalcade of Gospel Singers") organized by the

Bessie Griffin, "Queen of the Los Angeles Gospel Singers," not only performed in churches and auditoriums, but also took gospel music into nightclubs with the Gospel Pearls, formed in 1950. (J. C. DJEDJE)

Simmons and Akers Singers, who were associated with Eugene D. Smallwood's Opportunity Baptist Church. Griffin did not move permanently to Los Angeles until the late 1950s when her agent, record producer Robert "Bumps" Blackwell, made arrangements for her to star in the musical *Portraits in Bronze*. Upon her arrival, she quickly became an important gospel figure in the Los Angeles area, performing in churches and auditoriums. When Griffin joined the Gospel Pearls, a Los Angeles-based gospel group formed in 1950, much attention was given to them because of their nightclub appearances. Taking gospel music into clubs offered Griffin the opportunity to make a unique contribution to her profession, and it distinguished her from gospel singer Mahalia Jackson, to whom she was often compared. Both Griffin and Jackson were born in New Orleans, they had similar performance styles, and it was Jackson who introduced Griffin to the professional world of gospel music, but Jackson would never have performed in nightclubs.

Griffin recorded gospels, spirituals, and hymns. Some of her favorite songs included "The Days Are Passed and Gone," "It's Real," "Soon-ah Will Be Done with the Trouble of the World," "Sometimes I Feel Like a Motherless Chile," and "Come Ye Disconsolate." In addition to worldwide concert tours and television and Broadway appearances, Griffin received many commendations and accolades for her achievements in gospel music, as well as a Grammy nomination. As a result, she has been honored with such titles as "Good Queen Bess," the "Thunderbolt of Gospel Singing," and the "Queen of the Los Angeles Gospel Singers."

JACQUELINE COGDELL DJEDJE

Beginning as a dancer on Broadway, Reri Grist rose to a career on the operatic stage. (SCHOMBURG CENTER)

Grist, Reri (1932–)

Reri Grist was a successful product of the environment that nurtured her musical development from an early age. Beginning in musical theater, Grist went on to become a major figure on the 1960s opera stage.

Born in New York City in 1932, she danced in Broadway musicals, including *Carmen Jones*, *Shinbone Alley*, and *West Side Story*. She graduated from the High School for the Performing Arts and studied at Queens College; her voice teacher was Claire Gelda. Her successful transition to grand opera combined the power and stamina of a singer in musical theater with the facility and clarity of a coloratura. She made her operatic debut in 1959 as a soprano in the role of Blonde in Mozart's *The Abduction from the Seraglio* with the Santa Fe Opera Company, her San Francisco debut in 1963 as Susanna in Mozart's *The Marriage of Figaro*, and her Metropolitan Opera Company debut in 1966 as Rosina in Rossini's *The Barber of Seville*. She earned critical acclaim as Queen of the Night in Mozart's *The Magic Flute*, as Zerbinetta in Strauss' *Ariadne auf Naxos*, as Olympia in Offenbach's *The Tales of Hoffmann*, and as Norina in Donizetti's *Don Pasquale*. In New York she performed in oratorios and operas, including a City Center production of *Carmina Burana*. Favored by leading conductors, she was invited by Stravinsky to sing in his *Le Rossignol* and by Bernstein to sing in a New York Philharmonic performance of Mahler's Fourth Symphony. She toured widely in Europe, singing regularly in Cologne and as a member of the Zurich Opera. She settled in Berlin in the 1960s after her marriage to musicologist Ulf Thompson.

Grist gained the respect of critics and a reputation as a "demanding, no-nonsense artist for whom musical integrity was a high priority."

REBECCA T. CUREAU

H

Hall, Adelaide (1901–1993)

"Flashing eyes, beautiful, witty, vivacious, and she can sing, too!" This description of Adelaide Hall was characteristic of the reviews and comments in the early 1920s when she appeared on and off Broadway as singer, chorine, and comedienne. It was just as appropriate when she was ninety years old because Hall was still active as a performer in London, where she had lived since the 1930s.

Born on October 20, 1901, to William and Elizabeth Hall in Brooklyn, New York, Hall remained an active performer as an interpreter of popular ballads and stage songs for more than sixty-five years. She began her career as a member of the chorus line in Sissle and Blake's *Shuffle Along*, the 1921 African-American musical that set the pattern for such shows for the next decade. She later had a featured role in *Runnin' Wild* (1923). *Chocolate Kiddies* (1925), which introduced her to European audiences, was the beginning of her successful captivation of the London theater cognoscenti. It was followed by *Brown Buddies* (1928) at the Liberty Theatre in London and the 1928 version of Lew Leslie's *Blackbirds*, in which Hall replaced the previous star, **Florence Mills**, who had died.

During the late 1920s and the 1930s, Hall performed in shows and as a single who sang, danced, and wisecracked to audiences in Paris, London, Chicago, and New York. Her appearances in musicals were interspersed with those at the Cotton Club as vocalist with the Duke Ellington Orchestra. Her most memorable performance with Ellington was her haunting vocals on the "Creole Love Call." She also performed with the Mills Blues Rhythm Band during that period. Paris and London were like

Adelaide Hall delighted American audiences in such black musical-theater productions as Sissle and Blake's Shuffle Along. *Beginning in the late 1930s, she made her permanent home in London, with periodic trips to the United States to perform.* (SCHOMBURG CENTER)

magnets to the multitalented Hall, who also occasionally strummed the banjo in her act: She appeared at Paris's Alhambra Theater along with the Willis Lewis 10 Entertainers, "le plus sensationnel orchestre de couleur," and she claimed to have introduced the dance rage from Harlem–Truckin'–to Parisians. In 1936, Hall and her husband, Wilbur Hicks, opened the Big Apple Club and later the New Florida Club after they moved to London in 1938.

Hall remained in London from the late 1930s, but she returned to the United States to perform on Broadway on several occasions, including a dramatic role, Grandma Obeah, opposite **Lena Horne** in *Jamaica*. She was active as an entertainer with the European version of the United Service Organizations (USO) during World War II and has appeared in several British films and on British Broadcasting Company radio and television. She enjoyed an active participation in London night life as a vocalist renowned for her lush, sophisticated song styling. Her recordings are evidence of a vocalist of refined taste, romantic expressivity, and a sure sense of her musicianship. Her ability to keep abreast of contemporary trends in popular music was not unique but is certainly unusual for someone her age.

New York welcomed Hall home in spring 1992 for a solo performance.

Hall received belated recognition for her contributions to the British musical scene in 1989 when the British Broadcasting Company's Jazz Society honored her. However, she was never acknowledged as widely for her talents as she deserved, neither in her native United States nor in Europe. Nevertheless, she was still performing whenever she could at small jazz and supper clubs in London until shortly before her death in November 1993. She was buried in Brooklyn, New York, alongside her mother and sister.

DAPHNE DUVAL HARRISON

Hall, Danniebelle (1938–)

In the world of gospel music, Danniebelle Hall is no ordinary person. Despite humble beginnings, marked by abject poverty, Hall's music ministry has taken her to fifty countries on five continents.

Hall was born October 6, 1938, in Pittsburgh, Pennsylvania, the fourth of eight children, to William and Danniebelle Jones. Her father worked on the railroad; her mother was employed as a domestic.

The Jones family was overcome by hard times, forcing them to put their children into foster homes with relatives and friends of the Church of God where they worshiped. As a result, Hall was raised by an elderly couple whom she refers to simply as Mom and Dad Carter.

Even though Mom and Dad Carter were both legally blind and on welfare, they scraped up $185 to buy Hall a Wurlitzer baby-grand piano. Graduating from Peabody High School, she attended Mount Mercy College in Pittsburgh and played piano in the Church of God in the 1950s and '60s.

Hall studied music formally with pianist George Hornsby and, informally, with the many traveling gospel artists and groups who visited her church. In a typical year, Hall's church hosted concerts that included the Caravans, the Davis Sisters, and the James Cleveland Singers.

In 1958, Hall married, and had three children, Charlotte, Charles and Cynthia; her marriage ended in divorce. On rare occasions, her children traveled with her to local performances, especially during the summers. Relatives and friends helped Hall with her children during the school year.

By 1969, Hall had launched a solo singing career as part of her ministry: She played an important role in the Jesus People, a primarily white Christian movement that took her to white Presbyterian churches and then to the world at large. Hall's solo career led to the founding of her own group, the Danniebelles, an all-woman group that toured in and around the San Francisco Bay area and throughout the United States, the Philippines, Vietnam, Thailand, Japan, and Jamaica.

In 1973, Hall accepted an invitation from Andrae Crouch to join his group, the Disciples, with whom she toured extensively as their lead singer, performing at Carnegie Hall and at the White House for then President Jimmy Carter. Before Hall left the Disciples in 1978, Andrae Crouch had introduced her to many prominent musicians, including **Aretha Franklin**, Walter Hawkins and his family, and **Roberta Flack**. The influence of these artists is evident in Hall's music.

Hall has recorded eight solo albums. *Danniebelle* (1974), *This Moment* (1974), and a Christmas album, *He is King* (1975) were recorded on Light Records; *Unmistakably Danniebelle* (1976) for Onyx Records; and for Sparrow Records *Let Me Have a Dream* (1976) and *Live in Sweden* (1977). Her two CDs, *Designer's Original* (1992) and *The Best Gets Better* (1995), are on the CGI label. Hall's hit songs include "I Go to the Rock," "(Ain't no Devil in Hell Gonna Walk on) the Jesus in Me," "O Sé Baba," and her signature song "Ordinary People." She has appeared with **Roberta Flack**,

Though gospel singer Danniebelle Hall's foster parents were legally blind and on welfare, they scraped together the money to buy their daughter a Wurlitzer baby-grand piano. Despite her forty-year career as a gospel singer, Hall modestly calls herself "a pianist who accompanied herself with her voice." (DANNIEBELLE HALL)

Stevie Wonder, **Jennifer Holiday**, **Tramaine Hawkins**, The Winans, *Shirley Ceasar*, James Cleveland, Take 6, Edwin Hawkins, Bill Gaither, B. J. Thomas, and Debbie Boone.

Regarding her music ministry, Hall showed great humility when she said, "I don't consider myself a singer. I am a pianist who accompanies herself with her voice."

Despite the fact that Hall has appeared worldwide, she credits the success of her music to her recordings, which allow her to spread "the good news" to places where she cannot appear.

This grandmother of eight wants to cast an even wider net through an *Ordinary People* video and her first book. The working title of Hall's autobiography is *Some of the Things I Learned Along the Way.* She is not rushing the book nor the things she continues to learn.

"I've learned," she says, "that life is a constant evolution, a metamorphosis, change. I've learned that Jesus Christ loves us the way we are, but too much to leave us that way."

REGINA HARRIS BAIOCCHI

Hall, Juanita   (1901–1968)

Musical theater star Juanita Hall began her singing career in the Catholic church choir in Keyport, New Jersey; from there, she went to Juilliard School of Music in New York City.

In 1930, Hall appeared in *Green Pastures* with the Hall Johnson Choir and became Johnson's assistant conductor and stayed in that position until 1936. She also conducted other choirs, including the Works Progress Administration (WPA) Chorus, from 1935 to 1944 and the Westchester Chorale and Dramatics Association in 1941–42. In 1942, Hall formed her own group, the Juanita Hall Choir.

In addition to her distinguished career in musical theater and her work as a choral conductor, Hall performed successfully on radio and in nightclubs. Her biographical entry is in the *Theater* volume of this encyclopedia.

Handy, D. Antoinette   (1930–)

Classical and jazz flutist, lecturer, and director of the National Endowment for the Arts Music Program, Dorothy Antoinette Handy is both an artist and a scholar. A concert flutist for more than twenty years, she later turned her energies to lecturing about and documenting great black classical and jazz musicians.

Born in New Orleans on October 29, 1930, Handy first studied violin and piano with her mother. She went to **Spelman College** in Atlanta and then to the New England Conservatory of Music. Graduating from the conservatory in 1952 with a bachelor of music degree, in flute with orchestral concentration, she proceeded to receive her master of music degree from the equally well-known music department at Northwestern University in 1953 and earned an

A classical and jazz flutist, Antoinette Handy has performed with orchestras in Europe and the United States.   (PRIVATE COLLECTION)

Artist's Diploma from the National Conservatory in Paris in 1955.

As a classical flutist, Handy performed with many famous orchestras: the Chicago Civic Orchestra from 1952 to 1953, the International Orchestra of Paris in 1954, and the Musica Viva Orchestra of Geneva in 1955. She was a soloist in both Paris and Geneva and concluded her European residency with a nine-city solo tour of Germany.

In 1956, Handy returned to the United States to play with the Symphony of the Air on NBC in 1956, the Orchestra of America in New York from 1960 to 1962, the Symphony of the New World from 1968 to 1971, and the Richmond Symphony from 1966 to 1976. In 1971, she was awarded a Ford Foundation Humanities Fellowship at the University of North Carolina and subsequently performed and soloed at the Bach Festival Orchestra at Carmel, California.

Aside from her involvement with symphonies, Handy was a founding member of the Trio Pro Viva, which specializes in the music of black composers during the last two centuries, and has lectured and served music residencies at a number of colleges and universities.

But Handy's greatest contribution to music may very well be her remarkable efforts to document the lives and work of black musicians, particularly black women. Her 1981 book, *Black Women in American Bands and Orchestras,* is an indispensable resource. Without it, the efforts of many important African-American women in music would almost certainly have been forgotten. In 1983, she followed up with *The International Sweethearts of Rhythm,* a book chronicling the most important all-woman jazz band in America. Handy also

D. Antoinette Handy has made a remarkable effort to reclaim the lives and work of black women musicians. Among her many publications are three definitive books, Black Women in American Bands and Orchestras, The International Sweethearts of Rhythm, *and* Black Conductors. (PRIVATE COLLECTION)

published *Black Conductors* (1955), continuing in her mission to preserve the history of African-American music.

Handy has spread the word about black music in other ways as well. She was a radio commentator for the Richmond radio program "Black Virginia" and music journalist for the Richmond *Afro-American;* in Washington, D.C., she created three successful programs of black concert music for the Smithsonian Institution.

As a scholar and expert on black music, Handy was named assistant director of the music program for the powerful National Endowment for the Arts in 1984 and in 1990 was promoted to director of the music program, one of the NEA's largest programs, with a goal to assist and help develop outstanding American music and musicians. While now retired from the NEA, she remains a frequent lecturer at scholarly meetings.

ANDRA MEDEA

Harris, Hilda (1936–)

Very few jingle singers graduate to popular music, Broadway shows, solo concerts, television, and a Metropolitan Opera career. One exception is Hilda Genevieve Harris. Harris was born January 25, 1936, the second of four children, to Charles and Maxine Harris. Even though her father was a mechanic and her mother was a housewife, they recognized very early signs of a budding prima donna.

The Harris family worshiped at All Saints Episcopal Church in her native Warrenton, North Carolina. Even the formal hymns the choir sang lent themselves to Harris' soulful expression. After graduating from John Hawkins High School, Harris received a bachelor of arts degree from North Carolina Central University, where she studied voice with Howard Roberts.

Surprisingly Harris was not exposed to concert music as a child; the Harris family owned a radio, but no television. While her teachers exposed her to different types of music, Harris was in only one fully staged, full-length opera before she graduated from college, an opera by Gian Carlo Menotti that was presented by the drama depart-ment, not the music department, with piano only—not the full orchestra.

During the summers away from high school and college, Harris did factory work in New York. This was her way of staying in New York, the place where she dreamed of having a music career, and in 1958, she moved there, living at the 137th Street YWCA in Harlem and joining the choir at St. Phillip's Episcopal Church as a volunteer. When a paid soloist left the choir, Harris was awarded her position. This job helped finance Harris' first audition for a Broadway show, *Jamaica,* starring **Lena Horne.** Even though Harris did not get the part, she did meet Lola Hayes, a voice teacher whom she had heard about from her college voice teacher.

Despite her music degree, Harris started from ground zero with Hayes because, in her own words, Harris felt that she had "no vocal technique." She just sang what she felt. She credits Hayes with helping her find her true voice: For years, she considered herself a coloratura soprano; with Hayes, Harris discovered that she is a mezzo-soprano. Harris also studied with Marlena Malas.

It took Harris five years after college to feel secure about pursuing a solo career. During that period, she supported herself by singing jingles for AT&T, Coca-Cola, McDonald's, and various hair-care products.

Her jingle success led to more recordings: Harris sang background vocals alongside Luther Vandross, Patti Austin, Nick Ashford, and Valerie Simpson; when each of them launched his or her solo careers, Harris was hired for more background singing. Harris also worked with **Aretha Franklin,**

Dionne Warwick, Roberta Flack, and Quincy Jones.

Harris taught herself to make the mechanical transition from one singing style to another. In a typical day, Harris did "hard" singing with a group such as KISS in the morning and "soft" popular singing in the afternoon. While most purists would stay away from this kind of work, Harris learned to realign her "real" voice after such vocal workouts.

During the 1960s, Harris sang on Broadway in *Golden Boy* (1964), *Ben Franklin in Paris* (1964), *110 in the Shade* (1965), and *Mame* (1966) and off-Broadway in Irving Burgie's *Ballad for Bimshire* (1963) and *Jericho-Jim Crow* (1964). Her work led to a 1967 Carnegie Hall debut.

Harris has appeared on two soap operas, *The Edge of Night* and *Another World*. Other television credits include the NBC special *Kaleidoscope*, *Lamp Unto My Feet* with Alvin Ailey, *A Handful of Souls* (as **Rosa Parks**), and *The Questions of Abraham* (Hagar) on CBS. On stage, Harris premiered Ulysses Kay's opera *Jubilee* (Vyry), **Dorothy Rudd Moore's opera** *Frederick Douglass* (**Anna Douglass**), and Moore's song cycle *From the Dark Tower*, written for Harris.

Though a serious musician, Hilda Harris supported herself for years as a jingle singer for AT&T, Coca-Cola, McDonald's, and other companies. Finally, in 1977, Harris made her debut with the New York Metropolitan Opera Company. Today, she lives out her dreams as a concert artist and soloist with the Metropolitan and other companies. (HILDA HARRIS)

A banner decade for Harris was the 1970s, in part because of Harris' debut with the New York Metropolitan Opera Company in 1977 where she sang Schoolboy in Alban Berg's *Lulu*. Harris's petite size and mezzo soprano voice made her an ideal candidate for the numerous "pants roles" she sang. The Met cast Harris in *Le Nozze di Figaro, Roméo et Juliette, Faust, L'Enfant et les Sortilèges, Julius Caesar, Hansel und Gretel,* and the world premiere of John Corigliano's *The Ghosts of Versailles*.

In 1971, Harris took the title role of Bizet's *Carmen* at St. Gallen Opera in Switzerland, singing twenty-six performances in three months. Other roles followed with the Lyric Opera of Chicago, San Francisco Opera, New York City Opera, Opera South, Opera Ebony, and a host of companies worldwide.

Harris' operatic success led to work with various festivals at home and abroad. During the 1980s, she appeared with the New York Philharmonic, Chicago Symphony Orchestra, and other orchestras in the United States and Europe, as well as with several oratorio societies and the Boys Choir of Harlem.

Today Harris lives out her dreams as a soloist with the Met, maintains a private studio, and appears with various companies and ensembles. She is a soloist with the Chicago-based Black Music Repertory Ensemble and is adding to her discography that includes Hale Smith's *The Valley Wind* (on the CRI label), Harry Burleigh's *From the Southland* (Premiere), and Anthony Davis' *Life and Times of Malcolm X* (Grammavision). Harris is also a faculty member at Sarah Lawrence College, Manhattan School of Music, and the Chautauqua Institute in New York.

REGINA HARRIS BAIOCCHI

Harris, Margaret (1943–)

If the biography of Margaret Rosezarion Harris were titled *The Piano Prodigy*, it would tell only part of her story. Harris performs and conducts music in concert halls, on Broadway, for television, radio, and in just about every other venue and medium available.

Born in Chicago on September 15, 1943, only child of William D. and Clara L. Harris, Harris took her first bow at age three following a piano recital of eighteen pieces and three encores at Cosmopolitan Church. At ten, Harris won the Young People's Competition and performed Mozart's D-minor Piano Concerto with the Chicago Symphony Orchestra (CSO).

In 1953, her family left Chicago for Philadelphia where Harris studied with Madame Isabelle Vengerova at Curtis Institute. When Vengerova died, the family moved to New York, where Harris began a program at Juilliard, first with Jane Carlson and then with Edward Steuermann and Mieczyslaw Munz. Though employed by several New York churches as pianist/organist, she continued to travel as a soloist.

At Juilliard, Harris received a bachelor of science in piano (1964) and a master of science in piano (1965) summa cum laude as a Schepp Scholar. (In 1995, Harris was elected the first African-American trustee to the Leopold Schepp Foundation Board.) Before the ink was dry on her degree, Harris resumed her posts as organist/choir director for St. James Presbyterian, St. Martin's Episcopal, and St. Mark's Methodist churches in New York and Elmwood Presbyterian Church in East Orange, New Jersey.

In 1970, Harris made her Broadway debut as music director for *Hair*, later touring

Margaret Harris made her piano debut at three, and by the time she was ten, she was performing Mozart's D-minor Piano Concerto with the Chicago Symphony Orchestra. During her distinguished career as a composer, conductor, music director, and organist, Harris has conducted more American symphony orchestras than any other African-American woman. (MARGARET HARRIS)

with ten different companies of that play. *Hair*'s two-year run marked the beginning of Harris's Broadway career, which includes *Two Gentlemen of Verona* (1972–74), *Raisin* (1974–76), *Guys and Dolls* (1980), and James Baldwin's *Amen Corner* (1983–84).

Margaret Harris has conducted more American symphony orchestras than any other African-American woman—sixteen, in fact. The Chicago, Los Angeles, Detroit, St. Louis, Minnesota, San Diego, Wolf Trap, and American Symphony Orchestras have all played under Harris' baton. She also

travels worldwide to Canada, Israel, France, Spain, Italy, and the Scandinavian countries, concertizing and establishing new musical frontiers.

In 1975, Harris cofounded Opera Ebony in New York. Like Opera South, with which she also enjoys affiliation, Opera Ebony was founded to showcase the talent of African-American singers, composers, conductors, designers, artists, and technicians. Through her work with both companies, Harris has nurtured some of the finest African-American talent.

Harris' compositions include opera, piano concerti, musicals, spirituals, and television theme songs: *Requiem Mass*, *Mass in A*, and *Stabat Mater* are for soloists, double chorus, organ and orchestra; two commissioned ballets, *Goliath* and *Mandling/Halecord*; commercial titles including *Tell It Like It Is*, *The Three B's—Broadway, Black, and Beautiful*, *We Are D.C.'s Future*, and *Look and Long*.

Actress Ruby Dee commissioned Harris to write for a 1996–1997 premiere of the musical *John Boscoe*, a *Faust* adaptation about a singer who sells his soul to sing at Carnegie Hall; in the story the devil claims Boscoe's soul during the performance.

When Harris is not composing, she conducts piano or choral master classes. Harris has presented workshops for universities in Delaware, Illinois, and Washington, D.C. Her residencies are complemented by her work as consultant for Margaret R. Harris Enterprises and her distinguished visiting professorships at the University of West Florida, Virginia Polytechnical Institute, and Bronx Community College.

Radio, TV, and print media credits include *The Today Show*, *The David Frost Show*, and *Time*, *U.S. News and World*

Report, *Ebony*, and *Jet* magazines. In 1992, she hosted her own radio show, *Margaret on Music*, in New York.

Maestra Harris is still carving out a full life for herself as pianist, organist, conductor, composer, and lecturer. In August 1995, Harris was appointed music director and conductor of the United Negro College Fund Chorale in New York.

Few musicians possess the talent and versatility to produce religious and art music, show tunes and popular music, ragtime and blues; even fewer musicians enjoy the commercial success that is part of Margaret Harris' emerging legacy.

REGINA HARRIS BAIOCCHI

Harrison, Hazel (1883–1969)

There are no recordings of the performances of Hazel Harrison, but historical evidence indicates that she was a remarkable pianist. She was certainly an inspiring and effective teacher.

Harrison was born on May 12, 1883, in La Porte, Indiana. Her parents, Hiram James and Olive J. Wood, recognized her musical talent early, and she began to study the piano before she was five years old, soon becoming an accomplished pianist who performed at socials and in local musicales. Before long, she became a student of the well-known teacher Victor Heinze. While Harrison was in high school, Ferruccio Busoni, a great pianist and composer of the time, made a tour of America; through Heinze's efforts, Busoni agreed to listen to Harrison play. Favorably impressed, he urged her to complete high school and to concentrate on her musical technique, agreeing to see her again when she was older.

Three years after her high school graduation, Harrison was able to go to Europe, debuting at the Singakademie in Berlin to favorable reviews in October 1904, and returning to La Porte in January 1905. For six more years, Harrison taught, practiced, and gave recitals. In 1911, she returned to Europe, spending her first year in Berlin studying with a prominent German teacher who arranged for her to play again for Busoni. She then worked with Busoni for two years until the outbreak of World War I, when she was forced to return home.

Extraordinary pianist Hazel Harrison salted the standard classical repertoire with the compositions of black Americans and of then-radical composers such as Stravinsky and Ravel as she toured Europe and the United States in the 1910s and 1920s. (SCHOMBURG CENTER)

Beginning in 1914, Harrison toured the United States giving concerts. In addition to works from the standard classical repertoire, she included in her performances compositions by black Americans such as William Dawson, Hall Johnson, and Elnora Manson. She also had the courage to perform the more radical contemporary composers of her day such as Stravinsky, Ravel, and Laszlo. In 1922, she joined the staff of Pauline James Lee's Chicago University of Music.

In 1926, Harrison made her final trip to Europe, this time to study with a former student of Busoni's, Egon Petri. She stayed in Europe for ten months and returned to the United States to great acclaim. She was now recognized as a virtuoso and received many honors in the years that followed. During a **Young Women's Christian Association** leadership-of-women conference in 1929, she was chosen, from among women of all races, as a model for young people in the arts. In 1930, she made her Town Hall debut in New York City. She also performed that year at Boston's Jordan Hall, not a usual venue for black Americans at that time.

Another career began for Harrison in 1931, when she was forty-eight years old: She began to teach at Tuskegee Institute in Alabama. After five years there, she went to **Howard University**. At both schools she overcame resistance to her lack of a degree through her expertise, artistry, and practical experience. She was at Howard until 1955 and became something of a legend to its students. During that time, she took a three-year sabbatical to go back on the concert circuit. After her retirement from Howard, she lived briefly in New York but then, in 1958, went to teach at Alabama State College where she remained until 1963. After her retirement at the age of eighty, she performed no more. She died on April 28, 1969, at the age of eighty-five.

DEBORRA A. RICHARDSON

Hawkins, Tramaine (1951–)

Tramaine Aunzola Davis Hawkins, gospel singer and entertainer, was born October 11, 1951, in San Francisco, California. She is the daughter of Roland Duvall Davis and Lois Ruth Davis, who migrated to California from Houston, Texas, and Oklahoma City, Oklahoma, respectively. She is the mother of two children, a son Jamie who works with rap artist Hammer and a daughter Trystan.

Throughout her life, Hawkins has remained close to family and the church, institutions from which she has received much of her training and professional development in gospel music. From birth until 1971, she was affiliated with the Ephesians Church of God in Christ (COGIC) in Berkeley where her grandfather, Bishop Elmer Elijah Cleveland, served as pastor. During the 1970s and early 1980s, at the Love Center Church in Oakland, where her former husband, Walter Hawkins, is founder and pastor, she began to be recognized in the gospel music world. Since 1983, she has been a member of the Center of Hope Community Church, where her aunt Ernestine Cleveland Rheems is pastor. She has been singing contemporary gospel music since her early years as a vocalist with the Heavenly Tones.

Hawkins is fortunate to have worked with some of the most respected artists in contemporary gospel music: Andrae Crouch and the Disciples, the Edwin Hawkins Singers, and the Walter Hawkins Love Center Choir. While she sang on the first three *Love Alive* albums recorded by Walter Hawkins, it was her lead vocal performance on the songs "Changed" and "Going Up Yonder" on *Love Alive 1* (1975) that demonstrated her abilities as a soloist.

During the past ten years, not only has she been involved with numerous concert tours in the United States and Europe as well as television appearances, but she has also recorded several albums: *Tramaine* (1980), *Determined* (1983), *The Search Is Over* (1986), *Freedom* (1987), *The Joy That Floods My Soul* (1988), and *Tramaine Hawkins, LIVE* (1990). Some of the major awards that Hawkins has received include two Grammys, two Dove Awards, two Communications Excellence to Black Audiences (CEBA) Awards, an NAACP Image Award, a Stellar Award, a British Gospel Music Award, and several awards from James Cleveland's Gospel Music Workshop of America.

Considered to be more daring than most gospel artists, Hawkins has experimented with songs such as "Fall Down (Spirit of Love)," which some critics consider to be overly secular. However, her recording of "What Shall I Do" by Quincy Fielding has become a best-seller among churchgoers. For her 1990 album, she collaborated with musicians outside of the gospel music field—rock guitarist Carlos Santana, jazz organist Jimmy McGriff, and jazz tenor-saxophonist Stanley Turrentine. Regardless of what and with whom she performs, her singing maintains a spiritual feeling with clarity and strength. She calls it music that ministers to the heart.

JACQUELINE COGDELL DJEDJE

Hemphill, Jessie Mae (1933–)

Jessie Mae Hemphill has preserved a family tradition of music stretching over four generations and has helped to bring the sound of traditional Mississippi blues to modern listeners throughout the United States and abroad. Within this folk tradition she has created a unique style and has composed many original songs based on her life experiences. Her sound features melismatic, mostly pentatonic melody lines sung in a sweet voice, usually followed by repeated short figures on the electric guitar. Her powerful guitar rhythms, sometimes augmented by a tambourine attached to her foot, are influenced by the rhythms of fife and drum music, which she also plays.

Hemphill was born October 18, 1933, near Como, Mississippi, where she still lives. Her grandfather, Sid Hemphill (c. 1876–1963), was a prominent blind musician in the area and the son of a fiddler; he played fiddle, banjo, guitar, fife, panpipes, drums, and several other instruments, and for more than fifty years led a string band that also played fife-and-drum music. His three daughters, Sidney Lee, Rosa Lee, and Virgie Lee (Jessie Mae's mother), all learned to play guitar, drums, and various stringed instruments from him. Jessie Mae learned to play guitar and drums from her grandfather, her mother, and her aunts, especially her aunt Rosa Lee; her father, James Graham, was a blues pianist around Como and later in Memphis. Most of her music was confined to local house parties and picnics near Como and in Memphis, where she sometimes lived. She was briefly married when very young to L. D. Brooks and was known as Jessie Mae Brooks. She changed her name back to Hemphill in order to emphasize the

Jessie Mae Hemphill has preserved a family tradition of music stretching over four generations and has helped to bring the sound of traditional Mississippi blues to modern listeners around the world. (DAVID EVANS)

family's musical heritage when she decided to pursue a career in music in 1979. Since then, she has performed in concerts and festivals in more than twenty states, Canada, and nine European countries. In 1987 and 1988, she was voted winner of the Handy Award for Best Female Traditional Blues Artist. Hemphill has recorded two 45 rpm records and an album (*Feelin' Good*) for the High Water label of the United States, an album (*She-Wolf*) for the Vogue label of France, and various album tracks for the Black & Blue label of France and the Au-Go-Go label of Australia. Her album *Feelin' Good* won a Handy Award in 1991 in the Best Country Blues Album category. In December 1993, she suffered a stroke and has been inactive musically since then.

DAVID EVANS

Hendricks, Barbara (1948–)

Growing up black means being compassionate, Barbara Hendricks has stated. It is not a handicap, but it does include an obligation to give something back to the people.

The soprano was born on November 20, 1948, in Stephens, Arkansas, where her father served as Methodist minister. She enrolled at the University of Nebraska, carrying a double major in mathematics and chemistry, not taking her singing seriously until she was nineteen when friends urged her to study with Jennie Tourel.

Following their advice and with the resulting encouragement, Hendricks resolved to dedicate her attention to music. Although not wealthy during these student days, she invested in attending every concert and opera performance she could manage and began serious study of foreign languages, acting, music theory, and piano.

In 1973, when only twenty-five years old, Hendricks made her debut for twelve performances as St. Settlement in *Four Saints in Three Acts* by Virgil Thomson, an opera calling for an all-black cast. Following this, she performed in San Francisco's production of Cavalli's *Ormindo* (1974) and in various productions in England, the Netherlands, Germany, Austria, and the United States, with particular success in Paris as Juliette in Gounod's *Roméo et Juliette* (1982). In 1986, Hendricks returned to the Metropolitan Opera as Sophie in *Der Rosenkavalier* (Richard Strauss), moving to the Teatro alla Scala in Milan the next year to appear as Susanna in Mozart's *Le Nozze di Figaro*. A highlight of 1988 was the release on film of Puccini's *La Bohème*, directed by Luca Canonici, in which she was cast with José Carreras (because of health problems, the tenor was represented only on the sound track). She was offered the leading role in the film *Diva* (which was accepted by Wilhelmenia Fernandez); she declined so that she would not be thought a film actress who sings. Hendricks is attracted to films, however, because of the greater potential to pursue her interest in acting. For the same reason, she prefers the smaller opera houses and rarely schedules more than five operas per season.

Hendricks' recorded repertoire gives emphasis to French composers, as well as to Mozart, Gershwin, Handel, Schubert, and Puccini. Her first recordings to attract a large following were of Mahler's Fourth Symphony (London LDR-10004) in 1979, and Daniel del Tredici's *Final Alice* (London LDR-71018) in 1981.

Appointed Goodwill Ambassador by the United Nations, working for human rights, Hendricks was named Commandeur des Arts et des Lettres in 1986 by the French government and was awarded honorary doctorates by the Nebraska Wesleyan University (1988) and Belgium's Louvain University (1990).

She currently lives in Switzerland with her husband and children.

DOMINIQUE-RENÉ de LERMA

Hinderas, Natalie (1927–1987)

Born June 15, 1927, in Oberlin, Ohio, Natalie Henderson joined the musical household of Abram and Leota (Palmer) Henderson. They—her parents—were both students at Oberlin: Her father was a jazz pianist, and her mother was a classical pianist who taught at the Cleveland Institute of Music.

As a child, Hinderas was surrounded by music and musicians. She began to play the piano at the age of three, but her formal piano studies began at six; she also studied violin and voice at an early age. She was a child prodigy at the piano, who played a full-length public recital at the age of eight and a concerto with the Cleveland Women's Symphony at the age of twelve. Musically educated in the public schools of Oberlin, Ohio, she later received the B.Mus. in 1945 from Oberlin Conservatory as its youngest graduate (she had been admitted as a special student at the age of eight). Assuming the name Natalie Hinderas, she did postgraduate work in piano at the Juilliard School of Music with Olga Samaroff and at the Philadelphia Conservatory with Edward Steuermann. She also studied composition with Vincent Persichetti.

In 1954, she made her Town Hall debut and received critical acclaim. Thereafter, she toured extensively as a concert pianist in the United States, Europe, and the West Indies; the U.S. Department of State sponsored two tours abroad that included Africa and Asia as well as Europe. In the mid-1950s, Hinderas signed a contract with NBC to travel to their owned and operated stations in the various major cities to play solo recitals, concertos, and variety shows.

Hinderas made a debut with the Philadelphia Orchestra in four concerts in 1971, the first black female instrumental soloist to appear with the orchestra in subscription concerts; her debut piece was the contemporary Ginastera Concerto. Many concerts followed with the Los Angeles Philharmonic Orchestra, the Cleveland, Atlanta, New York, San Francisco, and Chicago symphony orchestras, and others. Her orchestral performances featured Rachmaninoff's

Concerto No. 2 in C minor, the Schumann piano concerto, Gershwin's *Rhapsody in Blue*, and George Walker's *Piano Concerto No. 1*, which she commissioned in 1975. Her recording debut came in 1971 with the album *Natalie Hinderas Plays Music by Black Composers* (DESTO); other recordings followed on the Orion and Columbia labels. She was hailed as an extremely intelligent and thorough pianist with comprehensive technical ability and honest musical instincts. Throughout her career, she promoted and recorded works by black performers and composers, among them R. Nathaniel Dett, William Grant Still, John W. Work, and George Walker, whose works she recorded.

She received numerous awards and fellowships, including the Leventritt, John Hay Whitney, Julius Rosenwald, Martha Baird Rockefeller, and Fulbright fellowships. She also received an honorary doctorate of music degree from Swarthmore College (1976). In 1968, Hinderas joined the faculty of Temple University, where she was a full professor at the time of her death on July 22, 1987.

MARVA GRIFFIN CARTER

Hobson, Ann (1943–)

During the 1960s, Ann Hobson broke ground as one of four African-American musicians in the nation's leading symphony orchestras. Born in Philadelphia on November 6, 1943, Hobson began to study the harp at age fourteen. During her senior year at Philadelphia's Girls High, she was noted as being of concert caliber. After high school, she enrolled at the Philadelphia Musical Academy and continued her harp study through the summer at the Maine Harp Colony (which had rejected her years earlier because of her race). In Maine, she met a teacher, Alice Chalifoux, whose protégée she later became; she transferred to the Cleveland Institute of Music in order to study with the noted harpist and teacher, who later recommended her for principal harpist of the National Symphony.

In 1966, Hobson was selected to fill a one-year assignment in this position but because of her fine musicianship, that initial year was extended for several seasons. In 1969, she competed against thirty harpists for the position of second harpist with the Boston Symphony Orchestra. Her competition performance was so outstanding, how-

Natalie Hinderas began as a child prodigy, giving her first full-length public recital at the age of eight. This highly respected pianist went on to become a strong advocate of the work of black composers. (SCHOMBURG CENTER)

ever, that she was offered a higher position as associate principal harpist and then eventually became principal harpist with the Boston Pops Orchestra.

In addition to her professional affiliation with the National Symphony and the Boston Symphony/Boston Pops Orchestras, Hobson has been a member of the Boston Symphony Chamber Players, and she founded the New England Harp Trio (cello, flute, harp) based in Boston. She has performed throughout the United States and, in 1979, traveled to Shanghai and Peking, China, where she also taught master classes. Throughout her career, she has taught privately and been affiliated with several outstanding musical institutions, including the Philadelphia Musical Academy and the New England Conservatory of Music.

Ann Hobson has recorded with the Boston Symphony Chamber Players on the Deutsche Grammophon label, performing Debussy, and has received numerous favorable reviews of her concert performances. After a 1977 appearance, the *Wichita Eagle* (Wichita, Kansas) wrote, "Miss Hobson is an incredible technician, but more, she is able to tear the harp out of its traditional raiment and give it new and vital voices."

She currently resides outside Boston.

IRENE JACKSON-BROWN

Holiday, Billie (1915–1959)

Billie Holiday never won a jazz popularity poll. Readers of *Metronome*, *Melody Maker*, and *Downbeat* magazines consistently chose Holiday second, third, even tenth after **Ella Fitzgerald**, Mildred Bailey, Helen O'Connell, and Jo Stafford, singers who typically performed with the commercially popular big bands. With jazz critics, however, there is little question that Billie Holiday was the greatest jazz singer ever recorded. Coming into her own a generation after the classic blues singers, like **Bessie Smith**, Holiday created a place for herself outside the confines of the big band "girl singer" role, setting standards by which other jazz singers continue to be judged and influencing singers as far-ranging in style as **Sarah Vaughan**, Frank Sinatra, **Carmen McRae**, and **Lena Horne**.

Holiday began to record during the big-band era, and although her work with Count Basie attests to her ability to perform with such ensembles, her style was better suited to small combos in which she found the freedom to be a true jazz soloist. Recordings made during her twenty-six-year career reveal her skill as a recomposer of melody and a rhythmic innovator, the hallmarks of any great jazz improviser.

Born Eleanora Fagan in Philadelphia, Pennsylvania, on April 7, 1915, to teenagers Sadie Fagan and Clarence Holiday, Billie grew up in Baltimore, Maryland, where she took the name of her screen idol, Billie Dove. Her father, later a guitarist with Fletcher Henderson's orchestra, never lived with the family, and Holiday was raised by her mother and other relatives. Her childhood was one of deprivation and even cruelty during a year spent at the Catholic-run House of the Good Shepherd for Colored Girls, ostensibly for truancy. As a teenager, she joined her mother, who had moved to New York City, and she may have worked for a time as a prostitute while learning to be a performer.

Her autobiography, *Lady Sings the Blues*, written with the help of journalist William Dufty and published in 1956, is often factually inaccurate, and the 1972 movie based

Though she never won a jazz popularity poll in Downbeat *or* Melody Maker, *jazz critics consider Billie Holiday the greatest jazz singer ever recorded.* (SCHOMBURG CENTER)

on it likewise served to sensationalize aspects of Holiday's tragic private life at the expense of her musical talent. Nonetheless, the autobiography provides a pointed critique of American society, with its portrayal of Holiday as a black performer facing racism and as a female performer facing sexism in the male-dominated world of jazz.

The beginnings of her career are unclear. Holiday claimed not to read music, but family friends remember her singing as a child, and by her early teens she was performing for tips and jamming with other musicians in Baltimore's waterfront entertainment district. In her autobiography, Holiday stresses the early influences of recordings by Louis Armstrong and Bessie Smith. Although not a true blues singer, Holiday certainly shares with blues singers like Smith an identification with the text, a gift for emphasizing particular words and syllables in performance, and a fondness for slow tempos. Similarly, although she did not imitate Louis Armstrong's virtuoso scatting technique, Holiday's singing is marked by rhythmic flexibility and the swing characteristic of Armstrong's trumpet performances. Holiday was not a big-voiced belter like Armstrong or Smith, but she used the distinctive timbre and limited range of her voice to their best advantage, producing solos marked by subtlety and nuance.

By 1931, Holiday was singing in New York City accompanied solely by piano. For a time she was part of a floor show featuring bassist George "Pops" Foster and tap dancer Charles Honi Coles. In 1933, John Hammond, jazz record producer and critic, heard the then eighteen-year-old Holiday singing in Monette Moore's club accompanied by the house pianist, Dot Hill. Hammond immediately wrote about her in the British journal *Melody Maker*, describing the individual vocal style and delivery that set Holiday apart from other mainstream pop singers of the time.

Hammond, who as a record producer was always looking for new talent, arranged for Holiday to record, and she cut two sides in 1933. Ironically, Hammond recorded Holiday within twenty-four hours of producing Bessie Smith's final recordings. Although Holiday's sidemen included Jack Teagarden, Benny Goodman, and Gene Krupa, the songs she was given to record, "Your Mother's Son-in-Law" and "Riffin' the Scotch," were second-rate Tin Pan Alley tunes. However, for her first time in front of a recording microphone, accompanied by musicians she did not know and in a manner to which she was unaccustomed, Holiday sounds assured and confident, if lacking in the rhythmic freedom that marks her later work.

Before Holiday returned to a recording studio in 1935, she took part in Duke Ellington's short film *Symphony in Black*, depicting African-American life. (The film received little distribution at the time but is now available on video.) Holiday performed "Big City Blues," a twelve-bar blues chorus sung during the second scene, entitled "A Triangle," and her brief appearance demonstrates her growing talent as a singer with a captivating stage presence. Holiday made one other screen appearance eleven years later, in the movie *New Orleans* (1946). Playing opposite her musical mentor Louis Armstrong, Holiday performed three numbers in an otherwise demeaning role as a singing maid with few substantive lines.

In July 1935, Hammond arranged for Holiday to return to the recording studio with pianist Teddy Wilson and his pick-up ensemble. Holiday found these musicians and their spontaneous approach suited to her style. She particularly enjoyed working with Count Basie's sideman, saxophonist Lester Young, whose vocal-like approach was ideal for providing instrumental responses and counter melodies during her solos, as in "When a Woman Loves a Man" or "I'll Never Be the Same." Young, who began to record with Holiday in 1937, gave her the nickname "Lady Day," by which she was known from then on. Between 1935 and 1938, she released some eighty titles on the Brunswick label for marketing to the black jukebox audience, earning a reputation as a one-take artist who learned material quickly and had a fantastic ear. Although still rarely given well-known songs to record, her performances demonstrated her improvisatory skill and contributed to her growing popularity with nightclub audiences. Also in 1935, she made the first of many successful appearances at Harlem's Apollo Theater. By 1936, she was recording under her own name, as well as with Teddy Wilson.

John Hammond also championed the work of Count Basie, and in 1937 he took

Billie Holiday enjoyed working with saxophonist Lester Young, whose vocal-like approach was ideal for providing instrumental responses and counter melodies to her solos. It was Young who gave her the nickname "Lady Day." (NATIONAL ARCHIVES)

Basie to hear Holiday and encouraged him to take her on as a singer with his band. Basie enthusiastically agreed, and Holiday performed with the band for a year. Because of contractual problems, the two were not able to record together, but three air checks from Savoy and Meadowbrook Ballroom performances show that Holiday was capable of meeting the rhythmic challenges of one of the hottest bands of the era. The reasons given for her departure vary, depending on the source, but Holiday and Basie remained friends, and she made occasional appearances with the band in the 1940s.

Holiday went on to perform with Artie Shaw's band in 1939, becoming one of the first black performers to integrate an all-white ensemble. Contractual problems again kept Holiday from recording with the band, however, and her time with Shaw's band was fraught with tensions over her style, which remained less popular with his big band audiences (who were used to a mainstream pop style), and over her race. Shaw hired white performer Helen Forrest as a back-up singer when establishments refused to allow Holiday to perform with the all-white ensemble or when conflicts over Holiday's approach to her material arose, and that did little to alleviate tensions. Holiday's descriptions of her time with Shaw, particularly on tour, are some of the most poignant parts of her autobiography.

By 1939, when she was just twenty-four, Holiday had gained significant recognition through her appearances at Café Society, a club opened by Barney Josephson in December 1938 for the express purpose of providing entertainment to integrated audiences. It was within this context that Holiday came to be identified with the song "Strange Fruit." Written by Lewis Allan, "Strange Fruit" is about lynching; in it, lynched bodies are described as "strange fruit," the "bitter crop" of Southern racial politics. The song was unusual for the directness of its message, and many critics, including Hammond, were uncomfortable with Holiday's adoption of it as a kind of theme song, which she performed in a dramatic manner. Columbia Records held her contract at the time and was unwilling to record "Strange Fruit," but Holiday managed to record the song on Milt Gabler's independent Commodore label. The recording sold well, with one of Holiday's blues numbers, "Fine and Mellow," on the flip side. Following her time at Café Society, Holiday became a much sought after performer in New York City and elsewhere.

She signed with Decca in 1944, a label with a reputation for mainstream popular music rather than jazz but where Gabler now worked. Holiday decided she wanted strings as part of her back-up, and Gabler complied. "Lover Man," her first recording in this new style, became her best-selling record to date. During her six years with Decca, Holiday recorded her own compositions, "God Bless the Child" and "Don't Explain," and had success with the material of others, such as "Good Morning, Heartache" by Irene Higginbotham (whom she had met when Higginbotham was married to Teddy Wilson), as well as some standards.

In 1947, Holiday entered a private clinic to try to kick her drug habit, but some three weeks following her discharge, she was arrested for possession. Circumstances surrounding her arrest are unclear, but rather than receive treatment, she was sentenced to a year and a day at the Federal Reformatory for Women at Alderson, West Virginia. She served nine and one-half months, and upon her release for good behavior, New York City authorities revoked her cabaret card, thus making it impossible for her to perform in local clubs. The loss of the nightclub venue was a blow to the singer, who had been one of the performing lights of the New York entertainment scene, but Holiday found work outside New York City and in special concerts in the city, such as appearances at Carnegie Hall, as well as on national and European tours.

Decca records let Holiday's contract lapse in 1950, and she was without a recording label until 1952, when she signed with

Norman Granz's Verve label. Granz wanted Holiday's recordings to recapture the spontaneity of the earlier sessions with Teddy Wilson, and so he shed the rehearsed orchestral arrangements of the Decca releases. With the formidable back-up talent of Oscar Peterson, Bobby Tucker, Ben Webster, Paul Quinichette, Harry "Sweets" Edison, and others, Holiday recorded some 100 songs for Granz. Although these recordings share the jamlike informality of the Brunswick releases, her material consisted of standards, like "Blue Moon" and "Stormy Weather," as well as remakes of some of her earlier numbers, such as "What a Little Moonlight Can Do," which provide an opportunity to hear how she continued to recompose her material.

In 1958, Holiday recorded her last and most popular album, *Lady in Satin*, featuring lush string arrangements by Ray Ellis. Holiday's voice is noticeably different from her Verve releases, and its cracked, almost harsh timbre, so apparent when accompanied by the strings, has led several critics to call it her worst album. Holiday's talent shines through the harsh timbre, however, and her rhythmic flexibility and careful shaping of the text remain as true as ever.

Prior to her *Lady in Satin* release, Holiday made one other recording that stands as a testament to her career as a jazz soloist. In December 1957, she took part in a special CBS program, *The Sound of Jazz*. Produced by Robert Herridge with the advice of Whitney Balliett and Nat Hentoff, the show presented nine performances by the leading jazz musicians of the time. Holiday performed her famous "Fine and Mellow" blues with assisting solos by Ben Webster, her old friend Lester Young, Vic Dickerson, Gerry Mulligan, Doc Cheatham, Coleman

Hawkins, and Roy Eldridge. On the program, which is available on videocassette, Holiday performs in a circle with the other musicians. Her singing is true and rhythmically flexible, and she takes obvious delight in the work of the others. On her remaining choruses, she enters, not as a singer carrying the blues text, but as a distinctive soloist in the jazz ensemble.

The two most recent biographies are Donald Clarke's 1994 *Wishing on the Moon: The Life and Times of Billie Holiday* and Stuart Nicholson's 1995 *Billie Holiday.*

Holiday died in New York City on July 17, 1959, from the long-term effects of drug addiction; she was only forty-four years old. A lifelong Roman Catholic, she is buried in Saint Raymond's Catholic Cemetery in the Bronx. Her funeral, a formal high requiem mass held at Saint Paul the Apostle Cathedral, was attended by thousands of friends and fans.

SUSAN C. COOK

Holt, Nora (1885–1974)

Music critic, composer, and performer Nora Douglas Holt lived by a creed that said, "Music is one of the greatest refiners of the race." During a long and successful career as a classical-music critic for the *Chicago Defender* (1917–23) and the *New York Amsterdam News* (1944–52), Holt challenged and inspired numerous young black musicians and urged her readers to culture themselves in the arts.

Born Nora Douglas in Kansas City, Kansas, in 1885, she was influenced to study piano at an early age by her mother, Grace (Brown), and her father, C. N. Douglas, presiding officer with the Puget Sound, African Methodist Episcopal (AME) Church.

Further encouragement came from her secondary school music teacher, N. Clark Smith, who took her to hear symphony concerts.

In 1916, she graduated from Western University in Quindaro, Kansas (B.A.), and in 1918 from the Chicago Musical College (M.Mus.). Holt is credited as being the first black musician to earn the M.Mus. degree.

For her master's thesis, Holt composed a symphonic rhapsody for string orchestra

As classical music critic for the Chicago Defender *(1917–23) and the* New York Amsterdam News *(1944–52), Nora Holt was dedicated to awakening musical tastes and encouraging black musicians.* (MOORLAND-SPINGARN)

based on the Negro spiritual "You May Bury Me in the East." Unfortunately, her music library and original manuscripts were stolen while she was traveling in Europe and the Far East in the early 1930s; however, one of her four "Negro Dances" for piano survives in her publication *Music and Poetry*, copies of which are housed in the James W. Johnson Memorial Collection of Yale University's Beinecke Library. Her musical settings for four Paul Laurence Dunbar poems, "My Love Is Like a Cry in the Night," "A Florida Night," "Who Knows," and "The Sandman," were very successful. "A Florida Night" became a favorite of the renowned black tenor Roland Hayes.

During her graduate studies (1917–18) under Felix Borowsky, musicologist, president of Chicago Musical College and, later, music critic for the *Chicago Sun-Times*, she began to demonstrate a growing curiosity for music criticism while her interest in composing and performing gradually diminished.

Holt joined the *Chicago Defender* in November 1917. Her first feature article, "Cultivating Symphony Concerts," appeared on November 10, 1917, on the "Woman's Page" under the byline Lena James Douglas. She had married George W. Holt (her third husband) a few months prior, however, and she later changed her name to Nora Douglas Holt.

As the only woman writing for a leading black newspaper in a male-dominated profession, she immediately recognized the enormity of the responsibilities she would encounter. Asked to summarize her philosophy on the role of the music critic, she said her goal was always to offer expert musical judgment, to teach and awaken musical interest in her public; to advance young artists and the music of African Americans, and, finally, to provide both black and white communities with quality appraisals in order to prove her competency as a critic.

Between 1917 and 1923, young and seasoned artists performed in the Windy City (many of whom she would review again during her tenure with the *New York Amsterdam News*), and Holt evaluated their performances by comparing them to what she believed were the necessary standards for measuring artistic growth.

Holt did not accept the insurgence of jazz and blues during the early 1920s and because of this was often perceived as snobbish. Unashamed, she considered herself an initiate and remained faithful to her creed to advance young black musicians into what she described as wholesome artistic realms.

On March 9, 1919, she invited several black Chicago musicians to her home to consider forming a national association to exchange views and ideas, evaluate standards in performance and teaching, and encourage black youth. This meeting resulted in the founding of the Chicago Musical Association, and Holt was voted its first president. In May of that year, other renowned musicians met in Washington, D.C., to consider forming a second temporary association, and Holt strongly objected because she thought it might lead to divisions within the association. In July, at her invitation, musicians met at her home to establish what is now the National Association of Negro Musicians (NANM). Among the charter members were Henry L. Grant, Nora Douglas Holt, Carl Diton, Alice Carter Simmons, Clarence C. White, Deacon Johnson, and R. Nathaniel Dett.

Music and Poetry was first published and edited by Holt in January 1921. Although the publication was short lived, it encouraged research and contained an array of articles by brilliant black artists with expertise in various genres, such as violin, voice, poetry, harmony, dance, and composition.

In 1923, Holt, now widowed, married Joseph Luther Ray, secretary to Bethlehem Steel magnate Charles Schwab, and retired as a music critic in order to honeymoon abroad. This marriage, however, lasted only one year, ending in divorce. Holt later returned to Europe, performing in the posh nightclubs of Paris, Monte Carlo, London, and Italy. She also went to the Far East to play for Chinese audiences in Shanghai. She returned to Chicago and Los Angeles intermittently over the next twelve years and finally settled in Los Angeles, where she taught in the California school system for several years.

She left California for New York City in 1944 in order to join the *New York Amsterdam News* as senior music critic. Her first article, "Carmen Jones, Magnificent with Quips, says Nora Holt," appeared on January 9, 1944.

Holt was the first black person to work as a music editor and critic under union contract with the American Newspaper Guild, CIO. In 1945, sponsored by composer Virgil Thomson, she became the first black member to join the Music Critics Circle of New York, and from 1953 to 1964 she was producer-musical director of radio station WLIB's "Concert Showcase."

Through her reviews, Holt welcomed hundreds of young musicians to New York City, some of whom were seasoned artists. Many were students of artists she had reviewed twenty-one years earlier in the *Chicago Defender* and who now taught in black colleges and universities in the South—

Howard, Fisk, Hampton, and Florida A & M universities as well as **Spelman**, Morehouse, and many white conservatories in the United States and Europe.

Nora Douglas Holt was indeed a pioneer who provided a rich legacy of music criticism.

RAWN SPEARMAN

Horn, Shirley (1934–)

Many long years of styling harmonious songs at the piano began to pay off handsomely in the late 1980s as Shirley Horn became a virtual overnight sensation with her much-acclaimed recordings for the Verve label. Beginning with the 1986 live album *I Thought about You: Live at Vine St.*, Horn began to craft an incandescent series of recordings, which included a rare guest appearance by her friend and supporter, the late trumpet master Miles Davis, along with the brothers Marsalis, Wynton and Branford, and harmonica man Toots Thielemans.

Author Kitty Grime summed it up succinctly when she wrote, "Shirley Horn must be *the* cult performer. A near-legendary figure, seldom seen outside Washington, she's just about everybody's favorite singer-player." Horn certainly was a favorite of Davis. When he made a guest appearance on her 1991 recording, *You Won't Forget Me*, it was the culmination of an artistic love affair that began decades earlier when, after hearing her 1960 debut album, *Embers and Ashes*, Davis insisted that she open engagements for his quintet at the Village Vanguard.

After that stint, Horn was in demand at jazz clubs across the country. She also found herself in the recording studio working with

Quincy Jones, then vice president of Mercury Records, which opened up the world of movie soundtracks, and she sang on *For Love of Ivy* and *A Dandy in Aspic*. Never one for the road, Horn took great comfort in her Washington, D.C., home life and was determined to raise her daughter, Rainy. This effectively kept her out of the music scene during the late 1960s and the entire decade of the 1970s.

Born, raised, and still living comfortably in Washington, D.C., Horn showed her talent at the piano at a very early age, even before kindergarten. As a teenager she studied composition at **Howard University**, eventually garnering a scholarship to Juilliard in New York City. A tight family budget forced her to return to Howard, however, and she later left school to pursue a professional career in local clubs.

Long one of the treasures of Washington night life, Horn's tender, swinging vocal style is second only to her enormous talent at the piano. So singular is her approach to the piano that she once became very uncomfortable in the studio when an insistent record producer wanted her to be accompanied by another pianist; she simply could not fathom another pianist backing her vocals.

Much more than a vocalist, Horn has made her mark as a pianist who sings, rather in the mold of Nat "King" Cole; unlike Cole, however, she never considered abandoning the piano in order to increase her visibility as a singer. Her piano talent received even greater recognition during the early 1990s, when she was called upon to back jazz vocal master **Carmen McRae** and harmonica player Toots Thielemans on their respective recordings.

Shirley Horn possesses an intuitive sense of swing that blends harmoniously with her honeyed voice. Her phrasing is impeccable, and her ease with a lyric, always tender and touching, is the mark of a true song stylist. Equally at home with Tin Pan Alley and jazz, Shirley Horn is one of the singular talents of jazz voice and piano.

WILLARD JENKINS

Horne, Lena (1917–)

"There were always people around reminding me that I was a symbol of certain Negro aspirations," Lena Horne said in a 1965 *Ebony* interview. "When those reminders were made too often I would try to assert myself and say, in effect: 'All right, I'm a symbol. But I'm a person, too. You can't push me so hard. I've got a right to my own happiness, too.'" Lena Horne's position as a symbol of and for her race has worked hand in hand with racism to limit her possibilities as a performer and a person. However, she has managed to go beyond those limitations to carve out an impressive stage, film, and recording career and a life of personal fulfillment.

Lena Calhoun Horne was born on June 17, 1917, in Brooklyn, New York. Her father was, in her words, a gambler and a racketeer, her mother was a struggling actress. Both of them, however, came from respectable middle-class families, and as a very little girl, Horne was surrounded by that respectability. She and her parents lived with her paternal grandparents until her mother and father divorced when she was three. Then Lena remained while her mother tried to make a career as an actress.

Cora Calhoun Horne was a suffragist and a bold defender of black rights. "My grandmother took me to her meetings," said Horne in an interview for *I Dream a World*, "from the time I was little until I was fifteen. She was in the Urban League, the NAACP, and the Ethical Culture Society. I was surrounded by adult activities. . . . if I hadn't had that from her, then the other side of my life, which was more bleak, might have finished me." There are probably few other Hollywood legends who were members of the **National Association for the Advancement of Colored People** at two years old.

Unfortunately, Horne was not able to stay permanently with her grandmother, or anyone else for that matter. When she was about seven, she rejoined her mother and spent the next few years traveling with her

Lena Horne began her career as a dancer at the Cotton Club, hired for her spectacular looks. She then studied music and honed her skills as a singer, becoming a successful recording artist and club and concert performer. (SCHOMBURG CENTER)

as she pursued her career as an actress. They had no home and, because of Jim Crow laws, could seldom find a hotel to stay in as they traveled. So they slept in the homes of relatives, friends, and even strangers, a common practice in the Southern black community where hospitality stretched to try to fill the void created by prejudice. Horne then spent several years in Brooklyn, living with relatives and attending the Brooklyn public schools and the Girls High School. When she was fourteen, her mother remarried, returning from a tour in Cuba with her new husband, Miguel Rodriguez. The new family moved to a poor section of the Bronx, having been rebuffed by Brooklyn's black middle class.

At sixteen, Horne had to quit school. Her mother had become very ill, and the household needed money. A friend of her mother's, Elida Webb, was choreographer at the Cotton Club and got young Horne a job, solely on the basis of her spectacular looks. While Horne was working there, she began to take music lessons. She said later that she was never a natural singer and that it took a lot of hard work and a number of years for her to hone her skills. In the meantime, she danced in the chorus on bills with Count Basie, Cab Calloway, **Billie Holiday**, and **Ethel Waters**. However, when she was only seventeen, she was cast in *Dance with Your Gods* (1934) on Broadway. At eighteen, she left the Cotton Club for good to be a singer with Noble Sissle's Society Orchestra in Philadelphia. Her father was not far away, operating a hotel in Pittsburgh. The two became reacquainted, and he remained an important part of her life until he died.

On the road with the orchestra, Horne was constantly confronted with the harsh realities of racism. Possibly to escape, she married a friend of her father's, Louis Jones. They remained married for four years, long enough for Horne to bear two children. In 1939, she took a starring role in the revue *Blackbirds of 1939*, and in 1940 she left her husband. When she first went to New York, she left her children with their father so that she could make a start and find a place for the three of them to live. Late in the year, she became chief vocalist for the Charlie Barnett band and began to record. Able to provide a home for her children, she went back to Pittsburgh to get them, but Jones would give up only her daughter. Horne agreed to settle for visiting rights with her son.

One of her most popular early records, "Haunted Town," was made with Barnett. Next, she went to the Café Society Downtown, an engagement that might be said to have made her name. There, she met Paul Robeson and Walter White, both on the same night. As her friends, they helped increase her awareness of the political struggles of black people. She also met and started dating boxer Joe Louis. Within the year, she received the offer of a booking at the Trocadero Club in California.

The decision to take the offer and go to Hollywood was a difficult one: She knew it might lead to work in films, but she had serious doubts about battling what she expected would be the rampant racism of the film community. Walter White persuaded her that she would be doing a service to her people if she could break into films. He made her think of the possibility as a challenge. Sure enough, two months after arriving in Los Angeles she was auditioning for Metro-Goldwyn-Mayer (MGM). Soon she signed a seven-year contract with a starting salary of $200 per week and a clause that said she did not have to perform in stereotypical roles. "My father had them scared to death. I think that was the first time a black man had ever come into Louis B. Mayer's office and said, 'I don't want my daughter in this mess.' . . . He was so articulate and so beautiful, they just said, 'Well, don't worry.'"

Then the problem was how to use her. She lost her first chance for a speaking role in a mixed-cast movie because she was too light. She did not get another shot until 1956. All her performances in between were guest spots in which she sang only. These scenes never included the principals of the film in any important way and were easily edited out so that the films could be shown in southern theaters. Horne did do one speaking part at MGM, an all-black film entitled *Cabin in the Sky* (1943), and she was loaned out for another, *Stormy Weather* (1943).

The guest spots had a tremendous impact. Her job, as Walter White had seen it, was to change the American image of black women, and she did. She fit white society's standards of beauty as well as the most beautiful white women did, but she was clearly a woman of color; she was also a woman of great charm and dignity who was conscious of her position as a representative of black America—her choices about the way she presented herself were influenced by that role. It seemed important at the time to show that a black woman did not have to sing spirituals or earthy, overtly sexual laments; Horne sang Cole Porter and Gershwin. It seemed important that a black woman could be cool, glamorous, and sophisticated; Horne always looked as though she had stepped out of the pages of *Vogue*. "The image that I chose to give them was of a woman who they could not reach."

When not singing on screen, she was singing in clubs. "Each year in New York's after-dark world of supper clubs," *Life* magazine reported in 1943, "there appears a girl singer who becomes a sensation overnight. She stands in the middle of a dance floor in a white dress and a soft light and begins to sing. The room is hushed and her voice is warm and haunting. Her white teeth gleam, her eyes move back and forth, and her softly sung words seem to linger like cigaret smoke. This year that girl is Lena Horne."

Horne turned out to have staying power. During the 1940s, she could command $10,000 a week at the clubs. Her recordings, including "Birth of the Blues," "Moanin' Low," "Little Girl Blue," and "Classics in Blue," were highly successful, and she was in demand on the radio. During World War II, she traveled extensively to entertain the troops, an experience that was not always salubrious. "When at a performance in Fort Riley, Kansas," Donald Bogle wrote in *Brown Sugar*, "she spotted German prisoners of war sitting in the best seats in the front of the house, she stepped from the stage, whisked past them, then sang to the black soldiers in the back."

In 1947, Horne secretly married Lennie Hayton, whom she had been seeing for years. Hayton was white, and Horne's position as symbol rose up to haunt her again. She did not reveal her marriage until 1950, and when she did, her mail filled with hate letters from white racists and bitter reproaches from black Americans. It was a reaction she had anticipated. "Isn't it ironic?" she said in a 1965 *Ebony* article. "For three years I preferred to let the world think I was a woman living in sin than admit that I had married a white man." While her comments in later years show that she clearly understood the source of the anger felt by other black people at her marriage, she had found that there were limits to her ability to tailor her life to fit what she and others thought of as her responsibilities as a public figure.

As the 1950s arrived, Horne was at the top of her form. By 1948, she received $60,000 a week for appearing at the Cibacabano in New York. In 1950, she made her first television appearance, on Ed Sullivan's *Toast of the Town*. In 1956, she had her first speaking role in a mixed-cast film, *Meet Me in Las Vegas*. In 1957, she starred on Broadway for the first time in *Jamaica*. However, she lost the film role she had most hoped for, the mulatto Julie in *Show Boat*, probably because of her marriage. Also, because she remained loyal to friends who were being blacklisted for supposed Communist sympathies, she was eventually blacklisted herself from television work. Her second appearance in that medium was nine years after her first, on *The Perry Como Show* in 1959.

As she went into the 1960s, Horne, like many others, became more and more involved in civil rights. She was at the march on Washington in 1963. In the atmosphere of change, she also separated from her husband. "I took a chance," she told *Ebony* in 1968. "I said, 'Lennie, I'm going through some changes as a black woman. I can't explain them. I don't know what they're going to mean, what they're going to do to me, but I've got to be by myself to work it out.'" They remained apart for three years and then came back together to go on with their twenty-four-year marriage. In the meantime, she toured for the **National Council of Negro Women**, speaking to black women all over the South. Her auto-biography, *Lena*, which she wrote with Richard Schickel, appeared in 1965. In these years, her music began to develop in different directions. The constraints of her position loosened, and she was able to explore areas she had once kept rigidly under control.

In 1970, Horne's father died, followed, in just a few months, by her son. Less than a year later, her husband died. The next few years were filled with grief and sorrow. She had lost the two people she most depended on and three of the people she most loved.

In 1974, Horne was back on Broadway, performing with Tony Bennett. Four years later, she played Glinda, the Good Witch, in the film *The Wiz*. On April 30, 1981, at the age of sixty-four, she opened on Broadway with *Lena Horne: The Lady and Her Music*, which became the longest-running one-woman show in Broadway history and won her a special Tony Award, the New York City Handel Medallion, the Drama Desk Award, and a Drama Critics' Circle citation. Shortly after the show closed, Lorne began to have heart troubles and was given a pacemaker. She has continued to appear on television regularly. She has received both an Image Award and the Spingarn Medal from the NAACP, and in 1979 she accepted an honorary doctorate from **Howard University**.

In 1994, Horne received raves again for a two-day sold-out concert at Carnegie Hall. The New York Times said, "Ms. Horne, who looks 20 years younger than she is, still exudes a sizzling glamour, and her voice remains in remarkable shape." This was again evident when the cable Arts & Entertainment network aired a Horne special taped at The Supperclub in New York. She

Legendary performer Lena Horne broke through countless racial barriers but had to live with the pressures of being a symbol to both black and white Americans. (SCHOMBURG CENTER)

was backed by the Count Basie Orchestra as she performed old standards and songs from a new jazz album, *We'll Be Together Again*.

It is difficult to assess the historical importance of Lena Horne's life and work. In part, this is because she is, even today, so remarkably contemporary. Thinking of her as a historical figure strains the imagination. Her image as a beautiful, proud, self-assured black woman suggests that nothing (not even history) could or would dare impinge on her. She responded to this idea when she talked about the time she struck a white man in a Hollywood nightclub for a racist insult. The incident was widely reported by journalists. "I got telegrams from black people saying, 'How wonderful, we didn't know.' I just automatically thought that black people knew that if you were black, you were going to catch hell. They thought because I was me I wasn't catching hell. It was a damn fight everywhere I was, every place I worked, in New York, in Hollywood, all over the world."

The mission Lena Horne accepted more than a half-century ago was to show that black people could be on top, could be winners. Her job was to make people look at the triumph and not just the struggle. She succeeded.

KATHLEEN THOMPSON

Houston, Whitney (1963–)

"Don't think it's all easy street," Whitney Houston told an *Upscale* interviewer in 1993. "I started out working in little night-clubs—sometimes getting paid, sometimes not—sometimes performing for 200 people, other times working in front of 10. Today, it's like people just want to jump out there and immediately become stars, but it takes time and it takes not giving up. It takes believing in one's self in spite of negativity and what people say."

Whitney Houston is the only artist in the world ever to have recorded seven consecutive number-one-hits. Her voice has set the standard for pop vocalists since she entered the music scene. Her beauty, grace, and unswerving commitment to her values and family have made her a role model for millions of Americans.

Born on August 9, 1963 in Newark, New Jersey, Whitney Houston is the daughter of gospel star Emily "Cissy" Houston and John Houston. She has two brothers, Mi-

chael and Gary; her cousin is **Dionne Warwick**, and **Aretha Franklin** is a close family friend. Gospel, soul, and R&B music were an everyday part of her life growing up. Her education included singing in the church choir and going to the studio and on the road with her mother.

At the age of eight, she sang her first solo, "Guide Me, O Thou Great Jehovah" at New Hope Baptist Church, where her mother was a minister. In 1979, she made her recording debut singing lead vocals on "Life's a Party," the title track for the Michael Zager Band's second album.

By fifteen Houston was singing background vocals at sessions for Chaka Khan and Lou Rawls. She also sang duets with Teddy Pendergrass and Jermaine Jackson. Throughout her teens, she received offers of recording contracts but, on the advice of her manager and her family, she held off until 1983 when Clive Davis signed her with Arista Records. As her manager Gene Harvey is quoted as telling the *Los Angeles Times*, "I felt it was too early. I didn't want her to deal with those kinds of pressures at that point." Even after signing with Arista, Whitney took her time before releasing an album. "It was Clive's philosophy and ours that we not push this girl out there right away. We decided to wait and do the best job we could, and if it took a little longer, so be it," Harvey is quoted as saying.

Her debut album, *Whitney Houston*, was released in 1985. It is the biggest-selling album ever by a woman and the top-selling debut album of all time. The single "Saving All My Love" won a Grammy Award. In 1987, *Whitney*, her second album, was the first album by a woman to debut at number one on the charts. The album included the hit singles "I Wanna Dance With Somebody

(Who Loves Me)," "Didn't We Almost Have It All," and "Where do Broken Hearts Go." In 1990, her third album, *I'm Your Baby Tonight*, reached double-platinum status. Touring with her road show, she sells out stadiums all over the world, from audiences of 65,000 in Brazil to 30,000 in Denmark.

As many pop stars have done before her, in 1992, Whitney Houston expanded her career to include film acting, starring in the hit movie *The Bodyguard* with Kevin Costner. She received good reviews for her debut performance, and her soundtrack album for the film sold twenty-eight million copies worldwide. She got "above-the-title" billing for her part in the 1995 film version of Terry McMillan's novel *Waiting to Exhale*, in which she costarred with **Angela Bassett**.

Awards and accolades have been a part of Houston's career since her first Grammy for her first hit single in 1985. Following that are a long string of awards including four more Grammy Awards, more than a dozen American Music Awards, MTV's Best Female Video Award, United Nations

Whitney Houston is the only artist ever to have recorded seven consecutive number-one hits. Her voice has set the standard for pop vocalists since she entered the music scene. (PRIVATE COLLECTION)

Children's Fund honoree, Stars Salute to Whitney Houston for her support of black colleges, several NAACP Image Awards, Soul Train Music Awards, Sammy Davis Jr. Entertainer of the Year Award, many Billboard Music Awards, People's Choice Awards, Emmy Awards, an American Black Achievement award, and the key to the city of Newark, New Jersey.

Although she is famous for her voice, Whitney Houston is also known for her values and her profound belief in God. She has established The Whitney Houston Foundation for Children, Inc., which is dedicated to promoting a positive self-image in children by providing opportunities for them to learn and express themselves in a safe and supportive environment; Houston's mother heads the foundation. Houston also supports the United Negro College Fund and AIDS research.

In 1992 Whitney Houston married hip-hop artist Bobby Brown, and in 1993 they had their first child, Bobbi Kristina Houston Brown.

Whitney Houston told *Upscale* that "when you become successful or famous, you do have a responsibility to those who are there to support you, to those who are trying to make it and to those who are looking to you for inspiration and encouragement. I think I definitely have a responsibility to our young people. I was raised and taught that you have to always look back and see what else you can do. It's not enough for me to just be a 'star.'"

HILARY MAC AUSTIN

Humes, Helen (1913–1981)

"I've been called a blues singer and a jazz singer and a ballad singer," Helen Humes

told Whitney Balliett. "Well, I'm all three, which means I'm just a singer." She did her "just singing" with the Harry James and Red Norvo orchestras and replaced **Billie Holiday** with Count Basie. Her distinguished career stretched over more than five decades.

Born in Louisville, Kentucky, on June 23, 1913, Helen Humes was the only child of lawyer John Henry Humes and his wife of Cherokee lineage, Emma Johnson, who taught school and had a musical bent. Though she had a German piano tutor at eleven, Helen already knew how to play the instrument and had begun to sing at church and then with the Booker T. Washington Community Center Band. She played the trumpet under the guidance of the band's Bessie Allen but preferred keyboards and mastered the harmonium and organ.

"Instant mastery," a Humes biographer's phrase, neatly describes the talent with which she met hurdles. Discovered by an Okeh Records producer when she was thirteen, she recorded blues numbers handed her moments before in a St. Louis studio. Her first recording was followed two years later by a single of "Race Track Blues" and "Black Cat Moan."

After high school and a few nonmusical jobs back home, she sang in a Buffalo, New York, club in 1936; in Louisville clubs and dance halls; and then with saxophonist Al Sears' band.

The Sears engagements led to the 1937 stint at Cincinnati's Cotton Club that so impressed Basie he offered her Holiday's vacated spot. She took him up on it, but not before spending a year with the James orchestra in New York.

Humes sang with Basie from 1938 to 1942 and intermittently to 1952. Jazz historian Linda Dahl writes that Humes' singing and that of her predecessor "were as unlike as their lifestyles." Billie's was "deep and shadowed, nearly always, with pain," Helen's "sunny, bouncing and infectious."

After 1942 she sang at New York's prominent Cafe Society club, then moved to California. She sang in films or on soundtracks that included *Panic in the Streets* (1944), *Jivin' in Behop* (with Dizzy Gillespie, 1947), *My Blue Heaven* (1950), *Harlem Jazz Festival* (1955), and *Basin Street Revue* (1956). In 1945, she ventured into lively rhythm-and-blues territory with the song for which many best remember her, "Ee Baba Reba," and her favorite, "If I Could Be with You." Very popular, too, was "Million Dollar Secret," which she wrote.

With the 1950s came her acclaimed Australian tour with vibraphonist Norvo, television work, and several singles that ranged from rock 'n' roll to ballad. Yet, that decade and the 1960s were a long, lean time for both jazz and Humes, despite tours and festival spots.

In 1973, however, she gained a new generation of devotees by singing at the Newport Jazz Festival. Now 60, she had her European debut tour that year, resulting in the *Helen Comes Back* album, released in France. The Grammy-nominated *Sneaking Around* soon followed and then a contract and recordings with Columbia. Louisville gave her a key to the city in 1975.

Helen Humes recalled unpaid royalties, past or current, with only slight ill humor. Throughout her career she seemed not to need a personal manager, nightlife, husband (though she said she had had one, a sailor), alcohol, nicotine, success, and even, very nearly, the calling of music itself.

Alberta Hunter was among the blues singers who began their careers in the dance halls and social clubs of Chicago and New York. Hunter later achieved success in the chic cabarets of Paris, London, and Copenhagen. (PRIVATE COLLECTION)

She died in Santa Monica, California, on September 13, 1981. Her final album, released that year, was titled simply *Helen*.

GARY HOUSTON

Hunter, Alberta (1895–1984)

Born in Memphis, Tennessee, on April 1, 1895, Alberta Hunter enjoyed a long and successful career primarily as a blues singer until her death on October 17, 1984, in New York City.

Hunter's career began around 1914 in Chicago and continued in New York in 1921. In both cities, she sang in clubs and cabarets, but after moving to New York she began to record for Gennett as well as other labels, accompanied by musicians such as Louis Armstrong, Sidney Bechet, and Fletcher Henderson. In order to record on labels other than Gennett to whom she was under contract, she used two different aliases, May Alix and Josephine Beatty.

From 1927 to 1953, Hunter sang both in Europe and the United States, including several United Service Organizations (USO) tours, and she appeared in the 1936 film *Radio Parade.* Hunter was semiretired from 1954 to 1977, having become a nurse; during this time she recorded only with **Lovie Austin** in 1961 and Jimmy Archey in 1962. She resumed her musical career in 1977 and continued to sing in clubs, make television appearances, and record until her death in 1984.

In addition to her vocal talent, Hunter also was a composer. She wrote at least one classic composition, "Downhearted Blues" in 1922, a composition that became famous after **Bessie Smith** recorded it in 1923.

EDDIE S. MEADOWS

I

International Sweethearts of Rhythm

The International Sweethearts of Rhythm was a late 1930s–40s black female swing band that was conceived, created, and managed (initially) by Laurence C. Jones. The band was originally based at Piney Woods Country Life School (founded in 1909 by Jones) in Piney Woods, Mississippi. A work-your-way-through coeducational institution (elementary, secondary, and, for a brief period, junior college), the doors of Jones' school were open to the materially impoverished, the social misfits, the physically disabled, and the blind, as well as the more affluent. Jones began to send out Piney Woods singing groups in the early 1920s on fund-raising missions of the school; noting the tremendous public response to the all-girl, all-white orchestras, including the Hormel Girls Caravan (Darlings of the Airwaves), Phil Spitalny, and Ina Ray Hutton orchestras, Jones decided to celebrate girls of tan and brown orchestrally. A fourteen- to sixteen-piece girls' swing band was culled from the school's forty-five-piece marching and concert bands, led by Piney Woods graduate Consuella Carter, who offered musical instruction on all instruments. The swingsters, whose ages ranged from fourteen to nineteen, became the school's primary musical messengers and fund-raisers during the 1938–39 school year. Thus began the extraordinary saga of the International Sweethearts of Rhythm. Originally appearing at dances, conventions, winter resorts, and all-day frolics throughout the South, by the winter of 1940, the band was completing a nationwide tour and competing successfully in various band polls (otherwise exclusively male).

Even while they still represented Piney Woods Country Life School, the International Sweethearts of Rhythm broke attendance records at such places as Washington, D.C.'s Howard, Chicago's Regal, and Detroit's Paradise theaters, as well as Los Angeles' Plantation Club. When the group went on to the "big time," seasoned performer Annie Mae Winburn was brought from Omaha, Nebraska, to front the band. (SCHOMBURG CENTER)

This 1948 USO photo announces in its caption that "The International Sweethearts of Rhythm returned last week from a six months' tour of Germany, France, Belgium and England where they entertained service men . . . these four trombonists were a lively part of the well known all-girl orchestra." (MOORLAND-SPINGARN)

The roster included saxophonists Willie Mae Wong, Alma Cortez, twins Irene and Ione Grisham, and sisters Lucy and Ernestine Snyder; trumpeters Sadie Pankey and Nova Lee McGee; trombonists Helen Jones, Ina Belle Byrd, and sisters Lena and Corine Posey; pianist Johnnie Mae Rice; bassist Bernice Rothchild; drummer Pauline Braddy; vocalist Virginia Audley; and entertainer Nina de la Cruz. Multitalented Edna Armstead Williams was designated leader/vocalist. Brought from Omaha, Nebraska, to chaperon was Rae Lee Jones and from

Ohio, as instructor in academic subjects, Vivian Crawford. Joining the band (and the school) later were saxophonists Helen Saine and sisters Judy and Grace Bayron. The first non-Piney Woods student to join the band was saxophonist Jennie Lee Morse; the second, vocalist Evelyn McGee.

Traveling in a unique palatial semitrailer, the band was soon declared one of the nation's best draws—a sweetheart for the box offices. They were breaking attendance records at such places as the District's Howard, Chicago's Regal, and Detroit's

Paradise theaters, as well as Los Angeles' Plantation Club. Replacements on all instruments remained on call back at Piney Woods Country Life School. By early 1941, school officials and supporters were raising questions about the girls' academic development. The girls were questioning graduation possibilities, as well as their wages. In April 1941, the following headline appeared in the black press: "Seventeen-Girl Band Which Quit School at Piney Woods Rehearses for Big Time." Homebase was now Arlington, Virginia. Seasoned performer Annie Mae Winburn was brought in from Omaha, Nebraska, to front the band. Veteran arranger Eddie Durham was brought in as music director, to be followed by Jesse Stone and Maurice King. Appearances now included New York City's Apollo Theater and the Savoy Ballroom; cross-country tours continued. Most memorable was a 1945 six-month United Service Organizations (USO) tour of France and Germany.

The first member who was not black was trumpeter Toby Butler, who joined in 1943. Following one year later was saxophonist Rosalind Cron. Other nonblack members included trumpeters Mim Polak, Nancy Brown, Norman Carson, and Flo Dreyer; saxophonist Pat Stulken; and drummer Fagel Lieberman. Other black performers who appeared on the band's roster before its demise in 1949 included saxophonists Vi Burnside, Marge Pettiford, Amy Garrison, Myrtle Young, and Geneva Perry; trumpeters Ernestine "Tiny" Davis, Marian Carter, Johnnie Mae Stansbury, Ray Carter, Jean Starr, and Augusta Perry; trombonists Jean Travis and Esther Cooke; bassists **Lucille Dixon**, Helen Coles, Margo Gipson, and Edna Smith; guitarists Roxanna Lucas and Carline Ray; pianist Jackie King; and vocalists Betty Sheppard and Betty Givens. Following three decades of undeserved obscurity, the International Sweethearts of Rhythm were saluted at the Third Women's Jazz Festival (March 1980) in Kansas City, Missouri, where pianist Marian McPartland released her booklet "The Untold Story of the International Sweethearts of Rhythm." Its activities were chronicled in **D. Antoinette Handy**'s 1981 publication *Black Women in American Bands and Orchestras* and its history documented in her 1983 publication *The International Sweethearts of Rhythm*. In 1984, Rosetta Records released a two-record album of sixteen cuts. The thirty-minute film *International Sweethearts of Rhythm*, produced and directed by Geta Schiller and Andrea Weiss, was released in 1986.

D. ANTOINETTE HANDY

J

Jackson, Janet (1966–)

"I'm in control of my own destiny. I'm the person who controls my career and life." And what an incredible career Janet Damita Jackson, youngest member of the famed Jackson family, has achieved.

Born on May 16, 1966, in Gary, Indiana, to Joseph and Katherine Jackson, Janet

Janet Jackson composed her first song, "Fantasy," at the age of eight. By 1986, when her blockbuster album Control *was released, Jackson was the top-selling musical artist in America.* (PRIVATE COLLECTION)

Jackson started her career at the tender age of seven. She and brother Randy sang Mickey and Sylvia's 1957 hit "Love Is Strange" during a Jackson Five engagement at the Grand Hotel in Las Vegas. She composed her first song, "Fantasy," when she was eight. In the meantime, she was appearing with her brothers on their television specials. But at the age of ten, Janet was bitten by the acting bug and played the role of Penny on the CBS sit-com *Good Times*. Appearances followed on television hits *Fame* and *Different Strokes*, as well as *A New Kind of Family*.

Persuaded by her father to return to singing, Jackson signed a contract with A & M records and released her debut album in 1982; *Dream Street*, her second album, was released in 1984. That same year, Jackson married James DeBarge, of the DeBarge singing group. The marriage, opposed by the Jackson family, was annulled within a year.

Jackson rebounded from her earlier lackluster albums and her transient marriage by releasing the blockbuster album *Control* in 1986. Working closely with the album's producers, Jimmy Jam (James Harris III) and Terry Lewis, both formerly of the Time, Jackson cowrote seven of the album's nine songs and was also involved in the production and arranging of what would become a multiplatinum milestone in her career. Five of the singles from *Control* became number one hits: "What Have You Done For Me

Lately?" "Nasty," "When I Think Of You," "Control," and "Let's Wait Awhile." Even the videos from *Control* sold more than a million copies, making Jackson the top-selling artist in America in 1986.

Jackson herself acknowledged the importance of this work as the cornerstone of her creative and emotional independence, because *Control* was made without assistance from anyone else in the Jackson family.

Jackson's *Rhythm Nation 1814* was released in 1989, also with Jam and Lewis. Touching upon socially conscious themes such as homelessness, drugs, and racism, Jackson again flexed her artistic muscle by cowriting seven of the album's songs. Hit singles from this album include "Alright," "Come Back To Me," and "Black Cat." She is also credited with coproduction of the quadruple platinum album.

A skilled dancer, Jackson has earned the Best Choreographed Video of the Year in MTV award for "Nasty" (from the *Control* album) and subsequently for "Rhythm Nation." A thirty-minute film based on *Rhythm Nation* won Jackson her first Grammy for Best Long Form Video. The choreography created by Jackson and Anthony Thomas certainly contributed to the sellout attendance of her 1990 world tour.

Leaving A & M in 1991, Jackson established her superstar status by signing a deal with Virgin Records reportedly worth anywhere from thirty-two to sixty million dollars.

In 1993, Janet Jackson appeared in the movie *Poetic Justice*. She and her celebrated brother, Michael, recently joined forces in the 1995 kinetic video, *Scream*.

Jackson moves easily and successfully from choreography to vocals to drama to composition. Her fans never have to ask, "What have you done for me lately?" They merely have to say, "Let's wait awhile." It won't be long before one of the highest paid women in the competitive field of pop music distinguishes herself once more.

RICHARD E. T. WADE

Jackson, Mahalia (1911–1972)

Mahalia Jackson, destined to become one of the greatest gospel singers of all time, was born in poverty in a three-room "shotgun" shack on Water Street between the railroad tracks and the Mississippi River levee in New Orleans. She was the third of six children. Her father, John A. Jackson, was a stevedore, barber, and preacher; her mother, Charity Clark, died at twenty-five when Mahalia was only four.

The church was always the central focus in Jackson's life, and she began to sing at the age of four in the children's choir at Plymouth Rock Baptist. After her mother's death, Mahalia was raised by her mother's sisters, Mahalia "Aunt Duke" Paul, for whom Mahalia was named, and Bessie Kimble, both of New Orleans. They lived in the section of the city upriver from Audubon Park that is known today as Black Pearl.

She attended McDonough School No. 24 until the eighth grade; then she worked as a laundress and cook. She attended Mt. Moriah Baptist Church, where she was very active, singing and "shouting its members" even before she was baptized in the Mississippi River at the age of twelve; she was also actively singing at other churches in the community. Even when she was young, her voice was recognized as something special.

As a young girl growing up in New Orleans, Jackson absorbed the musical sounds of her family's Baptist church, the Sanctified church next door, and the local legends-to-be King Oliver, Kid Ory, and Bunk Johnson; Louis Armstrong, not even in his teen years, was already playing trumpet in the New Orleans Waifs' Home Band; famous brass bands such as the Tuxedos, Eagle, and Eureka rode around town in advertising wagons and played at funerals, picnics, fish fries, lodge parties, and parades of all types; the Mardi Indians marched with their unique sounds on Fat Tuesday; musicians such as Jelly Roll Morton and King Oliver were playing in cabarets and cafes; and there was ragtime music on the showboats on the Mississippi.

Many people were buying gramophones at this time, and everybody had records of blues singers like **Bessie Smith** and **Ma Rainey**. Although Jackson grew up among people who were serious about religion, she was an admirer of Bessie Smith, and it was difficult not to hear the amalgam of sounds in her community. She was definitely influenced by this powerful music of the Delta.

Jackson experienced and was influenced by many styles of music at an early age; however, the most significant was that of the next-door Sanctified church, from which she could hear spirited singing and the drum, the cymbal, the tambourine, and the steel triangle. They did not have a choir or organ, however; the whole congregation participated by singing, clapping, and stamping their feet—in essence, utilizing the whole body. She has commented on several occasions that the church literally interprets the psalmist in the Bible, just as she does: "Make a joyful noise unto the Lord" and "Praise the Lord with the instruments." Jackson also said that the powerful beat and rhythms of the Sanctified church are retentions from the antebellum era of slavery and that the music is so expressive that it brought tears to her eyes.

The sacred and secular sounds in her community blended together, and when she left New Orleans, she carried this African-American musical matrix with her to Chicago in 1927, following the traditional pattern of African-American migration Jackson lived in Chicago with another aunt, Hannah Robinson, and worked as a laundress, a maid in a hotel, and a date packer; she also studied beauty culture. Soon after she arrived in Chicago, she joined the choir of the Greater Salem Baptist Church; after the director heard her sing "Hand Me Down My Silver Trumpet, Gabriel," she immediately became the choir's first soloist.

During the 1930s, she toured the "storefront church circuit," singing to congregations that could not afford conventional places of worship. She married her first husband in 1935 and in later years she married and divorced again. She also became a member of a gospel quintet, the Johnson Singers, at Greater Salem Baptist Church. In addition, she caught the attention of Professor Thomas A. Dorsey, later known as the "Father of Gospel Music." Dorsey was a gospel composer and publisher, who from then on served as her mentor and publisher. He wrote more than 400 songs and needed singers to sing and popularize them. Jackson, with singers **Roberta Martin** and **Sallie Martin**, began to perform and demonstrate Dorsey's songs for the Baptist conventions and various churches around the country. Dorsey was previously the accompanist for Ma Rainey, the classic blues singer, which accounts for his musical orientation and why he and his music were shunned by some middle-class congregations.

Jackson, Dorsey, and the other talented gospel singers and composers of this period revitalized African-American religious music by extending the developments that transpired within the sanctified churches to the more established denominations. They helped bring back into African-American church music the sounds and the structure of antebellum street cries and field hollers, folk spirituals and work songs; they borrowed freely from ragtime, blues, and jazz of the secular world; they helped keep alive the stylistic and aesthetic continuum that has characterized African-American music in the United States.

Jackson was criticized for hand clapping and stomping and for bringing "jazz into the church" because it was not dignified. Of course, being the feisty person that she was, she always retaliated, usually with scripture. Her favorite psalm to justify her performance practices was "Oh clap your hands, all ye people! Shout unto the Lord with the voice of triumph!" She said she had to praise God with her whole body, and she did.

Jackson bridged the gap between the sacred and the secular in her performance without compromising her deep-rooted fundamentalist faith. Numerous persons encouraged her to abandon her commitment to gospel music and switch from the church to the nightclub circuit. After hearing her sing in church, some of her relatives offered to teach her minstrel jazz tunes, and a jazz band leader offered her $100 per week. Decca Records wanted her to sing the blues and offered her $5,000 to play at the Village Vanguard. In addition, she was offered as much as $25,000 per performance in Las Vegas clubs. She turned down all offers. Mahalia knew that basically sacred gospels and secular blues flow from the same bed-

rock of experience. However, she explained the difference: "When you sing gospel you have a feeling there is a cure for what's wrong. But when you are through with the blues, you've got nothing to rest on."

Her first recording was for Decca, in 1934: "God Shall Wipe Away All Tears"; in 1946, she brought gospel singing out of the storefront and basement congregations by recording on the Apollo label "Move On Up a Little Higher," which sold more than eight million copies. This song made her commercially successful, and her career was

"When you sing gospel, you have a feeling there is a cure for what's wrong," said the great Mahalia Jackson, explaining her refusal to sing secular music. "But when you are through with the blues, you've got nothing to rest on." (MOORLAND-SPINGARN)

launched. Jackson, who had sung gospel songs in neighborhood churches since her childhood, turned her attention from her Chicago beauty parlor to push her professional career. African-American disc jockeys played her music; African-American ministers praised it from their pulpits. When sales passed one million, the African-American press hailed Jackson as "the only Negro whom Negroes have made famous." Few Euro-Americans had ever heard her; she had come to fame by singing only in African-American communities. From the start, audiences ackowledged her, as did London's *New Statesman*, as "the most majestic voice of faith" of her generation.

The obvious sincerity of Jackson's faith and belief moves audiences even when they cannot understand the lyrics. Her warm, uninhibited contralto voice carries a strong emotional message. Jackson's sound depends on the employment of the full range of expression of the human voice—from the rough growls employed by blues singers to the shouts and hollers of folk cries to the most lyrical, floating tones of which the voice is capable. She utilized to the fullest extent half-tones, *glissandi*, blue notes, humming, and moaning. Her performance also embodied pronunciation that was almost of the academy one instant and of the broadest Southern cottonfield dialect the next. Her style of singing has a broad rhythmic freedom and accents the lyric line to reinforce her emotional genuineness.

Many of these vocal characteristics were exemplified in Jackson's other multimillion sellers such as "Upper Room," "Didn't It Rain," "Even Me," and "Silent Night." Some of her earliest and best work, recorded originally at 78 rpm, has been reissued on LP and CD. On *Mahalia Jackson* (Grand Award 326), she sings "It's No Secret" and other songs that first gained her popularity in her own community. On *In the Upper Room* (Apollo 474), she performs "His Eye Is on the Sparrow" and, accompanied by a male quartet with a basso profundo, offers an unequaled version of the title song. She recorded about thirty albums (mostly for Columbia Records) during her career, and she acquired a dozen gold records (million sellers) from the 45 rpm records she recorded.

By the time of World War II, she was nationally known and was also recognized in many countries in Europe. After the war, with breakthroughs in communications, she became better known as a recording and performing artist. Jackson was also an entrepreneur/producer: She had her own CBS radio program and television show, which aired from 1954 to 1955. Thus she helped to prime the mass public for later gospel and soul singers. After attending beauty-culture school, she managed her own beauty shop and florist shop and also owned a substantial amount of real estate. She has appeared in movies such as *Imitation of Life*, *St. Louis Blues*, *The Best Man*, and *I Remember Chicago*. Three books have been published on her life, *Movin' On Up* (1966), *Just Mahalia, Baby* (1975), and *Got to Tell It: Mahalia Jackson, Queen of Gospel* (1992).

By 1953, Jackson received international acclaim on a European concert tour. When one of her recordings won the French Academy Award, Jackson consented to the European tour, though she was not convinced that foreign audiences would understand the sacred music of her people. In Paris, she had twenty-one curtain calls; she doubled the number of her originally scheduled performances when thousands were turned away from her concerts. Greetings came from Queen Elizabeth I and Winston Churchill before an Albert Hall concert; she also gave a command performance before the king and queen of Denmark.

For years, a Mahalia Jackson concert assured promoters of sell-out crowds at Carnegie Hall in New York, where she was a favorite. In Madison Square Garden, she moved a packed house from tears to thunderous applause. At the 1958 Newport Jazz Festival, the jazz world came to Mahalia on her own terms: Thousands of jazz buffs gave her standing ovations, and when she closed with "The Lord's Prayer," the crowd stood breathless. During two days in 1960, Mahalia taped a show for the Voice of America and gave two sell-out concerts at the hall of the Daughters of the American Revolution and one in Constitution Hall. She also appeared on many television shows.

With the advent of the civil-rights era, she yielded to the requests of Martin Luther King, Jr., and supported the liberation fight by traveling and singing at fund-raising rallies all over the nation with King. Mahalia Jackson would encourage the people with songs like "We Shall Overcome" and "If I Can Help Somebody"; she would also quietly slip money to leaders who she believed were "for real;" and she emerged as one of the symbols for the movement when in 1963 millions of television viewers watched as she accompanied King at the famous march on Washington. Immediately before King began his "I Have a Dream" speech at the Lincoln Memorial, Mahalia sang "I Been 'Buked and I Been Scorned." With the lyrics of this traditional spiritual, she summed up the frustrations and aspirations of the entire movement.

As an eighth-grade dropout, one of her major concerns was educating poor youth: She established the Mahalia Jackson Scholarship Fund and reportedly helped about fifty young adults to obtain college educations.

Jackson died of heart failure at the age of sixty in 1972. She was honored with funerals in Chicago and New Orleans and was finally entombed in Providence Memorial Park in Metairie, Louisiana. Jackson believed that she was "ordained to sing the gospel," but she did much more than just sing the gospel; she was an ambassador of goodwill wherever she traveled. People all over the world were attracted to her—Perhaps it was the simplicity of her ways; she said she was "just a good strong Louisiana woman who can cook rice so every grain stands by itself." Perhaps it was the explicit faith and conviction with which she delivered her messages in song. Jackson brought a wider acceptance and popularity to gospel music in the United States, which gave it more international prominence. She also helped make the gospel music industry a multimillion-dollar one while leaving her imprint on the African-American sacred-music culture. She achieved a universality by living faithfully within the confines of a particular tradition in singing the songs of her people in her own unique style. **Aretha Franklin** ended the funeral service by singing for Jackson one of Thomas Dorsey's songs that she loved so well, "Precious Lord, Take My Hand."

JOYCE MARIE JACKSON

James, Etta (1938–)

From her musical roots in the black gospel tradition, Etta James has forged a musical career that has spanned almost forty years. She is as comfortable with the gospel music she used to sing in church choir as she is with rhythm and blues, jazz, rock 'n' roll, ballads, and contemporary sounds. Critics have had a hard time defining her style, but there can be no doubt that the power, honesty, and sexual double entendres of her music evoke reminiscences of **Trixie Smith** and **Victoria Spivey**, the great classic blues singers of the 1920s.

Etta James was born in Los Angeles in 1938. Like many young African-American singers, she received her musical training in the church choir, at Saint Paul's Baptist Church. In fact, her musical style was developing in an era when gospel reformed the country's listening habits and when the term *race music* was replaced by *rhythm and blues*. When Etta was performing with her girlfriends on San Francisco's street corners, the stage was being set for her professional debut. Disk jockeys were becoming important players in the entertainment field, with recordings that reached larger and larger audiences who were avid for tunes to fuel the post-Depression dance crazes that swept the country.

James' career was launched at age fourteen when she became a member of Johnny Otis' rhythm and blues band, Etta and the Peaches, based in Los Angeles. Her first recording, "Roll with Me Henry," with the legendary band leader made her an instant success. Originally banned by radio stations coast to coast for its suggestive content, it was later released by Modern Records in 1954 as "The Wallflower," an answer to Hank Ballard's "Work with Me Annie," a 1954 hit. James's popularity was at its height in the 1950s. In fact, from then until the 1970s no other female rhythm-and-

Among female singers from the 1950s to the 1970s, only Dinah Washington and Ruth Brown had more top-ten rhythm-and-blues hits than Etta James. (SCHOMBURG CENTER)

blues artist, except **Dinah Washington** and **Ruth Brown**, had more top-ten hits. In the 1960s, she toured with Little Richard, James Brown, Little Willie John, and Johnny Guitar Watson. By 1969, James was one of *Billboard*'s top seven female artists.

As the 1960s wore on, however, it became apparent to the public that James was struggling with heroin addiction. As a result, she stopped recording and made very few public appearances from 1964 to 1968. She was eventually able to free herself from the habit through years in a drug rehabilitation program. In 1973, she picked up the pieces of her career and recorded her first album in two years, entitled *Etta James*, produced by Gabriel Mekler.

Once her rehabilitation was complete, there was no turning back. For the last twenty years, James has been active performing, touring widely in the United States and Europe and recording and appearing in concert halls, festivals, and clubs. In 1988, she cut her first solo album in more than ten years, *Seven Year Itch*. She has more than thirty albums and twenty charted hits to her credit. In 1990, the **National Association for the Advancement of Colored People** named her "Best Blues Artist" for her new album *Stickin' to My Guns*. In 1993 she was inducted into the Rock and Roll Hall of Fame.

ROBERT STEPHENS

Jennings, Patricia Prattis (1941–)

Patricia Prattis Jennings was apparently born with ink in her blood, fire in her fingers, and a passion for reading. She grew up to be an accomplished violinist, the first African-American member of the Pittsburgh Symphony Orchestra (Principal Keyboard), and the founder of *Symphonium* Newsletter.

Jennings was born July 16, 1941, in Pittsburgh, Pennsylvania, the only child of Helen Marie Sands and P. L. Prattis, whose home was filled with the warmth of a variety of sounds and aromas. Her father was editor of the *Pittsburgh Courier*, an avid reader, and a lover of concert music; her mother, an excellent cook and seamstress who made all Jenning's clothing, was also a trained pianist and a published poet.

At the age of six, Jennings began to study piano with Adele Rehard; she was such a natural pianist that a year later she had surpassed her mother. When she was eight, Jennings began violin lessons with then Pittsburgh Symphony Orchestra's (PSO)

violist, Kras Malno; during high school, she played piano for jazz and concert band under the baton of Carl McVicker, who also trained Billy Strayhorn and **Mary Lou Williams**; in 1955 and 1956, she played violin with PSO as a Pittsburgh Symphony Junior and in 1956 made her PSO debut as a pianist with Mozart's *Coronation Concerto*.

In the late 1950s and 1960s, Jennings spent her summers at the *Pittsburgh Courier*, doing everything except driving the trucks and running presses. These summers cultivated her love for the printed word and editing. Even though her love for books received stiff competition from bid whist, Jennings discovered that, "If I developed a love for reading I could conquer the world." She received undergraduate and graduate degrees in piano performance from Carnegie-Mellon University in Pittsburgh where she studied with Harry Franklin. Other teachers have included Sidney Foster, Americo Caramuta, and **Natalie Hinderas**.

In 1964, following a tour of Europe and the Middle East with PSO, Jennings became PSO's first African-American member. In those days the orchestra's season was quite short; Jennings supplemented her PSO salary by playing with Civic Light Opera and freelancing.

As the orchestral season grew, Jennings quickly emerged as a valuable member of the PSO, playing piano, organ, harpsichord, and celesta. In the 1970s, Jennings worked with PSO Music Director André Previn on a TV series called *Previn and the Pittsburgh*. The PBS series premiered with Jennings and Previn performing Mozart piano four-hands music. The Emmy-nominated series aired sixteen programs from 1977 to 1981.

The Jennings-Previn duo received many other accolades, leading to recordings on the

Philips label that included *Carnival of the Animals*. Soon, other engagements followed–with Benny Goodman at Avery Fisher Hall in New York, at the Concord and Chandler pavilions in California, festivals, and solo appearances nationwide. When the PSO toured the Far East in 1987, Jennings gave nine performances of Gershwin's *Concerto in F* to critical acclaim.

In 1988, Jennings attended the New York Philharmonic's Music Assistance Fund (MAF) Conference called "Toward Greater Participation of Black Americans in Symphony Orchestra." Meeting nearly 100 musicians, administrators, and educators who were considering the plight of African-American musicians was a turning point in Jennings's life.

She did not want to lose the contacts she made at MAF; in the fall of 1989, Jennings published the first issue of *Symphonium* Newsletter, providing information about African Americans in symphony orchestras. Jennings printed 250 copies of the first issue. Six years and seventeen issues later, *Symphonium*'s circulation had increased nearly four times.

In 1995 *Symphonium* was incorporated into *Collage*, a new, four-color magazine. *Collage* covers music, dance, visual arts, etc. The masthead presents it as "The National Journal of African Americans in the Arts." the staff includes publisher David Brown, Raoul Abdul, Dominique de Lerma, Rosalyn Story, and Jennings as editorial consultant.

In 1980, Jennings wrote *Gifts of Love*, a Christmas song, with lyricist Linda Marcus. Publisher Hal Leonard sold 17,000 copies the first year. *Gifts of Love* has been performed by Cleveland and Pittsburgh symphony orchestras and throughout the United States and Mexico.

Jennings is a compulsive letter writer. As early as 1973, Jennings began to compile her letters written to and from many people and organizations, including Arthur Fiedler, Larry King, Helen Gurly Brown, and Alex Trebek (Jennings is a *Jeopardy* TV show fan). She will publish these letters in a book to be titled *A Woman of Letters;* her account of the PSO's 1994 tour was published in a series called *Tour Diary* in the *Pittsburgh Post Gazette*.

Violinist Patricia Prattis Jennings was the first African-American member of the Pittsburgh Symphony Orchestra. In addition to her distinguished musical career, Jennings is an accomplished writer whose letters have been collected in a book, A Woman of Letters. (PATRICIA PRATTIS JENNINGS)

Jennings is a member of Sigma Alpha Iota, artistic director of the Manchester Craftsmen's Guild's Virtuoso Series, and a board member of the Pittsburgh Literary Council. She makes worldwide appearances and recordings with the PSO and as soloist. Jennings lives in Rosslyn Farms, Pennsylvania, with her second husband, Charles H. Johnson.

REGINA HARRIS BAIOCCHI

Jessye, Eva (1895–1992)

"Oh, I Can't Sit Down," the picnic song from *Porgy and Bess*, aptly characterizes the life of this black American musical phenomenon. For almost a century, Eva Jessye made a peerless contribution to the world of music, pushing herself and anyone associated with her at a relentlessly swift pace to achieve the perfection she demanded. A forceful woman, she was known to exclaim, "Time is fleeting! I have no time to waste or to spare!" and her achievements attest to that fact.

She was born Eva Alberta Jessye on January 20, 1895, in Coffeyville, Kansas, a small town bordering Oklahoma. Her father supported the family as a chicken picker. As a small child Eva sang and was an avid reader; she wrote her first poem at the age of seven and won a poetry contest when she was thirteen. By this time, her musical talents also had begun to surface—she organized a girls' quartet when she was twelve years old.

She studied choral music and music theory at the now defunct Western University in Quindaro, Kansas, graduating in 1914, and she received a degree from Langston University in Langston, Oklahoma.

Earning what was then a generous salary of $52.50 a month, Jessye taught elementa-

A monumental figure in black music, Eva Jessye was the first musical director of a motion picture starring black actors, Metro-Goldwyn-Mayer's Hallelujah, *written and directed by King Vidor. The Eva Jessye choir was the first to interpret the Virgil Thomson–Gertrude Stein opera* Four Saints in Three Acts *(1934), and was the official choir for the historic 1963 March on Washington.* (SCHOMBURG CENTER)

ry school in Taft, Oklahoma, and later was employed at schools in Haskell and Muskogee, Oklahoma, at Claflin College in Orangeburg, South Carolina, and at Morgan State College in Baltimore, Maryland, where she served as director of the music department. During that time, she also was on the staff of Baltimore's *Afro-American* newspaper.

In 1926, the young teacher decided to move to New York in search of musical and theatrical opportunities. Her first big break —at the Capitol Theatre playing with Major Bowles—was the occasion for her meeting and becoming the protégée of Will Marion Cook, an early black classical-jazz composer.

Eva Jessye immediately began to attract attention as a trail blazer. Her personality, her demeanor, and her talent declared to all: "I am a woman. I am a woman of African descent. I am a Black woman. And I am happy to be exactly as God made me." The music world was never the same.

An expert in harmonics, Jessye's literary and musical accomplishments spanned well over three quarters of a century. She was internationally renowned in the areas of poetry, musical composition, drama, and choral directing and was an acclaimed authority on American music and folklore; she also was an actress and an inspirational lecturer; in addition, she was known as the unofficial guardian of the *Porgy and Bess* score, having been appointed choral conductor by the composer, George Gershwin, and having officiated in that capacity since the premiere of the Gershwin-Heyward opera in 1935 and continuing through numerous productions around the world. Jessye contributed many authentic touches to the score, thereby deepening the cultural flavor of the African-American experience so miraculously discovered and translated by Gershwin. The choral pattern set in the original production by the Eva Jessye choir is still closely followed. At the thirtieth-anniversary celebration by the cast at the

Royal Alexandria Theatre in Toronto, Canada, then Vice President Hubert Humphrey wired Jessye to express his appreciation for her role in spreading Gershwin's great music around the country.

The artists Eva Jessye discovered, coached, and guided to success are legion. She was a pioneer in radio, writing and directing her own shows on major networks and also was the first musical director of a motion picture starring black actors, Metro-Goldwyn-Mayer's *Hallelujah*, written and directed by King Vidor. Finally, she and her choir were the first to interpret the 1934 Virgil Thomson–Gertrude Stein opera, *Four Saints in Three Acts*.

She was featured in 1944 in the first annual I Am an American Day initiated by Fiorello LaGuardia, the mayor of New York City. Jessye also wrote and directed the New York City theme song for Order of the Day, a postwar celebration sponsored by the Organization for American-Soviet Friendship held in 1944 at New York's Madison Square Garden and at the Watergate Hotel in Washington, D.C., with American and Soviet dignitaries participating. In 1963, she directed the official choir for the historic March on Washington, recordings of which were used by Tom Muboya in the struggle for independence in Kenya, and was cited by the cities of Detroit and Windsor, Canada, for her participation in their first annual freedom festival.

The Eva Jessye choir has performed in concert at major universities and colleges for more than forty years; in 1952, as the ensemble of the State Department-sponsored tour of *Porgy and Bess*, the choir was hailed by the Berlin press as ambassadors of good will.

In 1972, Jessye directed her original folk oratorio, "Paradise Lost and Regained," based on the epic poem by John Milton, at the Washington Cathedral, and it was hailed by the *Washington Post;* that same year, the Eva Jessye collection of Afro-American music was established at the University of Michigan. In May 1976, Jessye was awarded a Degree in Determination by the Department of Afro-American Studies at the University of Michigan, and she was cited by the International Women's Year for her contributions to the arts, women's progress, and peace. She was the recipient of numerous other awards from organizations and government agencies. In 1987, after receiving an honorary Doctor of Arts from Eastern Michigan University at the age of ninety-two, Jessye wrote in a letter, "You see I am still cuttin' cane and choppin' cotton—with might and main—with wide acclaim!"

Jessye was a constant, honored guest at conventions of the National Association of Negro Musicians in recent years at the special invitation of her good friend William Warfield, who is national president.

In 1990, she was selected as one of seventy-six black American women to be photographed in *I Dream a World: Portraits of Black Women Who Changed America;* her portrait also is featured for the month of January in the 1991 "I Dream a World" calendar.

Throughout her life, Eva Jessye shared her wisdom and her talents. Often to the amazement of many half her age, her resonant voice, the twinkle in her eye, the alertness of her mind, and the accuracy of her ear articulated the depth and breadth of her greatness. Professionally a very public person, Jessye never publicly dwelled on her personal life, although she outlived two husbands and had no children. She died on February 21, 1992.

FRANCES MARSH-ELLIS

K

King, Betty Jackson (1928–1994)

A typical weekend in the late 1940s found the Jackson family packing up the car for a short trip; it was not the average family vacation, but rather, a few days of concertizing. The members of the Jacksonian Trio were going out to display their musical talents as singers, keyboard artists, and composers. That is how Betty Jackson King cut her musical teeth.

She was born Betty Lou Jackson February 17, 1928, in Chicago. Betty Lou was the younger of two daughters born to Gertrude Jackson Taylor and the Rev. Frederick D. Jackson. While Mrs. Taylor taught Betty and Catherine piano, Rev. Jackson exposed them to classic literature, beginning with the Bible. The Jackson family lived in Vicksburg, Mississippi, and later on Chicago's south side, a mecca for African Americans after the Great Migration.

On Sunday mornings, the Jackson family worshiped at the People's Community Church and Center of Woodlawn. Rev. Jackson served as founding pastor; Mrs. Jackson was minister of music; Betty Lou and Catherine were known for their vocal and keyboard solos.

Often, worship services on the first Sunday of the month were followed by a quick dinner at the Jackson home. Then the family were off to round-robin concerts that involved most of the African-American churches on Chicago's southside.

These concerts typically consisted of choirs meeting at a designated church to show off their latest musical feats. This sometimes created an atmosphere for battles of the choirs, battles of the organists, and battles of the pianists—an exercise often referred to in jazz as "head-chopping." Other concerts consisted of genteel recitals that gave aspiring musicians a chance to debut.

King emerged early in life as an eager pianist-singer-composer. She was very passionate about her musical life. Though small in stature, she was a powerful keyboard artist who also showed a great command of choral conducting and singing. As a student at McCosh Grammar School and Englewood High School, she wrote music steadily.

Using an ensemble her mother founded, the Imperial Opera Company, King mounted full productions of her operas; soon, she expanded the range of genres in which she wrote to include piano/vocal, instrumental, choral, operatic, and other forms. She studied at Wilson Junior College and Roosevelt University in Illinois, receiving an B.Mus. from the latter in 1950 and an M.Mus. in 1952. She also studied at Peabody Conservatory in Maryland and Westminster Choir College in New Jersey. At about this time, she married vocalist Vincent King and had a daughter, Rochelle. In 1952, King's oratorio *Saul of Tarsus* was premiered by the Chicago Music Association. Among her other well-known compositions were the cantata *Simon of Cyrene*, the choral work *God's Trombones*, and arrangements of spirituals. By the 1960s, King enjoyed a national reputation. She received honors from the music industry, her religious congregation, and civic leaders nationwide.

One Sunday afternoon, as the southside faithful left a concert at the Congregational Church of Park Manor, a hit-and-run driver ended the life of King's sister, Catherine Jackson Adams. Though devastated by this tragedy, King responded by assuming Catherine's post as director of United Church of Christ's Chancel Choir, in addition to her own directorship at Park Manor.

King joined the National Association of Negro Musicians (NANM), serving as a national member and as a member of the local organization in Chicago, the Chicago Music Association. From 1979 to 1984, she served as president of the NANM, remaining active with NANM, the **NAACP**, and

Betty Jackson King cut her musical teeth as the youngest member of the Jackson Trio. She is pictured here on the right of her mother, Gertrude Jackson Taylor, and (far left) her older sister, Catherine Adams. Her compositions have included piano and vocal as well as instrumental and choral works. (REGINA BAIOCCHI)

American Women Composers for the rest of her life. She left her mark as an educator at the University of Chicago Laboratory School, Roosevelt University, Dillard University in Louisiana, and Wildwood High School in New Jersey, where she integrated the faculty.

In 1983 Roland Carter published *God Is God*, a collection of spirituals arranged by himself, Wendell Whalum, and King.

Plagued with kidney problems, King received dialysis treatments in Chicago and Wildwood, New Jersey, where she died on June 1, 1994.

King's legacy includes a rich catalogue of musical compositions, many spiritual arrangements, a history of building racial, sexual, and cultural bridges, and the publishing company, Jaxonian Press. At her death, Jaxonian Press was inherited by her niece, Arlene Sharp.

REGINA HARRIS BAIOCCHI

Kitt, Eartha (1928–)

From her initial stage appearances in the early 1950s to the recent and often ironic reflections on her life as America's black "sex kitt(en)," Eartha Kitt has maintained an awkward public stature, coupling ideals of black female liberation with lurid stereotypes of the mainstream sexual imagination. By simultaneously fulfilling and challenging the expectations of a male-centered popular culture, Kitt has negotiated a fine line between supplication and defiance, poignancy of insight and simple desires for public approval.

Born on January 26, 1928, in North, South Carolina, Kitt was raised in a foster family until 1936, when she moved to New York to live with her aunt. After attending Metropolitan High School (later the High School for the Performing Arts), she toured South America and Europe as a dancer and singer of "ethnic songs" with **Katherine Dunham** (1946–50). In Paris, she left the troupe in order to work in clubs and theater, notably on stage and on tour with Orson Welles. Returning to New York, Kitt appeared at the Village Vanguard—at the time, a popular folk venue—and with John Carradine in Leonard Sillman's Broadway show *New Faces of 1952* (film version, 1954).

These appearances vitalized her career as she quickly grew into a celebrated public figure. Articles, interviews, and reviews focused on her urbane sophistication, linguistic fluency, and haughty, aloof manner, all of which helped to shape a racially ambiguous image that stood at odds with the sambo stereotypes more commonly informing mainstream white perspectives. At the same time, gossipy references to her "feline seductiveness," alleged preference for white men, and contempt for her rural and racial past reinforced social hierarchies that placed male over female, urban over rural, white over black.

From the mid-1950s to the mid-1960s, Kitt worked regularly in nightclubs, cabarets, and hotels, both in the United States and abroad. Her appearances in film, on television (notably in the feline role of Catwoman on episodes of *Batman*, a television program from 1967), and on record—*The Bad Eartha* (1955), *Bad But Beautiful* (1961), *At the Plaza* (1965)—helped to reinforce her image as the sophisticated black seductress. Undermining both the sex kitten and uppity, color-struck themes, however, was her scandalous public appearance at a White House function hosted by Lady Bird

Johnson in 1968. Castigating a group of prominent women for their myopic views of American racial and social problems and an unjust Vietnam war, Kitt became the pariah of conservative politics as well as a hero of the antiwar and civil rights movements virtually overnight. For such acclaim, she would pay dearly, subjected to press ridicule, an alleged blacklisting, and investigations by both the CIA and FBI. Reviews of her activities after 1968 reveal, in fact, that Kitt worked principally overseas, although appearances in domestic clubs, film, and on television continued to a greater extent than has been commonly reported. Furthermore, while her 1972 performance in South Africa helped somewhat to restore her reputation in the American press—named in a *Life* essay, South Africa's "Honorary White"— her seemingly naive acceptance of white South African hospitality refueled skepticism about her sense of obligation to black Americans.

Aside from a brief return to Broadway in 1978, Kitt has worked mainly as a cabaret singer. Her Carnegie Hall appearance in 1985 represented a public revival of sorts, while her album *I Love Men* (1984) was popular in the gay disco community of the late 1980s.

As of 1993, Kitt lives on a 77-acre farm in Connecticut and spends some forty weeks a year on the road touring. Her career is managed by her daughter and namesake, Kitt, the product of her five-year marriage to Bill McDonald. She has published two autobiographies, *I'm Still Here* in 1989 and *Confessions of a Sex Kitten* in 1991. A five-compact disc retrospective of her work, entitled *Eartha Quake*, was released in 1993. She has one grandchild, Jason.

RONALD M. RADANO

Knight, Gladys (1944–)

Gladys Knight has been a singer for nearly a half-century. She wasn't always sure she could get where she wanted to go, but she hung in there.

Knight was born on May 28, 1944, in Atlanta, Georgia, to Merald Knight, Sr., and Elizabeth Woods Knight, singers in the Wings Over Jordan gospel group. She started to sing in her church choir at four and toured with the Morris Brown Choir from 1950 to 1953. In 1952, she won first place on the popular TV show *Ted Mack's Amateur Hour*, singing "Too Young," a song Nat King Cole had made famous. She often sang at church and social functions with her brother Merald, her sister Brenda, and her cousins Eleanor and William Guest; when they turned professional in 1957, another cousin, James "Pip" Wood, became their manager and gave his nickname to the group. Later, Eleanor and Brenda would leave to get married, and cousins Edward Patten and Langston George would replace them. George left the group in 1962, and from then on the Pips would remain a quartet.

There was nothing overnight about the Pips' success. In the early 1960s, several singles reached the Top 40, but number one was a long way away. Their live performances at Harlem's legendary Apollo impressed Motown producer Berry Gordy, and in 1965 he signed them to his subsidiary label Soul. Knight remembered the Apollo gigs fondly: "They were some of the first people to give us the opportunity. They were *fair* people. . . . They were as interested in your act as you were—sometimes more. And they would give people the encouragement they needed." The Pips had number-two hits with "I Heard It Through the Grapevine" in 1967 and "Neither One of Us

(Wants to Be the First to Say Goodbye)" in 1973 and then changed labels: Knight felt that Motown gave preferential treatment to Detroit-based acts and limited the Pips' potential for mainstream success by promoting them as an R&B group.

Recording for Buddah Records, the Pips finally topped the charts with "Midnight Train to Georgia" in October 1973. Awards and three more Top-10 singles followed, and in 1975 the group had its own TV variety show, but then things slowed down. Knight's film debut, *Pipe Dreams*, was a disappointment at the box office in 1976; still, the group kept working, and "Love Overboard" took them into the Top 20 again in 1988. Knight was still disturbed about the segregation of pop and R&B music on radio. "It's a need to keep black people, no matter what they do, in their place," she said. "I still have to go Top 10 R&B before I can cross over to pop. I resent that."

The Pips agreed to disband in 1991, but Knight had no intention of stepping out of the spotlight. Three years later, her album *Just for You* earned two Grammy nominations, and she had a recurring role on TV's *New York Undercover*. As spokesperson for Aunt Jemima pancake products, she drew criticism from some who believed she was perpetuating a stereotype of black women, comments she dismissed as "insulting." She doesn't worry about getting older. "The light came on when I turned forty, so I said, 'Shoot! If I'm learning all this and I know all that, wait till fifty comes, buddy!' Age ain't nothing but a number to me."

Gladys Knight began her career in her church choir at four. Her group, Gladys Knight and the Pips, which included her brother Merald, her sister Brenda, and her cousins Eleanor and William Guest, was named after their manager, James "Pip" Wood, another cousin. They were inducted into the Rock and Roll Hall of Fame in 1996.   (PRIVATE COLLECTION)

Gladys Knight and the Pips were inducted into the Rock and Roll Hall of Fame in a ceremony on January 17, 1996. Knight reminded the audience of some numbers: forty-three years with the Pips and nine different record companies.

INDIA COOPER

L

LaBelle, Patti (1944–)

Patti LaBelle is a Grammy-winning, bona-fide diva. Her voice is wide ranging, passionate, and, after more than thirty years in the business, showing no signs of becoming tame.

Patti LaBelle was born Patricia Louise Holte on May 24, 1944 (some sources list October 4), in Philadelphia, Pennsylvania. As a shy young girl, she first sang in front of the mirror and later in a choir at Beaulah Baptist Church in Philadelphia. In 1960, Patti and Cindy Birdsong (who joined the Supremes in 1967) were members of the Ordettes; a year later, the two were teamed with their friends Nona Hendryx and Sarah Dash as the BlueBelles; in 1962, the group became known as Patti LaBelle and the Blue-Belles.

The decade of the 1970s brought dramatic changes for the group. Under new management in 1970, it changed its name to LaBelle and burst on the scene provocatively dressed in leather, feathers, and glitter, singing disco anthems of progressive funk and rock. "Lady Marmalade," a widely played song, was a number-one hit for LaBelle in 1974. The group disbanded in 1977, however, as a result of artistic and personal differences.

Patti LaBelle, as a solo artist, continues to successfully record—winning her first Grammy in 1992—and perform before enthusiastic full houses. She also is an accomplished actress, having appeared in film (*A Soldier's Story*, *Beverly Hills Cop*), on Broadway (*Your Arms Too Short to Box with God*), and on television (most recently as Dwayne Wayne's mother on *A Different World*). She also has had her own television special and starred in the television series *Out All Night* (NBC).

In 1969, she married Armstead Edwards, who manages her career. They have three sons, Zuri, their natural child, and Stanley and Dodd, who are adopted.

In 1994 she opened a nightclub, Chez LaBelle, in Philadelphia. She performed a selection of her biggest hits at President Clinton's forty-eighth birthday (a $5,000 a plate celebration), before singing a rock/jazz/gospel-based version of "Happy Birthday."

LaBelle is well known for her support of numerous charitable and social organizations, including Big Sisters and the United Negro College Fund, as well as urban renewal projects and programs for the homeless in her native Philadelphia.

LAWRENCE J. SIMPSON

Lee, Julia (1902–1958)

Julia Lee, jazz pianist, vocalist, and composer for nearly three decades, was one of the most popular musicians in Kansas City, Missouri. Born there on October 31, 1902, she began to play the piano at age ten and as a teenager joined the George E. Lee Orchestra, her older brother's popular band. Lee worked with her brother from 1920 to

1934, when she struck out on her own as a result of her aversion to airplane travel.

Julia Lee recorded "Waco Blues" and "Just Wait til I'm Gone" in Chicago for the Okeh label in June 1923, becoming the first Kansas City jazz musician to record; however, because the records were not released, she is often not credited with that distinction. Lee reached the peak of her popularity between 1946 and 1949, selling nearly one million records; her first major recording, "Snatch and Grab It" (Capitol Records), sold more than 500,000 copies. During this period she toured the country and, in 1949, played at the White House during the term of fellow Missourian, President Harry S Truman. In 1957, she appeared in the Robert Altman film *The Delinquents*, performing "A Porter's Love Song."

Julia Lee had a distinctive and powerful singing style. She is best known for performing songs with suggestive lyrics, often using *double entendre*, for example, "King Size Papa" and "My Man Stands Out." Nonetheless, she was a fine and accomplished musician.

In 1919, Lee married Frank Duncan, catcher and manager of the Kansas City Monarchs of the Negro Baseball League. Their nine-year union resulted in the birth of one son, Frank Duncan, Jr.

Julia Lee, known as the Empress of Kansas City, of whom it was said that she liked her whiskey—and her men—straight, died of a heart attack in her Kansas City apartment on December 8, 1958.

LAWRENCE J. SIMPSON

Lightner, Gwendolyn (19??–)

Born in Brookport, Illinois, Gwendolyn Rosetta Capps Lightner (gospel pianist, arranger, and choir director) displayed talent for playing piano at an early age. "When I was small, we didn't have a piano. So I would make music on everything I saw—my father's razor stand, behind the stove, my mother's sewing machine, whatever. I would get there and imagine it was a piano and I would play and make music with my mouth." Little did she know that these early childhood experiences would serve as the foundation for a career that would include world concert tours and television appearances as pianist for the legendary gospel singer **Mahalia Jackson**.

Lightner is the daughter of Mace and Florence Capps; in personal interviews, she has declined to give her birthdate. She is married to Peter Lightner and is the mother of six children (Deborah, Ricke, Donna, Copelia, Raphael, and Barron). While two children (Ricke and Copelia) have begun to establish professional careers in music, the others are pursuing careers in the medical field, business, politics, and civil service.

As a youngster, Lightner studied Western art and music, church hymnody, and spirituals; after completing high school, she attended Southern Illinois University in Carbondale, Illinois, and Lyon and Healy Music School in Chicago. The move to Chicago during the early 1940s introduced her to gospel music through contacts with gospel giants in the city (e.g., Kenneth Morris, **Sallie Martin**, Mahalia Jackson, and **Roberta Martin**), and Lightner's membership with the Chicago gospel group the Emma L. Jackson Singers gave her the opportunity to travel to Los Angeles where she has remained since 1946.

Lightner's gospel music career blossomed after her move to the West Coast. Initially, she managed and taught music at a studio

(Los Angeles Gospel Music Mart) in the city; during the late 1940s, she was credited with introducing a new style of playing gospel music on the piano when she became the first pianist for the highly acclaimed Echoes of Eden Choir at Saint Paul Baptist Church (1947–49), a group that revolutionized the Los Angeles gospel music community. After leaving Saint Paul, she worked as choir director and pianist at Grace Memorial Church of God in Christ as well as Mount Moriah Baptist Church. Since 1956, she has been the minister of music at Bethany Baptist Church.

Among the Los Angeles-based groups with whom Lightner has been affiliated are the Rose of Sharon (1946–47), a female gospel trio; the J. Earle Hines Goodwill Singers (1947–49); the J. Earle Hines Goodwill Community Choir (1950s); and the Sallie Martin Singers (1952–53). Between 1957 and 1974, she and Thurston G. Frazier organized and served as codirectors of the Voices of Hope, a community choir initially established to raise funds for the March of Dimes; it later became well known on the West Coast as a result of numerous concert appearances and recordings on Capitol Records. During the 1950s, Lightner played piano on several gospel recordings by the Pilgrim Travelers, the Soul Stirrers, and Brother Joe May for Specialty Records; she recorded with **Doris Akers** on RCA Records in the 1960s. Nationally, she is probably known best for her work as pianist for the legendary gospel singer Mahalia Jackson (1968–72), including several world concert tours and many television appearances.

At present, Lightner instructs at Victory Baptist Day School and holds several offices within the Baptist church, including director of music for the Western Baptist State Convention and Congress of Christian Educa-

Gwendolyn Lightner is probably best known for her work from 1968 to 1972 as pianist for Mahalia Jackson, but her career has also included work with the Echoes of Eden Choir, the Rose of Sharon, and the Sallie Martin Singers and recordings with Doris Akers, the Pilgrim Travelers, and Brother Joe May. (J. C. DJEDJE)

tion and pianist for the National Baptist Convention, USA, and National Congress of Christian Education.

JACQUELINE COGDELL DJEDJE

Lincoln, Abbey (1930–)

Abbey Lincoln/Aminata Moseka is a uniquely talented vocalist, actress, and songwriter, as well as a student of African music. Scholar and night-life sophisticate, Aminata Moseka creates thoughtful cultural mirrors and shapes that are very reminiscent of the creative and explorative work of two other multidisciplined innovators,

Zora Neale Hurston and **Katherine Dunham**.

Born Gaby Lee in Chicago in 1930, Lincoln, who began her career during the 1950s, is often likened to **Billie Holiday** and **Betty Carter**, because her engaging dramatic

Vocalist, actor, and songwriter Abbey Lincoln has been compared to Billie Holiday and Betty Carter for her dramatic and innovative jazz song stylings. (SCHOMBURG CENTER)

interpretations goad, seduce, and inform; however, her voice is distinctively her own. Skilled and practiced control affords her a wide range of expression: Playful, sultry, angry, and despairing qualities all live in Lincoln's deep voice and share access to that instrument's clarity.

The 1965 film *Nothing But a Man* starred Lincoln, Ivan Dixon, and Gloria Foster, and she costarred with Sidney Poitier in the 1968 film *For Love of Ivy.*

Teamed for thirty years with a formidable array of forceful jazz instrumentalists, Abbey Lincoln works to create a space beyond the role of "singer with the band" to become a true collaborator. In the 1960 landmark recording *We Insist! Freedom Now,* with master drummer/composer Max Roach, she was at once a strong member of the ensemble sound, an innovative soloist, and the narrative center of the presentation.

People in Me, Talking to the Sun, The World Is Falling Down, and *You Gotta Pay the Band* are examples of Lincoln's strengths as a leader and songwriter.

WILLIAM LOWE

Liston, Melba   (1926–   )

"It's like Jackie Robinson," Melba Liston once said in an interview comparing the impossible standards set for female jazz instrumentalists to those set for African-American athletes. "You've got so much to prove before you get a chance. It shouldn't be like that. You go in there just like anybody else, and if you can't make it, then you get put out. But don't keep you out until you become a Charlie Parker or something. That's not fair!"

In spite of the unfair conditions and pressures she has faced in the male-dominated field of jazz, Melba Liston has become a pioneer female jazz trombonist of distinction and one of the greatest inspirations to female jazz writer/arrangers and brass players. Noted for eliciting a warm, robust tone from her instrument and putting together sensitive, personal, and often difficult arrangements, Liston has performed, composed, or arranged for Gerald Wilson, Dizzy Gillespie, Duke Ellington, Count Basie, Quincy Jones, Johnny Griffin, Clark Terry, Freddie Hubbard, Randy Weston, **Dinah Washington**, Gloria Lynne, Charlie Mingus, **Sarah Vaughan**, **Aretha Franklin**, Art Blakey, J. J. Johnson, Budd Johnson, Tony Bennett, and Jon Lucien, among others. She also has arranged symphonic music for Clark Terry and the Buffalo Symphony Orchestra, Randy Weston and the Boston Pops, and the Brooklyn Philharmonic.

Melba Doretta Liston was born in Kansas City, Missouri, on January 13, 1926, to Lucile and Frank Liston. Her father was a lawyer and a musician who played string instruments, and she grew up hearing Duke Ellington, Count Basie, Cab Calloway, and the swing music of the day. One of Liston's chief early influences was Ellington trombonist Lawrence Brown, and her mother bought Liston her first trombone when she was seven. Liston went on to excel at the trombone, an instrument that traditionally was considered unacceptable for women because it came out of the male brass band/marching band tradition.

Self-taught at first, Liston began to pick out church songs, such as "Deep River" and "Rocked in the Cradle of the Deep," as well as folk tunes. In 1937, her family moved to Los Angeles, where she joined a youth band that was sponsored by the parks and recreation department and that began to study

with Alma Hightower, who had been a friend of Bert Williams. Hightower taught the band comedy and straightman routines, to dance and sing, and to recite poetry by Paul Laurence Dunbar. The group played on street corners, at YMCA dances, and at supermarket openings. Even then, however, the taboo on women's involvement with the business side of music was evident: "The boys would steal all the money," Melba said in an interview, "'cause the girls weren't allowed to pass the hats."

The late 1930s and early 1940s were a time, she recalled, when "blacks didn't look forward to a musical career—especially a female! A female white didn't even look forward to it too tough. And I wasn't like Paul Robeson. . . . I wasn't one of those fighters. . . . The music that I gravitated to was what was available to me, what I was listening to at the little parties and dances and records, that seemed to be a possibility."

At sixteen, Melba joined the musicians union and got a job in the pit band in the Lincoln Theatre, playing for such acts as Dusty Fletcher and Pigmeat Markham. The theater closed, and in 1943 the members of the band joined the band of arranger/composer Gerald Wilson. Liston stayed with Wilson from 1943 to 1948, when the unit disbanded; she wrote and copied music for him while he taught her, he once said in an interview, "things that weren't in books."

Although highly respected by many musicians, Liston has said that she was a reluctant soloist, preferring pencil and paper and the chance to concentrate on her writing, making "the lines individually beautiful . . . all the parts sort of free and special—melodic," sometimes breaking up sections in order to blend one saxophone with the trumpets and one with the trombones. Undoubtedly, however, the conditions under which women jazz musicians had to labor also played some part in shaping this preference. "I was scared of the guys, too," Liston admitted in an interview. "They get so jealous of a girl. Once or twice, I had been threatened on the band from some of the older musicians, I mean, because I was a little old girl, I suppose. I would play my solo, and I would get an encore, and people would applaud, and then the older dude would go up there, and maybe he didn't get as much response, and once or twice I was threatened and had to run off the bandstand. So I really wasn't very aggressive about this solo business." It is widely agreed among musicians that Liston has never received the credit she deserves, and composer Hale Smith speculated in an interview that one reason for this was that "she could write most of the guys under the table without trying, and I'm talking about some of the best out there."

In 1947, while still with the Wilson band, Liston was persuaded to take some solos when she recorded with saxophonist Dexter Gordon in his Dial session. Later, in 1948 and 1949, she accompanied **Billie Holiday** on a Southern tour, as assistant director and arranger for Wilson's big band. In an interview she recalled that, as the band traveled deeper and deeper south, the audiences got smaller and smaller. "We sat in the bus for days in Charleston, South Carolina," she said, "and then came home." By the early 1950s, tired of the sexism of the music business and with her family encouraging her to leave the world of jazz, Liston got a job with the board of education in Los Angeles and stayed there for four years. She also married during this time, but in a business where steady work usually means long stretches of time on the road touring, riding buses, and doing one-nighters, she experienced the difficult struggle of work versus family life. It is not surprising, then, that Liston has been married three times. "Trying to do those kinds of ordinary things," she admitted in an interview, "didn't work too well."

Also during the 1950s, Liston appeared in the movies *The Prodigal* (1955) with Lana Turner and *The Ten Commandments* (1956); then Dizzy Gillespie asked her to join his band for two U.S. State Department Tours, one to the Middle East in 1956, the other to South America in 1957. On tour she arranged standards, ballads, and vocal backgrounds, work that fell to her, according to Liston, because she was a woman; she was not offered more dramatic kinds of pieces, she recalled, just the "mushy business." Nonetheless, her outstanding arrangements from this period include Claude Debussy's "My Reverie," "Stella by Starlight," and "Annie's Dance."

After the tours, Liston led her own allwoman unit for several months, and then in 1959 she joined a European tour of the Harold Arlen folk opera *Free and Easy* with Quincy Jones as music director. The group barnstormed through Europe for eleven months after the tour unexpectedly closed early. After returning to the United States in the early 1960s, she did arrangements for Johnny Griffin's album *White Gardenia*, a tribute to Billie Holiday, as well as for Riverside, Motown, and Bluenote records, for such artists as Ray Charles, **Dakota Staton**, Milt Jackson, Kim Weston, and Billy Eckstine. She also began a long and continuing association with pianist/composer Randy Weston. Liston has done arrangements for

A trombonist whose talent allowed her to crack that male-dominated musical province, Melba Liston has performed, composed, or arranged for a veritable Who's Who in American music, ranging from Duke Ellington and Count Basie to Aretha Franklin and the Boston Pops. (SCHOMBURG CENTER)

his albums *Little Niles, Blues to Africa, High Life, Uhuru Africa, Tanja, Open House at the Fivespot with Coleman Hawkins and Kenny Durham,* and most recently, *The Spirits of Our Ancestors* (1992), which features guest appearances by Dizzy Gillespie and Pharaoh Sanders. Liston also did the charts for his work, "Three African Queens," performed by Weston and the Boston Pops.

In the early 1970s, Liston visited Jamaica and was invited back in 1973 to start the African-American Division of the Jamaica School of Music. In 1978, she returned to the United States to play at the Kansas City Women's Jazz Festival, and in 1979 she moved back to New York City, where she led her own group, Melba Liston and Company.

In the mid-1980s, Liston suffered a stroke, which necessitated a lengthy convalescence. Later, in 1989, she moved back to Los Angeles, where, in 1990, she resumed writing. Liston wrote some arrangements for a 1991 New York City tribute to Dexter Gordon, and her first major undertaking was arranging the charts for the Randy Weston African Rhythms Orchestra concert "Blues to Africa," which, on September 13, 1991, inaugurated the first season of Jazz at Lincoln Center.

Like many women in jazz, Liston's multiple talents have enabled her to survive. When there was no work playing, her writing saved her, and when there was no work writing, out came her horn again. "The horn has always saved me from any sadness," she has said. "Anytime I need a lift, the trombone takes care of me. I'm not so good to it as it is to me. The trombone set me up for an arranger, and then when I'm writing I forget the trombone. But when things get dull, I go back to the trombone and it saves me again."

Passing the music and its history and traditions along to future generations has always been important to Liston, who has taught at Jazzmobile in New York City and the Pratt Institute Youth-In-Action Orchestra in Brooklyn. She also has been honored by several musical organizations. She received the Universal Jazz Coalition, Inc.

Award for Outstanding Contributions to Jazz at the fifth Annual Women's Jazz Festival on June 20, 1982; the Annual Black Musicians Conference Distinguished Achievement Award on April 23, 1984; a Triple Talent award, as arranger/composer/musician, at Freddie Jetts Pied Piper in 1971; and, in 1977, the Conductor/Christian Achievement Award for Outstanding Service. She also was a recipient of a certificate of award as an honored participant in the Philadelphia High School Gospel Choir Festival of 1976, and she was honored as a participant at the Jamaica Jazz Festival in 1975. In 1988, she was honored in the exhibition "Black Visions '88—Lady Legends in Jazz" in New York City.

SALLY PLACKSIN

Lucas, Marie (c. 1880–1947)

Marie Lucas, the celebrated conductor and society orchestra leader, was born to make music. Her father, Sam Lucas, was a renowned minstrel; her mother, Carrie Melvin, was equally talented, playing both the violin and cornet. When Marie started her young life in the 1880s in Denver, Colorado, Carrie and Sam Lucas began her musical training, laying a foundation that would serve their daughter well for the rest of her life.

After Lucas had exhausted their considerable knowledge, she furthered her musical education at schools in Nottingham, England, and at the Boston Conservatory.

Although she first performed publicly in 1883, at a concert with her father, Lucas made her professional debut in the musical show *The Red Moon*, written and produced by Robert Cole, J. Rosamond Johnson, and James Weldon Johnson, in 1909.

In 1915, Lucas began to garner rave reviews as the leader of the Ladies Orchestra at Harlem's Lafayette Theatre; she played piano and trombone and also served as an arranger. In 1916, the Quality Amusement Corporation, which managed several black theaters in the East, appointed Marie Lucas as its musical director.

Eager to pass along her knowledge, Lucas trained other young women for female theater orchestras in Philadelphia, Baltimore, Boston, and Washington, D.C. These orchestras performed admirably under her direction from 1915 to 1920. She also trained all-male theater bands, recruiting talent from as far away as Cuba.

As a credit to her vast talent, Duke Ellington, in his book *Music Is My Mistress* noted how impressed he was with one of her groups at the Howard Theatre "because all the musicians doubled on different instruments, something that was extraordinary in those days."

Following World War I, Lucas led a male dance band for a long stint at the Howard Theatre in Washington, D.C. In the 1930s, Lucas and Her Merry Makers, an all-male band, toured widely with great success.

Listed as a "composer and arranger" in *The Official Theatrical World of Colored Artists The World Over*, Marie Lucas shared the musical knowledge entrusted to her by her parents, thereby enabling hundreds of women and men to perform proudly in orchestras across the United States.

Marie Lucas died in New York City in 1947. Her legacy did not.

RICHARD E. T. WADE

M

Mabrey, Marsha (1949–)

Marsha Eve Mabrey is one of the foremost African-American orchestra conductors in the country. Her goal in life is to introduce people from all backgrounds and all walks of life to music in a way that makes them want to listen and encourages them to become performers themselves.

Mabrey was born in Pittsburgh on November 7, 1949, the oldest of three children, to Theodore Roosevelt and Ella Jones Mabrey. Her father was an aerospace engineer, and her mother was a medical secretary. Mabrey grew up in Niagara Falls, New York, and Ann Arbor, Michigan. She earned undergraduate (1971) and graduate (1972) degrees in instrumental music education from the University of Michigan at Ann Arbor; like her mentor there, Elizabeth A. H. Green, she played violin and viola. In 1976, she received a DMA in orchestral conducting from the University of Cincinnati; her doctoral thesis was *A History of Women Orchestral Conductors from 1800 to 1978.*

From 1972 to 1978, Mabrey taught in elementary schools in Ann Arbor and Denver. Between 1978 and 1989, she was the orchestra conductor and a faculty member at Winona State University in Minnesota, Grand Valley State University in Michigan, and the University of Oregon, and from 1989 to 1991 served as assistant dean at the University of Oregon School of Music.

Mabrey then joined the Detroit Symphony Orchestra as vice president for educational affairs. Among her other responsibilities in that position, she designed and managed the UNISYS African-American Composers Forum and Symposium, bringing together composers, performers, conductors, orchestral administrators, and

Marsha Mabrey is one of the foremost African-American orchestra conductors in the United States. (MARSHA MABREY)

the public for three days of panel discussions, chamber concerts, and performances of new music by African-American composers.

Since 1979, Mabrey has conducted nearly fifty orchestras, including the Oregon Symphony, the Savannah Symphony, the Women's Philharmonic in San Francisco, the Grand Rapids Symphony Orchestra, and the Sinfonietta Frankfurt. Mabrey was also music director and resident conductor for the Emerald Chamber Orchestra in Eugene, Oregon. She has a special interest in developing young musicians and has conducted many university and youth orchestras nationwide, including Interlochen in Michigan and Encore in Pennsylvania.

Mabrey has been a consultant for a variety of educational and performance programs. This work has taken her to the San Jose Symphony, the New World Symphony, and Duke University's and St. Augustine College's "William Grant Still Going On Project." In 1994 and 1995, Mabrey served as interim director of education with the Philadelphia Symphony Orchestra, where she coordinated concerts for students and children, competitions, open rehearsals, and other educational activities.

Marsha Mabrey is an inspiring role model for young musicians, not only because she is successful but also because she loves music and the work of making it.

REGINA HARRIS BAIOCCHI

Martin, Roberta Evelyn (1907–1969)

American composers of art music in the Western European tradition who studied with Nadia Boulanger take pride in having studied with the most important teacher of composition in the twentieth century. Gospel singers who sang with Roberta Martin are accorded a special position, for while **Mahalia Jackson** is considered the "Greatest Gospel singer of all time" and Thomas Andrew Dorsey is called the "Father of Gospel Music," Martin "created and left a dynasty of gospel singers and a portfolio of unduplicated gospel music." Equally significant is the fact that Martin was able to accomplish what few other composers have: the effective combination of emotion, style, and form.

Gospel singer, pianist, composer, and publisher Roberta Evelyn Martin was one of six children born to William and Anna Winston in Helena, Arkansas. She took piano lessons from her oldest brother's wife at the age of six and played for the local Sunday school. When she was eight, the family moved to Cairo, Illinois, and then to Chicago when she was ten; Roberta graduated from Wendell Phillips High School in Chicago, where she studied piano with the choral director, Mildred Bryant Jones. While preparing for a career as a concert pianist, she accepted her first church position as pianist for the Young People's Choir at Ebenezer Baptist Church.

Martin initially was not attracted to the new gospel music being sung in Sanctified churches. In 1932, when Thomas Dorsey and Theodore R. Frye organized one of the first gospel choirs at Chicago's Pilgrim Baptist Church, Martin was recruited as pianist; however, in 1933, after she heard the Bertha Wise Singers of Georgia, she adopted the Wise gospel piano style and, with the help of Frye, organized a group of male singers, first called the Martin-Frye Singers. The members were Willie Webb, Robert Anderson, Eugene Smith, and Narsalus McKissick. In 1935 she severed her relationship with Frye and renamed the group the

Roberta Martin Singers. In the 1940s, she added female singers Delois Barrett Campbell and Bessie Folk and refined the "Roberta Martin gospel style."

Her style is marked more by the potential of gospel than by its tradition, because she cultivated the well-modulated voice as opposed to the encumbered, raspy tone so often associated with gospel; she eschewed the low bass voice, instead creating a vocal harmony of soprano, alto, tenor, and high baritone; she favored the aggressive rather than passive lead, supported by background voices that more often hum a response than repeat the lyrics of the lead, thereby placing more emphasis on the lyrics and the leader; and she created a gospel piano style marked more by nuance and refinement than virtuosity and flamboyance. Her piano style was wholly adopted by her piano student and stepdaughter Lucy Smith Collier, the granddaughter of the legendary Chicago preacher Reverend Lucy Smith.

In 1939, Martin opened her publishing firm, the Roberta Martin Studio of Music, and one of her first successes came in 1941 with the publication of "He Knows How Much We Can Bear" by Phyllis Hall. She composed her first gospel song, "Try Jesus, He Satisfies," in 1943; before her death she had composed more than 100 songs under her own name and that of Fay Brown. Among her best-known compositions, in addition to "Try Jesus," are "God Is Still on the Throne" (1959), "No Other Help I Know" (1961), "Let It Be" (1959), and "Teach Me Lord" (1963). Less concerned with publishing her own compositions than those of other composers, her firm published compositions by James Cleveland, Alex Bradford, Lucy Matthews, Sammy Lewis, Kenneth Woods, and Dorothy Norwood.

Her most famous publication was her theme song, "Only a Look" by Anna Shepherd.

Martin began to record in the late 1930s, and during her career earned six gold records for selling a million copies of a song or an album. She received gold records for the songs "Only a Look" and "Old Ship of Zion" on the Apollo label and "Grace," "God Specializes," "God Is Still on the Throne," and "I'm So Grateful" on the Savoy label. Adamant that her name never appear on a marquee, she refused engagements at New York's Apollo Theatre and Las Vegas night clubs, but the Roberta Martin Singers appeared in almost every other gospel venue. From the huge tents of New York's Reverend A. A. Childs to the small churches of Cocoa, Florida, to the elegant auditoriums of Los Angeles to the domed cathedrals of Italy, where they were invited in 1963 to perform at the Spoleto Festival by its creator, Gian Carlo Menotti, the Roberta Martin Singers carried their gospel message throughout the world for over thirty-five years. Other singers associated with the group include Archie Dennis, Sadie Durrah, Gloria Griffin, Myrtle Jackson, Romance Watson, Louise McCord, Myrtle Scott, Delores Taliaferro (**Della Reese**), and James Lawrence. Roberta Martin was honored by a colloquium and concert at the Smithsonian Institution in 1982.

HORACE CLARENCE BOYER

Martin, Sallie (1895–1988)

Gospel singer and composer Sallie Martin is acknowledged as "the mother of gospel music" because of her ground-breaking work as a promoter and publisher. Born in Pittfield, Georgia, she eventually moved to Baltimore, Maryland, where she met and

Sallie Martin, known as "the mother of gospel music," helped to popularize that style as a promoter and publisher. She formed the first all-female gospel group and influenced many artists, including Dinah Washington. (MARY WILKES)

lished numerous choirs and created "the gospel highway circuit," a loosely formed network of churches and other performance venues that welcomed gospel music at a time when it was not always embraced by elite black congregations.

Martin, who had only a seventh-grade education, served as Dorsey's song demonstrator, promoter, and bookkeeper, and she is credited with encouraging him to copyright and publish his music. The pair cofounded the National Convention of Gospel Choirs and Choruses in 1933, the first such convention for gospel performers. Later, she joined with composer Kenneth Morris to found the Martin and Morris Publishing Company, which issued such classics as "Just a Closer Walk with Thee" and "Dig a Little Deeper." She is also credited with forming the first all-female gospel group, the Sallie Martin Singers. Among the many artists she influenced was blues great **Dinah Washington**, who performed with Martin as a teenager. Once, in assessing her life, Sallie Martin said, "I've never been the greatest . . . never claimed to be the greatest, yet and still I've been everywhere the greatest have been."

DEBORAH SMITH BARNEY

married Wallace Martin. The Martins, including one son, finally settled in Chicago, where, in 1932, Sallie Martin began her involvement in gospel music, winning a spot singing with a group headed by Thomas A. Dorsey, "the father of gospel music." With Dorsey, and later with singer/composer **Roberta Martin** (no relation), Sallie Martin helped popularize gospel music during its "golden age," 1945 to 1960. They estab-

Martin-Moore, Cora (1927–)

Cora Juanita Brewer Martin-Moore (gospel singer, choir director, composer, and publisher) was born November 4, 1927, in Chicago, Illinois, the oldest child of Lucious Bruer and Anne Claude James Bruer. When Martin-Moore was just a youngster, she was adopted by pioneer gospel singer **Sallie Martin** and is married to Henry A. Moore.

Martin-Moore began her musical career in Chicago as a member of Mount Pleasant

Baptist Church. Later, as a featured contralto soloist, she traveled extensively throughout the United States and made several recordings with her mother's group, the Sallie Martin Singers. Since moving to Los Angeles in 1947, she has been associated with Saint Paul Baptist Church, one of the first churches on the West Coast to promote and make recordings of gospel music (Capitol Records, 1947). She has served as a member of Saint Paul's legendary Echoes of Eden Choir (1947–58), director of the John L. Branham Crusaders Youth Choir (1952–58), and minister of music and director of the Echoes of Eden Choir (1958–present). In 1959, the latter group performed with Nat "King" Cole in the Hollywood Bowl.

Martin-Moore's formal educational training was obtained from several schools in the Los Angeles area: University of California, Los Angeles Extension; Los Angeles Southwest College (A.A. degree); and California State University, Dominguez Hills (B.A. degree). She has owned and managed a religious music studio and record shop (Los Angeles Gospel Music Mart) and served as an instructor at Crenshaw-Dorsey Community Adult School for over thirteen years.

Not only was Martin-Moore featured as a religious disc jockey for two years on her own gospel radio program, but she also has composed, arranged, and published a number of gospel songs, spirituals, and anthems, among them "Heaven Sweet Heaven" (1953), "Do You Know the Lord Jesus for Yourself?" (1955), "What a Wonderful Savior I've Found" (1957), and "He Is a Friend of Mine" (1965). Her song "He'll Wash You Whiter Than Snow" (1954) was featured in a Universal motion picture produced by Quincy Jones (*The Lost Man*,

1969) starring Sidney Poitier. During the 1970s she began to tour and perform as a solo artist, which led to two recordings with Savoy Records: *James Cleveland Presents Cora Martin* and *I Found God*. In 1974, she was awarded best soloist album by James Cleveland's Gospel Music Workshop of America (GMWA), and since 1987 she has been a member of the board of directors of GMWA. Also, she has received many tributes and proclamations from the city of Los Angeles.

Since arriving on the West Coast in the 1940s, Martin-Moore has become a nationally recognized gospel performer in her own

Cora Martin-Moore is among the second generation of gospel pioneers who serve as role models for today's young musicians. As such, she continues a tradition established by her adoptive mother Sallie Martin. (J.C. DJEDJE)

right. Along with others (e.g., James Cleveland, Albertina Walker, Delois Barrett Campbell) who had their early gospel music training in Chicago (a city now regarded as the birthplace and center for gospel music), she is among the second generation of gospel-music pioneers who serve as role models for today's young musicians, continuing a tradition established by her mother, Sallie Martin.

JACQUELINE COGDELL DJEDJE

Marvelettes, The

They were a girl group from the sixties, and they delivered the first number one hit for the starmakers at Motown. But they never quite got the attention and respect they deserved.

The Marvelettes came from Inkster, Michigan, a little town near Detroit. Inkster High School sponsored a talent contest in which the winners got to audition at Motown Records. (Motown was still struggling in those days, looking frantically for talent.)

Gladys Horton decided it would be fun to enter a girl group, so she gathered up five friends and they practiced some songs. They called themselves the Casinyets, which was short for "can't sing yet." They must have been able to sing a little because, although they didn't win first prize, they were allowed to audition anyway.

At their audition, the future Marvelettes sang a few songs that imitated current hits. Motown owner, Berry Gordy, told them to come back with some original material.

A member of the group, Georgia Dobbins, knew a song writer, so they looked over a few of his songs. She liked the title to a blues number called, "Please Mr. Postman," rewrote the tune and the lyrics to give

Though the Marvelettes never became a household word, this talented trio, consisting of Gladys Horton, Wanda Young, and Katherine Anderson, had several major hits, including "Please Mr. Postman" and "I'll Keep Holding On." (PRIVATE COLLECTION)

it a young, pop feel, taught the song to the other singers, and then dropped out of the group to care for her sick mother. The other girls went on to make it a hit in 1961.

The next year, they had more hits with "Playboy" and "Beachwood 4-5789." Then a few recordings didn't work out, and the pressures of touring and stardom began to take its toll on the singers. By 1965, the group was down to a trio—Gladys Horton, Wanda Young, and Katherine Anderson.

In that same year, the group came back with some rhythm-and-blues hits, including

"I'll Keep Holding On," and "Too Many Fish in the Sea," but their musical peak came in 1966 when they recorded the album "Sophisticated Soul" under the guidance of Smokey Robinson. It contained several popular hits and was considered one of the finest albums released by Motown in that period.

But the Marvelettes never entirely fulfilled their promise as a group. When they arrived at Motown, Gordy had already spent years grooming another girl group, the Supremes; while the Supremes had yet to produce a hit, Gordy was convinced that they would some day, and he lavished time and attention on them to the detriment of other Motown artists. Although the Marvelettes were given diamond rings and other flashy perks in their heyday, their feeling remained that the company never really took them seriously.

Another difficulty was that the Marvelettes, at heart, were country girls. They had little of the sophistication that characterized the Supremes. When the Marvelettes started, they didn't know how to dress or put on makeup; at Motown they never seemed to live down that image and gain the full respect they deserved.

Yet, the Marvelettes have endured. Not only did they once turn out hit after hit, their style continues to be in demand on the "oldies but goodies" circuit. Even now there are clone Marvelettes, belting out the songs that made the group so famous.

ANDRA MEDEA

Maynor, Dorothy (1910–1996)

Dorothy Maynor not only had a long and successful career as a concert singer, but she also established a school to ensure that other aspiring African Americans would have the opportunity to become artists as well.

Born Dorothy Leigh Mainor in Norfolk, Virginia, on September 3, 1910, Dorothy Maynor began vocal study at Hampton Institute at the age of fourteen in her native state and completed her formal education (B.S., 1933). Originally majoring in home economics, she attracted the attention of R. Nathaniel Dett, who enrolled her in the institute's choral ensemble and to whose music she remained dedicated.

Following additional vocal study at the Westminster Choir College, she was encouraged in her career by Serge Koussevitsky in 1939, who heard her at the Berkshire Music Festival, and she presented her recital debut that November at Town Hall. Her singing

Concert vocalist Dorothy Maynor performed throughout the world, but was never allowed to appear with a major opera company, because of her race. (SCHOMBERG CENTER)

In 1963, Dorothy Maynor gave up her performing career and started the Harlem School of the Arts, a school that offered classes in music, ballet, modern dance, drama, and art to poor children for minimal fees. At her death in 1996, the school had more than 1,000 students. (SCHOMBURG CENTER)

was characterized by a lyric legato with which she particularly endowed her French repertoire.

Her career included concerts and recitals throughout the Western hemisphere, Europe, and Australia, as well as broadcasts and telecasts. The repertoire included lieder, spirituals, sacred works of Bach and Handel, and opera arias (particularly "Depuis le jour" from Charpentier's *Louise*), but she never appeared on the opera stage.

Retired from concert life in 1963, she realized a long-standing dream by founding the Harlem School of the Arts, serving as its director until 1979. The school offered classes in music, ballet, modern dance, drama, and art to poor children for minimal fees, sometimes as little as 50 cents a lesson, and loaned or rented instruments to students who did not own one.

"In most schools, if you don't have a piano, you can't take lessons," Maynor told one interviewer. "But we say, 'Good, you come here and practice.'" In 1977 she raised more that $2 million to build a new facility for the school, which originally served twenty children and had grown to more than a thousand by 1996.

In 1975, she was appointed to the board of directors of the Metropolitan Opera. Honorary doctorates were bestowed on her by Bennett College, **Howard University**, **Oberlin College**, Carnegie-Mellon University, and Duquesne University.

Dorothy Maynor died February 19, 1996 in West Chester, Pennsylvania.

DOMINIQUE-RENÉ de LERMA

McLin, Lena (1928–)

Composer, conductor, and educator Lena Johnson McLin was born in Atlanta, Georgia, on September 5, 1928. As a young woman she moved to Chicago, where, for approximately nine years, she lived with her uncle, Thomas A. Dorsey, the father of gospel music.

She graduated from Booker T. Washington High School in Atlanta, and later received a B.A. from **Spelman College** in Atlanta and a master's degree from the American Conservatory of Music in Chicago; she completed additional graduate study at Chicago State University and Roosevelt University, both in Chicago, and received an honorary doctor of humanities degree from Virginia Union University in Richmond.

McLin taught for thirty-six consecutive years in the public high schools of Chicago, where she earned superior ratings annually at local music festivals. At Kenwood Academy, she created a conservatory-like environment with a curriculum for music majors,

an unusual achievement for a high school that is not focused on the performing arts.

McLin has served as a consultant for twenty years at forty-eight major universities, including Westminster Choir College in New Jersey, where she served for ten consecutive years. When she retired in 1991, many prominent former students attended the celebration, including opera stars Nicole Heaston and Mark Rucker and jazz singer Kim English. Her son, Nathaniel McLin, is a composer and critic of art and music, and her daughter, Beverly Leathers, is a composer and surgical assistant. In addition to composing music, McLin serves as a consultant and is a pastor at the Holy Vessel Baptist Church in Chicago.

Almost 100 of her more than 2,000 works have been published by Neil Kjos in San Diego, California. These works include art songs, cantatas, anthems, piano pieces, orchestral works, and arranged spirituals, as well as *Free at Last*, a cantata written in tribute to Martin Luther King, Jr., and *Pulse: A History of Music*.

SANDRA CANNON SCOTT

McRae, Carmen (1922–1994)

Carmen McRae was that rarest of jazz singers, as comfortable with modern pop songs and Tin Pan Alley tunes as she was with the tongue-twisting music of composer Thelonious Monk. Born and raised in New York, the crucible of modern jazz creativity, McRae studied piano extensively as a child, a talent she nurtured, often nudging aside her regular pianist during a set or concert.

Early on McRae came under the spell of the great **Billie Holiday**: To say that Billie Holiday was her greatest influence is to understate the case; McRae's albums, as well as a portion of nearly every nightclub set or concert she gave were devoted to the memory of Lady Day. McRae herself often summed it up by exclaiming, "'Lady' has always been my mentor."

Although Holiday's influence remains strong, make no mistake about it; Carmen McRae is one of the singular vocal talents in the history of jazz song. Her straightforward, no-frills approach to a vocal line and her tender touch with ballads are unmistakable McRae characteristics, and her often brusque, sassy manner, as well as her salty retorts to misbehaving audiences, are some of her most enduring qualities.

McRae's professional career began in 1944 with a stint as what was then called a girl singer with the Benny Carter Orchestra; thereafter, she worked with the big bands of Count Basie and later Mercer Ellington, the Duke's son. She became thoroughly immersed in the burgeoning bebop craze as an intermission singer and pianist at New York clubs, particularly those in Harlem. One of those clubs, Minton's Playhouse, is credited with having provided a nightly laboratory for such mid-to-late-1940s jazz explorers and alchemists as Charlie Parker, Dizzy Gillespie, Thelonious Monk, and drummer Kenny Clarke (to whom McRae was later

A singer whose name is mentioned in the same breath with Billie Holiday and Sarah Vaughan, Carmen McRae was comfortable with a wide range of musical styles, though she was best known for her jazz vocals. She is seen here with talk show host Dick Cavett. (SCHOMBURG CENTER)

married for a short time). These clubs were not merely places to work; it was here that McRae absorbed the coming sounds of be-bop and where she came under the influence of the great **Sarah Vaughan.**

"Sassy [as Vaughan was known] was a phenomenon," McRae said. "She took the art of improvisation and did it better than anybody. Plus, Sarah was blessed with the best voice *ever*. I, like many others, have always considered the human voice to be another instrument, and no one proved that better than Sarah. What great happiness she gave."

Accolades and recognition began to come McRae's way as early as 1954, when she was named "best new female singer" by *Down Beat* magazine following the release of her first recording as a lead singer. After that time, she recorded dozens of albums, ranging from ballad interpretations to lending her personalized touch and breathing new life into seemingly mundane pop material to her much-acclaimed 1990 recording of Thelonious Monk material.

Carmen McRae always enjoyed a particularly strong following in the Pacific Rim, most notably in northern California. She scored many of her triumphs at the famed Monterey Jazz Festival and at the 1962 festival worked opposite Louis Armstrong, performing an adaptation of Dave Brubeck's musical, *The Real Ambassadors*. A particular favorite in Japan, McRae traveled to the Far East on many occasions.

One of the hallmarks of McRae's art was her impeccable enunciation of a lyric. Ralph J. Gleason, San Francisco-based critic and longtime McRae admirer, stated it very eloquently when he said, "Carmen McRae sings the lyrics of a song like Sir Laurence Olivier delivering a Shakespearean speech.

She gives lessons in elocution. There are songs which take on multiple additional meanings by the manner in which Carmen McRae delivers the lines. You can hear a song for years and then hear Carmen sing it and all of a sudden the lyrics become a story, they literally come to life." A singer's singer in every sense of that overused cliché, Carmen McRae was a true original.

She died at her home in Beverly Hills, California, on November 10, 1944, after suffering a stroke.

WILLARD JENKINS

Mercer, Mabel (1900–1984)

"Mabel Mercer is a person of true maturity, of profound perception, of a lovingness seldom encountered and the guardian of the tenuous dreams created by the writers of songs." Thus composer Alec Wilder, many of whose songs were introduced by Mabel Mercer, described the singer, whose regal bearing, crisp diction, and attention to lyric interpretation made her the toast of café society and a major influence on such singers as Frank Sinatra, Nat "King" Cole, Peggy Lee, Johnny Mathis, Barbara Cook, Bobby Short, and **Leontyne Price**. Legend has it that **Billie Holiday** was nearly fired from a job because she spent so much time at the club across the street where Mercer was performing.

Born in Burton-on-Trent, Staffordshire, England, in 1900, Mabel Mercer was the daughter of an American jazz musician and a British variety actress. She attended a convent school in Manchester until age fourteen and then left school to go on tour with members of her family. After World War I, Mercer worked on the Continent as both a dancer and singer.

In 1924, she met Bricktop, who was herself an entertainer at that time. After Bricktop opened her famous Paris nightclub on the rue Pigalle in 1930, Mercer joined Bricktop and Louis Cole as an entertainer there, performing in ensemble and solo numbers. Her appearances at Bricktop's throughout most of the 1930s made Mercer a star and enabled her to develop her distinctive style and approach to a song. She characteristically performed seated, as if on a throne, wearing a dark dress, with her hands folded in her lap.

Mercer first appeared in the United States in 1938 at the New York City club Ruban Bleu in a successful engagement that lasted several weeks; she then traveled to the Bahamas for an appearance there. With the outbreak of World War II, she was unable to attain an entry permit to return to the United States until 1941.

Back in the States, Mercer returned to the Ruban Bleu for six months and then became a regular at Tony's, a club on West 52nd Street, from 1942 until 1949, when the building Tony's was in was torn down. Other engagements followed, notably at the Byline Room from 1949 to 1957 and later at Downstairs at the Upstairs, the St. Regis Room of the St. Regis Hotel, and the Café Carlyle.

In addition to her club appearances, Mercer appeared in 1972 in a PBS television special, *An Evening with Mabel Mercer & Bobby Short & Friends*. In 1977, she appeared at Carnegie Hall and then in London, where she also starred in a five-part BBC television series, *Miss Mercer in Mayfair*. After a three-year absence from performing, she appeared in 1982 at the Kool Jazz Festival in a program of songs by Alec Wilder. Her final public appearance was in November 1983 at a benefit for the SLE Foundation, which combats lupus. A video of her mid-1970s performances, *Mabel Mercer: A Singer's Singer*, was released in 1986.

Among the songs she introduced or saved from unjustified obscurity were "The End of a Love Affair" (by Edward Carolan "Bud" Redding), "While We're Young" (cowritten by Wilder), "Fly Me to the Moon" (by Bart Howard), "Remind Me" (by Jerome Kern and Dorothy Fields), "By Myself" (by Arthur Dietz and Howard Schwartz), and "Little Boy Blue" (by Richard Rodgers and Lorenz Hart); the last-named song was recorded by Frank Sinatra, **Lena Horne**, and Margaret Whiting after they heard Mercer's rendition of it.

She died April 20, 1984, in Pittsfield, Massachusetts, of respiratory arrest. A brief marriage to Kelsey Pharr, a jazz musician, had ended in divorce; she left no survivors.

BARBARA BERGERON

Molton, Flora (1908–1988)

Flora Molton was born in Louisa County, Virginia, in 1908. Partially blind at birth and plagued by impaired vision for all of her life, she grew up in a religious and musical family. Her father was a Baptist preacher in a local congregation, where her mother played the organ; he played the accordion, which was the first instrument that Flora mastered as a child. While in her teens, Flora Molton learned to play the guitar; she also joined the Holiness Church and there commenced her own career as a preacher.

In the late 1930s, she moved to Washington, D.C., where she continued to preach occasionally. During World War II, she began to perform her own unique brand of "holy blues" on the streets of the nation's

A founding member of the Society of Black Composers, Dorothy Rudd Moore says that the main influences on her music have been J. S. Bach and Duke Ellington. (SCHOMBURG CENTER)

streets, and appear at folk festivals with her bands. She also recorded an album and was the subject of a short documentary film. Flora Molton died at her home in Washington, D.C., in 1988.

WILLIAM BARLOW

Moore, Dorothy Rudd (1940–)

She is a poet, composer, singer, lecturer, and teacher, but ask her what she enjoys most, and Dorothy Rudd Moore will say that she thinks of herself primarily as a composer. However, although she is partial to her opera, *Frederick Douglass*, she insists that all of her compositions are her favorites because she thinks of them as her children.

Born on June 4, 1940, Dorothy Rudd spent her childhood in New Castle, Delaware, where the strong influence of her mother, a singer, seemed naturally to guide her toward a musical career. In 1963, she earned a B.M. in theory and composition from **Howard University**, having studied composition under Mark Fax, received a Lucy Moten Scholarship, and was accepted in the summer studies program at Fontainebleau where she studied under Nadia Boulanger. She later settled in New York City and studied composition with Chou Wen-chung and voice with Lola Hayes.

Moore has taught at the Harlem School of the Arts, New York University, and Bronx Community College, and she was a founding member of the Society of Black Composers. In 1975, she made her Carnegie Hall debut. She is married to Kermit Moore, a cellist and conductor.

As a composer, Moore leaves nothing to chance, working to achieve structure and logic. Although she bases her choice of style

capital to supplement her meager income. Her guitar style combined finger-picking techniques from her native Piedmont region with the Mississippi Delta slide technique. By the postwar era, she was also writing her own songs.

Molton teamed up with Ed Morris, a local guitarist, in the early 1960s. He was instrumental in getting her bookings in folk-music venues and organizing her initial backup bands. During this period, she wrote her best known songs, especially "The Train Song" and the tribute "Louis Armstrong." Throughout the next two decades, she continued to compose songs, play solo in the on the intent of a particular piece, the primary influences on her music have been J. S. Bach and Duke Ellington—Bach because of his structure and Ellington for both structure and inventiveness. Her works include a song cycle among other vocal music, a symphony, chamber music, and "Dream and Variations" for piano.

MELLASENAH MORRIS

Moore, Undine Smith   (1905–1989)

Undine Smith Moore, born on August 25, 1905, in Jarratt, Virginia, was a composer and educator. She earned bachelor of arts and bachelor of music degrees from Nashville's Fisk University, where she studied piano and organ with Alice M. Grass; Moore later studied at the Juilliard School of Music in New York City and the Eastman School of Music in Rochester, New York. She also received a master of arts degree and a professional diploma from Columbia University Teachers College.

Beginning her teaching career in the public schools in Goldsboro, North Carolina, Moore also taught at Virginia State College in Petersburg, Virginia, from 1927 until her retirement in 1972. She cofounded and codirected the Black Music Center at Virginia State College from 1969 to 1972.

Moore served as a visiting professor at Virginia Union University in Richmond, Virginia; Carleton College in Northfield, Minnesota; and **Howard**, Fisk, and Indiana universities. With Altona Trent-Johns, Moore founded the Black Man in American Music program at Virginia State College. She also has lectured extensively.

Her sixteen-part choral work "Scenes From the Life of a Martyr," written in honor of Dr. Martin Luther King, Jr., was premiered by the Richmond Symphony Orchestra and was performed three times in New York by the Voices of Saintpaulia, with a 120-voice choir, orchestra and soloists.

Moore died on February 6, 1989, in Petersburg, Virginia.

SANDRA CANNON SCOTT

N

Nickerson, Camille Lucie (1887–1982)

Music educator Camille Lucie Nickerson received her training in music at Oberlin Conservatory. During her notable career with her own school of music and later as part of the **Howard University** faculty, she composed and arranged a number of songs that are still sung by soloists and choral groups. Foremost among these are her Creole songs, often performed by the Robert Perry Singers in New Orleans.

Nickerson was also president of the National Association of Negro Musicians from 1935 until 1937. Her biographical entry is in the *Education* volume of this encyclopedia.

Norman, Jessye (1945–)

Overnight sensations are rare in opera, considering the time required for the voice to be trained and mature, the obligations for serious study of historical traditions and legacies, the commitment to comprehensive understandings of musical structures, the necessary mastery (not only of diction) of French, German, and Italian, and required stage experience as both recitalist and actor.

Jessye Norman, born September 15, 1945, in Augusta, Georgia, is one of those exceptions. Her vocal talents were discovered while she was still in high school, and she became a contestant in the **Marian Anderson** competitions at age sixteen. Although she did not win, she stopped on the trip to audition at Howard University for Carolyn Grant, who unconditionally accepted her for study. Grant did not immediately realize that the young soprano did not yet have her high school diploma, but this matter was promptly addressed. Her undergraduate studies culminated with the B.Mus. degree in 1967, after which she moved to Baltimore's Peabody Conservatory to study with former **Howard University** faculty member Alice Duschak. Thereafter she entered the graduate program at the University of Michigan, where her teachers were Elizabeth Mannion and Pierre Bernac.

While those degree plans were in progress, Norman secured a travel grant that allowed her to enter the 1968 International Music Competition in Munich. With performances of "Dido's Lament" (Purcell) and "Voi lo sapete" from Mascagni's *Cavalleria Rusticana*, she won first place and was immediately engaged for her operatic debut as Elisabeth in *Tannhäuser* by the Deutsche Oper (1969), later performing in *Aida, Don Carlo, L'Africaine,* and *Le Nozze di Figaro.* She first appeared at Milan's Teatro alla Scala in 1972 as Aida and, at London's Covent Garden, as Cassandre in *Les Troyens* (Berlioz), with New York and London recital debuts the next year. She was first seen on the American stage November 22, 1982, as both Jocasta in *Oedipus Rex* (Stravinsky) and Dido in *Dido and Aeneas* (Purcell) with the Opera Company of Philadelphia. Her Metropolitan Opera debut took place on September 26, 1983, returning to the role of Cassandre in Berlioz's *Les Troyens*, subsequently offering New Yorkers her interpretation of Didon in the same opera, as well as the Prima Donna and Ariadne in *Ariadne auf Naxos* (Richard Strauss). She was simultaneously active as recitalist, guest orchestral soloist, director of master classes, and recording artist, rapidly securing international respect as a musician of the highest rank.

Norman has made numerous recordings, including Beethoven's *Fidelio*; Berlioz's *Mort de Cléopatre*; Bizet's *Carmen*; Gluck's *Alceste*; Mahler's *Das Lied von der Erde*; Offenbach's *Tales of Hoffmann*; Purcell's *Dido and Aeneas*; Schoenberg's *Gurrelie-der*; Strauss' *Four Last Songs* and *Ariadne auf Naxos*; Verdi's *Aida*; Wagner's *Lohengrin* and *Die Walküre*; and Weber's *Euryanthe*. Other recordings include *Spirituals*, *Spirituals in Concert* (with **Kathleen Battle**), and *Jessye Norman at Notre-Dame*.

Hers is a voice that can range from a dark and lusty mezzo-soprano (Carmen, as an example) to a dramatic soprano that more than satisfies the highest ᵗ expectation of the Wagnerite. A person of commanding bearing, among her many strengths are an uncommon ability for emotional communication, a concern for repertoire beyond the traditionally expected, and an ability to bring new significance even into more popular repertoires.

DOMINIQUE-RENÉ de LERMA

O

Odetta (1930–)

Odetta sings folk songs and plays a guitar she calls "her baby" in a career that has spanned four decades. She has performed internationally, appeared in numerous films and plays, and lectured throughout the United States. Odetta has been said to be "authentic"; she is an artist who captured the soul of the folk revival movement and who has been embraced by the feminist community.

Odetta Holmes Felious Gordon was born on December 31, 1930, in Birmingham, Alabama. Odetta grew up in a southern Baptist music tradition that focused on the spiritual. Odetta and her family moved to Los Angeles, California, when she was six, and she began singing lessons at the age of thirteen. Odetta's father exposed her to big band and country music, and she also enjoyed listening to the Metropolitan Opera broadcasts on the radio.

Odetta was introduced to folk music while she was in the chorus of a production of *Finian's Rainbow* in Los Angeles. She traveled to San Francisco with a friend and emerged on the folk-music scene in San Francisco in 1953. Music critics have compared her to **Bessie Smith**. Odetta has said that her artistic progenitors are Paul Robeson for his political conviction and **Marian Anderson** for her character. Dignity, love of self, and political commitment permeate Odetta's songs and words.

Odetta has toured in Europe with two other vocal artists, Nina Simone and Miriam Makeba. She says that she is an "ancestor worshiper": She gives praise to and honors the ancestors who have taught her the importance of positive energy in vanquishing the negative forces that keep the struggle from advancing.

In 1974, she appeared in the made-for-television film *The Autobiography of Miss Jane Pittman*, which starred **Cicely Tyson**.

Since the 1950s, America's folk-music world has been enhanced by the proud presence of the magnificent Odetta. (SCHOMBURG CENTER)

199

In 1986, she marked forty years of performing with a concert that was released in 1987 as a live recording—*Movin' It On.*

NOMALONGA DALILI

Okoye, Nkeiru (1972–)

Before she turned twenty, Nkeiru Ndidikanma Okoye had written award-winning music and a directory of African-American women composers. Oberlin Conservatory Library used Okoye's resource guide as an acquisitions shopping list.

Her name, *Nkeiru* (in-KIR-oo), means "the future is more important than the past," *Ndidikanma* (in-DEE-dee-kahn-ma) means "patience is a virtue," and *Okoye* (oh-KOY-ya) means "born on market day." Okoye was born July 18, 1972 in New York, the younger of two daughters, to Emmanuelle and René Okoye. Her mother is an occupational therapist; her father, a member of the Igbo tribe of Nigeria, is an electrical engineer. Okoye was raised in Massapequa, New York, but spent her summers in the city of Enugu, Nigeria.

Okoye grew up viewing life from both sides of the Atlantic Ocean. When she was eight years old, she was a panelist on the Nigerian TV show "Junior Opinion," where she and other panelists gave advice to young telephone callers.

Okoye attended South Shore Christian Elementary School. Her high school days were spent at Amityville Memorial, Boces Cultural Center, and Manhattan School of Music, prep division. During high school, Okoye studied piano with Cecilia Brauer of the Metropolitan Opera Orchestra.

When she was thirteen, Okoye's first composition, *Phase II*, for piano and flute (written for herself and her sister) won first place in the NAACP's Afro-Academic Cultural, Technological, and Scientific Olympics (ACTSO). Okoye credits Everett Collins who encouraged her to participate in the ACTSO Competition, as her earliest mentor. Okoye was awarded a full scholarship to pursue a bachelor of music degree (1993) from Oberlin Conservatory of Music (Ohio), where she studied composition with Elizabeth Hinkle-Turner and piano with **Francis Walker.**

The summer of 1991 was a turning point in Okoye's life. Through a mutual friend, she met composer Noel DaCosta, who made her feel that the music she wanted to write was important. DaCosta introduced Okoye to a whole new world of African and African-American composers, including Howard Swanson, Hale Smith, and Wendell Logan.

When Okoye discovered a void in publications about African-American women, she wrote proposals to various foundations and received a grant from the Ford-Mellon Foundation in 1991 to write *Finding Aid for the Works of Black Women Composers,* a reference guide that helps readers identify and locate past and present composers. Information provided includes works lists, biographies, discographies, and organizational affiliations. Okoye's database lists hundreds of works by African and African-American women composers written in the 1800s and 1900s.

Okoye received a second grant from the Ford-Mellon Foundation in 1992 to obtain scores and recordings of works she had located and identified in her *Finding Aid.* Using Okoye's research, Oberlin Conservatory's library increased their holdings of works by black women. In 1995, Okoye received a master of arts in composition from Rutgers University, where she studied privately with Noel DaCosta.

From 1987 to 1995, Okoye wrote many award-winning compositions, including *Zeena* (1987, solo piano), *Freedom Celebration* (1988, dancer, voice, flute, percussion, piano), *The Graduate* (1989, for chamber orchestra, as realized on the Kawai K-1), and *The Heart of a Woman* (1995, soprano, oboe, two violins, bass, and piano).

In addition to four NAACP awards, Okoye's work has garnered recognition from the Long Island Composers' Alliance, the Midwest Composers' Symposium, and Ronald McDonald's Children's Charities. In 1995 the Rutgers University Orchestra premiered Okoye's *The Genesis*. Her ballet *Reign*, commissioned by Melanie Winstead in 1994, received its premiere from the Judah Dance Ensemble at the Abundant Life Family Worship Center in New Brunswick, New Jersey.

Okoye is currently in Los Angeles attending UCLA and pursuing a lifelong dream of writing film scores.

REGINA HARRIS BAIOCCHI

P

Perry, Julia Amanda (1924–1979)

A prolific composer and conductor extraordinaire, Julia A. Perry was born in Lexington, Kentucky, on March 25, 1924. She studied composition, conducting, piano, and voice at the Westminster Choir School in New Jersey, earning a master of music degree in 1948. Further study was done at the Juilliard School of Music in New York City and the Berkshire Music Center in Lenox, Massachusetts.

Perry's studies also took her to the Accademia Chigiana in Siena, Italy, where she studied with Emanuel Balaban, Aleco Galliera (conducting), Nadia Boulanger, Henry Switten, and Luigi Dallapiccola (composition). Her compositions include symphonic works, operas, and chamber music. *The Cask of Amontillado*, an opera, was finished at Columbia University on November 20, 1954.

In 1957, under the auspices of the United States Information Service, Perry conducted a series of European concerts, primarily performing her own works. She once referred to conducting as her "most rewarding performing medium." She also lectured extensively throughout Europe and America.

Perry's honors include two Guggenheim fellowships, an award from the National Institute of Arts and Letters, and a Boulanger Grand Prix. Her neoclassical style featured dissonant harmonies, contrapuntal textures, and intense lyricism. She also used black folk idioms in her *Soul Symphony*, which she composed in 1972.

Julia Perry died on April 29, 1979, in Akron, Ohio.

SANDRA CANNON SCOTT

Pierce, Billie Goodson (1907–1974)

Billie Goodson Pierce (a.k.a. Willie Madison Goodson) was born in Marianna, Florida, in 1907 and raised in Pensacola. She came from a musical family; her six sisters were all pianists. At ten, Billie temporarily worked as **Bessie Smith**'s accompanist; later in her career, she also accompanied blues great **Ida Cox**.

Drawn to the music of bands that traveled in and around the South, Billie decided to leave home at fifteen to play blues and ragtime jazz. For nearly ten years, she worked throughout the South in various bands, starting with the Mighty Wiggle Carnival Show, with her sister Edna, as a pianist, and then with Mack's Merrymakers, the Nighthawks Orchestra, the Joe Jesse Orchestra, the Douglas Orchestra, and Slim Hunter's Orchestra.

Her first job in New Orleans was as a substitute for her sister Sadie Goodson with Buddy Petit's Band on a steamliner—*The Madison*. She worked with Alphonse Picou in 1930 and then performed with Punch Miller and Billy, and Mary Mack's Merry Makers.

She had her own band in the mid-1930s with George Lewis (clarinet) and De De Pierce (trumpet). She married Pierce in 1935, and they gained international recognition. As the result of several recordings

The Pointer Sisters—Ruth, Anita, Bonnie and June—began to sing together in the 1960s and became known for their flamboyant '40s style and brilliant scat singing. (PRIVATE COLLECTION)

and tours, they became established successes in New Orleans and enjoyed fame throughout the 1960s.

Billie Pierce died on September 29, 1974, in New Orleans, shortly after her husband's death.

PAULETTE WALKER

Pointer Sisters, The

They can sing anything. Versatile, flamboyant, and consummate professionals, the Pointer Sisters have won acclaim for classic jazz, scat singing, rhythm-and-blues, and even country-and-western music. As singers, songwriters, and producers, they possess the talent and control to keep their group at the top of the charts and still change to meet their growing talents.

Ruth, Anita, Bonnie, and June Pointer were born between 1946 and 1954 in Oakland, California. Their parents were ministers, and the young girls had their first musical training in their father's church choir.

The singing group started in the late 1960s with sisters Bonnie and June; Anita joined soon after. Their first out-of-town engagement left them stranded in Houston when their prospective bookings fell through; a producer in California bailed them out and then found them work as backup singers for a number of popular singers and rock groups. Sister Ruth joined in 1972: "They seemed to be having a good time," she said later, "and I sure wasn't. I was a key punch operator at the time."

The Pointer Sisters did a lot of cabaret work in gay clubs in California, where they developed a forties, vampish style to match their fun, flamboyant jazz. They were witty, tough, and seductive, dressed in boas, and sang fast, brilliant, scat songs with razor-sharp harmonies.

Their first two singles were not successful, but in 1973 they broke through with "Yes We Can Can." Their debut album, *The Pointer Sisters*, went gold and made the top-twenty list. *Live at the (San Francisco) Opera House,* released the following year, earned them another gold album, with the hit single "That's A Plenty"; the same year they won a Grammy award in the country category with "Fairy Tale," written by Anita and Bonnie. In 1975, another hit—the driving number "How Long (Betcha Got a Chick on the Side)"—was later picked up by rap musicians.

By this time, however, the sisters began to feel the limits of the forties style, and becoming weary of constant touring, felt the need for a change.

In 1978, Bonnie left for a solo career at Motown, and the group temporarily disbanded. Bonnie's venture didn't work out very well, although she recorded one top-twenty hit. Meanwhile, the other sisters re-formed into a trio and became more successful than ever. Their album *Energy* went gold in 1979, followed by hits with "He's so Shy" (1980) and "Slow Hand" (1981). 1984 brought their biggest success, their album *Break Out,* which sold three million copies and contained four top-ten singles, including "Automatic," "Neutron Dance," and "I'm So Excited." Another single, "Jump (For My Love)," won a Grammy.

The Pointer Sisters are consummate professionals in everything they do—singing, songwriting, arranging, performing. They made it to the top with forties caricatures and shrugged off that image when they wanted to grow a new one. From their early club days, the Pointer Sisters have known how to cause a sensation.

ANDRA MEDEA

Price, Florence Smith (1888–1953)

Florence Smith Price was among the first black women composers to earn widespread recognition. Her award-winning compositions have been performed by major orchestras and renowned solo artists: The North Arkansas Symphony Orchestra, the Detroit Symphony, and pianists Althea Waites and Selma Epstein have given performances of her music.

Born on April 9, 1888, in Little Rock, Arkansas, she studied piano with her mother, Florence Smith, a concert pianist and accomplished soprano. A published composer while still in high school, Smith graduated in 1906 from the New England Conservatory of Music, where she studied piano, organ, and composition; her teachers included George Chadwick and Frederick Converse. She also studied at the Chicago Musical College, the American Conserva-

Among the first black women composers to earn widespread recognition, Florence Smith Price heard her Symphony in E Minor *performed by the Chicago Symphony Orchestra at the 1933 Chicago World's Fair.* (MOORLAND-SPINGARN)

tory of Music, and the Chicago Teachers College and she taught at Shorter College in Little Rock and at Clark College in Atlanta.

In 1912, Smith married Thomas Price, a lawyer in Little Rock, and devoted her time to composition and teaching in her private studio. She had two daughters, Florence and Edith, and a son who died during infancy. Price moved to Chicago in 1927 and remained there until her death in 1953.

Price won Holstein awards in 1925 and 1927. Her *Symphony in E Minor* won the Wanamaker Prize in 1932 and was premiered by the Chicago Symphony Orchestra at the 1933 Chicago World's Fair. Influenced by the more traditional melodic and

rhythmic characteristics of black music, her works are considered neoromantic and nationalistic. She wrote symphonies, concerti, sonatas, chamber music, choral music, and various pieces for organ, piano, and voice.

MELLASENAH MORRIS

Price, Leontyne (1927–)

"La diva di tutte le dive" (opera's foremost goddess) and "La prima donna assoluta" (the absolute first lady)—these are among the evaluations critics have made of soprano Mary Violet Leontyne Price, a native of Laurel, Mississippi, where she was born on February 10, 1927.

Her family life centered around the church, where both parents were active. She began piano lessons when only four and joined her mother in the church choir not many years later. In 1936, she attended a recital in Jackson, Mississippi, by **Marian Anderson**, and she firmly decided she would be a musician. At that time, the only role for a black woman in music other than performing was teaching, and with that major she attended Central State College in Ohio.

Before her graduation in 1949, she was encouraged to apply for admission to New York's Juilliard School of Music as a voice major. She was admitted, although she had learned no foreign languages and her only contact with opera had been the Saturday afternoon broadcasts from the Metropolitan Opera. Her student colleagues remember how cordially, but resolutely, she passed them in the hall, scores in her arms, on the way to the practice rooms to prepare for her lessons with Florence Kimball and to study for her classes.

She was cast in the role of Mistress Ford in a school production of Verdi's *Falstaff* and attracted the attention of the composer Virgil Thomson, who was seeking new singers for the 1952 revival of his *Four Saints in Three Acts*, an opera calling for an all-black cast. He engaged Price for the role of Cecilia, which she performed in New York and at the Paris International Arts Festival. In turn, this won her the role of Bess in Gershwin's *Porgy and Bess*, in which she toured to Berlin, Paris, Vienna, and Moscow in 1954. That November, she made her New York debut at Town Hall. The next February found her on national television, in the title role of Puccini's *Tosca*, later in Mozart's *Die*

"La diva di tutte le dive" (opera's foremost goddess) and "La prima donna assoluta" (the absolute first lady)—these are among the critics' descriptions of Leontyne Price. (MOORLAND-SPINGARN)

Zauberflöte and finally in *Don Giovanni*, and in Poulenc's *Dialogues des Carmélites*.

The San Francisco Opera engaged her as Madame Lidoine when they staged the Poulenc opera in 1957 and continued to call on her talents for *Il Trovatore* and *Madama Butterfly*. A European career was critical to the profession, and she appeared that year at the Arena di Verona, Covent Garden, and the Vienna Staatsoper. Her Chicago debut with the Lyric Opera was as Liù in Puccini's *Turandot* (1959).

Beginning in 1955, the Metropolitan Opera's roster listed black singers: Marian Anderson and Robert McFerrin (1955), **Mattiwilda Dobbs** (1956), Gloria Davy (1958), and **Martina Arroyo** (1959). In April of 1953, Price had, in fact, performed "Summertime" from *Porgy and Bess* in a broadcast gala to raise funds for the company, but her formal debut came with Verdi's *Il Trovatore* (January 27, 1961) when, in the role of Leonora, she won forty-two minutes of cheers from the audience. There was no doubt that she would open the Metropolitan Opera's next season (as Puccini's Minnie in *La Fanciulla del West*); and the next year, she opened again by repeating her 1957 Vienna role as Aida. During the final seasons that the Metropolitan remained in its old quarters, she was celebrated for her artistry in the Italian repertoires of Puccini's *Turandot* (Liù) and *Madama Butterfly* (Cio-Cio-San), and as Elvira in Verdi's *Ernani*, a role that entered her repertoire in the 1962 Salzburg Festival when she had been selected to sing it by conductor Herbert von Karajan.

When the Metropolitan Opera moved to Lincoln Center in 1966, she inaugurated the new hall in Samuel Barber's *Antony and Cleopatra*, which the composer had written specifically for her. Her international operatic career continued to set new vocal standards until January 3, 1985, when, as Aida at the Metropolitan Opera, she concluded an almost unprecedented one-third of a century on the stage.

She had demonstrated her interpretive leadership in the Italian repertoires of Verdi and Puccini and expanded the previously practiced limits to excel in German, Spanish, French, and Slavic works, as well as spirituals and other American music. Her principal opera roles, in addition to those mentioned, were the Prima Donna and Ariadne (*Ariadne auf Naxos*), Amelia (*Un Ballo in Maschera*), Fiordiligi (*Così fan Tutte*), Donna Anna (*Don Giovanni*), Tatiana (*Eugene Onegin*), Leonora (*La Forza del Destino*), and Manon (*Manon Lescaut*). These and other works are richly documented in her many recordings.

As her voice matured, it transformed from an almost coloratura soubrette to a *lirico spinto*, the luxuriously and richly textured sound that Verdi had desired, critics commented; but she unhesitatingly attributed her success to a voice that she described as "dark" and "smoky" and to the "luxury of her Blackness." Her continued work at the piano facilitated her deep knowledge of the structure of music. Her understanding of her own voice endowed her with the mechanics needed to accommodate its uniqueness. Moreover, her interpretations betrayed the profound intellectual probings to which she subjected every work from the recital, opera, and concert repertoires, in which she was first among the stars.

Her extraordinary voice and her deep commitment to excellence have helped Leontyne Price achieve one of the most brilliant operatic careers of our time. She is shown here, in 1955, as she sang Tosca *on the NBC network television.* (SCHOMBURG CENTER)

In 1992 RCA reissued on compact disc forty-seven arias by Price under the title *Leontyne Price: The Prima Donna Collection.* They were originally recorded between 1965 and 1979.

DOMINIQUE-RENÉ de LERMA

Q

Queen Latifah (1970–)

A rap artist, actor, and successful entrepreneur, Queen Latifah acquired her name over many years. When she was eight, a cousin dubbed her *Latifah*, which, in Arabic, means "delicate and sensitive." She added Queen at the beginning of her recording career to remind black Americans that they are the descendants of African kings and queens.

Queen Latifah was born Dana Owens in East Orange, New Jersey, in 1970. Her parents, Lance, a former Newark police officer, and Rita, a high-school art teacher, separated when she was eight. Her brother, Lancelot Hasaan Owens, died in a motorcycle accident in 1992 at the age of twenty-three.

While still in high school, Latifah performed as the human beat box in the rap group Ladies Fresh and met Mark James (DJ Mark, the 45 King). After high school she entered Borough of Manhattan Community College, but her career took off before she graduated. James had made a demo tape of Latifah's "Princess of the Posse" and taken it to Fred Brathwaite, host of the television show "Yo! MTV Raps," who played it for A&R executives at Tommy Boy Records. Tommy Boy signed Latifah immediately.

In 1988, Latifah released her first single, "Wrath of My Madness," which sold 40,000 copies; the following year she released her first album, *All Hail the Queen*, which ultimately sold a million copies and reached number six on *Billboard's* R&B

charts. In 1990, she rapped on David Bowie's single "Fame" and, in 1991, released her second album, *Nature of a Sista*, which included the hits "Latifah's Had It Up 2 Here" and "Fly Girl." The album *Black Reign* was released in 1993.

Queen Latifah was named Best New Artist of 1990 by the New Music Seminar in

Queen Latifah was born Dana Owens, but her cousin dubbed her Latifah, *which means "delicate and sensitive" in Arabic. Latifah added the "Queen" to remind black Americans that they are the descendants of African kings and queens.* (PRIVATE COLLECTION)

Manhattan and "Best Female Rapper" in the 1990 *Rolling Stone* readers poll, and two of her albums have been nominated for Grammy Awards.

In addition to her solo recording career, Queen Latifah created and is CEO of Flavor Unit Records and Management Company, which represents many artists, including the groups Naughty By Nature and Apache. She has also developed a very successful acting career, via the films *Jungle Fever*, *Juice*, *House Party 2*, and *My Life* and the television program *Fresh Prince of Bel Air;* she is currently starring in the hit comedy *Living Single*. Finally, on her list of additional credits, she owns Videos to Go, a video store that delivers tapes.

"Latifah's genius lies in intelligent lyrics that promote female self-respect, African-American cultural pride and the virtues of being positive," said *Newsmakers* in 1992. Those attributes go beyond just her lyrics and reflect her approach to life. *That's* her genius.

HILARY MAC AUSTIN

R

Rainey, Ma (1886–1939)

In a black theater in 1925, curtains open to reveal a huge hand-cranked Victrola. A slim chorus girl approaches the giant stage prop and puts an oversized record on the turntable, and from inside the machine a full, gravelly voice sings the popular hit "Moonshine Blues." Then the phonograph doors open and out steps a short, dark woman with broad features and luminous eyes, wearing a necklace of gold coins and a satin dress that glitters with spangles and sequins. Her name is Ma Rainey, the earliest well-known woman blues singer. Her style, the classic blues, was a female-dominated mixture of folk blues and black professional entertainment that flourished in the 1920s. She was a great vocalist, comedienne, and songwriter; a star in minstrelsy, vaudeville, and recording; a dancer, producer, and theater manager. She sang blues as early as 1902, earning the title Mother of the Blues, and leads a great tradition of women blues singers from **Bessie Smith** and Memphis Minnie to **Big Mama Thornton, Koko Taylor,** and many others.

She was born Gertrude Pridgett on April 26, 1886, in Columbus, Georgia, the second of Thomas and Ella Allen Pridgett's five children. Her family came from Alabama, and a grandmother may have been in show business after Emancipation. At the age of fourteen, she debuted in "A Bunch of Blackberries," a revue at the Springer Opera House in Columbus, and she trained professionally in southern minstrel shows, where she first heard the blues in Missouri around 1902 and added them to her act. On February 2, 1904, she married William "Pa" Rainey, a singing comedian, and performed with him as Rainey and Rainey, Assassinators of the Blues.

In her midteens she was already an established minstrel star and soon became leader of the famed Rabbit Foot Minstrels, black variety shows that included jugglers, acrobats, chorus lines, and comedians. But "Madame" Rainey was the star, singing blues and ragtime tunes, flirting outrageously with the young men in her band, and dancing nimbly despite her weight. The shows traveled by train, following cotton and tobacco harvests in the South and Midwest and performing under a large circus tent with a portable wooden stage and Coleman lanterns for footlights.

Sometime during her minstrel days, Rainey worked with Bessie Smith, whose fame would one day eclipse her own. Despite popular legend, she never kidnapped Smith or taught her to sing, but the two were close friends, and as a young chorus girl Smith clearly was impressed with the older star. They also may have been lovers: Both were bisexual, and Rainey later recorded a frankly lesbian song, "Prove It on Me."

Madame Rainey ran a disciplined show and paid employees on time, unlike many managers who stranded their companies on the road. Fellow performers have recalled her warmth and the way she encouraged younger musicians. She even adopted a son, Danny, billed as "the World's Youngest Juvenile Stepper," who sang, danced, and did female impersonations in her show. Because of her age (she was at least ten years older than most performers), her nurturing personality, and her act with Pa Rainey, she gained the nickname "Ma."

By the 1920s, she had separated from Pa Rainey, and in 1923, at the age of thirty-seven, she emerged from the rural tent-show circuit to national stardom through a recording contract with Chicago-based Paramount Records. Although popular Harlem entertainer **Mamie Smith** made the first black blues recording in 1920, sparking a nationwide blues craze, Ma Rainey brought an authentic Deep-South sound to the blues. Dubbing her "the Mother of the Blues," Paramount aggressively promoted her in the black press, especially the *Chicago Defender*. Her records were sold to Southerners by mail order and to Northerners through stores in black neighborhoods.

From 1923 to 1928, Rainey recorded at least ninety-two songs for Paramount with accompanists ranging from jazz greats to downhome slide guitarists and jug bands. Superbly backed by Louis Armstrong, she made the first recording of the blues standard "See, See Rider," and her rich contralto slurs and moans, and lisping diction deeply moved her audience, whether struggling down South or homesick up North.

Her brisk record sales resulted in tours on the Theater Owners' Booking Association (TOBA or Toby-time) circuit, a network of black vaudeville theaters in Southern and Midwestern cities. Working conditions could be feudal, and lesser acts grumbled that TOBA meant "tough on black asses,"

but these tours brought Ma Rainey standing-room-only audiences and national exposure. Her arranger and band director on the road was future gospel composer Thomas A. Dorsey.

A white singer with her talent would have earned more money, but Ma Rainey lived well. She dressed in diamonds and bought a house in Georgia and a $13,000 touring bus with a power generator to light her tent shows. Like most black musicians, though, she was paid a flat fee for recording sessions, and she never received royalties. Unlike most blues women of her day, she composed more than a third of the songs she recorded.

By the late 1920s, her style was threatened by competition from radio, talking pictures, and the emergence of swing music. Record companies began to record male country-blues singers for much lower fees, and in 1928 her Paramount contract was canceled. Ma Rainey continued to tour the ailing Toby-time and tent-show circuits, but Paramount went bankrupt in the early 1930s, and the Great Depression killed black vaudeville.

Her recording and vaudeville days were over, and when her sister, Malissa, died in 1935, Ma Rainey retired from active performance, returning to Columbus to live with her family; that same year her mother died. During this time, she purchased and managed the Lyric and Airdrome theaters in Rome, Georgia, and in later life she joined the Friendship Baptist Church where her brother, Thomas Pridgett, Jr., was a deacon. On December 22, 1939, at the age of fifty-three, she died of heart disease and was buried in the family plot in Porterdale Cemetery in Columbus. The black press ignored her passing, and her death certificate lists her occupation as housekeeping.

Ma Rainey was one of the last great minstrel artists and one of the first professional woman blues singers. She was Paramount's most recorded female star and one of its best-selling artists. Because of her lisp and heavy Georgia accent, because Paramount lacked the superior recording facilities of larger companies, and because her recordings were played so often, surviving seventy-eights are frequently scratchy or unclear, and her LP reissues suffer in comparison to Bessie Smith's. Nonetheless, her records should be heard and reheard for their timeless songs of wandering lives, broken family ties, and disappointed love affairs, as well as for their humor, strength, and resilience in new environments.

Ma Rainey has continued to influence other black artists. Country-blues singer Memphis Minnie recorded a tribute in 1940; poets Sterling Brown and Al Young wrote about her in the 1920s and 1960s, respectively; and August Wilson's critically acclaimed 1984 Broadway play, *Ma Rainey's Black Bottom*, testifies to her continuing vitality for black culture.

SANDRA LIEB

Ray, Carlene (19??–)

"Carlene Ray has been paying her own way in jazz, both as a bass player and singer, for probably a few more years than she cares to remember," Richard M. Sudhalter wrote in the *New York Post*. "She's worked with the best, and earned their respect. Survived the 'plays ok—for a woman' doldrums [and] come up spirited and unsoured. . . ."

Carlene Ray, whose musical credits include classical and pop as well as jazz, started out in a musical family. Born in New York City, she followed in her father's footsteps when she became a musician. Her father graduated from the Juilliard School of Music and played tuba, euphonium, and bass and gave his daughter her first music lesson. She also attended Juilliard, studied piano and composition, and earned her bachelor's degree; later, she received a masters in music degree in voice from Manhattan School of Music.

Starting out her professional career as a vocalist and pianist, Carlene Ray soon changed from piano to the rhythm guitar. Her first major big band gig was touring the United States with the famous all-woman, mostly black band **Sweethearts of Rhythm**. Next came a job as band vocalist with the Erskine Hawkins Orchestra.

Then, in 1956, she met the two loves of her life, her late husband, pianist-composer Luis Russell, and the Fender bass. She became known for her unique sound on the Fender because, in her lack of role models on the electric bass, she created the sound of a string bass. She later received a grant from the National Endowment for the Arts to study as an apprentice on the instrument which she had been imitating for years, the upright bass.

Building an impressive jazz portfolio, Ray toured with **Melba Liston** to both Europe and the Far East and with Carrie Smith to Europe. She played with the Sy Oliver Orchestra at the Newport Jazz Festival and with Sandra Reaves-Phillips at the Bern Jazz Festival; with **Ruth Brown** for the six years, leaving the group in February of 1995; with the Duke Ellington Band, led by Mercer Ellington; and with Skitch Henderson, Peter Duchin, and Tiny Grimes, among many others.

Ray's singing credits include solo and choral work in classical, jazz, and pop music. She was at home performing with the

Schola Cantorum Camarata Singers and with the American Opera Society, and as a backup singer, she has worked with **Della Reese**, Patti Page, and Quincy Jones. She played the bass for the Broadway production of *Purlie* and, between 1971 and 1984, she sang in the chorus and played in the orchestra for the Alvin Ailey American Dance Theater, receiving rave reviews for her solo singing.

Throughout her playing and singing career, Ray has continued to teach the future generation of musicians. She directed the college choir at Medgar Evers College, was an Adjunct Professor of Fundamental Guitar at Hunter College, was Artist-in-Residence at William Paterson College and currently teaches a singing course in the blues at the New School in New York City.

All of these experiences have led to a rich, full life for Ray, but she credits something quite different as the highlight of her career: In 1987, she received a National Endowment for the Arts Special Project Grant to create a Jazz Choral Workshop, which brought together nonprofessionals from all walks of life who "just liked to sing with other people." To communicate the joy of jazz and choral singing to a group of people new to the experience brought Ray some of the greatest fulfillment of her career.

HILARY MAC AUSTIN

Reese, Della (1931–)

Pop and soul singer and actress Della Reese was born Deloreese Patricia Early on July 6, 1931, in Detroit, Michigan. She began to sing professionally with **Mahalia Jackson**'s gospel troupe from 1945 to 1949 and then performed with Erskine Hawkins in the 1950s.

In addition to her recording credits, Della Reese has made numerous television appearances, including her own syndicated The Della Reese Show *(1969–70).* (PRIVATE COLLECTION)

In 1957, she began a solo career and achieved three top-forty hits in the late 1950s: "And That Reminds Me" (1957), which reached number twelve; "Don't You Know" (1959), which reached number two; and "Not One Minute More (1959), which reached number sixteen. Her RCA album *Della* (1960) reached the top forty and earned her a Grammy Award nomination for Female Vocal Album. Her other albums include *Special Delivery* (1961) and *Classic Della* (1962).

As an actress, Reese made many television appearances, including starring in the syndicated *The Della Reese Show* (1969–70) and performing as a series regular in *Chico and the Man* (NBC, 1976–78), *It Takes Two* (ABC, 1982–83), *Charlie & Co.* (CBS, 1986), and *The Royal Family* (1991–92). She made many guest appearances on television variety, talk, and panel shows including *The Ed Sullivan Show, Perry*

Como's Kraft Music Hall, To Tell the Truth, and *The Tonight Show Starring Johnny Carson*; in television movies and miniseries including ABC's *Nightmare in Badham County* (1976) and *Roots: The Next Generation* (1979); and as a guest star in drama and comedy series such as *The Bold Ones, Police Woman, McCloud, The Love Boat,* and notably *The A-Team,* in which she played the mother of series regular Mr. T., and *Touched by an Angel.*

Her film appearances include *Let's Rock* (1958) and *Harlem Nights* (1989).

BARBARA BERGERON

Reeves, Dianne (1956–)

No one comes to hear Dianne Reeves looking for the same old stuff. Embracing influences from jazz, classical European music, Brazilian, African, the Caribbean, and the greater African diaspora, Reeves is a jazz singer of unusual depth and breadth.

Born in Detroit in 1956, Reeves barely knew her father, who died when she was two. Her mother moved her and her sister back to Denver, where her mother's family still lived. Her maternal grandmother was the center of a large and loving extended family.

While Reeves sang to herself around the house, she didn't study singing formally until junior high school. At that time, she was enrolled in a piano class she dreaded; fortunately, she was allowed to switch to voice lessons after the music teacher heard her sing. Her mother and stepfather did not know about the switch until they arrived for her first recital. Instead of playing, she sang "That's All," accompanied by a lone piano. Her parents were moved to tears, and she had found her place in life.

By the time she was seventeen, Reeves was discovered by jazz trumpeter Clark Terry at a music educators' conference in Chicago. Terry invited Reeves to perform with his group, and she did, at the Wichita Jazz Festival and with the Denver Symphony.

In the mid-1970s, Reeves followed her career to Los Angeles, where she sang with a number of jazz musicians and joined a Latin jazz-rock group called Caldera. Later, she toured as the principal singer for the band of Brazilian jazz musician Sergio Mendes. In 1983, she began a two-and-one-half-year engagement performing and touring with Harry Belafonte. During this period Reeves' work began to be influenced by the rhythms and traditions from around the world.

Reeves recorded her first two albums under a small, independent label, produced in collaboration with her cousin, George Duke. Her first album, *Dianne Reeves,* came out in 1988 and included material written by Reeves, Herbie Hancock, and Stevie Wonder. This critically acclaimed album topped the jazz charts for eleven weeks.

In the album was a hit song, "Better Days," which was written for her grandmother, who died in 1980. As Reeves says, "I've had a chance to tell people about the beautiful aspects of growing older and wiser. We can't throw old people away; they're to be cherished." Reeves sings this tribute to her grandmother at every concert.

With her international vision, Reeves has gained an international audience. She was popular on the concert circuit in the United States and Japan and became the first black female jazz singer to perform in the Soviet Union.

Her latest album, *Art and Survival*, was released in 1994: Not satisfied with the usual love songs, her compositions range from swinging jazz to a cappella African chants. Speaking of one of the most popular songs on the album, "Old Souls," she says, "No matter how far we have come, we are still from Africa. This tune is my tribute to the ancestors, the spiritual guides and proctors who have always led me on my life's journey."

As her style continues to mature, Reeves becomes more honest, more daring, and more outspoken. She sings a hard-hitting song, "Endangered Species," which talks about the dangers of being a woman. She says, "At first I didn't feel strong enough to sing this song. But . . . I believe that the truth will set you free, but if you don't speak the truth it will kill you. I'd rather do some healing."

ANDRA MEDEA

Reeves, Martha (1941–)

Rock and roll wouldn't have been the same during the tumultuous sixties without the earthy soul of Martha Reeves, lead singer of Martha and the Vandellas.

Although Martha Rose Reeves was born in Eufaula, Alabama, on July 18, 1941, Detroit was the birthplace of her rhythm-and-blues career. It was there that she began singing with Rosalind Ashford during high school, and it was there, after graduation, that she went looking for a recording career.

Reeves's path to stardom, however, began with a stumble. After losing an audition at the famed Motown Recording Company, she found employment at Barry Gordy's fledgling empire, ironically enough, as a secretary.

Eventually, Martha and her group, the Del-Phis (consisting of Gloria Williams, Rosalind Ashford, and Annette Sterling) were tapped for background vocals on various Motown records, including Marvin Gaye's runaway hit, "Stubborn Kind of Fellow." Martha and the Del-Phis landed a contract with Check-Mate, a subsidiary of Chess Records and released a single; in 1962, Motown signed Reeves and her group to a contract.

After the group recorded "There He Is (At My Door)," a bust on the pop chart, Gloria Williams left the Del-Phis. Reeves renamed the group the Vandellas, taking "Van" from Van Dyke Avenue and "Della" from the name of singer **Della Reese**.

In 1963, with their recording "Come and Get These Memories," Martha and the Vandellas cracked the top thirty; "Heat Wave," released that summer, made it all the way to the top ten; "Dancing in the Streets" took the country by storm in 1964, followed by "Nowhere to Run" in 1965 and "Jimmy Mack" in 1967. From 1967 on, the group was known as Martha Reeves and the Vandellas and toured throughout Europe and the United States.

Reeves persevered through a series of Vandellas as well as her growing dissatisfaction with the management at Motown. The company continued to promote the Supremes at the expense of Martha and the Vandellas. "Honey Chile," released in 1977, was their last top-forty hit; the group disbanded that same year.

As determined as she was talented, Martha Reeves released a solo album, "Power of Love," in 1974. Ever popular, she has toured extensively on the oldies circuit, keeping her fans both here and abroad "dancing in the streets." In all, she tallied twelve albums, seven gold singles, and numerous Grammy nominations. Reeves appeared on the cable special *Legendary Ladies of Rock and Roll* in 1988.

Martha Reeves, along with the Vandellas, was inducted into the Rock and Roll Hall of Fame in 1995.

Riperton, Minnie (1948–1979)

Known for her angelic five-octave range, Minnie Riperton became one of the most memorable songstresses of the 1970s. Born in Chicago on November 8, 1948, she began her career by training in opera, but as a teenager she joined a girl-group known as the Gems.

Riperton later landed a job as a receptionist at Chess Records, where she did session background vocals for **Etta James** and Fontella Bass. After several session jobs, she joined the soul/psychedelic group Rotary Connection.

Beginning her solo career under the pseudonym Andrea Davis, the first solo album under her real name was the critically acclaimed *Come to My Garden*. Riperton augmented her career by touring with such luminaries as Quincy Jones and **Roberta Flack** and by doing session work with Stevie Wonder.

She moved to Epic Records in 1974 and recorded the aptly titled *Perfect Angel*. Produced by Stevie Wonder, *Perfect Angel* became Riperton's biggest seller, containing the haunting hit single "Lovin' You" (cowritten with her husband, Dicky Rudolph). Her next two Epic releases, *Adventures in Paradise* and *Stay in Love*, also sold well.

In 1976, Riperton was diagnosed with breast cancer, and she later became a spokesperson for the American Cancer Society. Still focused on her singing career, however, Riperton moved to Capitol Records, where she recorded the eponymous *Minnie* in 1979, which contained such classics as "Memory Lane" and "Lovers and Friends."

On July 12, 1979, shortly after the release of *Minnie*, Riperton succumbed to cancer; in 1980, Capitol Records released the posthumous *Love Lives Forever*, a collection of 1978 tracks with new, studio-dubbed backing.

Although considered more of a cult songstress than a superstar, Riperton's crystal-clear, angelic voice has influenced the likes of Teena Marie and Mariah Carey.

JOHN MURPH

Roberts, Kay George (1950–)

In the fourth century, Boethius said, "Music is number made audible." The truth of this adage is manifest in the life of mathematician-turned-conductor Maestro Kay George Roberts. Even though Roberts played violin as a child, she began her college career as a math major.

Roberts, born September 16, 1950, is the youngest of three daughters of Marion Taylor and Dr. Shearly Oliver Roberts of Nashville, Tennessee. Both parents worked at Fisk University in Nashville. Dr. Roberts made history by founding and chairing the psychology department; Mrs. Roberts was a librarian. Kay Roberts attended Pearl Elementary, Washington Park High School, and University School of Nashville, formerly George Peabody Demonstration School.

Roberts began violin lessons with Robert Holmes when she was in elementary school. Indeed, her earliest orchestral experience was in the all-black Cremona Strings, conducted by Holmes. Desegregating the Nashville Youth Symphony in 1964, she proved such a valuable player that the music director, Thor Johnson, chose her to become a member of the Nashville Symphony Orchestra (NSO). Under Arthur Fiedler's baton, Roberts represented the NSO in the World Symphony Orchestra, which consisted of 140 musicians from around the world who toured New York, Florida, and Washington, D.C.

In 1968 Roberts entered Fisk University to study mathematics, but the summer before her junior year, Roberts won a violin scholarship to attend Tanglewood. There she met Leonard Bernstein, who persuaded Roberts to change her major. Even though she was a natural mathematician, Roberts changed to music, against her father's wishes. Dr. Roberts was concerned that his daughter would not be able to support herself as a musician. He asked his daughter to continue her education in an academic environment, not a conservatory. In 1968, Roberts graduated with a B.A. in music, with a minor in psychology.

After graduating from Fisk, Roberts was awarded a Charles Ditson Scholarship to study violin at Yale University, from which in 1975 she received a master of music in violin performance. After taking a conducting class as an elective, Roberts realized what she wanted to do with her musical training. In 1976 Yale, where she studied with Otto-Werner Mueller, granted her a master of musical arts in conducting.

By 1978, Roberts was a member of the faculty at University of Massachusetts at Lowell, where she still teaches and conducts the university's orchestra. She has also con-

ducted community and youth orchestras nationwide.

Roberts attended conducting master classes led by Leonard Bernstein, Seiji Ozawa, and André Previn; she also studied early music with John Eliot Gardiner and the music of Debussy and contemporary styles with Pierre Boulez. After her conducting debut in 1976 with the Nashville Symphony Orchestra, Roberts served as music director and conductor of the New Hamp-

Orchestra conductor Kay George Roberts began her college career as a math major but won a violin scholarship to Tanglewood before she graduated. Leonard Bernstein persuaded Roberts to change her major, and thus began her career as a performer, teacher, and guest conductor for major U.S. orchestras. (PHOTO: VANDO ROBERTS)

shire Philharmonic from 1982 to 1987; she held the same position with the Cape Ann Symphony from 1986 to 1988.

Overseas, Roberts conducted the Bangkok Symphony Orchestra, the Cairo Conservatoire Orchestra in Egypt, and at the Lugano Festival in Switzerland, where she led the European debut of Frederick Tillis' *Concerto for Orchestra and Percussion*, featuring Max Roach.

In 1986, Roberts was the first woman to receive a doctorate in orchestral conducting from Yale. Since then, she has appeared as guest conductor for major U.S. orchestras including the Chicago, Cleveland, New York Philharmonic, Detroit, Grant Park, Dallas, Savannah, Chattanooga, Dayton Philharmonic, and the Women's Philharmonic of California.

While on sabbatical in 1989, Roberts founded Ensemble Americana, a chamber ensemble dedicated to performing and promoting contemporary American music in Germany. She also conducts the Artemis Ensemble of Stuttgart, Germany, a group whose mission is to perform and record music of women composers.

In 1990, Roberts was named one of the conductors of the Black Music Repertory Ensemble, a Chicago-based group sponsored by the Center for Black Music Research, and led the Black Music Repertory Ensemble in its New York debut at Lincoln Center and in a live television performance on NBC's *Today Show*.

The life of a guest conductor is much more transient than that of a resident music director. Roberts must gain the confidence of a large group of strangers and guide them through interpretations of a variety of music with minimal rehearsal time. Musicians describe Roberts as the performers' conductor,

who commands utmost respect through her solid musicianship, classic baton technique, and inimitable clarity. Music critics discuss Roberts in terms of her boundless energy and skills in interpretation. No one could fail to admire her success in getting paid to do what she enjoys most–conducting.

REGINA HARRIS BAIOCCHI

Ross, Diana (1944–)

Dreams do come true, even for a bus girl who clears tables in the cafeteria of Hudson's, Detroit's major department store—especially if that girl's name is Diane Ross.

Born on March 26, 1944, in Detroit, Michigan, to Fred and Ernestine Ross, Diane Ross actually received her show business name at birth through clerical, albeit prophetic, error: A clerk accidentally recorded "Diana" on her birth certificate. After entering the chic world of the Supremes, Ross chose *Diana* as her official name.

Her childhood was uneventful until 1950 when her mother, Ernestine, was sent to a hospital in Holland, Michigan, to recuperate from tuberculosis. Her five children were sent to an aunt, Beatrice, in Bessemer, Alabama. "My grandfather—Reverend William Moton—was minister of the Bessemer Baptist Church. I sang in his choir and maybe that's when I realized I loved to sing," Ross remembers.

The family was eventually reunited in Detroit and relocated to a three-bedroom apartment in a new division of the Brewster-Douglas Projects. Ross was fourteen at the time. Hardship did not translate into deprivation, Ross recalled in a *Woman's Day* interview: "We always had a good life. It wasn't like we had gobs of money. But we always had what we needed somehow. Later

Like so many great pop stars, Diana Ross began singing in her church choir, and it was in another church choir that she met Mary Wilson and Florence Ballard, who would become her fellow Supremes. Ross left the Supremes in 1969 and went on to a new career as solo performer and actress. (PRIVATE COLLECTION)

on, I found out that that neighborhood is called the ghetto. But basically, it was a warm, loving, family environment. There was always something exciting going on."

There was always something exciting going on in Ross' teenage years. She was accepted into Cass Technical High School where fashion design and the swim team took up a great deal of her time. Still, Ross found the time to sing in the Olivet Baptist Church, where she met Mary Wilson and Florence Ballard.

The three teenagers formed a trio and sang at social functions. In 1959, they joined with Betty Anderson to form the Primettes, a sister group to the Primes, led by Eddie Kendrick. Anderson was eventually replaced by Barbara Martin. The Primettes initially signed with LuPine Records and recorded "Tears of Sorrow," with Ross singing the lead. In 1960, Barry Gordy, Jr., of Motown Records changed the name of the group to the Supremes and signed them to a recording contract. Martin left the group in 1962.

The Supremes paid their dues by singing backup to the more established Motown stars such as Marvin Gaye and **Mary Wells**. They took their act on the road and released their first Motown single, "I Want a Guy," in 1961; however, it was not until 1964, through the wizardry of writers/producers Holland-Dozier-Holland, that the Supremes enjoyed their first million seller, "Where Did Our Love Go?" Within a year, six number-one hits were recorded by these Detroit divas: "Baby Love," "Come See About Me," "Stop! In the Name of Love," "Back in My Arms Again," and "I Hear a Symphony."

In 1969, the Supremes became Diana Ross and the Supremes. "Someday We'll Be Together" was their final recording. It went on to become their twelfth number-one song. By 1970, the spotlight was on Diana Ross alone.

As a solo performer, Ross ventured into new areas of success, while expanding upon her pop stardom. She earned an Academy Award nomination for her electric portrayal of **Billie Holiday** in *Lady Sings the Blues* (1972); her next movie, *Mahogany*, followed in 1975; *The Wiz* teamed Ross and superstar Michael Jackson in 1978. The first two films enjoyed popular, if not critical, success. The third was an expensive failure. In 1994, she portrayed a schizophrenic in a made-for-television movie, *Out of Darkness.*

Musically, Ross moved with ease from the nightclub circuit to lavish concert tours. Her first solo record to hit the charts was "Reach Out and Touch (Somebody's Hand)" in 1970; "Ain't No Mountain High Enough" shot to the number-one slot later that year; and "Touch Me in the Morning," released in 1973, met with resounding success and provided the singer with yet another number-one hit.

In 1972, Diana Ross was nominated for an Academy Award as Best Actress for her electric portrayal of Billie Holiday in Lady Sings the Blues. (PRIVATE COLLECTION)

Proving herself to be a singer of great versatility, Ross performed at the Newport Jazz Festival in 1994 to an enthusiastic audience and considerable acclaim. Her own concerts easily segued from Rodgers and Hart to pop to jazz to ballads—concerts in the late '70s often featured tributes to **Josephine Baker, Ethel Waters,** and **Bessie Smith.** In 1976, Diana Ross even ventured into the strobe-lit world of disco, recording what would become yet another number one hit, "Love Hangover." An extravagant television special, "An Evening With Diana Ross," aired in 1977.

In 1981, Ross left Motown, signing a $20-million contract with RCA for the United States and yet another contract with Capitol for the rest of the world. She recorded six number-one hits as a solo act, including the theme from "Mahogany," "Do You Know Where You're Going To?" (1976), and a tribute to the late Marvin Gaye, "Missing You" in 1985.

Somehow Ross found the time to write her autobiography, *Secrets of a Sparrow,* released in 1993. In it she writes candidly of her first marriage to Robert Ellis Silberstein in 1971 and their divorce in 1976, as well as her second marriage to Arne Naess, Jr., in 1985. Her children include Rhonda, fathered by Barry Gordy, Jr.; Suzanne, Tracee, and Chudney from the first marriage; and Ross Arne and Evan from the second.

Diana Ross is president of Diana Ross Enterprises. As shrewd as she is talented, she is now one of the richest women in the entertainment field. The recipient of numerous awards, including a Grammy Best Female Vocalist in 1970 and a Tony in 1972, she was inducted into the Rock and Roll Hall of Fame in 1988.

"I remember when I was such a little girl," Ross said in an interview for the book *Intimacies*, "I would walk a long, long way out of the neighborhood, away from Mama, just to see what the rest of the world looked like. Mama never scolded. She gave me that freedom. She always knew I would find my way back. I was trusted. And I never did get lost. I always did find my way home."

Diana Ross found her way home for the *25th Anniversary of Motown*, a spectacular television special that reunited Ross with the Supremes. She will be remembered always as the glamorous superstar who transcended the "girl-group" cliche to become a versatile performer in her own right.

RICHARD E.T. WHITE

Rush, Gertrude (1880–1918)

Gertrude E. Durden, composer and playwright, was born August 5, 1880, in Navasota, Texas, to Reverend Frank and Sarah E. (Reinhardt) Durden. After attending high schools in Parsons, Kansas, and Quincy, Illinois, she studied at the Westerman Music Conservatory in Des Moines, Iowa, and received her A.B. in 1914 from Des Moines College.

Gertrude E. Durden married James B. Rush, of Des Moines, on December 23, 1907. She taught in the government district schools in Oklahoma for four years and in the Oswego, Kansas, public schools for three years; became a lecturer in 1911, and started her career as a playwright when she staged *Paradise Lost* under the title *Satan's Revenge*. Her other writings include *Sermon on the Mount* (1907), *Uncrowned Heroines* (1912), and *Black Girls Burden* (1913). Rush was also a composer whose songs include: "If You But Knew," "Jesus Loves the Little Children," and "Christmas Day."

A member of the Associated Charities in the Interests of Poor Black People, the Colored Woman's Suffrage Club, and the Order of the Eastern Star, Rush organized the Woman's Law and Political Study Club, was a delegate to the Half-Century Exposition of Negro Emancipation in Philadelphia, and was a member of the committee that secured an appropriation for the Iowa Federation Home for Women and Girls.

Rush died on September 8, 1918, in Des Moines, Iowa.

JUDY WARWICK

Rushen, Patrice (1954–)

Patrice Rushen was giving classical piano recitals by the age of six. In her teens, she branched into jazz and soon evolved into a consummate, multifaceted artist, combining singing, composing, producing, arranging, and performing into a blend of rhythm and blues, jazz, and pop.

Born to Ruth and Allen Rushen on September 30, 1954, in Los Angeles, Patrice was enrolled in a special college eurhythmics course at age three. She began piano lessons at five and at a very early age developed the discipline that has allowed her to continue her growth and study of music as well as the development of her own unique style of music.

She has recorded nine albums, received two Grammy nominations for "Number One" (best rhythm-and-blues instrumental performance) and "Forget Me Nots" (best rhythm-and-blues vocal performance) in 1982, and developed a passion for film composing: "Film composing allows me to explore more aspects of music and meet a lot

Composer and instrumental recording artist Patrice Rushen was the first woman to be music director of a network television show, The Midnight Hour *for CBS. She is the only woman to emerge from jazz and rhythm-and-blues as a self-contained recording artist—responsible for composing, producing, and arranging her own work.* (SCHOMBURG CENTER)

more people," she explained in an interview. "As I get older, my priorities are shifting off myself and onto other people."

Her musical diversity handed Rushen a new challenge when she composed the score for Robert Townsend's film *Hollywood Shuffle* (1987). Her television composing credits include the series *Brewster Place* and the comedy special *Robert Townsend and His Partners in Crime*. She is distinguished as the first woman to be musical director of a network television show, *The Midnight Hour* for CBS, and has also been music director for Emmy Awards and the NAACP Image Awards ceremonies.

Rushen's early career included session work for such artists as **Diane Reeves**, Peabo Bryson, Jean-Luc Ponty, Teena Marie, Hubert Laws, Eddie Murphy, Terri Lyne Carrington, Lee Tineour, Con Funk Shun, Wayne Shorter, Flora Purim, Ronnie Laws, the Temptations, Sonny Rollins, and Herbie Hancock. A highly regarded arranger, Rushen has arranged strings and horns for Ramsey Lewis, Sheree Brown, the Dazz Band, and Prince. She is the only woman to emerge from jazz and rhythm-and-blues as a self-contained recording artist—responsible for composing, producing, and arranging her own work.

Patrice Rushen combines a career and marriage: She married Marc St. Louis, actor, concert-tour manager, and technician, in 1986.

REGINA JONES

S

Salt-N-Pepa

Salt-N-Pepa were the first female rappers to hit the big time, the first to have an album go platinum, and the first to crack the top forty on the music charts. As one writer put it, "With their sassy, sexy, bold, fun-loving, trash-talking, take-no-prisoners attitude, the group showed they were *women*, damn it, and proud of it."

Salt is Cheryl James, and Pepa is Sandi Denton. The future rappers were girls from middle-class families from Queens, both attending Queensborough Community College. Sandi (Pepa) was loud and outgoing, always the life of the party. Cheryl (Salt) was the opposite—quiet, soft-spoken, and conservatively dressed. Cheryl helped Sandi land a part-time job at Sears, and the two became best friends.

Also at Sears was another college student, Hurby (Luv Bug) Azor, who needed some rappers to complete a school recording project, so he drafted Sandi and her best friend Cheryl. The cut was "The Showstoppa," which was an answer to "The Show," by Dougie Fresh. It was 1986, and the single got all three—rappers and producer—a contract with Next Plateau Records.

The D.J. Salt-N-Pepa worked with in the beginning decided to leave the group in the tough early days. James and Denton replaced her with Dee Dee Roper, who took over the name Spinderella. Dee Dee was another quiet, middle-class girl from Queens, even younger than the others. Her skeptical father insisted that she finish school rather than get mixed up in show business, but even he was won over in time.

They released their debut album, *Hot, Cool, & Vicious*, in 1986. It included the single cuts, "My Mike Sounds Nice" and "Tramp," a scathing commentary on men

Salt-N-Pepa are Cheryl James (Salt) and Sandi Denton (Pepper), best friends who met at Queensborough Community College in New York. The third member of the group is Spinderella (Dee Dee Roper). They were the first female rappers to hit the big time and crack the top forty on the music charts. (PRIVATE COLLECTION)

who sleep around. Two years later, this album became the first female rap album to crack the top forty when "Push It" was remixed and released as a single. Originally, "Push It" was only the B-side of "Tramp" and was overlooked until it was remixed as a dance number. "Push It" went platinum and took the album platinum with it. The single also won a Grammy nomination for Best Rap Performance.

The group's next album was released in 1988 and was titled *A Salt with a Deadly Pepa*. A success from the start, it also hit the top forty.

In 1990 Salt-N-Pepa brought out *Black's Magic*, a third success. By now they had become the most popular female rap group in the country. One single, "Expression," set a record when it topped *Billboard's* rap chart for eight solid weeks. "Let's Talk about Sex" was another hit and a banner for AIDS awareness. The group followed up this success with *A Blitz of Salt-N-Pepa*, a collection of dance remixes of earlier numbers.

Now an artistic success, Salt-N-Pepa found it time to start taking care of other aspects of their work. For their two first albums, Azor was their producer and manager and he called all the shots; he told them what to sing, what to wear, and even who to associate with. In this they were very much like the girl groups of the 1960s, with a male figure directing the action from behind the scenes. With *Black's Magic* they had begun to write their own material, and Cheryl had begun to produce some of the cuts.

At the same time they began to assert themselves financially. They had signed their first contracts when they were young and naive, and people took advantage of their ignorance; this time they renegotiated their contract with Azor and went into a new distribution deal with London Records.

Next came a three-year hiatus for the group. All three of the members had babies; all three had their relationships come apart; still, they stood by each other and saw each through.

In 1994, they were back with *Very Necessary*. With a new, tougher attitude and more confident control, they brought down a string of hits. "Whatta Man" drew platinum, and "Shoop" reached gold.

In spite of all the challenges, Salt says, "The guys are in love with us, and the girls are proud of us. The guys may think we're sexy or whatever, but the girls think, 'Those are my girls. They're my homegirls!' They come up to us after the shows just to tell us they love us. Because they're proud. They're just bursting with pride."

ANDRA MEDEA

Although Philippa Duke Schuyler is best known as a concert pianist, she began to compose music at age three and continued to do so until her tragic death in 1967. (SCHOMBURG CENTER)

Schuyler, Philippa (1931–1967)

Philippa Duke Schuyler's career was as remarkable as her background was unusual. Her father was George S. Schuyler, a well-known black American writer; her mother, Josephine Cogdell, came from a wealthy white Texas ranching and banking family. Philippa was brought up in an atmosphere of intense interest in intellectual matters and the arts. Though her mother attributed the child's genius to a diet of raw foods, it is more likely to have resulted from constant intellectual challenge.

Schuyler was born on August 2, 1931. Newspaper and journal articles chronicled the prodigy's development as she crawled at four weeks, walked at eight months, read at two years, and played the piano at age three. At four, she could spell forty-letter words and was performing her own piano compositions over the radio. When she was seven, her IQ was measured as 180, and she was playing the piano on tour. She graduated from elementary school at ten, had written more than 100 compositions by thirteen and, for that birthday, completed her first orchestral work. Scored for 100 instruments, *Manhattan Nocturne* was performed by the New York Philharmonic under the direction of Rudolph Ganz during the last performance of the 1944–45 Young People's Concerts season.

Schuyler graduated from high school at fifteen. A few years later, she wrote *The Rhapsody of Youth* in honor of the inauguration of Haitian president Paul Magloire and was decorated with the Haitian Order of Honor and Merit. A young woman now, she continued to tour and was well received, visiting more than eighty countries. She was knighted in Haiti and gave command per-

Philippa Duke Schuyler wrote five books during her short life and was working as a news correspondent when she was killed at the age of thirty-five in a helicopter crash, trying to help remove Catholic schoolchildren from the site of fighting during the Vietnam War. (LIBRARY OF CONGRESS)

formances for Ethiopia's Emperor Haile Selassie and Belgium's Queen Elizabeth.

A devout Catholic, Schuyler wrote five books during her career, including one with her mother. She was fluent in several languages and in demand as a lecturer across the globe. The budding writer had begun to work as a news correspondent just before her death on May 9, 1967, in a helicopter crash in Da Nang during the Vietnam War: She was trying to help remove Catholic schoolchildren from the site of fighting in

Hue to the relative safety of a school in Da Nang.

Schuyler's best-known musical works include *Fairy Tale Symphony, Sleepy Hollow Sketches*, and *The Nile Fantasy*, also known as *Le Nile* and *White Nile Suite*.

A major biography of Schuyler was published in 1995—*Composition in Black and White: The Life of Philippa Schuyler*. The *New York Times Book Review* described it as ". . . [an] enthralling, heartbreaking book."

DEBORRA A. RICHARDSON

Scott, Hazel (1920–1981)

After making her music debut at age three, Hazel Dorothy Scott went on to become a star of Broadway, radio, television, and film. Described as gifted, sophisticated, elegant, glamorous, outspoken, and uncompromising, Scott was renowned not only for her outstanding achievements as musician, singer, and actress but also for her commitment to speaking out against racial injustice.

Hazel Scott was born in Port of Spain, Trinidad, on June 11, 1920. Under the guidance of her mother, Alma Long Scott, she began to play the piano at age two, and at age three she made her music debut in Trinidad. In 1924, her family moved to the United States where Scott—again thanks to her mother—began formal music training. Two years later, five-year-old Scott was making her American debut at New York's renowned Town Hall. Within three years, she had won a six-year scholarship to the Juilliard School of Music in New York City, but at the time the entrance age was sixteen. Around age fourteen, Scott joined her mother in Alma Long Scott's All-Woman Orchestra, where she played both piano and trumpet. By 1936, at age sixteen, Scott was not only a radio star on the Mutual Broadcasting System, but also was playing at the Roseland Dance Hall with the great Count Basie Orchestra.

In the late 1930s, Scott's career expanded when she appeared in the Broadway musical *Singing Out the News* and then, a few years later, *Priorities of 1942*. In 1939, she recorded her first record, with the sextet Rhythm Club of London. The early 1940s were busy years for Scott, with successful appearances in several films, including *Something to Shout About, I Dood It, Tropicana*, and *The Heat's On* in 1943,

*Hazel Scott was a star of Broadway, radio, television, and film. She is shown here entertaining at the Great Lakes Naval Training Station during World War II. (*NATIONAL ARCHIVES*)*

Broadway Rhythm in 1944, and *Rhapsody in Blue* in 1945. National recognition also came as a result of Scott's association with Barney Josephson's Café Society Downtown and Uptown in New York between 1939 and 1945.

In one of the year's most glittering social events, Hazel Scott married the charismatic preacher and powerful politician Adam Clayton Powell, Jr., in 1945. After the birth of their son, Adam Clayton Powell III, and following several years of separation, the couple divorced in 1956. During the late 1940s and early 1950s, Scott became the first black woman to have her own television show, but in 1950 she was accused of being a Communist sympathizer, and her show was canceled. Scott defended her participation in fund-raising performances for groups fighting for equal rights and was widely recognized for her efforts in the struggle for racial freedom and justice. Speaking of her contract, which during the 1940s contained a clause allowing her to refuse to perform before racially segregated audiences, Scott once said in an interview, "What justification can anyone have who comes to hear me and then objects to sitting next to another Negro?"

In 1967, following five years of living abroad, primarily in Paris, Scott returned to the United States. She appeared in television shows such as *Julia* and *The Bold Ones* and held nightclub residences at Emerson Ltd. in Washington, D.C., and Ali Baba East and Downbeat in New York City. In 1978, she was inducted into the Black Filmmakers Hall of Fame. Scott continued to perform until her death in the fall of 1981.

Famous for her ability to blend classics with high jazz as well as for her wit, personality, and talent, Hazel Dorothy Scott will be remembered for her dignity and determination in the struggle for racial equality and justice.

FENELLA MACFARLANE

Shipp, Olivia (1880–1979)

Olivia Shipp performed in jazz bands and chamber music ensembles, in theater orchestras and ragtime bands, from the turn of the century until the post-World War II era.

She was born Olivia Sophie L'Ange on May 17, 1880, in New Orleans. As a child, she taught herself to play keyboard on an old pump organ given to her family. She also took some voice lessons from Abbey Lyons, a member of the **Fisk Jubilee Singers**.

When the Black Patti Troubadour Company came through the city, Olivia L'Ange's sister, May, joined them as an actress, touring and then settling in New York to form the Bob and Kemp vaudeville team. (She adopted the name Kemp to protect her family from the stigma of association with show business.) When she left New Orleans, she promised to send for her sister as soon as she could; when Olivia was about twenty, May did so.

Olivia D'Ange worked in vaudeville while studying the piano. After hearing a cello in a vaudeville performance, she decided that that was the instrument she wanted most to play; she began to teach piano to another musician in exchange for cello lessons. Later, she used the money she earned from vaudeville and her music teaching to pay for lessons from an eminent Hungarian cellist, Professor Turkisher. She also studied with black cellists Wesley Johnson and Leonard Jeter. Through Jeter, she gained a position with the Martin-Smith Music School, serving as Jeter's assistant and as a member of the school's orchestra. She also performed with black violinist Charles Elgar and his chamber ensemble on radio and in a trio with two women on violin and piano. She too, adopted a stage name, Porter, and used that name until her marriage to a man named Shipp. Thereafter, she performed as Olivia Shipp.

Though not a member of the original group, Shipp played with the **Lafayette Theatre** Ladies' Orchestra in the late 1910s and early 1920s. In order to play with **Marie Lucas'** popular group, Shipp learned to play the bass violin, studying with a bassist for the New York Philharmonic.

Shipp worked with a variety of bands, orchestras, and small groups and also formed her own orchestra, Olivia Shipp's Jazz-Mines. Shipp's most important contribution was founding the Negro Women's Orchestral and Civic Association; with the backing of Local 802 of the American Federation of Musicians, it became an important performing group during the Harlem Renaissance.

Olivia Shipp died in February 1979, leaving a remarkable record of achievement.

KATHLEEN THOMPSON

Shirelles, The

Before the Shirelles recorded "Will You Love Me Tomorrow," the only black woman ever to hit the top of the pop charts was singing with four guys (Zola Taylor of the Platters). Because they were a "girl group," the Shirelles have seldom been recognized as the rock-and-roll pioneers that they were, but in a musical genre that was largely white and almost exclusively male, they were groundbreakers.

The Shirelles started out as a high school vocal group from Passaic, New Jersey. The members of the group—Addie Harris, Shirley Owens, Beverly Lee, and Doris Kenner, all born in 1940 or 1941—gave their first performance at a school talent show in 1958, where they performed a capella.

A classmate loved their style and wanted them to meet her mother, who owned a small record company, but the singers couldn't be bothered. They were more interested in cheerleading. The schoolmate kept pestering them, however, and they finally went to meet Florence Greenberg, who owned Tiara records. Greenberg signed them immediately, once their parents agreed.

Their first single was a song written by the group, "I Met Him on a Sunday"; it was released while they were still in school. The song did so well locally that Greenberg turned it over to a larger label to promote nationally. It went to forty-nine on the Pop chart and earned them their start as pop singers.

Their next few singles did not do well. Then Greenberg brought in Luther Dixon to produce their material. As was common in those days, the backstage producer took complete control. Their next hit was a song by Burt Bacharach, "Baby It's You," which was recorded so quickly that only Owens happened to be in the recording studio. The other girls weren't around, so Owens just sang along with the composer's demo tape. It hit number six on the charts.

The next year, their producer, who owed a favor to songwriters Carole King and Gerry Goffin, brought the Shirelles a King-Goffin song, "Will You Love Me Tomorrow?" The group hated it at first, but Dixon persuaded them to record it anyway. It be-

The Shirelles—Addie Harris, Shirley Owens, Beverly Lee, and Doris Kenner—were rock-and-roll pioneers because they were one of the first black "girl groups" to hit the big time. Their biggest hit "Soldier Boy," was an afterthought, thrown in during five minutes of studio time at the end of a recording session. They were inducted into the Rock and Roll Hall of Fame in 1996. (PRIVATE COLLECTION)

came a number one hit in 1962 and was the first number-one hit for a girl group and the first one for Goffin and King.

The Shirelles next recorded "Soldier Boy," written by Dixon and Florence Greenberg. The group had five minutes of studio time left at the end of a recording session, so the two producers tossed something together on the spot. The group recorded it in one take because there wasn't time for anything more. The Shirelles thought the song

was corny; in fact, when the group performed the song at the Apollo Theater in Harlem, they were embarrassed by it and afraid that black audiences would find it too lightweight, so they persuaded a young man from one of the other acts to "be" the soldier boy and do a comedy routine with them while they sang. They needn't have worried because the Apollo audience loved them— and "Soldier Boy." So did everyone else—it went to number one and became their biggest hit.

The Shirelles faced hard times after Dixon left their label; they had only one top-ten hit after his departure. But the biggest shock came when they reached twenty-one. Their earnings had supposedly been held in trust until they came of age, but when it came time to account, there were no earnings. The company claimed that it had all be used for expenses. The result was years of lawsuits that kept the group from recording for anyone. By the time they were free again, their career as hit-makers was over.

The Shirelles were young and unsophisticated, but they were singing at a time when roll-and-roll itself was young and unsophisticated. Their light, innocent songs were immensely popular with teenagers across America.

The Shirelles were inducted into the Rock and Roll Hall of Fame in a ceremony on January 17, 1996. At the ceremony Shirley Owens Alston expressed her gratitude for the award and then asked, "What took you so long?"

INDIA COOPER

Simmons, Dorothy (1910–)

Dorothy Vernell Simmons, gospel singer, choir director, and publisher, was born Sep-

A member of the Simmons-Akers Singers, one of the most sought-after gospel groups in the United States in the 1950s, Dorothy Simmons later became one of the first black performers to take gospel music to a western-music audience. (J. C. DJEDJE)

tember 10, 1910, in Powhatan, Louisiana, the only child of Martha Jones and George Smith. Simmons lived most of her early life in Louisiana, but after a brief stay in New Orleans, her family moved to Chicago when she was seven years old. She married Allen Simmons in 1940, and they have one son, Cornelius Webb, who is a salesman.

As a young person living in Chicago, Simmons learned much about singing from attending Tabernacle Baptist Church. In the early 1940s, she worked with **Sallie Martin** and Kenneth Morris at the Martin and Morris Music Studio in Chicago (a music store and publishing company), and she later joined a group organized by Kenneth Morris called the Martin and Morris Singers. She became a member of the Sallie Martin Singers when it was formed and traveled extensively with the group for several years. Her first trip to Los Angeles occurred in 1944 when the Sallie Martin Singers toured the city, and Simmons decided to move there in 1947. Around the same time, she and **Doris Akers** formed the Simmons-Akers Singers, a female gospel trio, which stayed together until the late 1950s. Through concert tours and recordings, the Simmons-Akers Singers became a highly respected, nationally known group. In addition, they served as choir directors at the Opportunity Baptist Church and Sky Pilot Church in Los Angeles and at the Upper Room Community Church in Richmond, California. They also organized their own publishing company and music store, the Simmons-Akers Music House in Los Angeles.

During the 1960s, Simmons established herself as a solo artist and moved to Colorado, where she became one of the first black performers to take gospel music to a western-music audience. Her Pilgrim Rest Baptist Church Choir in Denver had a weekly radio broadcast, and each month she appeared on two television stations. Because of this exposure and a guest appearance on a hootenanny television show in Denver, she regularly received generous offers to sing in nightclubs. However, she declined because of her belief that gospel singing should always be associated with and performed in a religious context. When Simmons returned to Los Angeles in the 1970s, she continued to perform in churches in the city and received formal training to become a licensed practitioner of the Religious Science Church. Simmons's musical career began to decline in the late 1970s.

Her high lyric-soprano voice, which seemed to be an inspiration from a higher source, is one of the reasons that the Simmons-Akers Singers were one of the most sought-after groups in the United States during the 1950s.

JACQUELINE COGDELL DJEDJE

Simone, Nina (1933–)

Born in Tryon, North Carolina, in 1933, Nina Simone exhibited musical talent at an early age. By the age of seven, she was a self-taught organist and pianist and a member of the church choir. Her early musical talents led to formal training at both Asheville (North Carolina) High School and the Juilliard School of Music in New York City. Simone's career began to blossom after her family moved to Philadelphia; thereafter she sang in nightclubs up and down the East Coast, primarily as a vocalist/pianist. Immersed in jazz, she became an eclectic vocalist in the 1960s, singing and recording compositions ranging from blues and jazz to soul. Specific examples include "I Loves You, Porgy" (1959) and "I Put a Spell on You," originally recorded by Screaming Jay Hawkins around 1965.

In 1967, after her switch from Phillips to RCA, she entered a very successful commercial period. Both commercial singles "Ain't Got No—I Got Life" from *Hair* and "To Love Somebody," originally recorded by the Bee Gees, were successful for Simone; in addition, the successful albums *Nina Simone Plays the Blues*, *Silk and Soul*, and

Here Comes the Sun all were issued between 1967 and 1972.

Simone's vocal style is characterized by a soul-searching, mostly alto, vocal range that appears to disdain ornamentation, preferring to squeeze meaning from individual words. Her vocal style emits a believable purity, giving the impression that she truly feels, or has lived, the text of her songs. The believable aspect of Simone's singing style is

Eclectic vocalist Nina Simone translated powerful political protest into great commercial success. (SCHOMBURG CENTER)

reflected in her social consciousness. In the 1960s, she made significant contributions to the civil rights movement via protest songs such as "Old Jim Crow," "Mississippi God-dam," and "Young, Gifted, and Black," and since the 1970s she has devoted more time to political causes. In part because of her political beliefs, since the late 1970s, Simone has released few albums in the United States: *Baltimore* (1978), *Let It Be Me* (1987), and *Single Woman* (1995); all of her other al-bums have been released in Europe. Her autobiography, *I Put a Spell on You*, was published in 1991.

EDDIE S. MEADOWS

Simpson, Valerie (1948–)

"It was a dream come true. We were just writers, and Motown was it. When they called us we didn't hesitate. With a whole slew of artists there our songs would get the chance to be recorded. It was the best thing that happened to us." This is how vocalist-songwriter Valerie Simpson has described her entry into the Motown studio stable with her eventual husband and songwriting partner, Nickolas Ashford.

Best known in the 1970s and 1980s for her in-studio and onstage partnership with Ashford, which produced a string of hits and opened many ears to her vivacious vocal charms, Valerie Simpson is a crafter of un-forgettable lyrics and haunting melodies. She was barely out of high school when she teamed up with Ashford to churn out hits, which they began selling at $75 each. Ash-ford and Simpson's first hit was "Let's Go Get Stoned," which was written for Ray Charles. Together they also produced such memorable pop classics as "Ain't No Moun-tain High Enough," "You're All I Need to Get By" for Marvin Gaye and Tammi Ter-rell, and **Diana Ross**'s anthem, "Reach Out (And Touch Somebody's Hand)," as well as her "Remember Me."

Both Simpson and Ashford wanted to strike out on solo and duo careers, but their contract with Motown kept them from do-ing so. Simpson managed to record two solo albums for Motown's Tamla label, *Exposed* in 1971 and 1972's *Valerie Simpson*, both of which have become collector's items. Shortly after the release of Simpson's epony-mous LP, the duo's desire to perform led them to leave Motown and move to a long-term deal with Warner Brothers. They later moved to Capitol Records, where Ashford and Simpson became hitmakers in their own right, scoring particularly big during the late 1970s and 1980s with such hits as "Send It," "Don't Cost You Nothing," "Is It Still Good to Ya," while at the same time making their mark due in no small part to Valerie Simp-son's soaring voice.

WILLARD JENKINS

Smith, Bessie (1894–1937)

Bessie Smith was the undisputed "Empress" of the blues in the 1920s. More than any other woman of her time, she came to sym-bolize African Americans' resurgent mili-tancy and racial pride. As a cultural leader, Smith assumed a role comparable to that of Jack Johnson, the first black heavyweight champion of the world whose defiance of white authority was legendary, and Marcus Garvey, the charismatic prophet of black nationalism—all three were highly visible in their advocacy of black pride and in their resistance to the unequal treatment and the inferior social status imposed on African Americans in the United States.

Bessie Smith was born in Chattanooga, Tennessee, on April 15, 1894. Her family was large, nine in all, and very poor. Her father, William Smith, was a Baptist preacher who operated a local mission; he died soon after Bessie Smith was born. Two other brothers as well as her mother died before Smith reached her teens. Her oldest sister, Viola, took over as the nominal head of the household, and Bessie Smith went to work on the city's street corners with her younger brother Andrew: She sang for tips, while he accompanied her on guitar.

During this period, Chattanooga was a rapidly growing yet rigidly segregated southern trade and transportation center; approximately half of the 30,000 inhabitants were black. They were crowded into the city's "Negro quarter," where unsanitary living conditions, disease, unemployment, poverty, and crime were common. Most of the jobs open to African Americans were low-paying manual or domestic jobs, and openings were scarce. The only other opportunity for lawful employment was in the segregated entertainment business. This was to be Smith's avenue of escape from the Chattanooga slums.

Bessie Smith broke into show business in her hometown at the age of eighteen with the help of her older brother, Clarence, who had earlier joined Moses Stokes' traveling minstrel troupe as a comedian. When he returned to Chattanooga with the show in 1912, he arranged for his sister to audition for it. She was initially hired as a dancer, and she went out on the road with the troupe that same year. One of its members was the famous **Ma Rainey**, at the time still married to Pa Rainey. Smith and Ma Rainey struck up a close friendship that lasted for the rest of their lives. Bessie Smith recorded two of Rainey's blues standards, "Moonshine Blues" and "Boll Weevil Blues." Smith, however, was not groomed for stardom by Ma Rainey. She had been singing publicly, if not professionally, for ten years before meeting Ma Rainey (the "mother of the blues"), and she toured with her briefly on only two occasions. Bessie Smith developed her own singing style through years of hard work, mostly on her own, just as she persistently made her own way in the world of show business.

In 1913, Smith relocated to Atlanta, where she soon became a fixture at Charles Bailey's 81 Theatre. Her starting salary was a mere $10 a week, but her evocative singing style brought in a deluge of tips to supplement her income. The song that she was most remembered for during her years in Atlanta is "Weary Blues," a common folk-blues song first published by St. Louis ragtime pianist Artie Matthews in 1915. By 1918, Smith was already a well-known headliner throughout the South and as far north as Baltimore. Two years later she became the star of her own musical troupe.

In the early 1920s, Bessie Smith moved to Philadelphia, where she performed regularly at the Standard and Dunbar theaters, as well as at Paradise Gardens, a popular nightclub in Atlantic City, New Jersey. Her initial attempts to break into the record industry were frustrated by a voice that sounded coarse by Tin Pan Alley standards and mannerisms that many considered plebeian. She auditioned material for the Emerson Record Company in 1921, but nothing was released in her name. She auditioned for Fred Hager at Okeh Records but was turned down because her voice was "too rough." Harry Pace of Black Swan Records rejected her on similar grounds. Early in 1923, however,

Smith was approached by the head of the Columbia Records segregated "race" catalogue, Frank Walker. He later claimed to have first heard her singing in a Selma, Alabama, gin mill in 1917, thereby implicitly taking credit for discovering her for the record industry. Actually, both Clarence Williams and Perry Bradford were active in attempting to negotiate a recording contract for Bessie Smith before Frank Walker showed any interest in her. Williams worked as Walker's assistant and served as the intermediary in locating her, which suggests that he may have had a hand in bringing her to Walker's attention. Williams talked Smith into taking him on as her manager,

When the great Bessie Smith toured the country, black people lined up around entire city blocks to her sing the blues. (SCHOMBURG CENTER)

and then he induced her to record material that he had copyrighted. When Smith discovered how much of her earnings from Columbia Records were earmarked for Williams' wallet, she terminated her contract with him and made new arrangements directly with Walker, who then handled her recording career from 1923 to 1931.

On February 11, 1923, her first recording session for Columbia, she recorded "Downhearted Blues" and "Gulf Coast Blues." Clarence Williams' piano accompaniment, even on the piece he had copyrighted as his own, "Gulf Coast Blues," is stiff, mechanical, and uninspired. Smith's vocals, however, are quite the opposite. In spite of the primitive acoustic recording techniques then available, her voice is both powerful and poignant, especially in her version of "Downhearted Blues." Her next session produced no real blues numbers, but instead a string of well-known vaudeville songs, including "Aggravatin' Papa," "Beale Street Mama," "Oh Daddy," and Clarence Williams' song "Baby, Won't You Please Come Home." Her undisputed masterpiece from this second session is her rendition of Porter Grainger's saucy "Tain't Nobody's Business If I Do."

By her third Columbia session, Smith had switched piano players, dumping Williams for Fletcher Henderson, probably because of the revelation of Williams' scheme to swindle her out of half of her recording fees but also because he was a mediocre pianist at best. Henderson had a shy and accommodating personal manner better suited to Smith's fiery temperament, and he was a better piano player. During this session, Smith returned to familiar blues material, recording a version of her standard, "Weary Blues," which she retitled "Mama Got the

Blues." In June 1923, Bessie Smith returned to the Columbia studios in New York for a fourth session, again accompanied by Fletcher Henderson on piano. A majority of the numbers she recorded were blues, among them the well-known "Jailhouse Blues."

The downhome folk lyrics from these songs, coupled with Smith's compelling blues vocals, struck a responsive chord among the black record-buying public. Her first Columbia record sold approximately 780,000 copies in six months. Throughout her career as a recording artist, she drew material from African-American oral tradition, a practice that helped to establish her strong personal bond with black audiences; she was the carrier of their cultural heritage.

The release of Bessie Smith's first recordings gave her stage career a dramatic boost, too: During the rest of 1923 and well into the next year, she toured constantly, in particular, to cities that had attracted large numbers of African-American migrants during World War I—St. Louis, Detroit, Cleveland, Pittsburgh, Cincinnati, Indianapolis, Kansas City, and especially Chicago. Black people lined up around an entire city block to hear her sing the blues, just as they waited in line to buy her latest record. She was also one of the few black performers of her era to stage shows for white audiences and was the first black woman to be broadcast live in concert on local radio stations in Atlanta and Memphis.

From the beginning, Smith's stage act included some dancing and an occasional husband-and-wife comedy routine with a male coworker. Perry Bradford recalled that she was "a whopping good foot dancer" when he first saw her in Atlanta; at the time, she was working with a male comedian named Buzzin Burton. Still, it was neither her dancing nor her humor that brought out the crowds but her vocal renditions of the blues. She sang them with a passionate conviction and stage presence. Her voice was rich and resonant; she concentrated on middle octave and center tones, although she had a much greater range. Like other great black vocalists, Smith could bend, stretch, and slur notes to achieve a desired effect. She used her voice as a jazz instrument, like the growl of a trombone. Many musicians who worked with her commented on these vocal pyrotechnics and on her ability to hold an audience spellbound.

In 1924 and 1925, Smith was back in the recording studio for a series of sessions that would prove to be, from a musical standpoint, the best of her career. Through her association with Fletcher Henderson, she began to use members of his New York-based dance orchestra as accompanists. Some of the most talented jazzmen in the country whose participation in her recording sessions vastly improved the quality of her accomplishments. They included cornetist Joe Smith, trombone player Charlie Green, clarinetist Buster Bailey, saxophonists Coleman Hawkins and Don Redman—as well as the era's premier jazz musician, Louis Armstrong. In addition, she found another pianist to her liking, Fred Longshaw. These men became key figures in Smith's best backup bands during the Columbia recording sessions from 1924 to 1930.

An especially memorable musical collaboration occurred in 1924, when Bessie Smith teamed up with Charlie Green and Joe Smith for the first in a series of recordings they would make together. On two of the 1924 recordings they made with Smith,

"Weeping Willow Blues" and "The Bye Bye Blues," they are featured together, and their endeavors produced an exceptional record. They created a spontaneous interplay between the two horns that embellished the accompaniment to the extent that even Smith's vocals sounded better than usual. The Empress was duly impressed; she would continue to request Green and Smith as backup musicians in her recording sessions up until the onset of the Depression. In 1925, Louis Armstrong backed up Bessie Smith in the recording studio on three separate occasions for a total of nine songs. The best titles they recorded were W.C. Handy's classic "St. Louis Blues," Ben Harney's satirical ragtime standard "You've Been a Good Old Wagon," and "Careless Love." Unfortunately, Armstrong and Smith never worked together after the 1925 recording sessions; hence, the nine Columbia releases produced in those sessions were the only collaboration of the decade's two most important black musicians.

The blues that Smith recorded from 1925 to 1930 give equal attention to social and sexual themes. The social material she drew from the daily plight of the African-American masses, as she saw it; topics such as poverty, bootlegging, prisons and injustice, drinking and gambling, unemployment, and hard times were all commonplace in her recordings. Some of her noteworthy releases include "Rent House Blues," which tells about receiving an eviction notice from the landlord, and "Workhouse Blues," which tells the story of confinement to a prison workhouse. Other prison-related material that she recorded during this period includes "Sing Sing Prison Blues," a grim reminder of the infamous New York State penitentiary, and "Woman's Trouble Blues," a story about the unjust incarceration of a young black woman.

Smith's biggest-selling blues number of the decade was "Backwater Blues," a song she wrote herself after seeing a flood along the Ohio River. It detailed the flood from the point of view of a female victim who had to be evacuated from her home before it was washed away by the raging flood waters. As if a prophecy, its release coincided with the worst flooding in the history of the Mississippi River, which may have accounted for some of its extraordinary sales.

Her accompanist and collaborator on "Backwater Blues" was the stride piano virtuoso James P. Johnson. Theirs was a brief but fruitful relationship, and Smith soon thereafter recorded one of his compositions, "Black Mountain Blues," a mischievous song about life in the "Negro quarters of the South." "Money Blues," "Pickpocket Blues," and "Dying Gambler Blues" deal with residents of the urban tenderloin; "Foolish Man Blues" is about homosexuality; and "Bedbug Blues" and "Washerwoman's Blues" tell two satirical stories about city life for migrant African Americans.

Her masterpiece of social protest from this period is a song she wrote entitled "Poor Man's Blues." Smith's biographer, Chris Albertson, maintained that "'Poor Man's Blues' could have been entitled 'Black Man's Blues.'" It was a song that much of the population could identify with, regardless of whom Smith had in mind when she wrote it.

Sex was one topic that Bessie Smith always dealt with candidly. At times, she employed risqué double entendres, as she did in her recording of "Kitchen Man" and the popular "Empty Bed Blues." When she turned to the subject of her personal relationships with men, however, she made several recordings that are critical of her male partners, like "Salt Water Blues" and "Sinful Blues"—though she did record some traditional material such as "My Man" and "Honey Man." She recorded numbers like "I Ain't Gonna Play No Second Fiddle" and "I've Been Mistreated and I Don't Like It," but she also recorded songs containing a sense of newly acquired independence and freedom of choice, as in "Young Women Blues" and "Reckless Blues."

Taken as a whole, the blues lyrics immortalized by Bessie Smith had two characteristics of great significance. First, they were drawn from the black oral tradition's repository of rural folk blues; hence, they were very familiar to African Americans. She avoided the more commercialized material from the vaudeville stage or Tin Pan Alley, concentrating instead on verse that evoked deeply felt responses from her audiences. The second characteristic of Smith's blues lyrics was that, although they often addressed far-reaching social issues and concerns, they expressed her own feelings and experiences as a black woman. Their individuality and emotional honesty appealed not only to African Americans, but also to certain sectors of the white population. Smith's blues verses were poetry set to music; they were like all great art in that they expressed human emotions that were universal.

Bessie Smith's personal life was full of the excesses, conflicts, and rebelliousness that she sang about with such conviction. She was married twice and not a stranger to heartbreak. Her first husband, Earl Love, died shortly after their marriage. When she moved to Philadelphia in 1922, she met and then married Jack Gee, a night watchman who claimed he was a policeman. They separated seven years later after a stormy

and exhausting marriage that often deteriorated into angry physical brawls. During this period of her life, Bessie also had numerous lovers, both male and female. Among her known male lovers were musicians Sidney Bechet, Porter Grainger, and Lonnie Johnson, all of whom worked with her in the 1920s. Her longest-lasting, and perhaps steadiest relationship with a man was with Richard Morgan, a Chicago-based bootlegger and patron of black music. Morgan became a friend in 1924 during her initial visits to Chicago; he remained close to her up until her death in 1937 and was, in fact, driving her car when the accident occurred that killed her.

Smith was open with her female lovers about her bisexuality but does not seem to have shared much of this information with the men in her life. The sexual liaisons she had with other women tended to be short-lived and relegated to a relatively secret zone of female social activity. Most often her liaisons occurred when Smith was on the road with a show and involved other women in the troupe. They lasted for the duration of the tour or until her husband discovered her indiscretions.

Bessie Smith indulged her appetites generally. She ate and drank with gusto and was especially fond of home-cooked Southern food and moonshine; she was a binge drinker who often drank to forget her troubles, though alcohol sometimes brought out a volcanic rage in her, and her drinking sprees often ended in violence. To compound the problem, Smith had a penchant for the night life of the urban underworld. This pattern of excess was part of Smith's chaotic lifestyle. To escape the pressures of fame, and perhaps also the painful memories of her childhood, she turned to drunken revelry, combined with sexual and culinary gratification. Whether she was attending a party in the sporting district where "the funk was flying," as she liked to put it, or holding court in the railroad car she toured the South in, the cycle of overindulgence hampered her development as a blues artist and damaged her health.

Smith became notorious for her extreme behavior. On the one hand, she could be fun-loving and generous to a fault, lavishing gifts on her companions, picking up all their bar tabs, even sending them on paid vacations. Yet, on several occasions she walked out on her road shows, leaving the cast and crew without money to pay their bills, and at times she fired her employees gratuitously. She displayed remarkable courage in the face of danger. During one altercation, she pursued a male attacker even after he had buried a knife in her side; another time she single-handedly repulsed a Ku Klux Klan raiding party with a barrage of scurrilous invective. She could also be a merciless bully and beat her adversaries senseless or attack them with no provocation. Great strength of character, courage, love, and will power were contradicted by deep hurt, anger, and an unremitting rage toward the society in which she lived.

With the onset of the Depression, Smith's fortunes plummeted along with those of most black entertainers. The advent of talking motion pictures was a death blow to vaudeville in general and black vaudeville in particular. The record industry also suffered serious setbacks. The sales of records dwindled considerably because of the overall economic decline and the gains made by radio in the entertainment business. Swing dance music, played by white orchestras, became the popular commercial music of the era,

and interest in the blues waned. Bessie Smith's recording contract with Columbia was terminated in 1931. She recorded once more in 1933 at a special session arranged and paid for by John Hammond, but other than that, her career as a recording artist was over. During one of her final recording sessions for Columbia, Smith made a record that was destined to become both her personal epitaph and a Depression-era classic; it was entitled "Nobody Knows You When You're Down and Out."

If Bessie Smith's final years did not yield to her the prominence and financial rewards commensurate with her vocal artistry, they were at least less turbulent and less emotionally traumatic for her than the previous decade had been. Her control of the drinking binges improved, and her relationship with Richard Morgan deepened into a loving and supportive companionship. Smith seemed to have mellowed with age, learning from her past mistakes. With the record contract gone, she found that even singing engagements in clubs were hard to secure. At times, she had to rely on Morgan for financial help. Smith continued to perform the blues up until her death at the age of forty-three in 1937. Her fatal automobile accident in Mississippi came at a time when her career was on the rebound.

While Bessie Smith never received official recognition in her lifetime, her important contributions to the blues idiom were eventually acknowledged by American music historians and scholars. Within African-American culture, she will always be the greatest woman blues singer, a heroine of her race who sang the common people's music like no one else. Her influence on American culture in general is impressive. More than any other black performer in the

1920s and 1930s, she was responsible for introducing the blues into the mainstream of popular American music. If Columbia Records reaped the financial benefits of this profitable enterprise, Smith and her public at least enjoyed the cultural fruits of these endeavors. Her music was not to be a passing commercial fad; it was an enduring and permeating contribution to the fabric of American music that would change the course of the entire culture over the next decades.

WILLIAM BARLOW

Smith, Mable Louise   (1924–1972)

Big Maybelle was born Mable Louise Smith on May 1, 1924, in Jackson, Tennessee, and died on January 23, 1972, following a diabetic coma.

Big Maybelle's earliest musical training was in the Sanctified Church choir in her hometown of Jackson, Tennessee. Her professional career was launched when she won first prize in the Memphis Cotton Carnival Singing Contest in 1932—she was just eight years old. Later, she worked with such noted groups as the Dave Clark Band (1930s), the **International Sweethearts of Rhythm** (1936–40), the Christene Chapman Orchestra (1944), the Tiny Bradshaw Orchestra (1947–50), and Jimmy Witherspoon.

Her career developed at an interesting time. During the 1930s there was a shift from smaller ensembles to swing bands. Along with this shift came a heavier reliance on male white singers and few if any contracts and engagements for blues singers. This was also a period when recording companies attempted to focus their markets by labeling music according to the market they hoped to attract. So, the term *rhythm and blues* was introduced to describe artists who considered themselves to be blues singers.

Big Maybelle's style was greatly influenced by the legacies of such artists as **Bessie Smith** and **Ma Rainey**, singers whose music not only validated African-American women performers as professional artists but also transformed and adapted the rhythms of southern-based blues to an urban landscape. Yet, her delivery was not jazz in the tradition of the classic female singers, or the shout of the male Kansas City singers; it was a style that relied on raw emotional power, a power that represented a combination of these various influences and one that was characteristic of the soul tradition that developed in the 1960s.

Although her recordings span a thirty-year period, Big Maybelle is best remembered for those done during her heyday in the 1950s. For example, while she is often remembered for *Candy* (Savoy 1195), recorded on May 20, 1956, she also charted hits with *Grabbin Blues* (Okeh 6931), recorded on January 3, 1953, *My Way Back Home* (Okeh 6955), recorded on May 30, 1953, and *My Country Man* (Okeh 7009), recorded on November 28, 1953. Other charted national hits include *Don't Pass Me By* (Rojac 14969), recorded on November 12, 1966, and *96 Tears* (Rojac 112), recorded on January 14, 1967.

Big Maybelle recorded eighteen 45-rpm records for a variety of labels from 1953 to 1967.

ROBERT STEPHENS

Smith, Mamie   (1893–1946)

In 1920, when Okeh Records released Mamie Smith's "Crazy Blues," it became one of the biggest popular hits of the early

1920s, sold close to a million copies, and set off a recording boom for black female blues singers.

Mamie Smith was born Mamie Gardener in Cincinnati, Ohio, on May 26, 1893. Not much is known about her family or childhood; however, she began her career in show business at the age of ten as a dancer with the Four Dancing Mitchells and soon thereafter left Cincinnati. By 1910 she was touring the Midwest and the East Coast as a member of the Smart Set Company, a black minstrel troupe. In 1912, she married singer William "Smitty" Smith, and at that time changed her stage name to Smith. A year later, the couple moved to New York, and Mamie commenced her career as a cabaret dancer, singer, and pianist.

Her first major break came in 1918, when she was hired by Perry Bradford, a black songwriter and show business entrepreneur, to appear in his musical, *Made in Harlem*. Bradford was so impressed with Smith that he chose her to be the black female artist to break the color line in the growing record industry based in New York. After her audition for Victor Records failed to make an impression, Bradford set up a session for her at Okeh Records, a small, independent label. Initially, Okeh was interested in Bradford's songs but wanted them to be recorded by the white vaudeville star Sophie Tucker. When Tucker could not make the recording sessions due to prior commitments, Mamie Smith was given the nod. Her first release for Okeh in the spring of 1920, "That Thing Called Love" and "You Can't Keep a Good Man Down," sold well enough to warrant another session later in the year. At that second session, she recorded "Crazy Blues," a Bradford composition she had popularized as "Harlem Blues" in the *Made in*

The release of "Crazy Blues" catapulted Mamie Smith into the national limelight. It was followed by thirty more recordings on the Okeh label. (SCHOMBURG CENTER)

Harlem musical; Bradford changed the name of the song to "Crazy Blues" to avoid copyright problems. Her backup band for the session, christened the Jazz Hounds, included Willie "the Lion" Smith on piano, Jimmy Dunn on cornet, and Dope Andrews on trombone—all well-known local jazz musicians.

"Crazy Blues" was a phenomenal success, catapulting Mamie Smith into the national limelight. In a matter of months, she became one of the best-known female vocalists in the country and during the next year made thirty more recordings for the Okeh label. In addition, she became the star attraction in a series of black vaudeville shows that toured the country, garnering rave reviews and packing the theaters wherever they appeared. These shows included *Follow Me* (1922), *Struttin' Along* (1923), *Dixie Review* (1924), *Syncopated Revue* (1925), and *Frolicking Around* (1926). During this period of her greatest renown, she continued to record for the Okeh label and began to record for Ajax Records (1924) and Victor Records (1926). In addition, her backup band, the Jazz Hounds, continued to attract the decade's most accomplished jazz musicians, men like pianist Fats Waller, saxophonist Coleman Hawkins, trumpeter Bubber Miley, and clarinetist Buster Bailey. Everywhere she appeared, Mamie Smith was lauded for her poise, beauty, and stage presence.

During the Depression, Mamie Smith's career slowed. She continued to record for Okeh Records up through 1931, about the time the bottom fell out of the "race" recording industry. She continued to star in black musical revues, including the *Sun Tan Frolics* (1929), *Fireworks of 1930*, *Rhumbaland Revue* (1931), and the *Yelping Hounds Revue* (1932–34). She married her third husband, Mr. Goldberg, in 1929; her second husband had been comedian Sam Gardner, whom she married in 1920 and divorced a few years later.

The highlights of her career in the 1930s were a tour of Europe in 1936 and a leading role in the 1939 film *Paradise in Harlem*, in which she sang the famous "Harlem Blues," backed up by the Lucky Millinder orchestra. Her film career continued to flourish in the early 1940s. During this period, she appeared in *Mystery in Swing* (1940), *Sunday Sinners* (1941), *Murder on Lenox Avenue* (1941), and *Because I Love You* (1943).

In 1944, Mamie Smith's health began to fail her, and she was admitted to the Harlem Hospital; after a prolonged illness, she died there in the fall of 1946.

WILLIAM BARLOW

Smith, Trixie (1895–1943)

Trixie Smith was a theatrical performer and blues singer. Born in Atlanta, she moved to the North and established herself as a singer in vaudeville by the time she was twenty. In the 1920s and 1930s, in addition to performing and recording as a singer, she pursued an active theatrical career, appearing in musical revues and plays and in one film, *The Black King* (1932). She appears to have performed both singing and character roles.

Her recording career began in January 1922 when she recorded for Black Swan, a black-owned record company. In February 1922, she won a blues singing contest sponsored by the Fifteenth Regiment of the New York Infantry at the Manhattan Casino in New York City, which helped both her recording and performing careers. After Paramount Records bought out financially troubled Black Swan, she recorded for Paramount until 1926. Her last records were made for Decca in the late 1930s. She went into semiretirement after 1940 and died suddenly in 1943.

Trixie Smith's singing voice was light and flexible, without the hard edge or the intense tone quality of other blues singers. She was an excellent performer of jazz-tinged blues and show tunes, recording with prominent jazz musicians, among them Louis Armstrong, Fletcher Henderson, and Sidney Bechet; however, the songs she wrote for herself ("Trixie's Blues," "Railroad Blues," and "Mining Camp Blues") exhibit a more traditional orientation and the ability to appeal directly to an audience, which is characteristic of the best of the blueswomen.

SUZANNE FLANDREAU

Smith, Willie Mae Ford (1904–1994)

The African-American gospel music movement of today is irrevocably linked with three names: Thomas A. Dorsey, **Sallie Martin**, and Willie Mae Ford Smith. These three were the leaders of a small group that met in Chicago in 1932 to organize the National Convention of Gospel Choirs and Choruses, the parent organization that brought forth such contemporary singers as the Winans, Take Six, and **Shirley Ceasar**. Of the three leaders, the most talented singer was Smith, who could have performed European classical music as easily as gospel, which would have been gospel's loss.

Willie Mae Ford Smith was born, one of fourteen children, in the small village of Rolling Rock, Mississippi, in 1904. As a child, she moved with her family to Memphis, Tennessee, and when she was twelve, the family settled in St. Louis. Her father, a devout deacon in the Baptist church, worked during the week as a railroad brakeman, and her mother was a homemaker until 1928, when she opened a restaurant in one of the poorer sections of St. Louis. Smith, an eighth-grade student at the time, left school to help her mother in the restaurant, bringing her formal education to a close.

Smith was not concerned with formal education because she had already chosen music as her vocation, performing as a soloist when she was ten. In 1922, she and her three sisters organized a group to sing black spirituals and the emerging gospel jubilee songs that were becoming popular. This group sang at the 1922 National Baptist Convention and created a sensation.

It was not until 1926, however, that Smith heard the kind of singing for which she had been searching. At the 1926 National Baptist Convention, Artelia Hutchins of Detroit, the cocomposer with Dorsey of "God Be with You," sang "Careless Soul, Why Do You Linger?" and Smith found her voice. From her Baptist background and the singing of Hutchins, Smith developed her dark contralto into a sonorous vehicle for delivering long melodic lines, executing mild embellishments, and expanding it from a whisper into a thunderous bell. She turned to the songs that she learned as a child and added the new elements she admired. In Smith's style, the hymn "What a Friend We Have in Jesus," traditionally sung in the slow and languorous eighteenth-century Baptist lining hymn manner, became a soliloquy of conviction and pride. She was the first gospel singer to add a gospel rhythm to the hymn "Blessed Assurance" and to improvise the chorus in such a way that it became a sing-along melody.

In 1929, she married James Peter Smith, who owned a small moving company. Shortly after her marriage, the stock market crashed, and in order to help with the finances of the family, she traveled to other cities to sing. She met Thomas A. Dorsey in Chicago in 1931 and was invited back to Chicago in 1932 to help with the organization of the National Convention of Gospel Choirs and Choruses. She was such a successful soloist, both in the rendition of songs and the ability to inspire audiences, that in 1936 Dorsey asked her to head the Soloists

Bureau and teach gospel singing. The following year, she set the standard for solo singing with her rendition of her own composition, "If You Just Keep Still." Smith served as the director of the Soloists Bureau for more than forty years. She organized a chapter of the National Convention of Gospel Choirs and Choruses in St. Louis and assisted Dorsey and Sallie Martin in traveling to cities in the Midwest to organize gospel groups.

In 1939, she joined the Pentecostal congregation of the Church of God Apostolic and took on the rhythm, bounce, and percussive attacks of the Sanctified singer. She was then able to render the Baptist hymn in the so-called Watts style or to bring a church into a holy dance through her short songs. She inspired a large number of singers, the first of whom was **Mahalia Jackson**. Jackson decided to leave her job as a beautician after consulting with Smith.

Unlike Jackson and **Roberta Martin**, with whom she sang for a while, Smith made very few recordings. None of these garnered much attention, and she therefore concentrated her efforts on preaching, having become an evangelist after joining the Sanctified church. She would sing and preach for a week at one church and offer singing lessons during the day. Many of her students attained the fame that eluded her. Among them were Edna Gallmon Cooke, Martha Bass (the mother of soul singer Fontella Bass), Myrtle Scott, the Oneal twins, and, perhaps her most famous student, Brother Joe May, who was the first to call her "Mother."

Smith is credited with the introduction of the song-and-sermonette form into gospel music, whereby the singer delivers a five- or ten-minute sermon before, during, or after the performance of a song.

She has appeared at the Newport Jazz Festival and Radio City Music Hall and in 1982 was celebrated in the gospel film documentary *Say Amen, Somebody*. In 1989, she was selected as one of the African-American women to be featured in Brian Lanker's collection of photographs called *I Dream a World*.

Smith died on February 2, 1994 of congestive heart failure, in the Tower Village Nursing Home in St. Louis. She continued to perform regularly at the Lively Stone Apostolic Church in St. Louis until the early 1990s.

HORACE CLARENCE BOYER

Snow, Valaida   (c.1909–1956)

Valaida Snow was born in Chattanooga, Tennessee, c. 1909. Although internationally known as Queen of the Trumpet, Snow was a versatile artist who claimed talents as a dancer, singer, conductor, arranger, and composer. She began her career in the 1920s in clubs in Pennsylvania and New Jersey and in 1922 made her debut in New York at Barron Wilkins' Harlem cabaret and showcased her versatility by dancing, singing, and playing the violin, topping the performance off with daring trumpet solos.

Snow was born into a family of musicians. Her mother tutored her on several instruments and her sisters, Alvaida, Hattie, and Lavaida, eventually became professional entertainers as well.

She toured internationally in the 1930s, 1940s, and 1950s and performed with jazz greats Count Basie, Earl Hines, Jack Carter, Teddy Weatherford, Willie Lewis, and Fletcher Henderson. Her fans in Europe called her Little Louis because of her Louis Armstrong-influenced trumpet style. She recorded more than forty titles for record companies in Denmark, England, and Sweden.

She made her Broadway debut as Mandy in *Chocolate Dandies* (1924) and later appeared in *Rhapsody in Black* (1924) and *Blackbirds* (1934) and in the films *Take It from Me* (1937), *Irresistible You, L'Alibi,* and *Pièges* (1939).

In 1941, when the United States entered World War II, Snow was interned in a Nazi concentration camp. She was released about a year later, and in unstable health, but nevertheless shortly resumed performing in theaters and clubs.

She married twice—first to dancer Ananias Berry and later to performer and producer Earle Edwards. Her last performance was a 1956 engagement at the Palace Theater in New York. She died May 30, 1956, of a cerebral hemorrhage.

PAULETTE WALKER

Spivey, Victoria (1906–1976)

Victoria Spivey had a long and colorful career as a blues singer, recording artist, and songwriter. She was born into a musical family in Houston, Texas, on October 6, 1906, and learned to play piano as a child. By her early teens she was performing in local clubs. She admired the recordings and performances of the older women blues singers. Hoping for such a career herself, she traveled to St. Louis in 1926 and wangled an audition with Jesse Johnson, the local agent for Okeh Records. Her first record, "Black Snake Blues," was a hit. She was hired as a songwriter for the St. Louis Pub-

lishing Company, and until 1929 she recorded extensively for Okeh.

In 1929, Spivey won an ingenue role in King Vidor's all-black film musical *Hallelujah!* though the role of the blues singer went to another actress. Throughout the Great Depression, when many musicians found work scarce, Spivey continued to record for various labels and to perform in clubs and touring shows, from *Dallas Tan Town Topics*, which toured Texas and Oklahoma in 1933, to the Minsky burlesque circuit. In 1938–39, she performed and toured in the Broadway show *Hellzapoppin'*. During these years she often appeared with her sisters, Addie and Leona, who were also blues singers, or with her husband, dancer Billy Adams.

Spivey continued to work in clubs until the 1950s, when she quit show business for church work, but in 1961 she returned, forming her own record label, Queen Vee. In 1962, it became Spivey Records, for which she produced recordings of well-known and up-and-coming blues musicians' lyrics and songs. She also recorded albums, performing her own songs for the Bluesville and Folkways labels. During the 1960s, she was a mainstay at colleges, folk clubs, and festivals, visiting Europe with the American Folk Blues Tour (1963) and performing at the Chicago (1969), Philadelphia (1971), and Ann Arbor (1973) blues festivals. She died suddenly of an internal hemorrhage in New York City on October 3, 1976.

Victoria Spivey had a high, rather nasal singing voice that was made more evocative by a characteristic moan she called her "tiger squall." She never entirely lost the Texas country-blues sound of her youth, and she was a mercurial performer, able to evoke whatever emotions each song required. Her best songs, among them "TB Blues" and "Murder in the First Degree," show an ability to portray even situations outside her personal experience vividly. The blues revival of the 1960s made it possible for her to receive the acclaim she deserved.

SUZANNE FLANDREAU

Staples, Mavis (c. 1940–)

Music critics unanimously applaud Mavis Staples as possessing one of the most dynamic and distinctive voices in contemporary music. Along with her father and siblings, Mavis was part of the Staple Singers, who enjoyed success with both gospel and popular music fans from the 1950s through the 1970s. She is also recognized as a solo performer of pop and gospel music.

In 1934, Roebuck "Pop" Staples moved his wife, Oceola, and children, Cleotha and Pervis, from his native Mississippi to Chicago. Once there, Yvonne, Mavis, and Cynthia were born, and eventually the children were taught to harmonize by their father. The Staple Singers performed in a style that

With her family, the Staple Singers, Mavis Staples told the black world in the sixties to "Respect Yourself." The Singers consisted of, left to right, Cleotha, Roebuck ("Pop"), Yvonne, and Mavis Staples. (STEVE HOLSEY)

In 1970, Mavis Staples began a solo career. Among her recordings that made the charts were "I Have Learned to Do Without You," "Endlessly," and "A Piece of the Action." (PRIVATE COLLECTION)

has been described by gospel-music historian Horace C. Boyer as "characterized by folk-style simple harmonies, rendered in a country and western twang, supporting a lead by the tenor voice of Roebuck or the hard gospel alto of Mavis." Roebuck's bluesy guitar and the group's pulsating rhythm section also were featured.

After performing in local Chicago churches, the Staple Singers recorded for a number of companies, beginning with United Records (1954) and Vee Jay Records (1955–61), with which they released several recordings, including "Uncloudy Day." Subsequent labels were Riverside (1961–64) and Epic (1964–68); for the latter, they recorded the classic "Why (Am I Treated So Bad)." Yet, it was the music they made for Stax Records (1968–74) that attracted mass audiences. While there, the Staple (the final "s" was dropped over the years) Singers were featured in the "Soul to Soul" and Wattstax concerts. Among their hits were "Respect Yourself," "If You're Ready (Come Go with Me)," and "I'll Take You There," all of which became number-one *Billboard* hits. Further success and another number-one hit came with their performance on the sound track for the comedy film *Let's Do It Again* for Curtom Records. Although some fans accused the singers of selling out when they switched from gospel to "message" music, the group insisted that although the beat had gotten funkier, the message of love had never changed. The Staple Singers continue to perform with various personnel changes (Pop has also recorded as a solo performer), but the group has not been able to replicate its earlier success.

Mavis' driving performance style and husky voice, reminiscent of two of her childhood gospel idols, **Dorothy Love Coates** and Ruth Davis, eventually led her to a solo career. Beginning in 1970, she recorded several critically acclaimed albums on the Volt, Warner Brothers, Phono, and Curtom labels. Among the recordings making the national rhythm-and-blues charts were "I Have Learned to Do Without You," "Endlessly," and "A Piece of the Action" from the movie of the same name. Mavis Staples also performs gospel music and has recorded with such major artists as **Aretha Franklin** (1988) and BeBe and CeCe Winans

(1991); with the latter, she sang on their remake of her family's hit of twenty years ago, "I'll Take You There."

Of her 1994 album *The Voice*, the reviewer for *Upscale* said, "[it will] carve her name even deeper in the living history of soul-filled rhythm and blues."

DEBORAH SMITH BARNEY

Staton, Dakota (1932–)

Born June 3, 1932, in Pittsburgh, Pennsylvania, Dakota Staton (Rabia Aliyah) is one of the best of several little-advertised jazz singers. Her artistic talents became evident at an early age as she began to sing and dance before she entered elementary school, and by the time she graduated from high school her jazz singing talent was sufficient to launch a professional career. She sang at jazz clubs, jazz festivals, and theaters throughout the United States and Canada while also studying music at the Fillon School of Music in Pittsburgh.

In 1954, at the age of twenty-two, Staton made her first recording. Thereafter, she made several additional recordings, receiving critical acclaim for her album *The Late, Late Show* (1957). Staton recorded with George Shearing in 1957 and at the Newport Jazz Festival in 1963; she also toured with Benny Goodman around 1960. In 1965, she moved to England, and from 1965 to the early 1970s she both lived and performed abroad, primarily in Australia, Europe, India, Pakistan, and the Far East.

Since returning to the United States in the early 1970s, Staton's recordings have become eclectic, including both jazz and two soul-jazz albums. She performs standards and incorporates elements of both **Dinah Washington** and **Sarah Vaughan** into her style. She displays excellent diction, has an excellent sense of rhythm and harmony, and often uses scat techniques in her voice stylings.

EDDIE S. MEADOWS

Sullivan, Maxine (1911–1987)

Born Marietta Williams on May 13, 1911, in Homestead, Pennsylvania, Maxine Sullivan grew up in a musical household; her father played mandolin, and several uncles played other instruments as well. One of her uncles, who played drums with vocalist Lois Deppe's band in 1922, formed a group of his own called the Red Hot Peppers, and young Maxine used to go along with the band and sing a few songs. Despite the fact that her voice was on the soft side and her repertoire did not contain any blues, Sullivan landed a job in the Benjamin Harrison Literary Club in downtown Pittsburgh. It was while she was working at this after-hours club that Gladys Mosier, pianist with Ina Ray Hutton's all-woman band, convinced Sullivan to go to New York, where Mosier arranged what turned out to be a successful audition with pianist/arranger Claude Thornhill. Thornhill wrote an arrangement of the old Scottish folk song "Loch Lomond" for Sullivan, and her 1937 recording became a hit. Sullivan was accompanied on the record by a small group, including bassist John Kirby. This was essentially the group that played at the Onyx Club on Fifty-second Street where Sullivan and Kirby often worked together. Later in 1937, Kirby and Sullivan were married.

Things were looking good for the newlyweds. They recorded frequently and even became costars of an NBC network radio show, *Flow Gently, Sweet Rhythm*. In 1939,

Sullivan took part in a stage production called *Swingin' the Dream*, a swing version of *A Midsummer Night's Dream* in which she played the part of Titania, queen of the fairies. She also appeared that year in two Hollywood films, *St. Louis Blues* and *Going Places*, in the latter costarring with Louis Armstrong and Ronald Reagan. Things stopped going well for the couple during this time, and they were divorced in 1941. Sullivan joined the Benny Carter Orchestra for one tour and then embarked on a solo career.

In 1950, Sullivan married stride pianist Cliff Jackson; the marriage lasted until Jackson's death in 1970. Sullivan took up the valve trombone in 1956 and later played flugelhorn and then pocket trumpet. Also in 1956, she retired from show business, choosing to devote her time and energies to raising her daughter and working with the local school board. In 1961, she became president of the Public School 136 Parent-Teachers Association in the Bronx.

Although she was retired, Sullivan made periodic appearances at clubs and festivals, and after her well-received performances and recordings with the World's Greatest Jazz Band in the late 1960s, she officially came out of retirement. She continued to perform, touring Europe and Japan, and to record until her death in New York City on April 7, 1987.

The 1937 hit recording of "Loch Lomond" type-cast Maxine Sullivan as a singer of folk songs such as "Molly Malone" and "If I Had a Ribbon Bow," which she sang in a suave, sweet, gently swinging style. In her comeback years, however, her voice acquired a huskiness that gave her jazz singing an authenticity that earlier had been lacking. Maxine Sullivan will be remembered not just as "the Loch Lomond girl" but also as a truly original vocal stylist whose best work was done in the later years of her long and distinguished career.

VINCENT PELOTE

Summer, Donna (1948–)

The year is 1978. As strobe lights toss out a million multicolored stars of glittering light across jam-packed dance clubs around the world, Donna Summer croons the opening strains of "Last Dance." Her little-girl, plaintive voice slowly but surely swells to big-girl brassiness as she invites the world to dance, invoking romance and vulnerability in an uptempo crescendo that brings the world to its feet. Not bad for a girl from Beantown.

La Donna Andrea Gaines was born in Boston, Massachusetts, on December 31, 1948. She used her voice to carve a niche for herself within a large family that included five sisters and one brother. By the age of ten, she was singing with gospel groups in local churches.

In 1967, after a brief stint with the group, Crow, she auditioned to replace **Melba Moore** in the Broadway version of *Hair*. Selected instead for the German cast, Summer found herself in Munich, Germany, in 1970, a providential setting. It was in Munich that La Donna Andrea Gaines married Helmid Sommer, an Austrian actor. They later divorced, but La Donna took the anglicized version of his surname for her now famous stage name, Donna Summer.

The run with *Hair* eventually ended, but Summer's career was just beginning. She balanced performances with the Vienna Folk Opera in *Porgy and Bess* and *Showboat* with back up work at Musicland studios, all the while taking care of her daughter, Mimi.

In Munich, Summer met producers Giorgio Moroder and Pete Bellotte. Under Moroder's guidance, Summer found herself properly positioned to ride the wave of popularity of Euro-Disco. In 1975, her steamy, sixteen-minute "Love To Love You, Baby," was released, or rather unleashed upon the world. In 1976, a million copies were sold in the United States alone, earning Summer a gold record. A diva was born.

Returning to the United States, Donna Summer went on to earn twenty-four gold and platinum certificates, seventeen awarded during the '70s. Her greatest hits

Donna Summer got her start in the German road company of Hair *in 1970. In 1975, she made the switch from musical comedy and opera to pop; her steamy "Love to Love You, Baby" earned her a gold record and made her a "queen of disco."*

include "I Feel Love" (1977); "MacArthur Park" (1978); "Hot Stuff," "Bad Girls," "Dim All the Lights" (1979), and "She Works Hard for the Money" (1983). In 1979, along with Barbra Streisand, Donna Summer recorded "No More Tears (Enough Is Enough)," which shot to the number-one spot on the chart.

Multitalented and ambitious, Summer appeared in the 1978 film, *Thank God It's Friday*, unfortunately to poor reviews. She rebounded to compose "Bad Girls," along with her future husband, Bruce Sudano, and Eddie Hokenson and Joe Esposito. Her songwriting skills continued to mature, as evidenced by "The Wanderer," released in 1980.

Even numerous awards, including four Grammys, and a legion of fans, could not protect Donna Summer from the downside of fame. The hectic tours, rumor mills, sex goddess image, and contract disputes exacted a toll in exhaustion, insomnia, headaches, and ulcers.

"I went from poverty to riches, but when I got there, I found it wasn't so great. I had neglected the spirit—my spiritual needs." Summer became a born-again Christian and lost her old image but not her talent. The 1983 hit "She Works Hard for the Money" was released after this milestone in her life.

Whatever lies in store in the future, this can be said: There was a phenomenon called disco; its diva was, and always will be, Donna Summer.

RICHARD R. T. WADE

Sweet Honey in the Rock

For nearly two decades, this black women's a cappella group has been singing songs of struggle. With a power rooted in the tradi-

With a power rooted in the tradition of the Southern black church, Sweet Honey in the Rock delivers sermons in song that challenge us to be counted in the fight for social justice. Pictured from left: Bernice Johnson Reagon, Aisha Kahlil, Shirley Childress Johnson, Evelyn Maria Harris, Nitanju Bolade-Casel, and Ysaye Maria Barnwell. (MOORLAND-SPINGARN)

tion of the Southern black church, Sweet Honey in the Rock delivers sermons in song that challenge us to be counted in the fight for social justice.

Since its founding in 1973 by **Bernice Johnson Reagon,** more than twenty women have been in the group. Though the exact cluster of talents has changed over time, in the early 1990s the group included Evelyn Harris, Ysaye Barnwell, Aisha Kahlil, Nitanju Bolade Casel, and sign-language interpreter Shirley Childress Johnson.

Using the power of the unaccompanied human voice, the women of Sweet Honey weave dazzling, breathtaking harmonies with a special sound that resonates with the history of the African diaspora. The group moves effortlessly through a repertoire that includes urban blues tunes, West African chants, field hollers, black gospel, reggae, and rap.

What distinguishes Sweet Honey in the Rock from other performers, however, are the messages contained in the group's songs.

The group's repertoire of original compositions tackles such issues as apartheid, economic injustice, the AIDS epidemic, homelessness, political prisoners, and the global struggle for human rights.

Sweet Honey in the Rock has built an international following through tours and performances in Africa, Asia, Europe, South America, and the Caribbean. They have performed in such historic venues as the Apollo Theater and Carnegie Hall, recorded nine albums, and received a Grammy Award for a 1988 recording of songs by Woody Guthrie and Leadbelly.

IVY YOUNG

T

Taylor, Gertrude Jackson (1903–)

For forty years, Gertrude Jackson Taylor produced operas, operettas, and concert versions of operas for black audiences on Chicago's south side. She contributed to the careers of dozens of musicians and to the cultural life of her community.

Taylor was born Gertrude Smith on April 24, 1903, in Chicago and baptized at Quinn A.M.E. Chapel. The Smiths lived on Chicago's south side in Englewood, a neighborhood that was then off-limits to African Americans. Because of Mr. Smith's light complexion (and the fact that he hired a white nanny/maid), neighbors assumed that Mrs. Smith was the family's domestic.

Ninety-two years of living did not cloud Gertrude Taylor's memory of music, nor of her parents. As a child, Taylor saw her father Charles Smith ride his bicycle to and from work, whistling a tune all the way; in the evenings, he would strum his guitar as he sang. Taylor's mother, Mary Rose, was her first piano teacher, an alto in the choir, and a composer. From the age of ten, young Gertrude studied piano with her mother and piano and organ with Antoinette Cone Tompkins, a Fisk University alumna. In her teens, she served as pianist/organist at both Salem Baptist Church and Quinn Chapel.

She attended Chicago schools and, in 1927, graduated from Roosevelt University with a B.Mus. in piano performance. Gertrude Smith then began graduate studies at Northwestern University, but, because of Northwestern's segregation policy, she was not permitted to stay in the "whites only" dormitory. Discouraged by the long commute to Northwestern, she continued her studies at the American Conservatory of Music.

In 1925, she married Rev. Frederick Jackson and had two children, **Betty Jackson King** and Catherine Jackson Adams. Both daughters grew to be pianists and singers. In the 1940s Taylor and her two daughters formed the Jacksonian Trio and traveled professionally throughout Illinois, Texas, Louisiana, Mississippi, and Tennessee. While they didn't make much money, the trio was able to build a studio in the Jackson home, which they used for opera rehearsals.

In 1930, Taylor founded and directed the Imperial Opera Company, which employed scores of singers, musicians, composers, designers, and technicians who were shunned by white opera companies. Until the 1970s, Taylor presented fully staged productions of *Swing Mikado*, *The Bohemian Girl*, *Chimes of Normandy*, and many other operas by and about African Americans. Imperial's roster included singers Mabel "Mother" Malarcher, John Burdett, Elroy Johnson, Helen Robbins White, Bernard Adams, Barbara Wright-Pryor, and Ron McKinley. Listed among the venues Imperial used are various churches and halls and the original band shell in Chicago's Grant Park, the site of Imperial's final curtain in 1950. In 1989,

When Gertrude Taylor went to graduate school in music at Northwestern University in 1927, she was not allowed to live in the "whites only" dormitory on campus. In 1930, Taylor founded and directed the Imperial Opera Company, which employed scores of singers, musicians, composers, designers, and technicians who were unable to work in white opera companies. (GERTRUDE TAYLOR)

the company reunited to mount Betty Jackson King's *Saul of Tarsus*.

On December 2, 1956, Taylor married Ozias Hummer Taylor, a baritone, choir director of Shiloh Baptist Church, and member of her Imperial Opera Company. However, not long after, Taylor followed a lifelong dream southward where she spent four years teaching at Southern Christian Institute. Returning to Chicago, Taylor resumed her post as choir director at Quinn Chapel, taught at the Jacksonian Center which was founded by her first husband, and served as minister of music at People's Community Church of Woodlawn where he had been pastor. Taylor maintained the center well after her husband's death—Taylor was widowed a second time in 1971.

Today, Taylor's home is filled with awards she has received over the past century. But no accurate picture of Gertrude Taylor may be drawn without considering her unrecorded arrangements and compositions. She is truly a product of the tradition that has kept spiritual and concert music alive aurally. Responding to questions, Taylor said, "Don't ask me to write down anything. I can answer any questions—as long as my memory holds—or get me to a piano or organ and I can tell the whole story."

The story, after all, is the music.

REGINA HARRIS BAIOCCHI

Taylor, Koko (1935–)

Koko Taylor is Chicago's reigning "Queen of the Blues." She was born Cora Walton on September 28, 1935, in Memphis, Tennessee. As a youth, she sang gospel music in a local church choir; she was also influenced by the recordings of **Bessie Smith** and "Memphis" Minnie Douglas. In 1953, Cora —or "Koko," a nickname her family gave her—moved to Chicago, where she married Robert "Pops" Taylor in 1956. She began to sing professionally in the late 1950s, and with the help of "Big" Bill Hill, a prominent Chicago blues disc jockey, made her first recordings for the U.S.A. and the Spivey labels in the early 1960s.

Her big breakthrough as a blues vocalist came in 1964, when she teamed up with composer/producer Willie Dixon of Chess

Records. A year later she released her first major hit, Dixon's classic "Wang Dang Doodle." Taylor remained with the Chess/Checker labels for ten years, during which time she worked with many of Chicago's best blues artists, including Buddy Guy, Matt Murphy, and Pinetop Perkins. In 1974, she signed with Alligator Records. By that time, Taylor had formed her own band and was performing throughout the country. Since then, she has recorded six albums for the Alligator label; these recordings have won for her four W.C. Handy blues awards and five Grammy nominations. Even today, Koko Taylor continues to be acclaimed as the undisputed "Queen of the Blues" wherever she performs. Her deep, resonant voice, punctuated by sustained growls, is instantly recognizable to blues enthusiasts not only in the United States, but throughout the world.

WILLIAM BARLOW

Tharpe, Sister Rosetta (c. 1915–1973)

Sister Rosetta Tharpe, performer and musician, helped bring gospel music from obscure African-American storefront churches to the national music stage. Some of her more popular recordings included "Rock Me," "That's All," "I Looked Down the Line," "Up Above My Head," and "This Train."

Influenced by the syncopated rhythms of such sanctified singers as Arizona Dranes, Tharpe created upbeat and jazzy religious songs. In the process, she ventured away from the deep and somber style that had characterized most religious music between the 1930s and 1950s. Tharpe rendered her upbeat style through abstract vocal phrasing and distinctive guitar playing.

Like blues guitarists such as Big Bill Broonzy and Lonnie Johnson, Tharpe viewed her guitar as much more than a source of background rhythm to support her lyrics. In the vast majority of the songs that comprised her repertoire, Tharpe foregrounded melody through guitar solos that featured single notes rather than chords. Moreover, Tharpe gave her guitar a clear and distinct presence by phrasing her guitar solos differently from her vocals.

Tharpe was born in Cotton Plant, Arkansas, on March 20, 1915 (1921?). The rhythmic power that became Tharpe's trademark was fostered in the Church of God in Christ (COGIC), where she began her career. In contrast to mainline black churches that stressed sedate religious worship, COGIC and other Pentecostal churches stressed the importance of emotional religious expression, encouraging the use of such rhythmic instruments as drums, trumpets, and tambourines in religious worship as a means of articulating devotion to God.

As a singing evangelist, Tharpe's mother, Katie Bell Nubin, was very active in COGIC. Tharpe accompanied her mother on her missionary travels as a youngster. By the time she was six, Tharpe was singing with her mother and touring sanctified churches. By the early thirties, she had migrated from Arkansas to Chicago with her mother and was accompanying herself on guitar when she performed in churches and revivals.

Tharpe gained national attention in 1938 when she did a revival show at the Cotton Club in New York City. The exposure she received helped propel her to national celebrity status. A recording contract with Decca Records in 1938 made Tharpe the first gospel singer to record with a major label. From the late 1930s through the 1960s, Tharpe performed in major entertainment venues in the United States and Europe that included concert halls, folk-jazz festivals, and radio and television programs.

Despite the national acclaim that Tharpe enjoyed, she did not let that notoriety determine the music she played. As an artist, Tharpe pushed her music to unexplored terrain. Although she was a gospel singer, Tharpe collaborated with artists of both sacred and secular music. She performed and recorded with boogie-woogie pianist Sammy Price and Lucky Millinder and his swing band, as well as such gospel groups as the Richmond Harmonizing Four and the Dixie Hummingbirds. For most of her career she was either a solo or lead singer, but in 1947 she teamed up with Marie Knight, a Sanctified church contralto. The two recorded together for several years.

While the exposure Tharpe enjoyed helped bring national recognition to gospel music, she unleashed controversy within African-American communities. As a type of religious music, gospel music primarily had predominated in black Baptist and Pentecostal churches before the 1940s. Unlike many of her gospel contemporaries, Tharpe ventured beyond the church to carry her music to such nonreligious venues as nightclubs and theaters that were frequented by black as well as white audiences. Many African Americans believed that singing gospel music in nightclubs turned sacred music merely into entertainment. These men and women viewed Tharpe's willingness to move beyond the church as blasphemous because it made a mockery of religion.

Tharpe died on October 9, 1973, in Philadelphia. Throughout her career she resisted the censure of her critics. The controversy she sparked involved more than concerns about the proper place of performance. Through both her music and performance,

The dynamic Sister Rosetta Tharpe helped bring gospel music from obscure black storefront churches to the national music stage. (SCHOMBURG CENTER)

she raised questions about the boundaries that separated the sacred and the secular. Tharpe dismissed the accusations directed against her by defending her behavior on evangelical grounds. She maintained that she had carried her music beyond the church in order to bring religion to, in her words, "the people who needed it."

JERMA JACKSON

Thornton, Willie Mae (1926–1984)

"Big Mama" Thornton was a wild rhythm-and-blues woman and one of the pioneers of rock 'n' roll. As was all too often true in the

1950s, however, although she had the style, the white performers made the money. Elvis Presley and Janis Joplin rose to fame performing her numbers, but Big Mama Thornton gained her share of success only late in life, and even when she got the credit due her, she never got the royalties.

Willie Mae Thornton was born in Montgomery, Alabama, in 1926, one of seven children. In her early teens, she won first prize in an amateur talent show and caught the attention of Sammy Green, who produced *The Hot Harlem Review*. She toured with the show until 1948, when she

Willie Mae "Big Mama" Thornton, a wild rhythm-and-blues singer, made the original recording of "Hound Dog," the song that was later "covered" by Elvis Presley and became a megahit. She never received more than $500 in royalties for it and died at fifty-seven in a boarding house. (AMY VAN SINGLE)

left and moved to Houston. There she sang with local bands and played in local clubs. In 1951, she recorded her first single from Houston, "All Right Baby"/"Bad Luck Got My Man."

She then recorded a string of records in the early 1950s, such as *Partnership Blues* and *No Jody for Me*. About this time, Thornton traveled to Los Angeles, where she joined the Johnny Otis Show, a touring rhythm-and-blues group.

If these songs and groups sound unfamiliar, there's a reason. In the forties and fifties, a lot of talented black musicians were never given air play; without promotion, rhythm-and-blues remained "specialty" music. Still, the Johnny Otis Show toured the country, and black audiences appreciated Thornton. When she made her debut at the Apollo Theater in Harlem, she delivered such a strong performance that she was promoted from opening act to headliner in a single night.

Otis produced Thornton's next record and invited two songwriters to drop by the session to write some material for her. They came back with "Hound Dog," written on a paper bag. Thornton didn't like it at first, but she recorded it. By 1953, it hit the top of the rhythm-and-blues charts. This same song became a megahit for Elvis Presley.

This was the time when rock 'n' roll was developing its roots, and many of those roots involved remaking black music for a white audience. Elvis Presley was intentionally packaged as a white musician who could sing black. Thornton did not share in the success. While rock 'n' roll flourished, rhythm-and-blues did not sell. In 1957, her recording company dropped her contract.

Thornton began to record on a series of small labels and to play in clubs in Los Angeles and San Francisco. In the early

1960s, she recorded wrote and "Ball and Chain;" unfortunately, the company didn't like her version and did not release the song, but they did hold on to the copyright. A few years later, Janis Joplin made the same song into a huge hit; Thornton could not collect any royalties from the Joplin version or any other.

Janis Joplin openly paid tribute to Thornton and put her name before the public. During this same era, interest was reviving in the blues. Thornton once again began to get recording contracts and concert dates. By the 1960s she was appearing at blues and jazz festivals around the world. The albums followed—*Big Mama in Europe, Big Mama Thornton and the Chicago Blues Band*, and *Stronger than Dirt*; in the 1970s, she released *She's Back, Sassy Mama*, and *Jail*, which was recorded live in two prisons. In 1980, she appeared at the Newport Jazz Festival, sharing the stage with **Koko Taylor** and **Sippie Wallace**.

Thornton remained wild and unpackageable to the end. At the Newport Jazz Festival, only a few years before she died, she appeared onstage in a thirties-style double-breasted suit and a ten-gallon hat, carrying a cane and a harmonica. Inevitably, the wild living eventually caught up with her. She died in a boarding house at the age of fifty-seven, her health ruined from years of hard drinking.

This woman who died in a boarding house helped pioneer a multi-billion dollar industry. "Hound Dog" was the only serious hit that Big Mama Thornton could claim as her own, and she never received more than $500 in royalties for it, but she helped set the style for a brand of music that has altered popular culture around the world.

ANDRA MEDEA

Turner, Tina (1939–)

During the mid-1980s, Tina Turner epitomized the meaning of the phoenix: This fiery, thoroughbred singer made one of the biggest comebacks in recording history with *Private Dancer*, an album that sold more than twenty-five million copies.

Born Anna Mae Bullock in the borough of Nutbush near Memphis, Tennessee, on November 26, 1939, Turner was not yet a teen when she began her career as a singer and dancer for local trombonist Bootsie Whitelaw. After her parents separated, she moved to St. Louis, Missouri, with her mother and sister. There she was befriended by Ike Turner, an established rhythm-and-blues singer and guitarist. While still in her teens she joined Ike's entourage, Kings of Rhythm, when she stepped in at the last moment of a performance to sing lead on "Fool in Love."

Renamed the Ike and Tina Turner Revue, the incendiary collaboration relocated to Los Angeles and became one of the biggest recording acts in both rhythm-and-blues and pop. With a mixture of raw soulful delta blues, edgy rock guitars, country rockabilly, and tinges of psychedelia, the revue became a favorite in both the United States and the United Kingdom. Churning out such hits as "I Want to Take You Higher," "Proud Mary," "Tra La La La," "Poor Love," "It's Gonna Work Out Fine," and "Nutbush City Limits," the Ike and Tina Turner Revue electrified audiences with Tina's raspy pipes and pulsating go-go acrobatic dancing. During her partnership with Ike, Turner recorded a solo record with Phil Spector titled "River Deep, Mountain High" and starred as the Acid Queen in the movie version of the Who's rock opera, *Tommy*.

Despite the magical chemistry that the Turners showcased onstage, behind closed doors she suffered physical, verbal, and emotional abuse from him. In 1975, she left him in Dallas in the middle of a tour. After her divorce, she tried to establish a solo career but was shunned by most promoters and booking agents in the United States. In the United Kingdom, however, her ties remained strong, and her appearances were not restricted to smaller clubs.

In 1979, Turner met Roger Davies, a young Australian manager who helped redirect her career from a lounge act back to its raw blend of rock and soul. He also steered her in the direction of England's new-wave sound. The following year, Turner relocated to Europe, where, with the help of Mick Jagger, Rod Stewart, Keith Richards, and David Bowie, she began to revive her career.

Paired with English newcomers Martyn Ware and Ian Craig Marsh (who later became known as the new-wave group Heaven 17), Turner provided vocals on the Temptations' classic "Ball of Confusion" for the synth new-wave group British Electric Foundation. After session work with Heaven 17, Turner landed a recording contract with Capitol Records and soon asked the duo to produce her version of Al Green's hit "Let's Stay Together." Not only did it become a hit, both in the United Kingdom and the United States, but it also served as a catalyst for a string of comeback hits. The single sold more than 250,000 copies and earned a U.K. Silver Disc Award. Very impressed with the results, Capitol Records decided to produce a full album of material.

Turner suddenly found herself working with eight different songwriters and four producers, including Mark Knopfler of Dire Straits. In May 1984, after only two weeks of production, Turner recorded the monumental *Private Dancer*, a multiplatinum album that took the world by storm. Supported by show-stopping videos, *Private Dancer* yielded such hits as "Better Be Good to Me," "Private Dancer," and "What's Love Got to Do with It," which won a Grammy Award for song of the year. Ironically, Turner initially did not like "What's Love Got to Do with It," claiming it was too tame. Turner won three Grammys in 1984—Record of the Year, Best Pop Vocal Performance, and Best Contemporary Rock Vocal Performance—capping one of the biggest comebacks in recording history. Turner also returned to acting in 1984, starring as Aunt Entity in the postatomic war action film *Mad Max: Beyond Thunderdome* (released in 1985). She also sang two songs on the soundtrack, "We Don't Need Another Hero" and "One of the Living."

In 1985, Turner was a featured artist on the single "We Are the World," a record that benefited hunger-relief efforts in drought-stricken parts of Africa. She also filmed a live performance special for Home Box Office (HBO), with guests David Bowie and Bryan Adams, and published her autobiography, *I, Tina.*

In September 1986, Turner released her second solo album for Capitol Records, *Break Every Rule.* Another top seller, it went platinum with the hits "Typical Male" and "Back Where You Started," which won a Grammy for Best Female Rock Performance. Turner promoted the album on an exhausting tour that covered 145 cities in twenty-five countries on five continents. The tour was recorded on a two-disk set, *Tina Live in Europe!* (released in 1988). At Brazil's Maracana Soccer Stadium in 1988,

In 1984, the amazing Tina Turner's comeback album Private Dancer *took the world by storm: At the Grammy Awards that year, Turner won Grammys for Record of the Year, Best Pop Vocal Performance, and Best Rock Vocal Performance. That same year, she returned to the world of film as Aunt Entity in* Mad Max: Beyond Thunderdome *(released in 1985).* (SCHOMBURG CENTER)

Turner played to the largest paying crowd for a solo artist in history. Turner announced that year that she was retiring from touring in order to focus on her acting career, but after working as a consultant on the autobiographical film of her life planned by Disney, she returned to the stage to support her 1989 *Foreign Affair* album. Europe's biggest tour ever, the *Foreign Affair* tour attracted more than three million fans to 121 sold-out performances.

In fall 1991, Capitol Records released a retrospective compact disc and home video, aptly titled *Simply the Best*. Recounting her comeback period, the release also featured three new tracks, "Love Thing," "I Want You Near Me," and "Way of the World." The album also featured new mixes of Turner's earlier hits "Nutbush City Limits" and "River Deep, Mountain High." That same year, she was inducted into the Rock and Roll Hall of Fame. In 1993 her autobiography *I, Tina: My Story* was made into a hit film starring **Angela Bassett**—*What's Love Got to Do With It?*

Tina Turner's saga provides the measuring stick for all comebacks. From a small town farm girl to an international superstar, Tina Turner is truly a living legend.

JOHN MURPH

V

Vaughan, Sarah (1924–1991)

Born in Newark, New Jersey, on March 17, 1924, Sarah Vaughan grew up in a musical family and became one of the most outstanding jazz recording artists. Her father was an amateur guitarist and singer of folk tunes; her mother, a pianist who sang in the church choir. Vaughan's musical career began with piano lessons at the age of seven, followed by organ lessons. At the age of twelve, she became the organist at the Mount Zion Baptist Church in Newark, also singing in the choir, often as a soloist. Sarah Vaughan's musical talents also blossomed outside the church because she played the piano in her high school orchestra and would, on selected occasions, sing popular songs at parties.

As a result of her eclectic musical talents, Vaughan was persuaded by friends to enter the famous amateur-night contest at Harlem's Apollo Theater. She entered on a Wednesday night in April 1943, when she was nineteen years old, winning the competition with her rendition of "Body and Soul"; in addition to receiving congratulations from **Ella Fitzgerald;** winner of a similar contest nine years earlier, Vaughan won $100 and a week's engagement at the Apollo. During her engagement, Billy Eckstine heard Vaughan sing and recommended her to his boss, Earl "Fatha" Hines (Eckstine was a vocalist for Hines). After a successful audition, Vaughan was given a job as a vocalist, doubling as a second pianist with the Hines band.

The job with Hines afforded valuable contacts with other young, creative, and soon-to-be giants of jazz, specifically, Dizzy Gillespie and Charles Parker, two of Hines' sidemen in his 1936 band. Vaughan was infatuated with the Gillespie and Parker approaches to both harmony and rhythm. After a year with the Hines band, Billy Eckstine, Vaughan's mentor from 1944 until her death in 1991, invited her to join his newly organized big band, a band that also included Gillespie and Parker. Vaughan was quoted once as saying, "I thought Bird and Diz were the end," and that, "at that time [her tenure with Hines and Eckstine], I was singing more off key than on. I think their playing influenced my singing. Horns always influenced me more than voices. All of them—Bird, Diz, Pres, Tatum, J. J. Johnson, Benny Green, Thad Jones—listening to them and others like them, listening to good jazz, inspired me." Indeed, throughout her recording career Vaughan was accompanied by Gillespie and Parker as well as Freddie Webster, Bud Powell, Thad Jones, Clifford Brown, and Frank Foster, among others.

After her years with the Hines, Eckstine, and John Kirby bands, Vaughan pursued a solo career. Soon after a stint at the Café Society in New York, she met her first husband, George Treadwell, who abandoned his own jazz career to become his wife's manager and music director. With Treadwell's support, Vaughan took voice and stagecraft lessons, updated her wardrobe, and improved her overall physical appearance. Thereafter, although the marriage did not last, a new, polished Sarah Vaughan emerged.

Arguably, Sarah Vaughan was the first vocalist to both understand and accentuate modern harmonic and rhythmic concepts. Although Louis Armstrong, **Billie Holiday**, and Ella Fitzgerald had taken jazz vocals to new heights, Vaughan was best suited to make it to new heights. Her vocal range encompassed three octaves, her command of dynamics enabled her to make quick transitions from soft to loud within a few measures, and she exuded impeccable pitch and a keen ear for harmonic changes. She also displayed an indelible feel for rhythm, alternating between tension and relaxation, from slow ballads to jump tunes. Sarah Vaughan was more than a vocalist; she was a musician's musician.

Beyond general observations of Vaughan's vocal stylistic interpretations, one also can draw specific conclusions from analyzing specific recordings. No researcher has introduced a methodology capable of discerning and explaining all of the intangibles of vocal stylistic interpretations of jazz, but the methodology espoused by Ruth Elaine King is well suited to describe the vocal stylings of Sarah Vaughan. King adapted Cantometrics, a system developed by Alan Lomax, and a system of notating modern music advocated by David Cope. King also developed seventeen new sets, patterned after Cantometrics, to analyze elements such as harmonic suggestion in the melodic line, position of the first tone in each phrase, text painting, vibrato, timbre, melodic and rhythmic imitation and deviation, and addi-

tional elements such as falls, smears, grace notes, lower and inverted mordents, bends, scoops, and slurs. King also compared Vaughan's early vocal style with two later recordings of the same compositions. Contrasting Vaughan's 1945 and 1963 recordings of "Lover Man" and her 1946 and 1978 versions of "Body and Soul," King was able to provide some insightful comparative comments.

In the 1945 recording of "Lover Man," one of her earliest recordings, one can hear undulated phrases (mostly two-measure phrases), a nasal-like tone quality, clear

The incomparable Sarah Vaughan had one of the biggest voices ever heard in popular music. Her control inspired awe in other musicians and fanatical devotion among audiences. "The Divine Sarah" was one of the greatest singers of all time. (SCHOMBURG CENTER)

enunciation, an interval range that commonly encompasses a perfect fifth to an octave, and a liberal interpretation of both the melody and rhythm. Also audible are a limited number of glissandos, falls, scoops, and inverted mordents. In short, here are the makings of an outstanding jazz vocalist, a goal that was realized soon after this recording. The 1963 recording of "Lover Man" differs in several ways from the 1945 recording: The 1963 tempo is slower, there is a key change from D to D flat, and Vaughan has developed both her vocal skill and her musicality, specifically, her explorations of vocal timbres and registers, her use of embellishments, and her use of vibrato. Also by 1963, perhaps due to Treadwell's urging, Vaughan had polished her stage presence, vocal skills, and musicianship.

The two recordings of "Body and Soul," 1946 and 1978, also offer an interesting insight into Vaughan's early and late vocal stylings: The 1946 version features the backing of a band, frequent beginning and ending of phrases on the lowest pitch of the phrase, a melodic range that extends beyond an octave, rhythmic deviation, and timbres primarily within the middle register; the 1978 version is characterized by musical contrast. Specifically, this rendition features Vaughan in a duet with Ray Brown (bass). She begins many of her phrases in both the lower and upper tonal ranges and demonstrates a wide variety of phrase contours. In addition, she uses rhythmic flexibility, timbre flexibility, a wide array of embellishments, and, on occasion, implies harmonies different from the original harmonies. In short, by 1978 Vaughan's style had matured and was characterized by freedom of interpretations including approaches to phrasing and articulation, phrase contour and length, and eclectic approaches to embellishments, reharmonization, and timbre.

The aforementioned concepts can be heard in all of her recordings after 1978, including *Sarah Vaughan: Celebration of Duke Ellington* (Pablo, 1979); *Send in the Clowns* (Pablo, 1981); and *Gershwin Live* (accompanied by the Los Angeles Philharmonic, conducted by Michael Tilson Thomas)(CBS, 1982).

EDDIE S. MEADOWS

Verrett, Shirley (1931–)

Concert singer, opera diva, and mezzo-soprano of international acclaim, Shirley Verrett has earned bravas in the great opera houses of the world. With her rich, sensuous voice and finely tuned intelligence, she has earned superlatives from audiences and critics.

Born in New Orleans, Louisiana, in 1931, Verrett was the daughter of Leon Solomon Verrett and Elvira Harris Verrett. Her father was a building contractor and the musical director of the Seventh Day Adventist church. Neither her father nor the church approved of opera singers, so Verrett's musical training was confined to the choirs her father directed. But she came from a talented family: Her four brothers and her sister were musically gifted, and several of her relatives and ancestors were New Orleans jazz musicians.

When Verrett was still a child, her family moved away from New Orleans and settled in Los Angeles. After attending the Los Angeles public schools, she went to Ventura College, where, at the insistence of her father, she studied business administration. Graduating with an Associate in Arts degree, she returned to Los Angeles and opened a real-estate office. Within a year her business was prospering. There was only one problem: She didn't want it.

Verrett kept asking herself, "What am I doing this for?" In her spare time, she began to explore her love of singing, studying under Anna Fitziu, a former Metropolitan Opera soprano.

Fitziu used her contacts to get Verrett an appearance on Arthur Godfrey's network television show, *Talent Scouts*, where she sang an aria from the opera *Samson and Delilah*. This won the attention of Madame Marian Szekely-Freschl, a noted voice teacher on the staff of the Juilliard School of Music. In 1955, Verrett gave up any thought of being a real-estate agent and followed her dream to New York.

Becoming an opera singer is not like becoming a pop star. Verrett spent six hard years at Juilliard, developing her voice and refining her art. During her first two years, her work was confined to student performances and recitals. Her first professional appearance came in 1957, at the Antioch College Shakespearean Festival in Yellow Springs, Ohio. The following year she made her New York operatic debut at City Center and, later in 1958, made her recital debut at the equally famous Town Hall in New York. She was not an instant success but received cautious, studied reviews.

Still, by 1960 Verrett had begun to be known as a singer with promise. That year, she was chosen by conductor Leopold Stokowski to be soloist for the Philadelphia Orchestra. By the time she was awarded her diploma in voice in 1961, she had begun to make a start on her professional career.

The warm depth of her voice and the intelligence of her presentation continued to win her roles. In 1962, she first performed the leading role in *Carmen* at the Festival of Two Worlds in Spoleto, Italy. The opening night audience was enthusiastic, but the critics remained reserved. Still, they noted that this was her first attempt at this demanding role and that she showed promise for the future. In fact, Carmen was to become one of her signature roles.

In the following years, her talent matured, and the critics were won over. She toured the Soviet Union in 1963, and audiences were wildly enthusiastic. At the Bolshoi Theater of Moscow, one of the most famous houses in Europe, she received a twenty-minute standing ovation. When she returned to New York in the role of Carmen, one critic described her as "the finest Carmen seen or heard in New York (in) this generation"; another critic described her Lincoln Center performance as "Simply without flaws, simply a great event in the annals of American music-making."

Verrett made her Metropolitan Opera debut in 1968 as Carmen and in 1978 and 1979 she performed there in Donizetti's *La Favorita* and in the title role in Bellini's *Norma*. At this time, Verrett divided her performances between operatic parts and recitals or concert singing. By the 1960s, she also began to record albums. In 1964, a collection of hymns, *How Great Thou Art*, followed by *Carnegie Hall Recital* in 1965. She recorded operas, recitals, and even protest songs. Still, her greatest acclaim has come from her live performances.

Verrett has achieved equal applause for singing parts from composers as diverse as Verdi and Beethoven. As a concert singer, Verrett performed with many of the great symphony orchestras of the world, including the Montreal Symphony, the Chicago

Symphony Orchestra, and the Los Angeles Philharmonic.

A recipient of the **Marian Anderson** award when she was a struggling student, Verrett appeared in a concert honoring Marian Anderson on the latter's eightieth birthday in 1982.

Now established as one of the great divas, her recital tours each year took her to the great opera houses of the country. In an honor enjoyed by few opera greats, Verrett had a series of operas staged especially for her at the Paris Opera House during the 1986–87 season.

In 1991 she performed songs by George Gershwin in Moscow, and in 1994 she sang the role of Nettie in the Lincoln Center production of Rodgers and Hammerstein's *Carousel*.

The world of real estate will never know what it lost in Shirley Verrett, but what the world of music gained is clear.

ANDRA MEDEA

W

Walker, Frances (1924–)

Frances Walker (Slocum) retired in 1990 from the piano faculty at **Oberlin College** after a forty-year career as a teacher and concert pianist. Born in Washington, D.C., on March 6, 1924, to parents of West Indian background, she was raised in a solidly middle-class environment. Her father, a prominent physician and amateur pianist, encouraged the music interests of both Frances and her brother, George, an accomplished concert pianist and composer.

Frances Walker's formal musical training began at an early age with private teachers in Washington, D.C. While still a student at Dunbar High School, she studied in the junior division of the **Howard University** School of Music, regarded as a spawning ground for many of the nation's talented musicians. Upon graduation, she entered the renowned Oberlin Conservatory and received a bachelor's of music in 1945. She continued studying privately at the Curtis Institute of Music (Philadelphia) and entered Columbia University Teachers College, earning both an M.A. in 1952 and a professional diploma in 1971.

In addition to Oberlin, where she returned to teach in 1976, Walker held faculty appointments at Barber-Scotia College (North Carolina), Tougaloo College (Mississippi), Lincoln University (Pennsylvania), and Rutgers University (New Jersey). During the early 1960s, she also taught piano at the Third Street Settlement House in New York City.

At age thirty-five, she made her debut in New York's Carnegie Hall and continued to concertize in the United States and Europe until her retirement. Besides being known for her performances of European classical composers, particularly Brahms, Schumann, Prokofiev, and Rachmaninoff, her repertoire included the work of several important African-American composers, including Samuel Coleridge-Taylor, William Grant Still, George Walker, and **Margaret Bonds**, whose setting of the spiritual "Wade in the Water," entitled "Troubled Water," often was featured by Walker on her concert program.

Frances Walker has recorded two albums. One, featuring compositions written for her by Wendell Logan, is titled *Five Pieces for Piano* (Orion ORS 80373); the other is a two-album set, *Samuel Coleridge-Taylor, Twenty-Four Negro Melodies*, and *William Grant Still, Traceries* (Orion ORAS 78305/306). Walker has been quoted as saying that the black pianist is not accorded the luxury of being a specialist, limiting his or her repertoire to a specific composer or period. Among African-American pianists, she noted, "there is no Mozart or Beethoven specialist." However, she has performed on programs dedicated to black composers, such as the February 29, 1976, piano festival in Harlem, where she was a featured pianist, and an April 1975 concert at the National Gallery of Art in Washington, D.C.

IRENE JACKSON-BROWN

Wallace, Sippie (1898–1986)

Eminent blues artist Beulah ("Sippie") Wallace was born to George and Fanny Thomas on November 1, 1898, in Houston, Texas, the fourth child of the religious couple who neither approved of nor indulged in the Saturday night house parties that spawned such blues notables as "Ragtime" Henry Thomas and Blind Lemon Jefferson. Although the Thomases did not live to see it, two of their sons, George, Jr., and Hersal, and one of their daughters, Beulah, rose to stardom as a trio on the vaudeville circuit.

Walker, nicknamed Sippie by her siblings, spent her preteen years singing and playing in the family church, Shiloh Baptist. Her musical career was encouraged by her older brother and sister, George, Jr., and Lillie. When George, Jr., went to New Orleans to pursue his musical career in 1912, Sippie soon followed him there. In New Orleans she met and married Frank Seals. It was an unsuccessful marriage, which she later described as a mistake. Both of her parents had died when she returned home around 1918 to live with her siblings, but the stage-struck young woman could not forget her experiences in the Storyville District of New Orleans, where George's friends included King Oliver and the soon-to-be-famous Louis Armstrong.

Sippie Wallace began her road show career as maid and stage assistant to Madam Dante, a snakedancer with Philip's Reptile Show. With Madam Dante, Wallace traveled around Texas, where she soon gained a reputation as the "Texas Nightingale," singing with small bands at picnics, dances, and holiday celebrations. Later, she began to sing in tent shows around the state and no longer needed to work as a maid.

Wallace's first recordings demonstrate her status as a mature, seasoned performer who had honed her craft. She owed a lot to her brother, George, who was a respected composer and music publisher when he sent for her to come to Chicago. George was on the recording staff of the music division of the W. W. Kimball Company as well as director of his own orchestra when Sippie, her niece, Hociel, and brother Hersal arrived in Chicago. Under George's influence, the three siblings formed a trio. Sippie and George developed their songwriting partnership to produce the popular songs

Blues singer Sippie Wallace had a successful career in the 1920s, but the Depression stalled her progress. She made a comeback in the mid-1960s, when a new generation of blues enthusiasts discovered her mix of southwestern rolling honky-tonk and Chicago shouting moan. (DAPHNE HARRISON)

"Shorty George" and "Underworld Blues," and the musically talented Thomases quickly became famous as recording artists. Sippie Wallace's first recordings, "Shorty George" and "Up the Country Blues" on the Okeh label, were very popular. "Shorty George" purportedly sold 100,000 copies, quite a feat for a newcomer.

Wallace's blues style was a mix of south-western rolling honky-tonk and Chicago shouting moan, a seductive brew that fit her personality. She had a strong, smooth voice and good articulation that pushed the words straight forward. Her ability to shift moods with a song was a dimension missing in other singers. Her unorthodox sense of timing and accentuation of words gave her lyrics push and tension. Many of the ideas for her blues songs came as she mulled over her personal concerns. She repeatedly said about songwriting that she would be "thinking it over in my mind . . . and it would just come to me to make a song about what was troubling me."

Wallace's second marriage was to Houstonian Matthew "Matt" Wallace, whose penchant for gambling created financial problems for the couple, problems Wallace wrote about in her 1926 release, "Jack o' Diamond Blues." Wallace was promoted as a recording artist in 1923 and 1924, and this enhanced her stage career as well. Soon she was a regular headliner on the Theater Owners Booking Association (TOBA) circuit, and Detroit replaced Chicago as home base for her, Matt, Hociel, and Hersal. The next few years were her peak years on the stage, but her success was at times overshadowed by great sorrow, as the three siblings who had been instrumental in her development as a singer died in close succession. In 1925, she was summoned to the bedside of her dying older sister, Lillie; then, in June 1926, her beloved Hersal died from a case of food poisoning at age sixteen; and, in 1928, George was run down by a streetcar in Chicago, bringing an end to the brilliant trio.

In 1929, Wallace was put under contract by Victor records. There she made four sides, but only two were issued, the popular "I'm a Mighty Tight Woman" and "You Gonna Need My Help." "Mighty Tight Woman," one of the few erotic blues tunes recorded by Wallace, demonstrated her superb vocal phrasing and her talent at the piano. Unfortunately, her career greatly suffered during the Great Depression. Because she had not developed the versatility of style and the repertoire of an Edith Wilson or an **Alberta Hunter**, she could not find employment as a comedienne or sultry chanteuse. Wallace's stage bookings finally petered out, and by 1932 she had slipped into obscurity along with many of her singing sisters. Her husband, family, and church became the focal points of her life, as, for the next three decades, Wallace turned her songwriting and piano-playing abilities toward church music.

Sippie Wallace, the blues singer, might have remained in obscurity, except for an occasional club date in Detroit, had it not been for the issuance of two recordings. In 1945, Mercury Records issued her great recording "Bedroom Blues," which was excellent but did not sell well. Her next recording, on Detroit's Fine Arts Label in 1959, suffered the same fate, but it must have convinced her friend **Victoria Spivey** to keep urging her to come out of retirement and try the folk-blues festival circuit that was sweeping the country. As a result, Wallace went to Europe in 1966 and captivated a new, younger generation of blues enthusiasts. The Storyville recording of her Copenhagen performance demonstrated that the second coming of Sippie Wallace was long overdue: She presented new renditions of her old classics and introduced "Women Be Wise, Don't Advertise Yo' Man," the blues song that inspired a young white singer named Bonnie Raitt. One reviewer wrote, "Visiting Europe in 1966, Sippie Wallace astonished by the breadth of her singing and a delivery recalling **Bessie Smith**." In 1977, bathed in the spotlight of Lincoln Center's Avery Fisher Hall, Sippie Wallace, at eighty, could still evoke the deepest emotions as she sang the blues.

In numerous ways, Sippie Wallace was the archetypal woman blues singer—gutsy, yet tender; bereft, but not downtrodden; disappointed, yet hopeful; long on talent, short on funds; legendary, but not widely acclaimed; exploited, but not resentful; independent, yet vulnerable. Her life story is not resplendent with dramatic events that capture the imagination. Indeed, it might have been considered quite pedestrian had it not been for her musical talent, which did not save her from toil or drudgery or grief but did enable her to communicate her feelings about life's triumphs and disasters. Old age and crippling arthritis did not stop Wallace from singing the blues whenever and wherever she was called. In the spring of 1986, six months before her death, Wallace sang to an audience in Germany, "Women Be Wise, Don't Advertise Yo' Man."

DAPHNE DUVAL HARRISON

Ward, Clara (1924–1973)

The famous Ward Singers were one of the finest groups during gospel's golden age, the period from 1945 to 1960, and Clara Ward was a major gospel talent: arranger, composer, pianist, and group leader. Her vocal style was closely echoed by **Aretha Franklin**; similarly the stylistic mannerisms of her star soloist, **Marion Williams,** inspired Little Richard. Traces of the Ward Singers can be detected in popular and gospel music, twenty years after Ward's death.

The group was formed by Gertrude Murphy Ward (1901–1983), a native of South Carolina who, with her husband, George, had moved to Philadelphia, where her daughters, Willia (1921–) and Clara (1924–1973), were born. In 1931, while working in a local dry-cleaning establishment, Gertrude Ward felt herself summoned to "sing the gospel and help save dying men." She became an early exponent of the gospel style pioneered by Thomas A. Dorsey and **Sallie Martin,** and she formed a trio with her daughters. Eventually Clara became both the piano accompanist and the star attraction. By the late 1930s, the group was touring the South during summer vacation.

In 1943, the trio made a triumphant debut at the National Baptist Convention, and by that time Clara had become a remarkable soloist. However, although she became a mistress of the newest gospel sounds, she tended to favor the traditional hymns and the moans of Dr. Watts. Her inspiration was Mary Johnson Davis, the most audacious of the early gospel divas. Davis, a Pittsburgh soprano, specialized in melisma, the elaborate spinning out of syllables, also known as "slurs" or "flowers and frills," and she had an equally strong impact on **Mahalia Jackson**'s early career. Clara also learned from **Roberta Martin**, a major gospel pianist and founder of a unique group, the Roberta Martin Singers of Chicago. Clara toured a few times as a Martin Singer, and in 1946 Roberta presented her and Delois Barrett Campbell, the Martin Singers' soprano, in a dual concert. Five years later, the Ward group returned and packed Chicago's churches for five straight weeks.

In 1946, Gertrude Ward began to recruit other members, and for the next decade she signed an unparalleled array of talent. The first was Henrietta Waddy (1901–1981), another South Carolina native who performed in traditional church fashion, albeit with great charm and showmanship. Others included stylists of Clara Ward's calibre; the most famous was Marion Williams, lead singer of the group's greatest hits, but others included Martha Bass, a St. Louis contralto with the immense, bluesy authority of her mentor, **Willie Mae Ford Smith**; Thelma Jackson, a powerful mezzo-soprano; Frances Steadman, a debonair contralto who recalled her twin inspirations, Roberta Martin and **Billie Holiday**; Kitty Parham, a flamboyant performer in the style of **Dorothy Love Coates**; Gloria Griffin, later a soloist with the Roberta Martin group; and Ethel Gilbert, a pianist, soloist, and evangelist who generally was considered to be the most spiritual member of the group.

Beginning in 1948, the Wards made a series of classic records, most of them led by Marion Williams, including "Surely God Is Able," "I'm Climbing Higher and Higher," and "Packin' Up." Under her own name, Clara recorded an equally distinguished repertory, including new compositions "How I Got Over" and "Come in the Room" and traditional hymns. Her finest solos on "The Day Is Past and Gone," "The Fountain," and "Precious Lord" were later duplicated, virtually note for note, in Aretha Franklin's first recording session. The Wards were not merely celebrated for their musicianship,

however. Fierce competition required heavy doses of religious drama, and they became preeminent church-wreckers—If Marion Williams did not "shout" the people with her rockers, Clara would perform a hymn; if all else failed, Madame Gertrude Ward (as she had become known) would start up a congregational number. The Wards also specialized in flamboyant wardrobes and hairstyles, which may have diverted attention from their musical excellence. In any case, people often turned out simply to see their costumes.

Madame Ward became a leading gospel promoter, and her Cavalcades, featuring the best-selling groups and quartets, drew astonishing crowds, up to 25,000 at a time. She also was an imperious taskmaster, however, and notoriously stingy. In 1958, Marion Williams, Frances Steadman, Kitty Parham, and Henrietta Waddy quit and formed their own group, the Stars of Faith (under Steadman's leadership, the group still performs, appearing mostly in Europe). "It's a sit-down strike!" complained Madame Ward, the aggrieved gospel capitalist. She recruited new members—the most gifted were Jessie Tucker, a wide-ranging soprano from Atlanta, and Christine Jackson, a Florida native reminiscent of Marion Williams—but the old magic was gone.

The group shifted gears. Calling themselves the Clara Ward Singers, they entered the secular arena and greatly magnified their patented flamboyance. In their glittering robes and outlandish hairdos, the new group became a star attraction in Las Vegas, where their club repertoire was restricted to pop-gospel, spirituals, and inspirational ballads. During this time, they moved from Philadelphia to Los Angeles. The members included Vermettya Royster (Jacksonville,

Florida), Voyla Crowley (Columbus, Ohio), soprano Mildred Means (Detroit), soprano Agnes Jackson (St. Louis), Geraldine Jones (Tampa, Florida), Mavelyn Simpson (Baltimore), and Alice Houston (Oakland, California). This group continues to perform under the leadership of Madeleine Thompson, a Philadelphia native who first heard the originals when she was a schoolgirl. In 1991, they released an album comprising the Wards biggest hits. Other albums include *The Best of the Ward Singers, Clara Ward Memorial Album, Gospel Warriors, The Gospel Sound,* and *The Great Gospel Women.*

Clara Ward adjusted to show business, but her heart remained with the Baptist hymns. "That's all I like to sing," she once told an interviewer; everything else was just a job. Clara recorded a few more hymns before her untimely death in 1973, a tragic event that prompted Gertrude Ward's last attempt at spectacle. There were two funerals, one in Los Angeles where Marion Williams recreated "Surely God Is Able," and another in Philadelphia which was graced by Clara's idol, Mary Johnson Davis, and her prize student, Aretha Franklin. After that Madame Ward mostly kept to herself. Occasionally, she toured with Clara's group, reminding folk that "before there was a Clara Ward, I was telling the world it's a God somewhere." Whenever singers or friends would visit, she would insist on taking them to the cemetery where Clara lay buried "with all the stars." She outlived her daughter by one decade, dying in 1983.

ANTHONY HEILBUT

Warwick, Dionne (1940–)

Born Marie Dionne Warrick on December 12, 1940, to Mancel and Lee Warrick, War-

Twice in a lifetime, Dionne Warwick has risen to the top as a singer of popular music. Now, her Warwick Foundation raises funds to fight AIDS. (SCHOMBURG CENTER)

wick grew up in East Orange, New Jersey, singing in the Methodist church in which her parents were active members. Her mother was business manager for a well-known gospel group, the Drinkard Singers, and as a child, Warwick often served as a replacement singer. By the time she was fourteen, when she formed her own group with her sister, Dee Dee, and a cousin, Cissy Houston, she was an experienced entertainer. The group, called the Gospelaires, sang backup for such performers as the Drifters and Sam "the Man" Taylor on the stage of the Apollo Theater and in New York recording studios.

Warwick left the group to attend Hartt College of Music at the University of Hartford in West Hartford, Connecticut, on a four-year scholarship to study music education. However, during summer vacation recording sessions with the Gospelaires, composer Burt Bacharach heard her. She was wearing jeans and pigtails and singing louder—and better—than anyone else. The composer and his lyricist partner, Hal David, asked Warwick to make demonstration records for them. They then promoted the demos to record companies and, in 1962, were offered a contract by Scepter Records. (Marie Dionne Warrick became Dionne Warwick because Scepter misspelled her name on the record label.) Their first single, "Don't Make Me Over," was a hit, as were thirty others by the trio that, for most of the 1960s and early 1970s, could do no wrong.

In the mid-1960s, *Time* magazine called Warwick "the best new female pop-jazz-gospel-rhythm-and-blues singer performing today." She collected many Grammy awards and gold and platinum records and was one of the strongest black women in the entertainment business. She had a sense of who she was and how she should be treated, but when she found out, in 1972, that the partnership of Bacharach and David had split up by reading it in the papers, she was devastated. "I thought I was their friend," she told *Rolling Stone*, "but I was wrong. They didn't care about Dionne Warwick." She sued the pair for breach of contract. Then, less than three years after the Bacharach-David breakup, Warwick's eight-year marriage to Bill Elliot, father of her sons, David and Damion, ended in divorce. In 1977, her father died unexpectedly, and the next day, her mother suffered a serious stroke. To make matters worse, the woman who was accustomed to having two or three hits a year had only three hits in half a decade, between 1972 and 1979.

Then she changed record labels. Her first album with Arista, *Dionne*, produced by Barry Manilow, went platinum. One single from the album, "I'll Never Love This Way Again," went gold and hit the top five. Since then, Warwick has had a half-dozen successful albums with Arista.

During the 1980s, Warwick began to become involved with political and social issues. In 1985, she was one of the performers of the song "We Are the World," recorded to benefit hunger relief in Africa. In that same year, she recorded "That's What Friends Are For" with her friends Stevie Wonder, **Gladys Knight**, and Elton John and donated the proceeds to the American Foundation for AIDS Research. The song was written by Burt Bacharach, with whom she had reconciled, and his wife, Carole Bayer Sager. It raised more than $1.5 million. In 1986, she won the Entertainer of the Year Award at the nineteenth annual Image Awards sponsored by the **National Association for the Advancement of Colored People** (NAACP). In 1987, she announced the first of a series of concerts with friends to further benefit acquired immune deficiency syndrome (AIDS) research and education and has established the Warwick Foundation to help fight the disease.

Dionne Warwick has never been easy to label, but she is a force in contemporary music and a strong presence in the public consciousness. "Talent will prevail," she says of herself. "Nobody, bar none, can do what Dionne Warwick does." So far, she's right.

KATHLEEN THOMPSON

Washington, Dinah (1924–1963)

Known as "Queen of the Blues," Dinah Washington, née Ruth Lee Jones, was one of four children born to Alice Jones in Tuscaloosa, Alabama. Like many other black families at that time, they moved to Chicago in 1928. Although they were financially burdened, the Jones family shared a musical talent that provided them with some monetary relief. In addition to domestic work, Alice Jones played piano at St. Luke's Baptist Church for extra money. She taught Ruth to play the piano, and while still in elementary school, Ruth was singing and playing solos at the church. She was so popular that her mother formed a singing group with her to tour the country, giving recitals in black churches.

Still known as Ruth Jones, she made little money singing gospel in churches. The family lived in poverty, a condition that left her bitter for years. She became intrigued with the secular music that was becoming popular in Chicago, soon began to idolize **Billie Holiday**, and began to sing popular songs, much to her mother's displeasure. At fifteen, she won an amateur contest at Chicago's Regal Theater by singing "I Can't Face the Music"; she then performed, without her mother's knowledge, at various local night clubs, using a different name so that her mother would not find out.

In 1940, Ruth Jones was discovered by **Sallie Martin**, one of the foremost figures in gospel music. Martin placed her in the first all-woman gospel group, the Sallie Martin Colored Ladies Quartet, with whom she performed for about three years. Still unable to earn a sufficient income, Ruth left Sallie Martin to perform in nightclubs on Chicago's south side. During this time, she met John Young, who became her agent and the first of seven men she married. The others were George Jenkins, Robert Grayson, Walter Buchanan, Eddie Chamblee, Rafael Campos, and Dick "Night Train" Lane.

Contrary to popular belief, it was not Lionel Hampton who changed her name from Ruth Jones to Dinah Washington: Washington herself stated that the change occurred in 1942 while she was singing at the Garrick Lounge in Chicago. She credits Joe Sherman, the club's manager, with changing her name for billing and promotional purposes. She did, however, tour with Hampton's orchestra as the featured vocalist from 1942 to 1945, leaving because of contractual and monetary disputes with Hampton; according to legend, she had to use a gun to persuade Hampton to release her from her contract.

As a soloist, Washington first recorded in December 1945, for Apollo Records, blues songs such as "Wise Woman Blues," "My Lovin' Papa," and "Mellow Mama Blues." In early 1946, she was approached by Ben Bart of Mercury Records, who offered her an exclusive recording contract. This was the beginning of Washington's career as a major popular vocalist, acquiring such accolades as "the poor man's **Lena Horne**" and "Queen of the Blues." During her sixteen-year tenure at Mercury, she placed forty-five songs on *Billboard*'s Rhythm-and-Blues charts, including "Am I Asking Too Much," "Baby, Get Lost," "What a Diff'rence a Day Makes," and "This Bitter Earth." Her biggest hit with the label was "Baby, You've Got What It Takes," a duet she recorded with Brook Benton in 1960. Many of her hits were recorded with leading musicians like Count Basie, Dizzy Gillespie, and Mitch Miller.

Although she was infamous for having a volatile temper, Washington was also known to shower her close friends and associates with lavish gifts: She gave free concerts in the black community, financially supported Martin Luther King, Jr.'s activities during the Civil Rights Movement, and unselfishly helped build the careers of many now-famous entertainers like Slappy White, Redd Foxx, Johnny Mathis, **Lola Falana, Leslie Uggams,** Patti Austin, and Quincy Jones.

In spite of being called "Queen of the Blues," Washington's repertoire was not confined to the blues genre; in fact, she once said in an interview that she did not consider herself a blues singer but rather "a pop singer with conviction." Washington recorded many pop songs and covers of hits by white singers such as "Harbor Lights," "Pennies from Heaven," and "September in the Rain," but Mercury continued to market her solely as a rhythm-and-blues vocalist.

Unhappy with Mercury's promotional activities, Washington left Mercury for Roulette Records in 1961 but was unable to duplicate her previous success. It was during this time that her financial status declined and her health began to deteriorate from years of touring. Overweight for most of her career, she also taxed her health by taking diet and sleeping pills, mercury shots, and drinking heavily. In 1963, while making plans for a huge Christmas party at her Detroit home, Washington was found dead from an accidental overdose of sleeping pills.

Because of her immense popularity and unique vocal quality, many singers, including **Della Reese,** claim to have been directly influenced by Dinah Washington. Many of her songs have been remade by other vocal-

During her sixteen years with Mercury Records, Dinah Washington had forty-six hits on Billboard's rhythm-and-blues charts, including "What a Diff'rence a Day Makes" and "Baby, You've Got What It Takes." She also helped build the careers of many other entertainers, such as Slappy White, Redd Foxx, Johnny Mathis, Lola Falana, Leslie Uggams, Patti Austin, and Quincy Jones. (SCHOMBURG CENTER)

ists and most of her original recordings are still available to the public.

FRANK WILLIAM JOHNSON

Washington, Isabel (1908–)

Though 1929 was not a good year for the economy, it was a great year for Isabel Washington: She was picked from the chorus at the Alhambra to star in *Harlem,* a Broadway play written by novelist Wallace Thurman and *New York Times* feature writer William Jourdan Rapp. Brooks Atkinson wrote that she radiated "the more scarlet aspects of Harlem life with an abandon seldom seen before." A few months later, the *Times* reviewer described her performance in *Bomboola* as "outstanding," "sparkling," and "lustrous," and surmised that if the show were "revised to accommodate her talent," it would "be something to mention in a breath with that permanent criterion, *Blackbirds*." Then she got a part in **Bessie Smith**'s film *St. Louis Blues*. When Isabel auditioned, she was considered too light. She agreed to be darkened, saying, "I can be dipped." The year 1929 was also the year that Isabel turned 21.

She was born in Savannah, Georgia, by her own account, on May 23, 1908. Her mother died when she was still young, and she and her older sister, **Fredi Washington**, went to a Catholic boarding school in Philadelphia. Practically from the moment they moved to the North to live with their maternal grandmother, the Washington sisters set Harlem to talking about their beauty, grace, and spirit. Fredi, who had embarked on a stage career, did not want Isabel to follow in her footsteps. Fredi wanted to save her from heartbreak, but Washington was persistent. "I had a voice and I could dance."

Isabel Washington began her career as a recording artist at fifteen, recording two songs that Fletcher Henderson wrote especially for her in 1923. Working at Black Swan, W. C. Handy's record company, after school, she would sing to herself while stuffing envelopes. Henderson, the house pianist, who had one of the finest jazz bands during the 1920s, liked her voice and urged her to record for him. Paramount later reissued "I Want to Go" and "That's Why I'm Loving You," first recorded on the Black Swan label.

In the early 1930s, Washington was a soubrette at two of the leading Harlem nightspots, Connie's Inn and the Cotton Club and in 1931 appeared with her sister in *Singin' the Blues*, which boasted songs by Jimmy McHugh and Dorothy Fields, lyricists for the Cotton Club. Eubie Blake's orchestra provided the music. Atkinson referred to Washington as "Harlem's most vivid nightingale" who gave "the blues the exultation of the spirituals." She replaced Revella Hughes in the 1932 revival of *Shuffle Along*, singing in the quartet, and she later was offered the role of Julie in *Show Boat*, but "Adam told me if I took it, we couldn't get married."

Isabel Washington married the Reverend Adam Clayton Powell, Jr., in 1933. Powell had to fight his father's congregation, which opposed his marriage to the Broadway star and divorced Cotton Club chorine with a son. After her marriage, Isabel Powell devoted her talent to the choir at her husband's Abyssinian Baptist Church, which at one time included a young **Diahann Carroll**. The marriage lasted twelve years, and Isabel Powell helped create a closer tie between church and stage.

BARBARA LEWIS

Webster, Katie (1939–)

The career of "Swamp-Boogie Queen" Katie Webster, featuring her telltale vocals and her barrelhouse, boogie-woogie piano, never would have started had it not been for her perseverance, especially because her deeply religious father had renounced his career as a ragtime piano player to become a minister in the sanctified Church of God in Christ. Her mother was also a gospel and classical pianist.

Born Kathryn Jewel Thorne on September 1, 1939, in Houston, Texas, she began musical training early but was forced to confine her interests to playing gospel and classical music at the insistence of her parents. So convinced were her parents that the blues was "the devil's music," the family piano was locked so that Katie could be monitored by her mother when she played. On the sly, however, Webster listened to the early rock 'n' roll of Fats Domino, Little Richard, Ray Charles, and Sam Cooke.

Webster's parents and nine siblings moved to Oakland, California, leaving the young girl with less strict relatives in Texas; it did not take the blues enthusiast long to launch her professional career. Her ability to read music landed her a debut job with a jazz band. By age thirteen, she was touring and performing in clubs from Dallas to southern Louisiana with a jazz band. About the same time, Ashton Savoy, one of southern Louisiana's most prominent rhythm-and-blues musicians, discovered the young pianist and took her to Louisiana to feature her piano on several of his recordings. Thorne had married pianist Earl Webster when she was fifteen, and although the marriage ended, she continued to use her married name professionally.

Two years later, she moved to Lake Charles, Louisiana, and was employed extensively as a studio musician for such Louisiana labels as Excello, Goldband, and Jin. As a result of exposure on these labels in the late 1950s and early 1960s, Webster garnered hundreds of recording sessions on 45s with such bluesmen as Guitar Junior (Lonnie Brooks), Clarence Garlow, Jimmy Wilson, Slim Harpo, Lazy Lester, Mad Dog Sheffield, Lightnin' Slim, and Clifton Chenier.

At the same time, Webster, leading her own band, The Uptighters, performed regular gigs in Lake Charles' major venue, The Bamboo Club. In 1964, her idol Otis Redding did a one-nighter at the club and an enthusiastic crowd called for Webster to sit in with the guest musician. So impressed was Redding with the pianist that she joined his tour the next morning and spent most of the next three years with Redding until his death in a plane crash in 1967. They became close spiritual friends because their fathers were both ministers.

Two reasons are given for Webster's failure to be on the plane with Redding: She was eight months pregnant, and she either declined the offer to accompany him or overslept and missed the plane. Whichever is true, Redding's death affected Webster to such an extent that she stopped performing for several years.

In 1982, after another hiatus from music to take care of her ailing parents in the San Francisco Bay area, Webster made her debut tour of Europe, to which she has since returned numerous times. Also that year, between jaunts to Europe, Webster gave her first performance since Redding's death at the San Francisco Blues Festival and performed at various clubs. In 1986, the Bay Area Women in Music group awarded Webster the Performer of the Year award, marking one of the rare times a blues artist has been so honored.

Webster has released numerous albums on the Ornament, Arhoolie, and Alligator labels. Her rousing keyboard style features her father's driving, clustered-chord bass riffs in her left hand and a unique fusion of gospel, blues, and boogie techniques in her right. Webster has been referred to as a female Muddy Waters, but she has definitely developed her own unique piano style accompanied by crisply intimate, throaty vocals tending her lyrics. In live performance, she thrives.

EVAN MORSE

Wells, Mary (1943–1992)

Mary Wells, a rhythm-and-blues sensation before her twenty-first birthday, was "a hometown girl made good," Mary Wilson, one of the Supremes, would recall. "And she was the first female there in a man's world, so she really gave us initiative."

Born in Detroit on May 13, 1943, Wells was bedridden for two years in early childhood, first with spinal meningitis and then tuberculosis. Her experiences with doctors and hospitals led her to think about becoming a scientist, but then she noticed the exciting things that were happening at a recording studio just a few blocks from home. Wells had been singing in church and school choirs since the age of three; "And all the entertainers looked so glamorous and wonderful, so I started writing songs," she would remember. The determined teenager took herself over to Barry Gordy's office to sell him "Bye Bye Baby," which she had written for her idol Jackie Wilson, one of the singers whose records he produced. To audition the song for Gordy, Wells had to sing it herself, because she couldn't read music or play an instrument. Gordy not only wanted the song, he wanted the singer too; he signed Wells to Motown, the new label he was starting.

"Bye Bye Baby" went to forty-five on the Hot 100 chart in 1961. But her career really took off after Gordy made Smokey Robinson her writer and producer. In 1962, they had three singles in the top ten. Wells was Motown's first female star. In 1964, the year Wells turned twenty-one, she and Robinson teamed up for "My Guy." The biggest hit of her career, it kept the Beatles out of the number one spot on the charts for two weeks. When she toured England with those superstars in the fall, she became the first Motown artist to perform overseas.

At contract-renegotiation time, Wells felt that Motown offered less than she deserved. When 20th Century Fox Records offered her a large advance, she signed with them; Motown's first female star had become its first major loss. She would change labels several more times, but none of her other professional associations would take her anywhere near the heights she had reached with Motown. She also tried to establish herself as an actress, without success.

Wells' personal life was a troubled one. Her family was poor, and her childhood home unhappy. A teenage marriage to Motown backup singer Herman Griffin had ended after two years; she had been pregnant twice during that time, but her husband insisted she have abortions because of her career. During the 1970s, she married gospel singer Cecil Womack, left the business for several years to stay at home with their three children, and then divorced him. Her fourth child was born while she was living with Cecil's brother Curtis. In the darkest corners of her life were a suicide attempt and heroin addiction. In 1990, she was diagnosed with throat cancer; with no insurance and no income, she lost her home. After her desperate situation became known, industry colleagues raised more than $50,000 toward her medical expenses. She died on July 30, 1992. Her daughter Stacy said that she never complained during her illness. "She only cried because she couldn't do what she liked to do, which was sing."

INDIA COOPER

Williams, Eva Taylor (1895–1977)

The contralto voice one observer called "rich and thrilling" shifted easily from blues to ballads; the woman behind it made her mark upon the 1920s and 1930s Harlem Renaissance not only onstage and in the recording studio but also on the radio's airwaves. Indeed, in 1929 she became the first black woman soloist to be broadcast both nationally and internationally and, during 1932–33, she hosted her own radio program.

She was born Irene Gibbons Williams on January 22, 1895, in St. Louis, one of Frank and Julia Gibbons' twelve children. At the age of three, she joined a vaudeville troupe, Josephine Gassman and Her Pickaninnies, on that city's Orpheum Theater stage; for the years up to World War I, the little girl went on national tours with Gassman on the Orpheum circuit and to Europe and the Pacific islands.

Despite this early and long association, she attended Sumner High School in St. Louis and, in 1911, was in New York as a chorus girl in *Vera Violetta*, with Al Jolson.

Ten years later, she settled in New York with her husband, bandleader Clarence Williams, to whom she remained married until his death in 1965. For the next two decades, she sang with Williams in his various groups, such as the Clarence Williams Trio, the Clarence Williams Quartet, and the Blue Five, both in person and on radio. In 1926, she was on the Lincoln Theater stage in the *Clarence Williams Revue*.

Taylor also performed blues and ballads in clubs and in Broadway shows, including *Bottomland* (1927) and the **Florence Mills** vehicles *Shuffle Along* (1921), *Queen O'Hearts* (1928), and *Dixie to Broadway* (1924), as well as the out-of-town Miller & Lyles variety shows *Step On It* (1922) and *Keep Shufflin'* (1929), the latter with Fats Waller.

Taylor made her radio debut with the Trio in 1922; that performance led to many more, with different combinations of artists and on several stations. She was staff soloist for a time at WEAF/WJZ radio and hosted the *Eva Taylor Crooner Show* at that station in 1932–33.

Taylor recorded on an extensive list of record labels—Black Swan, Okeh, Columbia, Edison, Victor, Velvetone, Vocalion, Bluebird, and ARC. She wrote such songs as "May We Meet Again, Florence Mills" and remained a frequent stage and club entertainer, performing with her husband in 1939 at Carnegie Hall. Her work teamed her with Jolson, Mills, **Bessie Smith**, **Ethel Waters**, King Oliver, Cab Calloway, and many others of note. Best known as Eva Taylor, she also recorded as Irene Gibbons, Irene Williams, and Catherine Henderson, and with the Charleston Chasers and the Riffers.

Taylor retired from public performance in the World War II years when she entertained in the New York buildings of the Hospital Reserve Corps. Her retirement was to be broken often, as in the case of 1948's Bessie Smith Memorial Concert. As late in her life as the 1970s, she went to Scandinavia for broadcasts and concerts with the Sweet Peruna Jazz Band and Maggie's Blue Five.

Eva Taylor Williams died October 31, 1977, in Mineola, New York.

GARY HOUSTON

Williams, Marion (1927–1994)

Marion Williams was one of the finest vocalists gospel has produced; yet, her impact extended beyond gospel. Much of the falsetto ecstasy inherent in rock 'n' roll can be traced to the style she forged while performing with the Ward Singers in the 1950s. Her greatest strength, however, was her musicianship. She was simply the finest improviser within the gospel tradition, at once the most rhythmic and the bluesiest. Her only equal was **Mahalia Jackson**.

For black, female, and jazz musicians, history was made when three works by jazz composer Mary Lou Williams were presented at Carnegie Hall by the New York Philharmonic Orchestra in 1946. This performance completely eroded the whites-only barrier to the Carnegie Hall stage. (LORNA MCDANIEL)

Marion Williams was born on August 29, 1927, in Miami, Florida, the daughter of a West Indian barber and a South Carolinian laundress. Her father died when she was nine (she still remembers helping him campaign for Franklin Delano Roosevelt). A major influence was her great-aunt, Rebecca Edwards, a native of Cat Island who ran a preschool for the neighborhood children. Despite Edwards' plans for her, Marion was forced to leave school at fourteen to help support her mother. In an interview, she said that for years she worked in the laundry "from sun-up to sun-down," adding, "When I was coming up, we didn't know anything about what they call adolescence." She began to sing as a child, dividing her time among local Sanctified congregations. An older brother had more secular interests, however, and he placed a jukebox ("we called it a piccolo") in the family's yard. So, as a girl, Marion was exposed to blues and jazz, although her only musical thoughts were of gospel. Jon Pareles of the *New York Times* has called her the equal of any living blues singer, and Whitney Balliett of the *New Yorker* considered her one of the greatest jazz singers. Yet, she never performed a worldly song, except for "God Bless the Child," which she transformed into a gospel moan.

Marion Williams was exposed to the pioneer gospel singers, Sanctified shouters like **Sister Rosetta Tharpe**, Baptist moaners like Mary Johnson Davis, and various male quartets. In 1947, she joined the Ward Singers, and for the next eleven years she was the group's undisputed star. The Ward sound, conceived by **Clara Ward**, was executed by Marion. Her wide vocal range and mastery of tonal colors were featured as prominently in the background as when she sang lead.

Her years of studying preachers paid off; she had no trouble holding her own with the mightiest gospel men. Indeed, her stylistic versatility, encompassing lyrical poignance and a backwoods energy, inspired numerous male performers, from the gospel singer Professor Alex Bradford to Little Richard and the Isley Brothers. Her most famous recordings with the Wards were "Surely God Is Able," "I'm Climbing Higher and Higher," and "Packin' Up."

In 1958, she and several other Ward Singers formed their own group, the Stars of Faith. She stayed with them for six years, a period most notable for her appearance in *Black Nativity*, the first gospel song play. After 1965, she performed as a soloist, appearing at numerous festivals in America and Europe. She also was one of the first gospel singers to perform in Africa (1966).

In later years, Marion Williams received great attention for her performances of a cappella moans. Her slurs and grunts recalled old field recordings, but her stylistic authority was such that one doubts whether these traditional hymns have ever been so compellingly sung. In such performances, she recalled her musical ancestors, not merely the gospel pioneers but the nameless workers in fields and factories who expected their songs to "lift heavy burdens."

In her last years, Williams finally got a "foretaste of glory." In 1991, she was featured in the movie *Fried Green Tomatoes*, which was dedicated to her; in 1992, the *Rolling Stone Album Guide* awarded her four "Spirit Feel" albums, *I've Come So Far*, *Born to Sing the Gospel*, *Surely God is Able*, and *Strong Again*, five stars apiece, and pronounced her "the greatest singer ever"; in 1993, she became the first vocalist to receive the MacArthur "genius" fellowship.

Later that year, she became the first gospel singer to receive the Kennedy Center Honors; her two best-known acolytes, **Aretha Franklin** and Little Richard, performed some of her hit songs.

However, she had been in ill health for years, undergoing dialysis three times a week since 1988. (Astonishingly, she recorded some of her best albums during this period.) In February 1994, she entered Philadelphia's Einstein Hospital, where she died on July 2.

ANTHONY HEILBUT

Williams, Mary Lou (1910–1981)

Mary Lou Williams takes her rightful place as one of the most highly regarded performers, arrangers, and composers of black American music. Her niche as projector and protector of jazz is indisputable, and her importance in the history of jazz continues to be seen in the homage paid to her by scores of her musical progeny.

Her first professional period as arranger/pianist began in 1928 when she joined Andy Kirk's band, the Twelve Clouds of Joy. The second period (1941–54) was framed by her composition *Zodiac Suite* and her hiatus in Europe. In 1954, she withdrew from performing for three years in order to explore a religious life, and her last creative period began in 1957 with her return to New York and to performance.

She was born Mary Elfreida Scruggs on May 8, 1910, in Atlanta, Georgia. Her mother, a classically trained pianist, realized when Mary was three years old that her daughter possessed a special musical gift to remember melodies. She was advised to keep Mary away from formal instruction that might restrict imaginative improvisation—and she did just that. At about the age of four, Mary and her mother moved to Pittsburgh where "the little piano girl" interacted with the great stride players, including Earl "Fatha" Hines, Count Basie, Art Tatum, and Duke Ellington. Much later, as an adult artist, Mary Lou Williams, in discussing the tension between notated music and aural sound, said, "My mother ended up not playing [the piano] at all, just reading music." During her career, however, Williams judiciously mediated the use of notation and improvisation in her arranging and composition.

As a preteen, Williams joined the Buzz and Harris act managed by the Theater Owners Booking Association (TOBA). By the age of seventeen, she had married John Williams, an alto and baritone saxophone player and leader of the Holder Band (later to be Andy Kirk's Band), and moved with him to Kansas City. She worked there until 1941, when she returned to Pittsburgh and wrote for Benny Goodman ("Roll 'Em"), Louis Armstrong, Tommy Dorsey, and Duke Ellington ("Trumpet No End"). "Trumpet No End" is a piece for the four trumpets that her second husband, Shorty Baker, played when they worked together in New York at the beginning of her second creative period, which began in 1941. It was during this period that she composed the *Zodiac Suite*, the first of many large compositions comprising several movements; it is a suite of dances named after the twelve signs of the zodiac with each sign dedicated to a musician or friend.

The first three dances of the suite were written for her radio show (WNEW), and a single piece was presented on the air each Sunday. "Capricorn," however, was a piece created for dancer **Pearl Primus**, who performed, as did Mary Lou Williams, at the

Café Society. Interestingly, another black dancer/anthropologist, **Katherine Dunham**, choreographed the "Scorpio" movement of the *Zodiac Suite*.

In 1946, the three items "Aquarius," "Scorpio," and "Pisces" were scored for a Carnegie Hall performance by the New York Philharmonic Orchestra. Williams often recounted that she had to copy the "Scorpio" movement overnight herself for the large orchestra (100 parts). Although black musicians had performed on stage at Carnegie Hall on several occasions since 1919 (for example, Clef Club Orchestra, H. T. Burleigh), this symbolic performance completely eroded the whites-only barrier to Carnegie's stage, and it is especially important that a jazz composer, a black woman, created a composition for symphony orchestra at that time.

From 1952 to 1957, Mary Lou Williams sought privacy and opted not to play publicly, explaining later that "she had stopped to pray." She did return to playing in 1957, and at the urging of her friends Dizzy and Lorraine Gillespie, "Virgo," "Libra," and "Aries" of the *Zodiac Suite* were resurrected, performed at the Newport Jazz Festival, and recorded on Verve Records.

After Williams converted to Roman Catholicism in 1956, her focus and inspiration changed. During her third creative period, she produced three large liturgical works in jazz style. The versatility of *Mary Lou's Mass* made it suitable for professional, amateur, or children's choirs along with a jazz combo or other instruments. Williams, in preparation for a concert involving an inexperienced school choir, often refined the teacher-trained choir shortly before the concert. Performances were held at New York's Saint Patrick's Cathedral, at the First Kansas

City, Missouri, Woman's Jazz Festival (1978), and in several churches throughout the United States.

During this period, Williams lived in New York's Hamilton Terrace, where a concern for young people and the infirm became foremost in her mind, and she worked to ease the suffering of society. She also established the Bel Canto Foundation, a shop that collected donated articles for impoverished musicians.

Mary Lou Williams admired beautiful bass lines and composed a huge repository of bass lines for her compositional use. She often worked alone with bassists Percy Heath, Bob Cranshaw, and Buster Williams and with female bassist/singer Charlene Ray.

Her pedagogy of jazz taught that there were no positive developments immediately after bebop, the era that, in her thinking, was the pinnacle and end of the creative surge in jazz. She saw the musical detour away from bebop as a serious cultural loss that impeded not just the continuity of the music but also the functioning of the black family. To her way of thinking, the electric sounds of the new music, rock 'n' roll, were expressive of violence and, unlike pure acoustical sound, created confusion. She promoted jazz as an art form born of suffering, and she celebrated the blues as a major healing force basic to the structure of jazz. She taught that good music must "swing" and not bounce in a meaningless and "corny" way—that the spiritual science of music, with its deepest realization in improvisation, emanates from a personal will and system of belief. She often expressed this idea to timid students by saying, "Just put your hands on the keys—and you will play."

We find in Williams' musical language the ability to shift to any style and harmonic structure in the history of jazz from the stride of the ragtime era (with foot pumping of the loud pedal), to the boogie-woogie left-hand span of ten notes, or to the clustered and dissonant chords of avant-garde.

Musicians from all eras honored Mary Lou Williams, and they continue to pay her homage by "signifying on" and by revising her piano treatments and tunes. In 1976, the respected avant-garde pianist Cecil Taylor approached Williams with the idea of a collaboration. The astounding Carnegie Hall concert and its recording, *Embraced*, that came out of that meeting are a testament to the continuing connection among black pianists and to the depth of Williams' belief in the blues as the foundation of black music. Her historic repertoire serves as the framework of the concert, overlaid with Taylor's virtuoso and layered sounds. By manipulating the stereophonic channels (restricting the sound to the left channel), one can hear the echoes of the roots of jazz engulfed within a dramatic and contemporary setting.

During her rich and productive concert, club, and recording career, Mary Lou Williams also worked for periods in the public schools of Pittsburgh, the University of Massachusetts at Amherst, and, from 1976 until her death on May 28, 1981, at Duke University in Durham, North Carolina. Williams' friend, manager, and spiritual advisor, Father Peter O'Brien, a Jesuit priest, participated with her in concert and classroom lecture/performances in which together they demonstrated the history of jazz. She received two Guggenheim Foundation grants as well as several honorary degrees. Mary Lou Williams Lane in Kansas City, the city of her first creative period, is named after her.

LORNA McDANIEL

Wilson, Cassandra (1957?–)

In the late 1980s, commentators were wondering under headlines like "Sham or shaman?" whether Cassandra Wilson was, purely speaking, a jazz singer. Her dusky contralto voice not only roved unpredictably through standards of the genre, but also invaded pop, folk, and the musicals of Hollywood and Broadway.

Not much later her impact was seen differently. Some began to feel that Wilson, crossover artist or not, was actually restoring to jazz a "singability" it had not had since the 1940s.

Cassandra Wilson was born and raised in Jackson, Mississippi, in a middle-class family. Her father was a musician and her mother a Motown fan. As a child, she listened to Duke Ellington, Thelonious Monk, **Nancy Wilson**, **Ella Fitzgerald**, and **Sarah Vaughn**. She started to study classical piano at six or seven, and while she was under folk music's thrall, her father taught her chords on the guitar, the instrument with which she would write some twenty tunes between ages eleven and fifteen.

In the 1970s, Wilson graduated from Jackson State University, married, spent a year in New Orleans, did some work in television, and moved to East Orange, New Jersey. Eventually she moved to Brooklyn Heights, New York. The marriage did not last, but her connection to jazz did.

At a New York jazz session, Wilson met composer/alto saxophonist Steve Coleman, an encounter that led to their collaboration on several recordings, including her debut album, 1985's *Motherland Pulse*, and then *World Expansion*, *On the Edge of Tomorrow* and *Point of View*.

Wilson's singing reflected both earlier influences and those of **Betty Carter** and Abbey Lincoln. She also learned from such musicians as Grachan Moncur, Greg Osby, and two who urged her to sing more songs of her own, Coleman and Henry Threadgill.

Wilson likes jazz standards—and nonjazz standards that she, of course, jazzes up. Her 1988 *Blue Skies* was a whole album of them, containing "I Didn't Know What Time It Was," "I've Grown Accustomed to His Face," and "Shall We Dance?" *Billboard* magazine picked it as the year's number-one jazz album.

At the same time, she has written, cowritten, or arranged roughly half of her twenty or so albums. Her lyrics for "You Belong To You" on the album *Days Aweigh* in 1987 declared, "I used to think that I was just a puppet on a wing/Now I find I'm the one who holds the strings."

Wilson reached a new plateau of success with 1994's *Blue Light 'Til Dawn*, which richly combined her own songs with others' and addressed what she called "something primordial—basic man-woman energy." On it are Robert Johnson's "Hellbound On My Trail" and Joni Mitchell's "Black Crow." Its release was followed by a six-week European tour and her acting debut in the Arnold Schwarzenegger comedy film *Junior*.

Wilson is so gifted that her particular musical destiny now is believed to affect that of jazz overall. This perhaps led one writer to call Wilson "the most cutting-edge young jazz singer in the business today" and another to say she is "the most accomplished jazz vocalist of her generation."

GARY HOUSTON

Wilson, Nancy (1937–)

Born February 20, 1937, in Chillicothe, Ohio, Nancy Wilson began her musical career primarily in Columbus, Ohio. She was active as a vocalist during her teenage years, singing in nightclubs and making local television appearances, and in 1956–58 she toured the Midwest and Canada with Rusty Bryant's band. In 1959, her biggest career break came when she met Cannonball Adderley. When she sat in with the Adderley band in a 1959 gig in Columbus, Adderley was so impressed that he invited Wilson to record an album with him. She soon signed a contract with Capitol Records and in 1962 recorded an album with Adderley. Wilson's career blossomed. She received rave reviews from several prominent jazz musicians, and thereafter she was booked for numerous appearances in concert halls, nightclubs, and jazz clubs throughout the United States and Europe. Her recording career also blossomed, including several new albums, one with George Shearing.

Wilson's vocal style displays remarkable versatility, giving equal emphasis to both jazz and popular music. She relies upon a keen ear for both tonal and timbre nuances, an emotional intensity that draws emotion and meaning from each word of the text, and a stage presence that evokes a belief that Wilson has lived the words that she sings. It is also significant that after an experiment with popular music, primarily in the 1970s, Wilson resumed her jazz career with several leading jazz musicians in the early 1980s. She toured Japan with Hank Jones in 1981–82 and performed with the Art Farmer/

After early encouragement from jazz great Cannonball Adderley, Nancy Wilson has been successful as both a jazz and popular singer. She has worked in nightclubs, jazz clubs, and concert halls throughout the United States, Europe, and Japan, in addition to her recording career. (SCHOMBURG CENTER)

Benny Golson quintet at the Playboy Jazz Festival in 1982. Since the early 1980s, Wilson has concentrated on both jazz and popular music, singing in concert halls, nightclubs, and making television appearances.

Her 1991 album *With My Lover Beside Me* premiered several songs with lyrics by the late Johnny Mercer that had been found after his death.

EDDIE S. MEADOWS

Chronology

1619

Twenty Africans, three of them women, are put ashore by a Dutch ship at Jamestown, Virginia.

1667

"Pinkster Day," a slave celebration that includes dancing and singing, is mentioned in a book of sermons by Adrian Fischer.

1693

The Society of Negroes begins meeting in Massachusetts, each slave attending with the permission of his or her master, on Sunday evenings to pray, sing, and listen to sermons.

1741

The earliest reported "Negro election day" is held in Salem, Massachusetts. The celebration, in addition to a mock election and a parade, includes singing and dancing.

1816

A part of the upper tier of the New Orleans Opera House is reserved for African Americans.

1818

A visitor, Benjamin Henry Latrobe, sees and describes the gathering of hundreds of dancers in the Place Congo after Sunday church service. He talks specifically about women dancers.

1821

The African Grove Company, with women among its members, begins to perform. The company includes music in its productions.

1828

St. Thomas Episcopal Church, a black church in Philadelphia, hires a young black woman, Ann Appo, as organist.

1830s

The Negro Philharmonic Society is organized in New Orleans. It has more than 100 members.

The minstrel show, based on African-American music and dance, becomes popular. The performers are all white men.

Sacred music concerts at Boston's Belknap Church are under the direction of Susan Paul, daughter of its black minister.

1830s–60s

Sojourner Truth writes and sings antislavery songs around the country.

1834

Black musicians begin to perform on showboats along the Mississippi River.

1841

An anonymous monograph, *Sketches of the Higher Classes of Colored Society in Philadelphia*, emphasizes that young black women in this class are expected to be skilled musicians, in order to entertain at home.

A black choir of 150 men and women perform Handel's *Messiah* at the First African Presbyterian Church in Philadelphia.

1842

Charles Dickens writes about Almack's—later called Dickens' Place—where the black owner presents shows for his patrons, performed by the waitresses.

All-woman choirs perform sacred music at the black Convent of the Holy Family in New Orleans.

1850s

Harriet Tubman sings her signature song to signal her presence to slaves.

1851

Elizabeth Taylor Greenfield, "The Black Swan," makes her singing debut in Buffalo, New York. She is the first black woman concert singer and the first to have a career of any kind on the stage.

1853

The Luca Family, a troupe that includes father, mother, aunt, and three sons, performs concert music and antislavery songs at an antislavery convention in the Old Tabernacle on Broadway in New York.

1854

Elizabeth Taylor Greenfield becomes the first black woman music producer when she presents Thomas Bowers in concert.

Elizabeth Taylor Greenfield gives a command performance at Buckingham Palace for Queen Victoria.

1859

The Luca Family performs with the white Hutchinson family in Ohio.

1865

Nellie Brown (Mitchell) is the soprano soloist for four white churches in Boston.

After the Civil War, black male entertainers begin to form minstrel troupes, including Lew Johnson's Plantation Minstrel Company and the Georgia Minstrels.

1867

Singers from Fisk University who will later become the **Fisk Jubilee Singers** make their debut in Nashville.

Slave Songs of the United States is published. Young black teacher **Charlotte Forten** is a contributor.

1870

Annie Pindell's "Seek Ye the Lodge Where the Red Men Dwell" is the only antebellum song by a black composer in *The Complete Catalogue of Sheet Music and Musical Works Published by the Board of Music Trade of the United States of America.*

1871

The Fisk Jubilee Singers go on tour.

1872

Hampton Institute Singers, following in the footsteps of the Fisk Jubilee Singers, go on tour.

1875

Anna and Emma Hyers found the Coloured Operatic and Dramatic Company to present musical plays about the black experience. This is the first black repertory company.

1880s

Historians report that a black woman named Mama Lou sang traditional spirituals and work songs for patrons of a St. Louis brothel. She is credited with writing "Ta-ra-ra-boom-de-ay" and "A Hot Time in the Old Town Tonight" and probably "Frankie and Johnny."

1884

Rachel Washington, the first black graduate of the Boston Conservatory, publishes *Musical Truth; The Rudiments of Music*.

The first "Ladies' Orchestra" to play popular music is formed in Chelsea, Massachusetts.

1885

Flora Batson becomes a featured singer with Bergen Star Company.

1888

Sissieretta Jones makes her debut in New York City.

1890s

W. C. Handy reports the presence of a "lady trombonist" in the band of a minstrel show.

1891

The Creole Show is the first minstrel show/musical comedy with a chorus of black women and a black woman performing one of the principal roles.

1892

Sissieretta Jones performs before President Benjamin Harrison at the White House.

1896

Sissieretta Jones' Black Patti Troubadours opens its first season.

1898

A Trip to Coontown, the first musical comedy written by, directed, acted, and produced by black theater artists, features a female chorus.

Abbie Mitchell appears in *Clorindy, the Origin of the Cakewalk*, the music for which is written by her future husband, Will Marion Cooke.

1901

Soprano Emma Azalia Hackley makes her concert debut in Denver.

A group of black women singers, calling themselves the Louisiana Amazon Guards, begin three years of touring Europe before settling for a year in Russia. Coretta Alfred remains in Russia and builds a successful operatic career there.

1902

Anita Patti Brown is soloist with Chicago's black symphony orchestra, which continues in existence until about 1905.

1903

In Dahomey plays in London with **Aida Overton Walker** in a principal role. It is the first black American musical to be performed abroad.

Soprano Anita Patti Brown gives her debut recital in Chicago.

Harriet Gibbs Marshal founds the Washington Conservatory of Music to train black musicians.

1905

Abbie Mitchell is vocalist for the Memphis Players, the first modern jazz band, at its New York debut. **Ida Forsyne** dances.

The Creole Belles, under the leadership of **Georgette Harvey**, tour Europe and settle in Russia, as did the Amazon Guards. Harvey remains, pursuing a nightclub career, until the 1917 revolution.

1912

Helen Elise Smith joins David I. Martin to form the Martin-Smith School of Music, which quickly becomes one of the most important black musical institutions in the United States.

1915

Marie Lucas becomes conductor of the Lafayette Ladies' Orchestra at the Lafayette Theatre in Harlem.

1916

Lauretta Green opens the Butler Dance Studio, the first black-owned professional studio for children.

1919

Nora Douglas Holt founds the National Association of Negro Musicians.

Concert pianist **Hazel Harrison** makes her American debut in Chicago after returning from a successful stay in Europe.

1920

Mamie Smith records "Crazy Blues" on the Okeh label. It is the first blues record.

1921

Shuffle Along heads **Florence Mills** (a lead) and **Josephine Baker** and **Adelaide Hall** (chorus girls) toward stardom.

Pace Phonograph Company, the first black record company, is founded, using the Black Swan label.

Lil Hardin (Armstrong) joins King Oliver's jazz band, after studying concert music at Fisk University.

1922

Florence Mills opens in *The Plantation Revue* in Harlem before moving to Broadway.

1923

Bessie Smith records "Down Hearted Blues" and sells 800,000 copies. It is her first record for Columbia and is written by **Alberta Hunter** and **Lovie Austin**.

Elida Webb, the first known black professional choreographer in the United States, choreographs *Runnin' Wild* on Broadway.

Gertrude "Ma" Rainey makes her first recording.

Lovie Austin begins her tenure as recording pianist for Paramount Records, playing, composing, and creating arrangements for such vocalists as Ma Rainey, **Ida Cox,** and **Ethel Waters.**

1924

Florence Mills wows them in *Dixie to Broadway*, which is based on her London hit *Dover Street to Dixie*.

Valaida Snow makes her Broadway debut in *Chocolate Dandies*.

1925

Josephine Baker is a sensation in *La Revue Négre* in Paris, launching a legendary European career.

Lillian Evanti makes her professional singing debut in *Lakmé* with the Paris Opera.

Pianist Lil Hardin Armstrong records with Louis Armstrong, her husband, with composer credits on many of the numbers.

Florence Mills captivates London in *Blackbirds of 1926*.

1927

The Rodman Wanamaker Musical Composition Prizes for black composers are established.

Florence Mills dies. More than 150,000 people crowd the streets to make her funeral the largest in Harlem history.

1928

The first of the Blackbirds revues opens in New York. It will showcase a number of black performers, including Adelaide Hall and Aida Ward.

1930

Caterina Jarboro is the first African American to sing with a major opera company when she sings the role of Aida at the Puccini Opera House in Milan.

1931

Katherine Dunham forms the Negro Dance Group in Chicago.

1933

Ethel Waters is the only black cast member in Irving Berlin's *As Thousands Cheer*. She stops the show with "Heat Wave" and sings "Supper Time," about an African-American woman whose husband has been lynched.

Margaret Bonds is the first black guest soloist with the Chicago Symphony Orchestra when she performs at the World's Fair.

Chicago Symphony performs **Florence Price's** *Symphony in E minor*.

1934

On the same night, **Pearl Bailey** wins Amateur Night at the Apollo Theatre and **Ella Fitzgerald** is discovered when she wins Amateur Night at the Harlem Opera House.

Mahalia Jackson makes her first recording, which includes the song "God Shall Wipe Away All Tears."

The Gertrude Stein–Virgil Thomson opera *Four Saints in Three Acts* opens with a black cast. The members of the cast are gathered from New York's black churches.

Gershwin's *Porgy and Bess*, with libretto by Dorothy and DuBose Heyward, opens at the Alvin Theatre. **Eva Jessye** is choral director and **Anne Wiggins Brown** creates the role of Bess. The cast also includes Georgette Harvey and **Abbie Mitchell**.

1936

Maud Cuney Hare publishes *Negro Musicians and Their Music*.

1937

Billie Holiday opens at the Apollo Theatre with the Count Basie Orchestra.

1938

Billie Holiday performs with Artie Shaw, becoming one of the first black vocalists to sing with a major white band.

Rosetta Tharpe is the first gospel singer to record with a major record label. She is also a hit performer at Harlem's Cotton Club.

1940

Ethel Waters and Katherine Dunham star in Broadway musical *Cabin in the Sky*.

The Cotton Club closes.

1941

The National Negro Opera Company is founded by **Mary Cardwell Dawson**. It is the first permanent black opera company in the United States.

Bebop begins to emerge from Harlem jazz sessions.

1942

Billboard creates a rating chart for black music.

1943

Lillian Evanti performs in *La Traviata* with the National Negro Opera Company and receives rave reviews for her performance.

Carmen Jones opens on Broadway with Muriel Smith and **Muriel Rahn** alternating in the title role. The black adaptation of Bizet's opera *Carmen* is a triumph.

1944

Pearl Primus debuts on Broadway as a dancer at the Belasco Theatre.

Philippa Duke Schuyler composes "Manhattan Nocturne" for her thirteenth birthday.

1945

Sarah Vaughan's career is launched when she wins an Amateur Night contest at the Apollo and is hired by Earl Hines' Band.

Nora Douglas Holt is the first African American accepted into the Music Critics Circle of New York.

Mahalia Jackson has her first remarkably successful record, selling more than a million copies of "Move on Up a Little Higher."

1946

Camilla Williams signs with the New York City Opera, becoming the first black woman to sign a contract with a major American opera company.

Pearl Bailey makes her Broadway debut in *St. Louis Woman* and steals the show from the leads.

Dinah Washington makes her first recording, on her way to the title "Queen of the Blues."

1948

Doris Akers and **Dorothy Simmons** create the Simmons-Akers Singers, a gospel group.

1949

The term *rhythm-and-blues* replaces *race records* in the *Billboard* charts.

The first black-owned radio station, WERD-AM, begins operation in Atlanta.

1950

Mahalia Jackson appears at Carnegie Hall, in the biggest gospel concert to date.

Jazz pianist **Hazel Scott** is the first black woman to host a nationally syndicated television show. It is a musical variety show.

1951

In one of the first appearances by black concert singers on television, Muriel Rahn and William Warfield go on *The Ed Sullivan Show*.

Janet Collins joins the Metropolitan Opera and becomes the first black prima ballerina in the United States.

1953

"Hound Dog," as sung by **"Big Mama" Thornton**, is number one on *Billboard*'s R&B charts for seven weeks.

Vivian Carter Bracken is one of the founders of Vee Jay Records, which will represent such black performers as the **Staple Singers** and introduce the Beatles to the United States.

1954
The National Negro Network begins broadcasting on radio.

1955
Marian Anderson is the first black singer to perform with the Metropolitan Opera Company, in Verdi's *Un Ballo in Maschera*.

Leontyne Price appears on national television in the title role of Puccini's *Tosca*.

1956
Ruth Brown has her first top-forty hit, "Lucky Lips."

Mattiwilda Dobbs debuts at the Metropolitan Opera.

1957
Lena Horne has a huge personal success in a weak musical called *Jamaica*.

1959
Ruth Bowen opens a talent agency for black artists called Queen Artists. It becomes the largest black-owned entertainment agency in the world.

Martina Arroyo makes her Metropolitan Opera debut in *Don Carlos*.

Reri Grist makes her operatic debut with the Santa Fe Opera Company.

1960
The Ike and **Tina Turner** Revue begins touring.

Shirley Caesar records "Hallelujah, It's Done" in her trademark song-and-sermonette style.

1961
Leontyne Price makes her Metropolitan Opera debut in *Il Trovatore* by Verdi.

Grace Bumbry debuts in Richard Wagner's *Tannhäuser* at the Bayreuth Festival. Her casting is controversial, but she receives forty-two curtain calls.

Florence Ballard, **Diana Ross**, and Mary Wilson form the Supremes.

The Marvelettes have their—and Motown's—first top-forty number-one record with "Please Mr. Postman."

Singer/actor **Diahann Carroll** stars in a racially mixed cast in the musical *No Strings*.

Soprano **Adele Addison** is soloist at the opening concert of Philharmonic Hall at Lincoln Center in New York.

1963
Billboard stops publishing a separate chart for R&B because there are so many crossover hits. The R&B chart will be back in 1965.

Dorothy Maynor founds the Harlem School of the Arts.

1964
The Supremes record "Where Did Our Love Go?", their first number-one hit.

1966
Reri Grist makes her Metropolitan Opera debut in *The Barber of Seville*.

1967
Pearl Bailey heads the all-black cast of *Hello, Dolly!* on Broadway, for which she receives a special Tony.

Leslie Uggams dazzles critics and audience alike in *Hallelujah, Baby*, a musical survey of black history with a racially mixed cast.

1969

Undine Moore founds the Black Music Center at Virginia State University.

"Someday We'll Be Together" is the twelfth number-one hit for the group now called Diana Ross and the Supremes. It is also the last, as Diana Ross leaves the group.

Melba Moore breaks into the big time as Lutiebelle in *Purlie*, the musical version of Ossie Davis' *Purlie Victorious*. She wins Tony, Drama Desk, and Theatre World awards and tops *Variety*'s Drama Critics Poll.

1972

Kathleen Battle makes her solo debut singing Brahms' *German Requiem* at Spoleto, Italy.

1973

Bernice Johnson Reagon forms **Sweet Honey in the Rock**, an a cappella singing group.

The Pointer Sisters release their first album.

Diana Ross has her first number-one solo single, "Touch Me in the Morning."

At the Grammy Awards, **Gladys Knight** and the Pips win both Best Pop Vocal Performance and Best R&B Vocal Performance, for "Neither One of Us (Wants to Be the First to Say Good-bye)" and "Midnight Train to Georgia," respectively.

Barbara Hendricks, at the age of twenty-five, makes her Metropolitan Opera debut.

1974

Labelle is the first black rock group to perform at the New York Metropolitan Opera House.

Dorothy Maynor and Martina Arroyo release "There's a Meeting Here Tonight," a historic blending of two great black voices.

1975

Donna Summer appears on the scene with "Love to Love You Baby," which reaches number two on the pop charts.

1977

Supremes break up.

Kathleen Battle makes her Metropolitan Opera debut.

1978

Nell Carter is a smash hit in *Ain't Misbehavin'*.

A Taste of Honey is the first black group to receive the Grammy for Best New Artist.

1979

Lisa Lee forms Us Girls, one of the first all-woman rap groups.

1980

Donna Summer is the first woman to have three number-one singles in one year.

1981

In *Dreamgirls*, **Jennifer Holiday** stops the show every night with "And I Am Telling You I'm Not Going" and, according to the *New York Times*, makes "Broadway history."

Judith Jameson leads a smashing cast in *Sophisticated Ladies*, the first hit musical with Duke Ellington music.

1982

Jessye Norman makes her American opera debut with the Opera Company of Philadelphia.

1984

Tina Turner's comeback album, *Private Dancer*, is released. It becomes multiplatinum and wins three Grammy awards.

The folk musician **"Libba" Cotten** wins a Grammy for *Elizabeth Cotton Live!*, which is voted the best ethnic or traditional folk recording of the year.

1985

Leontyne Price makes her farewell appearance at the Metropolitan Opera.

Whitney Houston's debut album goes to number one for fourteen weeks and stays in the top forty for more than a year.

Roxanne Shante releases "Roxanne's Revenge," an answer to UTFO's "Roxanne, Roxanne."

1986

Salt-N-Pepa are the first female rappers to go platinum, with *Hot, Cool, and Vicious.*

Janet Jackson releases *Control*, which has five top-five singles and sells more than eight million copies.

1987

Aretha Franklin is the first woman inducted into the Rock and Roll Hall of Fame.

Whitney Houston's *Whitney* debuts at number one, the first album by a woman to do so.

1988

Tracy Chapman's first album soars to the top of the charts and wins her two Grammy Awards.

Barbara Hendricks appears in the film version of Puccini's *La Bohème.*

1989

Judith Jameson becomes director of the Alvin Ailey American Dance Theater.

Rhythm-and-blues singer Ruth Brown wins a Tony for her performance in the musical *Black and Blue.*

Queen Latifah's first album, *All Hail the Queen*, is released and goes gold. It addresses issues such as poverty, urban decay, and the liberation of women.

1990

Queen Latifah becomes a crossover hit when she raps on David Bowie's "Fame 90."

1991

Toni Morrison writes the lyrics for *Honey and Rue*, performed by Kathleen Battle at Carnegie Hall.

Patrice Rushen becomes the first woman to be musical director of a network television show on *The Midnight Hour.*

Janet Jackson signs a contract with Virgin Records that is reportedly worth between $32 million and $60 million.

1993

Angela Bassett stars in the Tina Turner biographical film *What's Love Got to Do With It?*

Several black women appear at President Clinton's inaugural festivities, including **En Vogue**.

1994

Whitney Houston goes to Johannesburg, South Africa, to perform at at "Whitney—The Concert for a New South Africa."

Toni Braxton wins two Grammy Awards for the first single from her debut album, "Another Sad Love Song." The album goes platinum.

1995

Gladys Knight and the Pips and the **Shirelles** are inducted into the Rock and Roll Hall of fame.

Bibliography

GENERAL BOOKS USEFUL TO THE STUDY OF BLACK WOMEN IN AMERICA

Reference Books

African-Americans: Voices of Triumph. Three volume set: *Perseverance, Leadership*, and *Creative Fire*. By the editors of Time-Life Books, Alexandria, Va., 1993.

Estell, Kenneth, ed., *The African-American Almanac*. Detroit, Mich., 1994.

Harley, Sharon. *The Timetables of African-American History: A Chronology of the Most Important People and Events in African-American History*. New York, 1995.

Hine, Darlene Clark. *Hine Sight: Black Women and the Re-Construction of American History*. Brooklyn, N.Y., 1994.

Hine, Darlene Clark, ed., Elsa Barkley Brown and Rosalyn Terborg-Penn, assoc. eds. *Black Women in America: An Historical Encyclopedia*. Brooklyn, N.Y., 1993.

Hornsby, Alton, Jr. *Chronology of African-American History: Significant Events and People from 1619 to the Present*. Detroit, Mich., 1991.

Kranz, Rachel. *Biographical Dictionary of Black Americans*. New York, 1992.

Lanker, Brian. *I Dream a World: Portraits of Black Women Who Changed America*. New York, 1989.

Logan, Rayford W., and Michael R. Winston, eds. *Dictionary of American Negro Biography*, New York, 1982.

Low, W. Augustus, and Virgil A. Clift, eds. *Encyclopedia of Black America*. New York, 1981.

Salem, Dorothy C., ed. *African American Women: A Biographical Dictionary*. New York, 1993.

Salzman, Jack, David Lionel Smith, and Cornel West. *Encyclopedia of African-American Culture and History*. Five Volumes. New York, 1996.

Smith, Jessie Carney, ed., *Notable Black American Women*. Two Volumes. Detroit, Mich., Book I, 1993; Book II, 1996.

General Books about Black Women

Giddings, Paula. *When and Where I Enter: The Impact of Black Women on Race and Sex in America*, New York, 1984.

Guy-Sheftall, Beverly. *Words of Fire: An Anthology of African-American Feminist Thought*. New York, 1995.

Hine, Darlene Clark, Wilma King, and Linda Reed, eds. *"We Specialize in the Wholly Impossible": A Reader in Black Women's History*. Brooklyn, N.Y., 1995.

Jones, Jacqueline. *Labor of Love, Labor of Sorrow: Black Women, Work, and the Family from Slavery to the Present*. New York, 1985.

Lerner, Gerda, ed. *Black Women in White America: A Documentary History*. New York, 1972.

BOOKS WHICH INCLUDE INFORMATION ON BLACK WOMEN MUSICIANS

Bronson, Fred. *The Billboard Book of Number One Hits*. New York, 1988.

Dahl, Linda. *Stormy Weather*. New York, 1984.

Epstein, Dena J. *Sinful Tunes and Spirituals: Black Folk Music to the Civil War*. Chicago, 1977.

Gaar, Gillian G. *She's a Rebel*. Seattle, Wash., 1992.

Greig, Charlotte. *Will You Still Love Me Tomorrow?* London, 1989.

Handy, D. Antoinette. *Black Women in American Bands and Orchestras*. Metuchen, N.J., 1981.

Harris, Sheldon. *Blues Who's Who*. New Rochelle, N.Y., 1979.

Harrison, Daphne Duval. *Black Pearls: Blues Queens of the 1920s*. New Brunswick, N.J., 1988.

Southern, Eileen. *Biographical Dictionary of Afro-American and African Musicians*. Westport, Connecticut, 1982.

Southern, Eileen. *The Music of Black Americans: A History*. New York, 1971.

The New Grove Dictionary of American Music. Edited by H. Wiley Hitchcock and Stanley Sadie. New York, 1986.

Who's Who in Rock & Roll. Tobler, John, ed. New York, 1991.

Contents of the Set

(ORGANIZED BY VOLUME)

Dance, Sports, and Visual Arts

Dance

Sports

Visual Arts

Education

Religion and Community

Social Activism

Science, Health, and Medicine

Contents of the Set

(LISTED ALPHABETICALLY BY ENTRY)

Index

Page numbers in **boldface** indicate main entries. Page numbers in *italics* indicate illustrations.